Lecture Notes in Artificial Intelligence 11248

Subseries of Lecture Notes in Computer Science

More information about this series at http://www.springer.com/series/1244

Manasawee Kaenampornpan · Rainer Malaka
Duc Dung Nguyen · Nicolas Schwind (Eds.)

Multi-disciplinary Trends in Artificial Intelligence

12th International Conference, MIWAI 2018
Hanoi, Vietnam, November 18–20, 2018
Proceedings

Springer

Editors
Manasawee Kaenampornpan
Mahasarakham University
Maha Sarakham, Thailand

Rainer Malaka
Center for Computing Technologies
University of Bremen
Bremen, Germany

Duc Dung Nguyen
Vietnam Academy of Science
and Technology
Hanoi, Vietnam

Nicolas Schwind Ⓘ
AIST Tokyo
Tokyo, Japan

ISSN 0302-9743 ISSN 1611-3349 (electronic)
Lecture Notes in Artificial Intelligence
ISBN 978-3-030-03013-1 ISBN 978-3-030-03014-8 (eBook)
https://doi.org/10.1007/978-3-030-03014-8

Library of Congress Control Number: 2018958766

LNCS Sublibrary: SL7 – Artificial Intelligence

This Springer imprint is published by the registered company Springer Nature Switzerland AG
The registered company address is: Gewerbestrasse 11, 6330 Cham, Switzerland

Preface

Artificial intelligence (AI) research has broad applications in real-world problems. Examples include control, planning and scheduling, pattern recognition, knowledge mining, software applications, strategy games, and others. The ever-evolving needs in society and business both on a local and on a global scale demand better technologies for solving more and more complex problems. Such needs can be found in all industrial sectors and in any part of the world.

The MIWAI series of conferences consist of yearly events bringing together AI researchers and practioners from around the world, providing participants with opportunities to exchange new ideas and to establish collaborations worldwide. By promoting AI research in both theoretical and applied research, the conference aims to be a meeting place where excellence in AI research meets the needs for solving dynamic and complex problems in the real world. The range of AI topics covered by MIWAI is quite broad, including machine learning, computer vision, knowledge representation and reasoning, natural language processing, pattern recognition, planning and scheduling, and multi-agent systems, among others. Thanks to MIWAI the academic researchers, developers, and industrial practitioners thus have extensive opportunities to present their original work, technological advances, and practical problems. Participants can learn from each other and exchange their experiences in order to finetune their activities and help each other better. The main purposes of the series are also to inform research students about cutting-edge AI research via the presence of outstanding international invited speakers, and to raise the standards of practice of AI research by providing researchers and students with feedback from an internationally renowned Program Committee.

MIWAI was initiated in Thailand in 2007, and back then it was the acronym for "Mahasarakham International Workshop on Artificial Intelligence." In 2011 MIWAI was held outside of Thailand for the first time, in Hyderabad, India, so that it became the "Multi-disciplinary International Workshop on Artificial Intelligence." Then the event took place in various Asian countries, subsequently in Ho Chi Minh City, Vietnam (2012), Krabi, Thailand (2013), Bangalore, India (2014), Fuzhou, China (2015), Chiang Mai, Thailand (2016), and Brunei (2017). The 12th edition of MIWAI was held in Hanoi, Vietnam, in November 2018, and was renamed to the "Multi-disciplinary International Conference on Artificial Intelligence." This volume contains papers selected for presentation at MIWAI 2018.

We received submissions from 18 countries in Asia, Europe, and Africa. Among the 65 submissions, 19 received highly positive reviews and were accepted as regular papers, leading to an acceptance rate of 29%. Among the remaining submissions, 13 received positive reviews and were deemed suitable for publication as short papers. Each submission was carefully reviewed by at least two members from a Program Committee consisting of 76 AI experts from 22 countries, and some papers received up to four reviews when necessary. The reviewing process was double-blind. Many submissions, despite presenting promising research, were not included so as to maintain a high-quality program. Regular papers are allocated up to 14 pages in the proceedings, while short papers are allocated seven pages. From the list of accepted papers, three regular papers and four short papers were withdrawn. This volume contains the remaining 16 regular papers and nine short papers.

In addition to the papers published in the proceedings, the technical program included a keynote talk from Prof. Phan Minh Dung, Asian Institute of Technology, Thailand. We would like to thank the keynote speaker for accepting our invitation. We are also thankful to the local organizers in Hanoi for the excellent hospitality and for making all the necessary arrangements for the conference. Last but not least, we thank the MIWAI 2018 Program Committee for their excellent work in reviewing the papers, and to the authors for their high-quality submissions. The contributions from members of both parties were crucial for making MIWAI 2018 a successful conference.

September 2018   Manasawee Kaenampornpan
                                                               Rainer Malaka
                                                          Duc Dung Nguyen
                                                            Nicolas Schwind

Organization

Honorary Advisor

Sujin Butdisuwan   Mahasarakham University, Thailand

Steering Committee

Arun Agarwal	University of Hyderabad, India
Rajkumar Buyya	University of Melbourne, Australia
Patrick Doherty	University of Linkoping, Sweden
Rina Dechter	University of California, Irvine, USA
Leon Van Der Torre	University of Luxembourg, Luxembourg
Peter Haddawy	Mahidol University, Thailand
James F. Peters	University of Manitoba, Canada
Jérôme Lang	University of Paris-Dauphine, France
Somnuk Phon-Amnuaisuk	Universiti Teknologi Brunei, Brunei
C. Raghavendra Rao	University of Hyderabad, India
Srinivasan Ramani	International Institute of Information Technology Bangalore, India

Conveners

Richard Booth	Cardiff University, UK
Chattrakul Sombattheera	Mahasarakham University, Thailand

General Chairs

Duc Dung Nguyen	Institute of Information Technology, Vietnam Academy of Science and Technology, Vietnam
Rainer Malaka	University of Bremen, Germany

Program Chairs

Manasawee Kaenampornpan	Mahasarakham University, Thailand
Nicolas Schwind	National Institute of Advanced Industrial Science and Technology, Japan

Organizing Chairs

Phatthanaphong   Mahasarakham University, Thailand
  Chomphuwiset
Khachakrit Liemthaisong   Mahasarakham University, Thailand

Local Chairs

Quang Doan Nhat   Hanoi University of Science and Technology, Vietnam
Luong Chi Mai   Hanoi University of Science and Technology, Vietnam

Publicity Chairs

Olarik Surinta   Mahasarakham University, Thailand
Supakit Nootyaskool   King Mongkut's Institute of Technology, Thailand

Finance Chair

Rapeeporn Chamchong   Mahasarakham University, Thailand

Webmasters

Chaya Hiruncharoenvate   Mahasarakham University, Thailand
Panich Sudkhot   Mahasarakham University, Thailand

Program Committee

Arun Agarwal   University of Hyderabad, India, India
Thien Wan Au   Universiti Teknologi Brunei, Brunei
Joscha Bach   MIT Media Lab, USA
Costin Badica   University of Craiova, Romania
Raj Bhatnagar   University of Cincinnati, USA
Richard Booth   Cardiff University, UK
Zied Bouraoui   CRIL-CNRS and University of Artois, France
Gauvain Bourgne   CNRS and Sorbonnes Universités, UPMC Paris 06,
                                LIP6, France
Rapeeporn Chamchong   Mahasarakham University, Thailand
Zhicong Chen   Fuzhou University, China
Phatthanaphong   Mahasarakham University, Thailand
  Chomphuwiset
Maxime Clement   National Institute of Informatics, Japan
Broderick Crawford   Pontificia Universidad Catolica de Valparaiso, Chile
Tiago de Lima   CRIL-CNRS and University of Artois, France
Marina De Vos   University of Bath, UK
Emir Demirović   University of Melbourne, Australia
Sang Dinh   Hanoi University of Science and Technology, Vietnam

Thanh Ha Do   VNU University of Science, Vietnam
Nhat-Quang Doan   Hanoi University of Science and Technology, Vietnam
Vlad Estivill-Castro   Griffith University, Australia
Peter Haddawy   Mahidol University, Thailand
Tran Thị Thanh Hai   MICA Institute, Vietnam
Xinyi Huang   Fujian Normal University, China
Zhisheng Huang   Vrije University Amsterdam, The Netherlands
Jason Jung   Chung-Ang University, South Korea
Manasawee   Mahasarakham University, Thailand
   Kaenampornpan
Satish Kolhe   North Maharashtra University, India
Anh Cuong Le   Ton Duc Thang University, Vietnam
Thai Le   Ho Chi Minh City University of Science, Vietnam
Thi-Lan Le   MICA Institute, Hanoi University of Science
                                 and Technology, Vietnam
Théo Le Calvar   LERIA, University of Angers, France
Phuong Le-Hong   Hanoi University of Science, Vietnam
Tek Yong Lim   Multimedia University, Malaysia
Pawan Lingras   Saint Mary's University, Canada
Martin Lukac   Nazarbayev University, Kazakhstan
Rainer Malaka   University of Bremen, Germany
Jérôme Mengin   IRIT, University of Toulouse, France
Sebastian Moreno   Universidad Adolfo Ibañez, Chile
Kavi Narayana Murthy   University of Hyderabad, India
Sven Naumann   University of Trier, Germany
Abhaya Nayak   Macquarie University, Australia
Naveen Nekuri   Sasi Institute of Technology and Engineering, India
Thi Phuong Nghiem   Hanoi University of Science and Technology, Vietnam
Dung Duc Nguyen   Institute of Information Technology, Vietnam
                                 Academy of Science and Technology, Vietnam
Thi-Oanh Nguyen   Hanoi University of Science and Technology, Vietnam
Viet Anh Nguyen   Institute of Information Technology, Vietnam
                                 Academy of Science and Technology, Vietnam
Maria do Carmo Nicoletti   Universidade Federal de S. Carlos and Faculdade de
                                 Campo Limpo Paulista, Brazil
Tiago Oliveira   National Institute of Informatics, Japan
Laurent Perrussel   IRIT, University of Toulouse, France
Nguyen-Khang Pham   Can Tho University, Vietnam
Somnuk Phon-Amnuaisuk   Universiti Teknologi Brunei, Brunei
M. V. N. K. Prasad   Institute for Development and Research in Banking
                                 Technology, India
Tho Quan   Ho Chi Minh City University of Technology, Vietnam
Sheela Ramanna   University of Winnipeg, Canada
Tony Ribeiro   Institut de Recherche en Communications et
                                 Cybernétique de Nantes, École Centrale de Nantes,
                                 France

Alexis Robbes	University of Tours, France
Harvey Rosas	University of Valparaiso, Chile
Andre Rossi	University of Bretagne-Sud, France
Adrien Rougny	National Institute of Advanced Industrial Science and Technology, Japan
Jose H. Saito	Universidade Federal de São Carlos, Brazil
Yuko Sakurai	National Institute of Advanced Industrial Science and Technology, Japan
Aknine Samir	LIRIS, Lyon 1 University, France
Sebastian Sardina	RMIT University, Australia
Nicolas Schwind	National Institute of Advanced Industrial Science and Technology, Japan
Jun Shen	University of Wollongong, Australia
Alok Singh	University of Hyderabad, India
Vivek Kumar Singh	Banaras Hindu University, India
Dominik Slezak	University of Warsaw and Infobright, Poland
Chattrakul Sombattheera	Mahasarakham University, Thailand
Virach Sornlertlamvanich	Sirindhorn International Institute of Technology, Thammasat University, Thailand
Frieder Stolzenburg	Harz University of Applied Sciences, Germany
Olarik Surinta	Mahasarakham University, Thailand
Ilias Tachmazidis	University of Huddersfield, UK
Jaree Thongkam	Mahasarakham University, Thailand
Anni-Yasmin Turhan	TU Dresden, Germany
Suguru Ueda	Saga University, Japan
Chau Vo	Ho Chi Minh City University of Technology, Vietnam National University, Vietnam
Viet-Vu Vu	Vietnam National University, Vietnam
Rajeev Wankar	University of Hyderabad, India
Jingtao Yao	University of Regina, Canada
Wai Yeap	Auckland University of Technology, New Zealand
Kevin Kam Fung Yuen	Singapore University of Social Sciences, Singapore

Additional Reviewers

Dennis Pfisterer	Thanongchai Siriapisith
Felix Putze	Giang Son Tran
Snehalata Shirude	Kishor Wagh

An Introduction to Argumentation and Practical Reasoning (Keynote Abstract)

Phan Minh Dung[1] and Phan Minh Thang[2]

[1] Computer Science and Information Management Program,
Asian Institute of Technology (AIT), Thailand
[2] International College, Burapha University, Chonburi, Thailand

Abstract. Arguing could be viewed as one of the most important intellectual activities of humans during their entire lives. People of all walks of life get involved in argumentation on a daily basis. But often when we are aware that we need arguments, we are in trouble (and often the lawyers are happy). In this talk we will present an introduction into the theory of argumentation and its potential application in practical reasoning. We will start with a light-hearted introduction to argumentation and practical reasoning in our daily lives. We then introduce the theory of argumentation where an argument system is viewed as a pair of a set of argument and a binary attack relation between arguments. The semantics of argumentation rests on the acceptability of arguments, their structure and attack relations. We present an axiomatic analysis of semantics of argumentation.

Contents

Short Papers

Regular Papers

Partial Ellipse Filter for Maximizing Region Similarity for Noise Removal and Color Regulation

Nam Anh Dao[✉] [iD]

Electric Power University, Hanoi, Vietnam
anhdn@epu.edu.vn

Abstract. Ellipse filters can be implemented for partition of image patch. We introduce a method for automatically obtaining a set of neighbor patches for an image pixel in form of ellipses for noise removal and color regulation. Comparing neighborhood similarity of patches of the set allows selecting an optimal patch. The evaluation of similarity is developed from bilateral filter with additional orientation condition. Through the development of the image filter model it is shown that the image noise can be removed better with the ellipse patches that are allocated in different directions. Our first finding is that it is enough to select 4 or 8 major orientations to determine the best ellipse patch for each pixel. Secondly, by operating convolution weighted by intensity similarity and the spatial distance, this is capable to detect particular oriented patch with the best neighbor similarity and ameliorate the elimination of different noise types. These filters also permit remaining color harmony and edge contrast for color correction. In particular, the validity of the method is demonstrated by presenting experimental results on a benchmark database.

Keywords: Ellipse filter · Bilateral filter · Noise removal · Patch similarity Oriented ellipse · Color correction

1 Introduction

Image noise appears where there is random alteration of brightness or color in digital images. In most cases, the noise is ordinarily found as random speckles on a stable region in result of the sensor and chip in digital camera or a scanner. Sometimes small noises can hold appearance analogous to salt and pepper. In regular noise model the allocation of noise is characterized by Gaussian distribution [1]. Whilst they remain in most all kinds of image applications including industrial inspection, medical imaging, traffic, sport and entertainment, the noise can extremely reduce image quality. This demands accurate noise detection with a removal process for images to provide a smooth analytic task. The task is not always simple even for specialists, because the variation of noise. Thus, it is a widely recognized need among computer vision experts for assistance to eliminate image noise. The focus of this paper is the ellipse filter which can manage practical reasoning through efficient argumentation. It shows how analysis by ellipse regions can add value to noise distribution estimation and improvement of

M. Kaenampornpan et al. (Eds.): MIWAI 2018, LNAI 11248, pp. 3–18, 2018.
https://doi.org/10.1007/978-3-030-03014-8_1

color correction. Orientation based splitting regions and analysis of such regions become fundamental due to their natural formulation and visual representation. Furthermore, similarity level of patch relies upon patch definition and the features under which the noise is estimated.

We have recently developed a new method of noise estimation based on a special patch similarity estimation, which allows us to capture the most related region with less noise. The proposed approach is extended from the original bilateral filter with multivariate Gaussian distribution [2] and applies it for noise estimation. We show how distinctive patterns such as edges and corners can be identified to distinguish with noise. Thus the method will engage in long and careful consideration on a designing the filter for noise removal by: (a) delivering a circumstantial justification for setting ellipse patches around considered pixel; (b) constructing elements of filter based on ellipse patches to determine level of similarity by checking intensity and location distance, where each ellipse patch covers a particular direction and combination of the patches can mask all neighbor pixels; (c) reporting test results of the ellipse filter for major noise types; (d) in addition to noise removal, integration of the ellipse filter with PDF color transfer is proposed for improvement of color regulation.

This paper is organized as follows. The most recent advances of bilateral filter are discussed in the Sect. 2, where the behavior of the filter is analyzed to note its strengths and limitations. Section 3 describes essentials of the proposed ellipse filter applied for noise removal and color correction. Experimental results by applying the method within a benchmark database and their analysis are presented in Sect. 4. Finally, the paper is concluded in Sect. 5.

2 Motivation and Related Works

We present major applications of the bilateral filter (BF) [3]. There are many technique reasons for demanding a strong estimation of noise to avoid image quality decrease. Some of these are found in the literature on methods for de-noising: iterative reconstruction techniques by [4, 5]. The bilateral filter is described by [6, 7] as an efficient method for blurring image while preserving edges. Formal description of the filter for noise removal is as follows:

$$u(x) = v(x) + noise(x) \tag{1}$$

$$f(x) = p(v|u) \approx \frac{1}{C} \int_{|x-y| \leq w} u(y) \exp\left(-\frac{(x-y)^2}{2\pi\sigma_s^2}\right) \exp\left(-\frac{(u(x)-u(y))^2}{2\pi\sigma_r^2}\right) dy \tag{2}$$

$$C(x) = \int_{|x-y| \leq w} \exp\left(-\frac{(x-y)^2}{2\pi\sigma_s^2}\right) \exp\left(-\frac{(u(x)-u(y))^2}{2\pi\sigma_r^2}\right) dy \tag{3}$$

where $u(x)$ is the observed image intensity including original image $v(x)$ and the noise; x, y denote 2D location of pixels, w is radius of patch window and C is a normalization factor. The capability of the filter for de-noising is the primary target of the filter and it is demonstrated in tracking, medical imaging, and more.

It can be used for a range of different imaging applications: mesh de-noising [8], tone mapping [3], image up-sampling [9], detail enhancement [10, 11], artistic rendering [12] and stylization [13]. Instead of weighting by the intensity, joint bilateral filter [14], [15] uses flash image $F(x)$ for estimation of ambient image by (4). Furthermore, in a case of texture analysis [16] a texture description image $G(x)$ is employed for the weight by (5).

$$f(x) = \frac{1}{C} \int_{|x-y| \leq w} u(y) \exp\left(-\frac{(x-y)^2}{2\pi\sigma_s^2}\right) \exp\left(-\frac{(F(x)-F(y))^2}{2\pi\sigma_r^2}\right) dy \qquad (4)$$

$$f(x) = \frac{1}{C} \int_{|x-y| \leq w} u(y) \exp\left(-\frac{(x-y)^2}{2\pi\sigma_s^2}\right) \exp\left(-\frac{(G(x)-G(y))^2}{2\pi\sigma_r^2}\right) dy \qquad (5)$$

The method involves patch shift mechanism to find relevant texture or smooth patch for each pixel that is required to form a guidance image. The next group of methods is related to spatial weighting. A multi-scale dual bilateral filter is proposed for fuse high spatial resolution panchromatic image and high spectral resolution multi-spectral image [17]. The filter expands its size sparsely according to resembling ratio for fusing image while keeping edge. Then, for filling the holes and eliminating the noise in depth maps a directional filter is proposed to vary adaptively according to the direction of the edge [18]. The method is development of the joint trilateral filter [19] with four spatial directions. In a similar way, a directional bilateral filter [20] applies an oriented Gaussian domain kernel locally by a structure tensor. The last two methods with variation of direction are using partial filters whose center is allocated in the considered pixel. A filter of this type makes neighbor region in form of ellipse which is symmetric thought the pixel. So, the filter performs the same weights for two neighbor pixels which are located symmetrically and this lacks of distinct weights for the neighbor pixels.

3 The Method

As shall be discussed, a gray image $u(x)$ is presented in 2D space, where locations x and y from (1) are vectors by (6). The standard spatial deviation σ_s^2 is in a form of vector by (6) to display neighbor region by an ellipse but not a cycle for the original version of BF where they are the same, $\sigma_1^2 = \sigma_2^2$.

$$x = \begin{bmatrix} x_1 \\ x_2 \end{bmatrix}, \; y = \begin{bmatrix} y_1 \\ y_2 \end{bmatrix}, \; \sigma_s^2 = \begin{bmatrix} \sigma_1^2 & 0 \\ 0 & \sigma_2^2 \end{bmatrix} \qquad (6)$$

3.1   The Partial Filter

The Gaussian weighting of the BF for pixel x and its neighbor y is marked by $s(x, y)$ in (7) now has its details in (8) by (6). Thus, modification of (6) allows us to have formulas (8) for the standard spatial deviation σ_s:

$$s(x, y) = \exp\left(-\frac{(x - y)^2}{2\pi\sigma_s^2}\right) = \exp\left(\frac{-1}{2\pi}\begin{bmatrix} x_1 - y_1 \\ x_2 - y_2 \end{bmatrix}^T \begin{bmatrix} \sigma_1^2 & 0 \\ 0 & \sigma_2^2 \end{bmatrix}^{-1} \begin{bmatrix} x_1 - y_1 \\ x_2 - y_2 \end{bmatrix}\right) \quad (7)$$

$$\sigma_s = \begin{bmatrix} \sigma_1^2 & 0 \\ 0 & \sigma_2^2 \end{bmatrix}^{1/2} = \sqrt{(\sigma_1^2.\sigma_2^2 - 0.0)} = \sigma_1\sigma_2, \quad \frac{1}{\sigma_s^2} = \begin{bmatrix} \sigma_1^2 & 0 \\ 0 & \sigma_2^2 \end{bmatrix}^{-1} = \begin{bmatrix} \frac{1}{\sigma_1^2} & 0 \\ 0 & \frac{1}{\sigma_2^2} \end{bmatrix} \quad (8)$$

In order to calculate the spatial weight $s(x, y)$ by (7), formulas (8) allow modification of (7) to get formulas (9) and then (10):

$$s = \exp\left(\frac{-1}{2\pi}\begin{bmatrix} x_1 - y_1 \\ x_2 - y_2 \end{bmatrix}^T \begin{bmatrix} \frac{1}{\sigma_1^2} & 0 \\ 0 & \frac{1}{\sigma_2^2} \end{bmatrix}\begin{bmatrix} x_1 - y_1 \\ x_2 - y_2 \end{bmatrix}\right) = \exp\left(\frac{-1}{2\sigma_1^2}(x_1 - y_1)^2 \frac{-1}{2\sigma_2^2}(x_2 - y_2)^2\right)$$

$$(9)$$

$$s = \exp\left(-\frac{(x_1 - y_1)^2}{2\sigma_1^2}\right)\exp\left(-\frac{(x_2 - y_2)^2}{2\sigma_1^2}\right) \quad (10)$$

Further taking logarithm to (10) and moving sign $(-)$ from the right part to the left part of equation we have (11):

$$\log s = -\frac{(x_1 - y_1)^2}{2\sigma_1^2} - \frac{(x_2 - y_2)^2}{2\sigma_2^2}, \quad \log\frac{1}{s} = \frac{(x_1 - y_1)^2}{2\sigma_1^2} + \frac{(x_2 - y_2)^2}{2\sigma_2^2} \quad (11)$$

Division of both sides of (11) by the $\log\frac{1}{s}$ allows us getting a simple expression (12). Now with introducing radius r_1 and r_2, $r_1^2 = 2\sigma_1^2 \log\frac{1}{s}$; $r_2^2 = 2\sigma_2^2 \log\frac{1}{s}$, an ellipse is presented by (13). The ellipse holds center allocated at the pixel x and keep its axis along horizontal or vertical direction.

$$1 = \frac{(x_1 - y_1)^2}{2\sigma_1^2 \log\frac{1}{s}} + \frac{(x_2 - y_2)^2}{2\sigma_2^2 \log\frac{1}{s}} \quad (12)$$

$$1 = \frac{(x_1 - y_1)^2}{r_1^2} + \frac{(x_2 - y_2)^2}{r_2^2} \quad (13)$$

For accessing partial region of neighbor pixel in a particular direction, the center of the ellipse can be moved from x to a new position $c = (c_1, c_2)$. Formula (14) expresses turning the ellipse for an angle θ at the center c. Back to the formula (10), the ellipse parameters (14) permit to present the spatial weighting by (15). Here we keep the new center c in a distance by a half of radius w from (2) to make the fitter allocated mostly in a particular direction of the considered pixel x.

$$1 = \frac{((x_1 - c_1) \cos \theta - (y_1 - c_1) \sin \theta)^2}{r_1^2} + \frac{((x_2 - c_2) \sin \theta + (y_2 - c_2) \cos \theta)^2}{r_2^2} \quad (14)$$

$$s_{c.\theta}(x, y) = \exp\left(-\frac{((x_1 - c_1) \cos \theta - (y_1 - c_2) \sin \theta)^2}{2\sigma_1^2}\right) \exp\left(-\frac{((x_1 - c_1) \sin \theta + (y_1 - c_2) \cos \theta)^2}{2\sigma_2^2}\right) \quad (15)$$

We employ the modification of the spatial weighting to get a new form of the bilateral filter by (16) with its partial weighting factor (17):

$$f_u(x, c, \theta) = \frac{1}{C_u(x, c, \theta)} \int_{|x-y| \le w} u(y) s_{c,\theta}(x, y) \exp\left(-\frac{(u(x) - u(y))^2}{2\pi\sigma_r^2}\right) dy \quad (16)$$

$$C_u(x, c, \theta) = \int_{|x-y| \le w} s_{c,\theta}(x, y) \exp\left(-\frac{(u(x) - u(y))^2}{2\pi\sigma_r^2}\right) dy \quad (17)$$

In our extension to oriented filter, a series of angles is considered to check patch similarity in different directions. Thus, we present the series by (18). The center of each filter is allocated in a distance by a half of the window radius w, and the coordinates of the ellipse center can be formulated by (19):

$$\theta_k = k\frac{2\pi}{n}, k = 1, ..n; \quad (18)$$

$$c_1^k = x_1 + \frac{w}{2} \cos \theta_k; \quad c_2^k = x_2 + \frac{w}{2} \sin \theta_k \quad (19)$$

Let's denote D for spatial domain of the BF (2) and D_k – the spatial domain of partial ellipse filter (20). The series of ellipse filters are designed in the way so that union of all partial domains D_k must cover the D by (20), allowing formula (21) to be effective.

$$\bigcup_{k=1,n} D_k \approx D \quad (20)$$

$$f_u(x) = p(v|u) = \frac{1}{n} \sum_{k=1,n} p(v|u, D_k) = \frac{1}{n} \sum_{k=1,n} f_u(x, c, d_k) \quad (21)$$

3.2 Maximizing Region Similarity

In particular, partial filters help to detect the direction which produces the best value of similarity by the ellipse filter (16). By selecting the partial filter which has max value for the weights C by (22) the partial filter detects the neighbor region with the most similarity.

$$ind(x) = \arg\max_{k=1,n} C_u(x, c, \theta_k) \tag{22}$$

$$f_u(x) = p(v|u, D_{ind}) \frac{\sum_{k=1,n} p(v|u, D_k)}{p(v|u, D_{ind})} = f_u(x, c, \theta_{ind}) \frac{1}{n} \sum_{k=1,n} \frac{f_u(x, c, \theta_k)}{f_u(x, c, \theta_{ind})} \tag{23}$$

In particular, partial filters help to detect the direction which produces the best value of similarity by the ellipse filter (16). By selecting the partial filter which has max value for the weights C by (17) the partial filter detects the neighbor region with the most similarity. So that we have (24). Then the filter produces final value for the pixel x by (25). This is especially effective for the pixel located nearby edges.

$$f_u(x, c, \theta_k) < f_u(x, c, \theta_{ind}), \frac{f_u(x, c, \theta_k)}{f_u(x, c, \theta_{ind})} < 1, k \neq ind \tag{24}$$

$$f_u^*(x) = f_u(x, c, \theta_{ind}) \tag{25}$$

In Fig. 1a, the red contour illustrates spatial domain of the BF, the other blue contours display a set of four ellipse filters in different directions. Figure 1b demonstrates a simple image with a foreground in blue and background in white; the top ellipse filter obtains the most neighbor pixels having similar color to the pixel drawn by a red dot. Notice that the formula (16) for the partial weighting factor consists of spatial weights for the domain in form of ellipse, multiplied with responsive intensity distinction. Though the parameter C is used as normalization factor for original BF, here this is the critical factor for selecting the best suitable sub-region of neighbor pixels by (22).

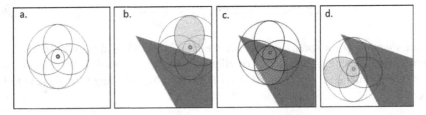

Fig. 1. (a) The BF's domain is marked by a red contour, four ellipse filters are printed by blue contours. (b) The top ellipse filter delivers the best value of similarity for pixel marked by a red dot. (c) The bottom ellipse filter is advanced than others for this case. (d) The left ellipse produces the best value of similarity. (Color figure online)

3.3 Algorithm and Parameters for Noise Removal

This is essential to improve quality of noise removal respecting images edges. However, there is time consuming which is proportional with the number of ellipse filters used for sub-region division. A solution for decreasing computing time is to use the ellipse filters to apply to gray version if the input is color image to search the sub-region with the most similarity, then apply the filters for color version. As such, the speed of the method will be improved. Algorithm 1 resumes our method by description of the ellipse filters for noise removal optimization with analytical fundaments discussed above. The number of filters n from (18) can be 4 or 8 since four cardinal directions are the directions North, East, South, and West.

ALGORITHM 1. Ellipse Filters (EF) for noise removal optimization

Input: Noise image u, window size w, deviations σ_s, σ_r, number of ellipse filters n.
Output: The image v cleared of noise.

```
1    start
2        θ=floor(2π/n);
3        for each k=1..n        // A. Create ellipse filters
4            filter(k) = CreateEllipseFiter (θ,w);// by (16)
5        end
6        for each=1..n           // B. Fill by ellipse filters
7            vf(k)=PartialGrayFill (u, Filter(k)); // (20, 21)
8        end
9        for each pixel x of v   // C. Select the best result of ellipse filters
10           v(x)=PartialColorFill (vf(1:n));     // (24, 25)
11       end
12   end
```

Also, the four intermediate directions are North East, South East, South West, and North West. Figures 2 and 3 demonstrate examples of the series of 4 and 8 filters accordingly. The center of ellipse c from (19) was addressed to be valued by half of the radius of window w $(0.5 * w)$ to keep the ellipse domain allocated in a direction by the view from center of window. However the domain should cover the center so we decrease the distance a little by $(0.4 * w)$. The width of ellipse must be large enough to make sure the combination of series of ellipse can cover most spatial domain of BF, while it should not too small to hold neighbor pixels. This concerns setting deviations $@_s$, $@_r$ for the algorithm. The parameters were implemented by our experiments for the algorithm. Reports and discussion are provided in the Sect. 4.

Fig. 2. Series of 4 ellipse filters with window size by 21 pixels are in the right. The original Gaussian filter is presented in the left.

Fig. 3. Series of 8 ellipse filters with window size by 21 pixels.

3.4 Color Correction by the Partial Filter

An alternative application of the described partial filters is color correction from which we can perform color regulation for an image by color structure of a reference image. The idea is to use the available color style of the reference image to produce a new version for considered image, retaining the image content but having new color style. Thus, the color regulation would eventually grant natural conformity, giving variety of applications from photo editing and web designing to video processing.

A relatively low-cost and comfortable method for changing the color style is the global approach, which is based on global color features of given image and a reference image to design color transform rules. Analysis of local image features exposes divergent color styles in different region of the image: a smooth color for an image object, and a set of repeated colors for a texture object. The advantages of local color analysis enhanced with directional aspect over global approach include detailed color style, comfort for texture and especially for edge regions. In order to transfer color style adaptively for variety of color styles in region level it is necessary to consider not only global features but also local directional features. Just a special algorithm was designed for color regulation as follows. The first color style transfer is produced by probability density function (PDF) for colors of images. The PDF of a continuous distribution of a color value z is defined as the derivative of the distribution of the image $dis(u)$ by (26). The PDF of the target image t is used for finding new color for given image u by transfer function $tran(u)$ so that the new image obtains similar PDF of the target image v by (27).

$$pdf_u(z) = \lim_{\Delta \to 0} \frac{p(z < dis(u) \le z + \Delta)}{\Delta} \tag{26}$$

$$pdf_t(z) \approx pdf_v(z), \ t = tran(u) \tag{27}$$

Depending on the directional model and the number of arcs n used, local region D surrounding a pixel x is split into partial elliptic regions D_k by (20) to check similarity in each partial region by (28).

$$f_t(x) = p(r|t) = \frac{1}{n} \sum_{k=1,n} p(r|v, D_k) = \frac{1}{n} \sum_{k=1,n} f_t(x, c, d_k) \tag{28}$$

where the partial filters f_t are similar to the f_u in (23) by (29, 30). Their expected estimation of color similarity is given by checking each pixel y in the partial region and have certain arc θ predefined for each partial region.

$$f_t(x, c, \theta) = \frac{1}{C_t(x, c, \theta)} \int_{|x-y| \le w} t(y) s_{c,\theta}(x, y) \exp\left(-\frac{(t(x) - t(y))^2}{2\pi\sigma_r^2}\right) dy \tag{29}$$

$$C_t(x, c, \theta) = \int_{|x-y| \le w} s_{c,\theta}(x, y) \exp\left(-\frac{(t(x) - t(y))^2}{2\pi\sigma_r^2}\right) dy \tag{30}$$

The partial region of the most similarity with index *ind* by (22) can selectively modify color of the target pixel x by assigning the value f_t at the selected arc θ_{ind}:

$$f_t^*(x) = f_t(x, c, \theta_{ind}) \tag{31}$$

Since our solution combines both global and local color analysis, it is definitely imperative that selection of the best partial region is based on the local feature of the original image u by (22) while the modification with PDF by (27) adheres to the global color stability, given interoperated color modification by (31). The color regulation is related directly to the reference image v.

When the PDF of the original image u and v are independent, the global transfer by PDF may lead to inconsistency of coloring for image objects which are not addressed in the method. When considering inexpensive and object related detector for the coloring issue, saliency map [21] shows high potential solution with evaluating visual attention for images. We propose a simple color regulator for run-time efficiency which uses saliency map s extracted from the original image u for weighting the relevance of major objects in the image. Adding the saliency based weight for color modified version by (32) similar to [22]; the final color regulation is produced. Here, color is changed by PDF, ellipse filters and saliency map. There is good agreement in the retrieved final image between the global PDF and local directional filter, but with object consideration by saliency:

$$t_{fin} = s(x) \cdot f_t^*(x) + (1 - s(x)) \cdot u(x) \tag{32}$$

Algorithm 2 highlights the main tasks of color regulation with available ellipse filters from Algorithm 1.

ALGORITHM 2. Ellipse Filters (EF) for Color Regulation

Input: Color image u, target color image v, ellipse filters *filters*.
Output: The image t having structure of u and color by v.

```
1    start
2            // A. Estimate the best arc for each pixel
3            ind(x) = FindTheBestArc(u(x)); // (22)
4            // B. Calculate saliency map
5            s(x) = CalculateSaliencyMap(u(x));
6            // C. PDF based color transfer
7            t(x)=pdfColorTransfer(u);
8            // D. Integration of partial filter with PDF and saliency
9            r(x)=PartialColorFill (t(x),ind(x),filters, s(x)); // (32)
10   end
```

---

4 Experimental Results and Discussion

Based upon the fundamental analysis from session 3, it is intuitive to carry out experiments of noise removal and color regulation using the described partial filters. Considering that each kind of experiments needs appropriate dataset, we initially selected suitable image benchmarks which were collected for specific purposes.

4.1 Noise Removal

The proposed algorithm is tested over a benchmark image database [23]. The goal is to estimate performance on the noise removal. Noise is added to each image of the database. There are three types of noise which are used the test: salt & pepper, Gaussian noise and speckle. We further apply the ellipse filters to remove noise in two options: four ellipse filters and eight filters. We also implement the bilateral filter [3] by codes of Lanman [24] and non-local mean (NLM) [25] by codes of [26] for each case.

Naturally, local mean filter inspects neighbor pixels in the region that surrounds a target pixel to take the mean value. The filter smooths image and blurs image edges. To keep contrast in edge region, the NLM searches the similar pixels for a target pixel and takes the average value. Figure 4 demonstrates two examples from our test with salt and pepper noise. Noise of salt & pepper is added to the images in column a. Column b shows extracted part from patch of image in the column a. Column c displays results of the bilateral fitter with deviation $@_s = 0.5$, $@_r = 0.5$. We present results of four ellipse filters and eight ellipse filters in column d, and e accordingly. The salt & pepper noise is removed mostly from images in column c, though blurring effect is observed for edges. Images in column d and e are mostly free of noise with less blurring effect. The edges are remained well in images in the last column. Similarly for Gaussian noise we illustrate examples in Fig. 5. The noise with deviation 0.01 is added to images in column a, details of noise effect are seen well in column b. The images in column c are cleared of the noise but edges are blurred. Images in column d keep edges better then images in column c.

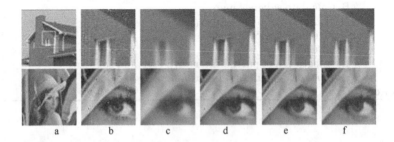

a   b   c   d   e   f

Fig. 4. (a) Noise of salt & pepper is added to the image with a patch in center, marked by a white border. (b) Extraction of the patch of the image. (c) Result of the BF. (d) Result of Non-local mean. (e) Result made by our 4 ellipse filters. (f) Result of 8 ellipse filters.

Speckle noise is the focus for our illustration in Fig. 6. Images in column a and their extractions are shown in column b. The noise is removed mostly for images in column c with blurred edges. Noise is not removed fully for images in column d and partially removed in column e. To quantitatively evaluate the quality of the noise removal generated for each noise type we use Peak Signal to Noise Ratio (PSNR) [27], Structural SIMilarity (SSIM) [28], Sum of Absolute Differences (SAD) [29], and Mean Squared Error (MSE) [30]. The measure of the metrics are as follows:

$$PSNR = 10 \log_{10} \frac{(2^n - 1)^2}{\sqrt{MSE}} \tag{33}$$

$$SSIM = \frac{(2\mu_x\mu_y + c_1)(2\varsigma_{xy} + c_2)}{(\mu_x^2 + \mu_{yc}^2 + c_1)(\sigma_x^2 + \sigma_y^2 + c_2)} \tag{34}$$

$$SAD = \frac{1}{mn} \sum_1^m \sum_1^n |A(i,j) - B(i,j)| \tag{35}$$

$$MSE = \frac{1}{mn} \sum_1^m \sum_1^n (A(i,j) - B(i,j))^2 \tag{36}$$

The quality measurements for both techniques can be seen in Table 1. It is clear that the method uses a number of filters to search the best solution from temporal results and it takes more time than the BF. In the table we mark the best score by bold numbers. As shown in Fig. 7a measurements of PSNR and SSIM are presented for four test cases. We display statistics of SAD and MSE in Fig. 7b.

New image noise removal and ellipse filters have been implemented for USC-SIPI Image Database [23] with the ability to increase reservation of edges which are usually blurred by BF. Designing the ellipse filters in relation to Gaussian distribution of pixel similarity in neighbor region, we considered coverage of the combination of spatial domain of ellipse filters to be equivalent with spatial domain of the original Gaussian filter. We then splitting the whole region of neighbor pixels of studied pixel into sub-regions in four or eight directions based on ellipse filters whose major axis go through the pixel. The efficacy to the filters has been compared with the original bilateral filter and non-local mean filter. In particular, similarity metrics by PSNR, SAD and MSE have showed the improvement of capability of keeping edges un-blurred in comparison to the BF and NLM for three types of noises. When the BF uses local intensity distinction for blurring, the NLM searches the most similar patch. Our method applies oriented local fitters to determine level of similarity in ellipse patches. The method requires more time than BF and NLM, as using multiple filters (4 or 8) instead of one. However the quality is improved. The ellipse filters, on the other hand, are capable to manage color regulation with assistance of saliency map.

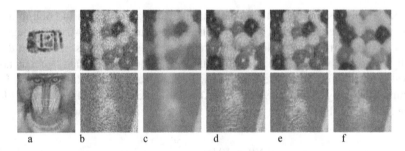

Fig. 5. (a) Gaussian noise is added to the image with a patch in center, marked by a white border. (b) Extraction of the patch of the image. (c) Result of the bilateral filter. (d) Result by non-local mean. (e) Result made by our 4 ellipse filters. (f) Result of 8 ellipse filters.

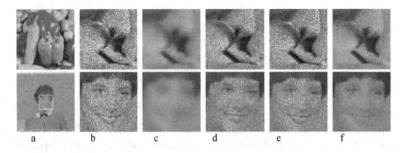

Fig. 6. (a) Speckle noise is added to the image with a patch in center, marked by a white border. (b) The extracted patch. (c) BF. (d) NLM. (e) EF(4). (f) EF(8).

4.2   Color Regulation

Local directional features by the partial regions also improve the color correction. Our experiments for color regulation used mainly integrating global color transfer PDF with partial filters and weighting by saliency map were carried out on color images of a MSRA database [31]. Color images in various themes of the database have played a role of original image, and reference images were designed for variety of color structure. A color image with different textured regions is illustrated in Fig. 8a. An image having distinct set of colors was used for reference as shown in Fig. 8b.

Color transfer by PDF [32] was carried out for the color image and reference image to change the color, as shown in Fig. 8c. Our method was applied for the same images producing a color image, as shown in Fig. 8d, demonstrated contrast of different areas while smoothing is kept inside areas. Figure 8d shows the lack of artifacts which are observable in Fig. 8c in result of PDF transfer. The color inside a region is relatively harmonious, but the edges between regions of image exported by our method in Fig. 8d are in contrast. Figure 9 shows a series of examples of the saliency benchmark, modified by PDF transform and our method for the same reference image. The themes of images are diverse: mountain/lake and interiors/exteriors. The directional filters demonstrated their capability of improving color similarity and harmonic smoothing inside region while keeping edges and contrast between regions.

Table 1. Performance statistics

	Metrics	PSNR	SSIM	SAD	MSE	Time (s)
3 types of noise	BF	74.05	0.99989	0.0372	0.00332	7.6
	NLM	73.79	**0.99995**	0.0417	0.00389	**3.4**
	EF(4)	74.69	0.99992	0.0336	0.00303	26.3
	EF(8)	**75.07**	0.99993	**0.0328**	**0.00282**	47.6
Salt & pepper	BF	74.53	0.99992	0.0332	0.00299	7.7
	NLM	78.04	**0.99998**	**0.0189**	**0.00116**	**3.4**
	EF(4)	76.78	0.99996	0.0230	0.00203	26.3
	EF(8)	**77.73**	0.99997	0.0203	0.00168	46.1
Gaussian noise	BF	74.06	0.99989	0.0373	0.00325	7.5
	NLM	73.04	**0.99996**	0.0441	0.00335	**3.3**
	EF(4)	74.33	0.99994	0.0348	0.00297	26.2
	EF(8)	**74.55**	0.99995	**0.0346**	**0.00278**	47.6
Speckle	BF	**73.54**	**0.99987**	**0.0413**	**0.00372**	7.5
	NLM	70.29	0.99990	0.0620	0.00717	**3.3**
	EF(4)	72.96	0.99986	0.0430	0.00407	26.4
	EF(8)	72.92	0.99986	0.0436	0.00401	49.2

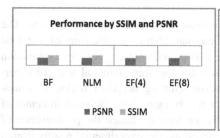

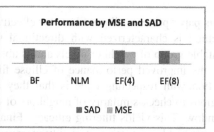

a.   SSIM and PSNR.   b. MSE and SAD.

Fig. 7. Statistics of experiments for three types of noises.

a.   b.   c.   d.

Fig. 8. Example of color correction. (a) Original image. (b) Reference image. (c) Result of PDF transfer. (d) Result of our proposed method. (Color figure online)

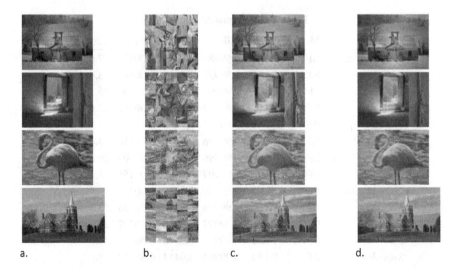

a.   b.   c.   d.

Fig. 9. Examples of color correction. (a) Original images. (b) Reference images. (c) Results of PDF transfer. (d) Results of our proposed method. (Color figure online)

5   Conclusions

This paper presents ellipse filters for effective noise removal and color correction. The method is characterized with directional Gaussian filters for selection of the best suitable group of neighbor pixels and is able to cope with noise types. An explanation for the improved performance of ellipse filters for the noise removal and color correction with respecting edge is that they allow splitting neighbor region into sub-regions to check similarity of neighbors of each sub-region with the pixel in center of window. This yields filtering efficacy. Finally we have evaluated the performance of the method by a number of quality measurements and the experimental results from a benchmark database have showed remarkable performance. The ellipse filters can be applied for other computer vision tasks like detection of abnormality in medical images or object following in video clips. This is our research plan for future research.

Acknowledgements. The support of the 2018 Electric Power University Research Program, which is funding the projects, is gratefully acknowledged.

References

1. Hazewinkel, M. (ed.): Encyclopedia of Mathematics. Springer Science Business Media B. V., Kluwer Aca. Pub., Heidelberg (1994)
2. Genz, A., Bretz, F.: Computation of Multivariate Normal and t Probabilities. Lecture Notes in Statistics. Springer, Heidelberg (2009). https://doi.org/10.1007/978-3-642-01689-9
3. Durand, F., Dorsey, J.: Fast bilateral filtering for the display of high-dynamic-range images. ACM Trans. Graph. **21**(3), 257–266 (2002)

4. Koehler, T., Brendel, B., Roessl, E.: A iterative reconstruction for differential phase contrast imaging using spherically symmetric basis functions. Med. Phys. **38**, 4542–4545 (2011)
5. Hahn, D., et al.: Statistical iterative reconstruction algorithm for x-ray phase-contrast CT. Sci. Rep. **5**, 10452 (2015)
6. Yaroslavsky, L.P.: Digital Picture Processing: An Introduction. Springer Series in Information Sciences. Springer, Heidelberg (1985). https://doi.org/10.1007/978-3-642-81929-2
7. Tomasi, C., Manduchi, R.: Bilateral filtering for gray and color images. In: Proceedings of the ICCV 1998, pp. 839–846 (1998)
8. Fleishman, S., Drori, I., Cohen-Or, D.: Bilateral mesh de-noising. ACM Trans. Graph. **22**(3), 950–953 (2003)
9. Kopf, J., Cohen, M., Lischinski, D., Uyttendaele, M.: Joint bilateral upsampling. ACM Trans. Graph. **26**(3), 96 (2007)
10. Bae, S., Paris, S., Durand, F.: Two-scale tone management for photographic look. ACM Trans. Graph. **25**(3), 637–645 (2006)
11. Fattal, R., Agrawala, M., Rusinkiewicz, S.: Multiscale shape and detail enhancement from multi-light image collections. ACM Trans. Graph. **26**(3), 51:1–51:9 (2007)
12. Kang, H., Lee, S., Chui, C.: Flow-based image abstraction. IEEE Trans. Vis. Comput. Graph. **15**, 62–76 (2009)
13. Winnemoller, H., Olsen, S.C., Gooch, B.: Real-time video abstraction. ACM Trans. Graph. **25**(3), 1221–1226 (2006). Proceedings of the SIGGRAPH Conference
14. Eisemann, E., Durand, F.: Flash photography enhancement via intrinsic relighting. ACM Trans. Graph. **23**(3), 673–678 (2004)
15. Petschnigg, G., Szeliski, R., Agrawala, M., Cohen, M., Hoppe, H., Toyama, K.: Digital photography with flash and no-flash image pairs. ACM Trans. Graph. **23**, 664–672 (2004)
16. Cho, H., Lee, H., Kang, H., Lee, S.: Bilateral texture filtering. ACM (TOG) **33**(4), 128 (2014)
17. Hu, J., Li, S.: Fusion of panchromatic and multispectral images using multiscale dual bilateral filter. In: ICIP 2011, pp. 1489–1492 (2011)
18. Le, A.V., Jung, S.-W., Won, C.S.: Directional joint bilateral filter for depth images. Sensors **14**, 11362–11378 (2014). https://doi.org/10.3390/s140711362
19. Jung, S.-W.: Enhancement of image and depth map using adaptive joint trilateral filter. IEEE Trans. Circuits Syst. Video Technol. **23**, 258–269 (2013)
20. Venkatesh, M., Seelamantula, C.S.: Directional bilateral filters. In: CVPR (2014)
21. Goferman, S., Zelnik-manor, L., Tal, A.: Context-aware saliency detection. In: IEEE Conference on Computer Vision and Pattern Recognition (2010)
22. Nam Anh, D.: Smooth context based color transfer. Int. J. Comput. Appl. **116**(15), 29–37 (2015). https://doi.org/10.5120/20413-2825
23. USC-SIPI Image Database. http://sipi.usc.edu/database/
24. Lanman, D.R.: BFILTER2 Two dimensional bilateral filtering. Brown University (2006)
25. Buades, A., Coll, B., Morel, J.-M.: Non-local means denoising. IPOL **1**, 208–212 (2011)
26. Darbon, J., Cunha, A., Chan, T.F., Osher, S., Jensen, G.J.: Fast nonlocal filtering applied to electron cryomicroscopy. In: Biomedical Imaging: From Nano to Macro (2008)
27. Huynh-Thu, Q., Ghanbari, M.: Scope of validity of PSNR in image/video quality assessment. Electron. Lett. **44**(13), 800 (2008). https://doi.org/10.1049/el:20080522
28. Wang, Z., Bovik, A.C., Sheikh, H.R., Simoncelli, E.P.: Image quality assessment: from error visibility to structural similarity. IEEE TIP **13**(4), 600–612 (2004)
29. Richardson, I.E.G.: H.264 and MPEG-4 Video Compression: Video Coding for Next-generation Multimedia. Wiley, Chichester (2003)

30. Lehmann, E.L., Casella, G.: Theory of Point Estimation. STS. Springer, New York (1998). https://doi.org/10.1007/b98854
31. Liu, T., Sun, J., Zheng, N.N., Tang, X., Shum, H.Y.: Learning to detect a salient object. In: IEEE CVPR (2007)
32. Pitié, F., Kokaram, A.C., Dahyot, R.: N-dimensional probability density function transfer and its application to colour transfer. In: IEEE International Conference on Computer Vision, vol. 2, pp. 1434–1439 (2005)

Work Flexibility, Telepresence in the Office for Remote Workers: A Case Study from Austria

Michal Beno$^{(\boxtimes)}$

VSM/City University of Seattle, Panonska cesta 17, 851 04 Bratislava, Slovakia
michal.beno@vsm-student.sk

Abstract. There is an increasing need for technology to support remote workers in professional and personal activities, so as to reduce the consumption of fuel, reduce traffic and environmental issues, and enable the workers to stay in contact with their colleagues. Telepresence robotics helps the remote worker by providing a virtual presence, or telepresence, in the office. This tool is a robot controlled by computer, tablet or smartphone and includes a video camera, screen, speakers and microphones for mutual interaction, thereby allowing remote workers and their colleagues to see, hear and speak to each other. In this paper, we describe this technology. The home office is still taboo for many employers. Our experiment has found a solution, because the employee can have a presence in the office and always have audio and video contact. Telepresence robots were introduced a number of years ago, and these robots now allow any employee to be present in the office from anywhere in the world and at any time. This study is a small-scale exploratory case study that examines the use of a robot to interact with colleagues in a traditional office. One of the natural consequences of this kind of workplace flexibility is that less office space is required. We conducted the experiment with a Double 2 Robot over a period of three working days. Based on the data collected from this study, we present a set of guidelines for the use of this technology, and we try to find a solution that will allow the employee to have a presence in the office and enjoy the benefits of this even if he/she is not physically present.

Keywords: Telepresence robot · Double 2 · Remote work · Home office

1 Introduction

Technology has had a significant impact on work, making it possible to work from the home and other locations [1], i.e. work can be done anywhere at any time [2]. The information age, where information and communication technology (ICT) play a vital role, allows people to perform their daily work both in the office and away from it using ICT tools. This has many advantages, especially flexibility, easier circumstances, productivity, communication capability and saving the time spent commuting.

Teleworking, as it is commonly referred to in Europe, or telecommuting in the United States, is a work phenomenon that allows human beings to work outside a localised workplace rather than inside it, using ICT equipment. The term

© Springer Nature Switzerland AG 2018
M. Kaenampornpan et al. (Eds.): MIWAI 2018, LNAI 11248, pp. 19–31, 2018.
https://doi.org/10.1007/978-3-030-03014-8_2

telecommuting first appeared in the USA in the 70s [3]. Currently, it is used worldwide in different concepts such as telework, e-Work, online work, nomadic work, mobile work and by various professions such as programmers, technicians, customer service staff, marketing consultants, purchasing agents, journalists, market investigators, publishers, interpreters, brokers and accountants.

The concept of telepresence is not new. Marvin Minsky [4], a founder of MIT's artificial intelligence laboratory, referred to the concept as "telepresence", instead of "teleoperator" or "telefactor", because telepresence emphasises the importance of high-quality sensory feedback and suggests the possibility of future instruments that will feel and work so much like the worker's own hands that one would not notice any significant difference. Telepresence is not science fiction. The first robotic-assisted remote telepresence surgery using an early prototype of the da Vinci robot developed by the Stanford Research Institute was performed successfully by Drs Rick Satawa and John Bowersox in 1996 [5]. The first ever self-driving business collaboration robot, iRobot AVA 500, has been available for a number of years and offers a useful range of services [6].

Telepresence is a mix of technologies that allows users to be present remotely. Widely used telepresence tools are videoconference applications like Appear.in, Skype, Messenger, Google Hangouts and Viber. We describe telepresence robots as embodied videoconferencing on wheels. Instead of legs, the worker moves on stabilised wheels, instead of a face, he/she has an iPad screen, instead of eyes, a camera, instead of a mouth, a speaker, and instead of ears, a tiny microphone. Over the past decade, companies such as Anybots, Double Robotics, Mantaro, Revolve Robotics, Vecna, Awabot, Inbot Technology and iRobot have produced these robots for use in a wide variety of situations from conversations in the office to patient rounds at medical facilities. The quest of developing a user-friendly interface for telepresence robots [7] and special interfaces for disabled people [8] has motivated significant research efforts.

Our goal was firstly to understand how the Robot Double 2 works, including its utilisation. The next task was what it can do when the employee cannot be in the office and wants a robot to do his work instead. Generally, human beings are concerned about the idea that robots will take over their jobs. But in this case, robots are helping employees to keep their jobs and do them better.

In the following section, we briefly outline the methodology that we used in our research project. The third section gives a brief overview of the concept of a telepresence robots. In the fourth section, a case study is presented to investigate the features of the telepresence robot from the perspective of the remote worker in its utilisation and application in communication with colleagues. We tried to find out the benefits and limitations of a robotic experience. The paper closes with our conclusions.

2   Methodology

In order to investigate real-world experience with a virtual robot in the globalised world of modern workplace e-working, the research team sought a company where the robot was distributed by the company on the basis of a remote worker's need, for a period of three working days. The use of the robot requires financial resources, which were covered by several donations from different companies to assist in the renting of this tool, the Double 2 from Germany, as displayed in Fig. 1. The Double 2 is an iPad mounted on wheels. The head has a fitting for a regular-sized iPad, which is connected to the Double 2 via Bluetooth, and the iPad's camera and microphone provide video and audio to the controller. The tool requires a connection to the Internet. To control the robot, the employee needs another iPad or an iPhone and the free iOS app for iPhone or iPad [9], or can use Web-based controls via Google Chrome, in which case the up and down arrows on the computer keyboard are used for forward and reverse movement, and the right and left arrows for turning.

Fig. 1. Double 2 (Source: [10])

The telepresence robot used in our study helped to place the person at a remote location instantly, thereby providing him with a virtual presence, or telepresence. The robot was computer controlled, with the iPad attached to the robot. The arrangement included a video camera, screen, speakers and microphones, so that people interacting with the robot could see, hear and talk to its operator, and the operator could simultaneously see what the robot was "seeing", "saying" and "hearing".

Since the robot is controlled from a remote location with assisted teleoperation, the robot follows the steering commands of the operator, except for situations where there is a high likelihood of collision. This can easily occur if the user is not experienced in navigating the robot, the network connection is delayed or an obstacle appears unexpectedly in the robot's path.

The robot driver uses his own communications video application to drive the robot, using arrow keys to move the robot forward, back, left or right. The robot driver can also use a mouse to indicate a "Click and Go" velocity based on the angle and magnitude of the distance from the centre point at the bottom of the video window. Double 2 uses the WebRTC standard for video and audio. It is therefore encrypted and always secure. The encryption used is an AES cipher with 128-bit keys to encrypt audio and video, plus HMAC-SHA1 to verify data integrity. Video and audio connections are end-to-end and peer-to-peer encrypted whenever possible.

This study sought to explore and understand the phenomena of remote workers using robots to be present and participate in the traditional workplace in the real world. The study was qualitative and exploratory, and the following research questions were investigated: What is the robot like to use? What can the worker do when he/she needs to be in the office, but cannot be there? Does this flexibility reduce office space? What are the benefits and the limitations of a robotic experience?

A small-scale exploratory case study was conducted in an international Austrian sports company with twelve hours of interviews and twelve hours of observation over a period of three days. A total of four participants shared their experiences during this experiment: one remote worker (author, male, 37 years old) and three office-based workers (male supervisor, 47 years old; and two female office workers, 26 years old and 36 years old).

All interviews were semi-structured and lasted sixty minutes. Interview topics included motivation for using the robot, technical aspects, benefits and disadvantages. Interviews took place in multiple sites at the home and in the office.

Observations took place in one home where the remote worker was controlling the robot and in one room at the office where the robot was deployed and actively at work. The observations lasted sixty minutes over the period of three days. Observation notes were recorded and analysed on the same day.

Interviews and observations were recorded, transcribed and coded to identify patterns, similarities and dissimilarities.

3 Telepresence Robots

The most popular teleconferencing tools at the moment, such as Skype and Messenger, are in our opinion limited in various respects. This classic kind of telepresence is very easy to use, but not very effective. Even when video is added to the audio communication, the remote worker often cannot see or hear all the other colleagues at the remote location and may feel like a passive observer who is not able to move around or explore the environment.

Phone communication enables us to hear another person and to note the tone of voice. Visual communication is even more powerful. When we see a face, we are able to distinguish a whole range of emotions or their absence, we see body language, interest or lack of interest, and much other information. Direct eye contact has been shown to increase the perception of credibility [11]. McNelley [12] emphasises that 93% of subjects state that participants would prefer to communicate with eye contact.

Telepresence robotics, remote presence and virtual presence are terms that describe technologies that allow the remote operator to control a robotic platform from a distance and to interact with remote participants using audio [13] and video. We describe telepresence robotics as a smart form of robotic remote control by a human operator that influences video/audio conferencing and networked connectivity to enable communicate without geographical and virtual borders. This tool is an interesting variant based on the integration of ICT on to robotic platforms, providing the user with a higher degree of interaction with the remote environment [14]. According to Melendez-Fernandez et al. [15], robotic telepresence is a promising approach for diverse applications, including assisting elderly people, telework and remote surveillance. The concept of home telehealth services is one solution that is worth investigating [16–21]. Research by Tsai et al. [19] highlights the aim of telepresence: bringing together two people situated in separate locations.

Teleoperated robots are already used in many areas and applications. In addition to industry and corporations, telepresence is becoming common in the field of social interactions, such as business meetings or the workplace. Instances of the use of telepresence robots in the workplaces of different companies are presented in Table 1.

Table 1. Related work

Author	Title
Guizzo [22]	*When my avatar went to work* (The author shares his experience of using a robot during a week in his office, which he concludes can bring benefits, especially to the remote teammate)
Lee and Takayama [23]	*Now, I have a body: uses and social norms for mobile remote presence in the workplace*
Tsui et al. [24]	*Exploring use cases for telepresence robots*
Tsui et al. [25]	*Towards measuring the quality of interaction: Communication through telepresence robots*
Herring [26]	*Telepresence robots for academics*

In this work [23–26], different situations in which people interact with robots both in public and in the academic environment are analysed.

The possible applications of telepresence robots are very wide and promising [20]. Users of these robots are usually social-service providers, doctors, academics, other professionals, or simply workers where the people do not meet and where specially equipped rooms or computers, rather than videoconferencing or other telepresence solutions, are used.

This tool allows for virtual inclusion by enabling the user to be in virtual attendance in a remote location and have the freedom to move around. Luta et al. [27] stress that telepresence robots give humans the sensation of being present in another location by allowing the user to see, hear and move around the surroundings with the robot at will. Using an Internet-connected telepresence robot enables users to see, hear and move or navigate. Nowadays, a number of manufacturers make and sell these tools in different models and various shapes and sizes, such as Amy Robotics, AXYN Robotique, MantaroBot, Suitable Technologies, Double Robotics and Ava Robotics [28]. International and local companies have explored the use of this modern tool [29–31]. According to a report by Tractica [32], the market and applications for telepresence robots are developing rapidly. Based on Wintergreen Research [33] data, the market for telepresence reached $1.4 billion in 2016 and will reach $8 billion in 2020. As stated by the study The Telepresence Revolution [34], telepresence in the US and UK can prevent the generation of millions of metric tons of CO_2, therefore the potential financial benefits from telepresence run into billions of dollars. This tool offers a rapid return on investment, reduces air travel, improves productivity and improves and increases work-life balance.

4 Findings

For about 45 years, since the beginning of telecommuting, humans have been working at locations away from the main office, in the car, in the train, at the airport or in the hotel. Digitisation makes mobile working much easier. It seems that for many jobs, it makes almost no difference when or where they are done, and they can be carried out via email, chat or videoconference. Employees can optimise family and work demands, and although supervisors may initially fear a loss of control, this is not the case. A study by Stanford University finds that working from home boosts employees' happiness and productivity [35]. "Through remote work, companies can meet the needs of each jobholder. A robot could be a way to make this possible," is the hope expressed by the supervisor.

A remote worker describes this modern tool as an iPad on a Segway: "Well, that's basically what it is. There is a pair of squat wheels at the bottom and a telescoping pole that extend from 91 cm to 152 cm. At the top of the pole, there is a jig for an iPad. You log in like a Skype call. I used the website for logging in, and after that you are presented with controls to move it, and the loudspeaker optimises the sound." This employee has been a remote worker for eight years: He talks with his colleagues on the phone, they tweet each other, use emails, and Skype, but, as he emphasises, "Well, I am often left out of crucial face-to-face meetings, spontaneous brainstorming sessions, I miss the gossip and the birthday parties… I have to be responsive to my team when we need to solve problems." Before he tried the robot, he was sure that, on the basis of what others had said, he would not like using it or that it would be a waste of time. "At the beginning, I was disoriented and felt helpless, but after a while I got used to it. It was thrilling, fascinating, as if I was in the office."

For the past eight years, the manager of the department has been letting two of its employees work remotely at least three days a week in order to help them to manage stress better and to integrate their work and home lives, thereby reducing the time spent commuting to work. He emphasises that, "On the days when the employees are not in the office, they could have the option of using a robot to make them feel like they are physically here among their colleagues." When the team initially transitioned to a flexible work arrangement, the director said, "We relied on tools like videoconferencing. But even the most advanced technology cannot replicate the experience of walking around in the office." With regard to videoconferencing, he added, "People forget that you are here," even though you may be "waiting, trying to get attention through singing or waving on the screen". But the colleagues stress that, "With the robot, we treat you like you were physically here, no chance to forget you."

Our results show that the remote employee controls the robot, so that the robot holds the screen and moves around the office. The technology not only facilitates collaboration among the team, but also encourages a kind of team bonding. Office worker 1 illustrates it as follows, "It is like part of a science fiction movie. A monitor on a pole with wheels moving around in the office." The colleagues start a conversation with, "Hi Michi, how you doing?". The Segway rolls a little closer. The screen on the top shows a man wearing small headphones. "Unfortunately, I can't shake hands with you," he says, and the colleagues start to laugh. While the supervisor admits there was some amusement when the robot was first introduced, he was surprised how quickly his staff adjusted to it. As explained by two office workers, they found it difficult to become accustomed to the remote worker rolling from one person to another and talking to them by means of a small monitor. Office worker 2 remembers her first meeting with the remote worker. "When he came around the corner punctually at the agreed time and I talked to him over the screen, it was unusual for me in the beginning ... but after 15 min it was the same as always, it was as if Michi was actually here." The remote worker said, "Once it was all up and running, it was a lot of fun and, to be honest, I forgot the fact that I was there remotely ... it was like being there in my office."

According to the interview, the remote worker and the director both believe that, "This tool could pop up elsewhere, alleviating some of the most common issues associated with working from home, like loneliness, less interaction with colleagues and less of a feeling of belonging." Typically, social isolation [36] and loneliness are major social issues leading to many forms of suffering, e.g. anxiety, depression, burnout [37, 38]. Generally, work such as telework, remote work and e-Work lead to increased productivity [39–41], but the supervisor states that, "Right now, it is too early to say whether the robot will significantly increase productivity among remote workers. It is possible that many employees will prefer sitting at home and controlling the robot remotely rather than coming to the office. For this reason, each organisation has to set the rules for this kind of option, however in my opinion the robot is not designed to replace your workers, but on the contrary to help us and enable us to lead less stressful lives."

The most interesting issue was that the use of a robot requires less space, and all the respondents agree that this type of work flexibility may make the office much emptier. Especially on Mondays and Fridays many desks are unoccupied, because the traffic is heavier on these days, and workers therefore choose these days to work remotely from home. This is something that many companies still find difficult to accept.

Double 2 is an ideal robot for remote workers who frequently need to interact with co-workers in the office. But a question we asked the co-workers was why a telepresence robot should be used in the first place when FaceTime, Google Hangout, Viber, Skype or other videoconferencing tools work just as well. The unanimous answer was that it has one major advantage: "mobility". An important point that must be considered is whether the people in the work environment are even ready to have a robot in the office. In our study, the colleagues thought that having this modern tool in the office was an indication of futuristic thinking. The remote worker expressed it more precisely. "I am starting to see how a remote-controlled robot can be different from a Skype call ... you do not have to rely on others, but the door has to be kept open ... it is not like a phone call; you can just exist remotely, and then interact with your colleagues whenever you or they choose to do so."

Let us have a look at the remote worker's experience of utilising a robot. His day working from home starts as usual by logging into the VPN and checking the mail, but instead of greeting colleagues on the phone or Skype, "I navigated myself into the office," he said. "I simply connected my robot and said, 'Good morning everybody, what a lovely day'. It was a big difference in terms of presence," the remote worker explained. As stated, the colleagues were really curious about interacting with him. After being at meetings and connecting throughout the day, he felt that working remotely through the robot was actually quite comparable with a normal day at the office. Having control over when he wanted to connect provided a good balance of social time, and he could also disconnect to have lunch or get some other work done. The sound and video quality were clear and strong.

The remote worker thinks that the robot solution is legitimate. "However, one of the main problems of a home office is that there is no informal conversation," he stressed. This is an important disadvantage, because many new ideas often arise from casual conversation. We believe that a key aspect of a telepresence robot is the level of attention required from the person participating remotely. The manager said, "What telepresence technology has given us goes far beyond our initial expectations with this experiment, which was to make meaningful technological accommodation for our remote worker."

The remote worker emphasised that, "a telepresence robot can be used to provide yourself with a "far reaching" pair of mobile "eyes" and "ears", enabling you to have a remote presence at any location with an Internet connection. The user has complete control to move the robot around the office in Schwechat and to view anything at the robot's location". He pointed out further: "Forget video conferencing. Now there's an even better way to telecommute, one that allows you to move, interact and engage as if you were right in the same room as your colleagues. Perhaps even cooler, it allows you to ride a Segway from afar." The supervisor stresses that "telepresence robots go beyond a simple video conference call, because the operator has full control of what he/she wishes to see".

As reported in our results, a telepresence robot in teleworking makes experiential learning easier, as it is no longer necessary to factor airfare, hotel, bus and food expenses into the cost of experiential learning. A robotic telepresence allows the user to participate in professional conferences without leaving home. Furthermore, mobility has been of great assistance in allowing companies to hire the best person for the job, regardless of where he/she lives. Now companies can utilise the insights and person- ality of such people even easier, by involving them in impromptu discussions, ad hoc meetings and even lunch outings. For the first time, remote employees can really feel that they are part of the team. In the past, remote employees often could not enjoy the benefit of group work and interaction. Now robots can be wheeled to one side for team projects, private conversations and other personal engagements, things that are simply not possible with video conferencing. This allows for a more seamless, and efficient, work experience, and allows those present at the meeting to benefit from the employee's full range of talents. Robotic telepresence limits the ability for employees to take on tasks, therefore forcing them to focus on the project, and people, at hand. That in turn makes the meetings less arduous and more productive overall. As the world continues to move towards mobility and remote work environments, we believe that robotic telepresence offers a wonderful way to retain our human connections, albeit with the help of technology. This is undoubtedly a type of advancement that will become more common in offices around the world.

The results of our experiment indicate the following positive aspects and current limitations of telepresence in teleworking, as highlighted in Table 2.

Table 2. Positive aspects and current limitations

Positive aspects	Current limitations
• reduces travel costs • eliminates fatigue caused by long journeys to and from work • gains more flexibility • makes telework easier, working anywhere/anytime • increases teleworkers' socialisation in the office (crucial conversations) • solves "watercooler conversation" • is better than video conferencing • reduces CO_2 emissions • allows people who are unavoidably elsewhere to be virtually present at meetings or in the office • has a great deal of future potential for workplace • attends meetings	• quality of audio/video could be improved • robots cannot manage doors, stairs, lifts, time stamp clock etc. • shows little capacity for spontaneous social interaction • has short autonomous battery life • tends to be expensive • must be integrated with corporate security systems • learning to pilot the robot is demanding, and office conditions are not always ideal, because of obstacles, sloping floors, uneven WiFi signal, iPhone, etc. • security risks • relies on colleagues help in the case of collision

Table compiled by author

In summary we now provide nine rules that are important for workers to work effectively from home: check the suitability of your equipment, start work on time, develop self-confidence, take responsibility, set clear goals, communicate clearly, establish a work routine, work carefully and manage yourself. On the basis of the manager's views, we outline the following rules from the employer's point of view: make clear agreements, working from a home office must be a voluntary decision, trust employees, measure employee performance, do not neglect leadership, take the duty of caring for employees seriously, create a new culture of meetings, strengthen the community, welcome the employees and review corporate culture.

5   Discussion and Conclusions

The biggest challenge in developing telepresence is to achieve a sense of really being present. The important question is whether telepresence can in fact be considered a true substitute for being present in person. Will it be possible to work with human beings naturally and comfortably if you are really only present as a robot? The big advantage of telepresence is that when a job is too big, too small or too problematic for human beings, the telepresence robot will allow one to make the necessary adjustments for such a situation, thereby making life easier for the workers. We can make use of telepresence in any human environment and save billions of dollars by employing remote-controlled robots. Telepresence will improve and preserve old jobs and create new ones. This technology promises wealth and freedom, but is there a dark side, are there associated disadvantages that we should question? However, telepresence does offer a freer market for human skills, rendering each worker less vulnerable to the moods and fortunes of just a single employer.

Telepresence robotics has always been a "when, not if" technology. Unfortunately, until recently the answer has been "not yet" [13]. We believe that the development of this tool will continue to advance in the future. This technology allows the user to access a robot remotely from anywhere in the world. On the basis of the results of our investigation, we firmly believe that this tool is well suited for use by remote workers and has a role to play, not only in formal meetings in an office environment, but also in informal meetings (stand-up meetings).

In general, different people from various environments are putting telepresence robots into action. School districts, corporate offices, hospitals, medical clinics, nursing homes, business warehouses and others are seeking the potential benefits that can be gained by taking prudent advantage of the progress made within the field of telepresence robotics. But what positive features does a telepresence robot bring for the business? According to our data, the robot owner appreciates the savings in cost, time and energy, as well as the enhanced communication and presence that telepresence robotics can bring to almost any area or location. In addition to the personal and psychological benefits of being present in the workplace, according to our results robotic teleworking also offers benefits such as making experiential learning easier, allowing employers to hire the best and most experienced and skilled persons, offering more seamless work experience, and cutting down on multitasking.

The guidelines, utilisation and results in this paper were derived from a case study of the use of a robot in a corporate office environment. This paper presents the results of our experiment on the use of the telepresence robot Double 2 (which provides light, manoeuvrable, low-cost and simple operation and interaction) in an office in Austria, while being operated by a remote worker at home. Our results indicate that telepresence is an intriguing addition to the office, and the team found it to be highly effective. For the remote employee, the flexibility it provides in workplace arrangements increases morale, job satisfaction and productivity, reduces feelings of isolation, increases interaction with colleagues and gives a greater sense of belonging. What telepresence technology has given the team goes far beyond the company's initial intention of accommodating remote workers in a meaningful technological way. The motivation to try out this technology was the increasing number of remote workers in the company.

This technology allows workers to work from different remote locations at different times, and also to avoid being passive, as is the case with teleconferencing tools; instead the remote worker can move around and explore new parts of the office. The robot gives the user a physical presence by means of the ability to carry on live conversations with individuals and groups. In our opinion, this tool is probably most suitable to be used fairly infrequently. It is unlikely that telepresence will be used in the near future as a permanent substitution for going to the office. It is a useful device, however, for getting in touch with other workers and for attending meetings, for example, when illness, bad weather or disability force people to stay at home.

A survey done in 2015 shows that workers in more businesses are switching to remote work; the possibility of working flexible hours and at various locations are among the most important benefits for employees [42]. The results of a 2014 SHRM survey reveal that 48% of employers offer one or more flexible work arrangements to employees [43]. Gallup [44] found in 2016 that 43% of employees work remotely at least part of the time. We believe that this form of work is something of a controversial topic: Employees feel the most satisfaction when they work remotely (even if only on a part-time basis), while employers are not wholeheartedly in favour of it. In general, managers fear that this flexibility could leave them with an office without any workers in it. We believe, however, that the telepresence robot is not designed to replace humans, but to enhance their performance and enable all to lead less stressful lives.

Our work clearly has certain limitations and although we have experienced some challenges with this technology, workers still see the robot as a tool that can be utilised in many different applications, such as facilitating accessibility to meetings and conferences. Telepresence would naturally, for example, offer great benefits to those who wish to read a paper at a conference, perhaps in a foreign country many thousands of kilometres away, but cannot attend the conference in person. To be able to present the paper remotely via a telepresence robot would undoubtedly be a great advantage. Using robots for more effective teleworking is a reality. As technology advances, more people will spend more time working from remote locations and will use robots to increase the effectiveness of their presence. We have observed that there is a growing demand for the introduction of robots. We anticipate that this study will stimulate interest in the utilisation of the robot by remote workers because mobility has come to telepresence, and that development is opening up a wide range of uses for businesses.

References

1. Grant, C.A., Wallace, L.M., Spurgeon, P.C.: An exploration of the psychological factors affecting remote e-worker's job effectiveness, well-being and work-life balance. Empl. Relat. 35(5), 527–546 (2013)
2. Kurland, N., Bailyn, L.: Telework, the advantages and challenges of working here, there, anywhere and anytime. In: Organisational Dynamics, Autumn, pp. 53–68 (1999)
3. Nilles, J.M., Carlson, R.F., Gay, P., Hanneman, G.J.: The Telecommunications-Transportation Tradeoff. An Interdisciplinary Research Program of University of Southern California, Los Angeles. NSF-RA-5-74-020 (1973–1974)
4. Minsky, M.: Telepresence. Omni 2(9), 45–52 (1980)
5. Laparoscopy.org: Laparoscopy today (2006). http://laparoscopy.blogs.com/laparoscopy_today/LaparoscopyTodayPDFs/Laparoscopy4-1.pdf. Accessed 1 May 2018
6. Cangeloso, S.: iRobot Ava 500: the first ever self-driving telepresence robot (2013). http://www.extremetech.com/extreme/157602-irobot-ava-500-the-first-ever-self-driving-telepresence-robot. Accessed 1 May 2018
7. Do, H., et al.: An open platform telepresence robot with natural human interface. In: IEEE 3rd Annual International Conference on Cyber Technology in Automation, Control and Intelligent Systems (CYBER), pp. 81–86 (2013)

8. Leeb, R., Tonin, L., Rohm, M., Desideri, L., Carlson, T., Millán, J.d.R.: Towards independence: a BCI telepresence robot for people with severe motor disabilities. Proc. IEEE **103**(6), 969–982 (2015). https://doi.org/10.1109/jproc.2015.2419736

9. Apple.com: App store preview. https://itunes.apple.com/us/app/double/id589230178. Accessed 29 Apr 2018

10. Fernanbieter.de: Double 2 (Tagesmiete) (2018). http://shop.fernarbeiter.de/produkt/double-2-tagesmiete. Accessed 29 Apr 2018

11. Aguinis, H., Simonsen, M.M., Pierce, Ch.A.: Effects of nonverbal behaviour on perceptions of power bases. J. Soc. Psychol. **138**(4), 455–469 (1998)

12. McNelley, S.: Immersive group telepresence and the perception of eye contact (2005). http://www.dvetelepresence.com/files/eyeGazeStudy.pdf. Accessed 29 Apr 2018

13. Robotic Telepresence: State of the Industry (2013). http://www.webtorials.com/main/resource/papers/telepresence/paper11/Robotic_Telepresence.pdf. Accessed 29 Apr 2018

14. González-Jiménez, J., Galindo, C., Ruiz-Sarmiento, J.R.: Technical improvements of the Giraff telepresence robot based on user's evaluation. In: IEEE RO-MAN (2012)

15. Melendez-Fernandenz, F., Galindo, C., González-Jiménez, J.: A web-based solution for robotic telepresence. Int. J. Adv. Robot. Syst. **14**(6), 1–19 (2017)

16. Katevas, N.I.: Mobinet: the European research network on mobile robotics technology in health care services. In: ICORR 1999: International Conference on Rehabilitation Robotics, Stanford, CA, pp. 142–148 (1999)

17. Pollack, M.E., et al.: Pearl: a mobile robotic assistance for the elderly. In: Proceedings AAAI Workshop on Automation as Caregiver (2002)

18. Cesta, A., et al.: The RobotCare project cognitive systems for the care of the elderly. In: Proceedings International Conference on Aging, Disability and Independence (2003)

19. Tsai, T.-Ch., Hsu, Y.-L., Ma, A.-I., King, T., Wu, Ch.-H.: Developing a telepresence robot for interpersonal communication with the elderly in a home environment. Telemed. e-Health **13**(4), 407–424 (2007)

20. Luta, R.B.G., Bugtai, N.T., Ong, A.P.R.: Recent developments of telepresence robots for healthcare. In: 1st DLSU Graduate Research Conference (2016a). https://drive.google.com/file/d/0B8C6ZqhO1U0tUDY4aWJSNU9Da28/view. Accessed 29 Apr 2018

21. Laniel, S., Letourneau, D., Labbe, M., Grondin, F., Michaud, F.: Enhancing a beam telepresence robot for remote home care applications. In: 2017 International Conference on Virtual Rehabilitation (ICVR) (2017)

22. Guizzo, E.: When my avatar went to work. IEEE Spectr. **47**(9), 26–50 (2010)

23. Lee, M.K., Takayama, L.: Now, I have body: uses and social norms for mobile remote presence in the workplace. In: 29th International Conference on Human Factors in Computing Systems (CHI) (2011)

24. Tsui, K.M., Desai, M., Yanco, H.A., Uhlik, C.: Exploring use cases for telepresence robots. In: 6th International Conference on Human-Robot Interaction (HRI) (2011)

25. Tsui, K.M., Desai, M., Yanco, H.A.: Towards measuring the quality of interaction: communication through telepresence robots. In: Performance Metrics for Intelligent Systems Workshop (PerMIS) (2012)

26. Herring, S.C.: Telepresence robots for academics. In: ASIST 2013. https://asis.org/asist2013/proceedings/submissions/posters/140poster.pdf. Accessed 29 Apr 2018

27. Luta, R.B.G., Lindo, D.E.G., Ong, A.P.R., Bugtai, N.T.: Design of a telepresence robot utilizing wireless technology for a sustainable development. In: 4th DLSU Innovation and Technology Fair 2016. https://www.dlsu.edu.ph/conferences/ditech/2016/_pdf/paper-14.pdf. Accessed 29 Apr 2018

28. TelepresenceRobots.com: Manufactures (2016). https://telepresencerobots.com/manufactur ers. Accessed 29 Apr 2018

29. Malczewski, K.: The rise of telepresence robots for business and beyond (2014). http://factor-tech.com/connected-world/6231-the-rise-of-telepresence-robots-for-business-and-beyond/. Accessed 29 Apr 2018
30. Seitz, P.: Telepresence robots poised to multiply (2015). https://www.investors.com/news/technology/irobot-others-riding-telepresence-robot-growth/. Accessed 29 Apr 2018
31. Jetro: Market report smart robots (2018). https://www.jetro.go.jp/ext_images/en/invest/attract/pdf/mr_smartrobot.pdf. Accessed 29 Apr 2018
32. Tractica.com, Telepresence robots (2015). https://www.tractica.com/research/telepresence-robots/. Accessed 29 Apr 2018
33. WinterGreenReseach, Telepresence Robots Market Shares, Strategies, and Forecasts, Worldwide (2017). http://www.wintergreenresearch.com/telepresence-robots. Accessed 29 Apr 2018
34. The Telepresence Revolution, Carbon Disclosure Project Study (2010). https://www.att.com/Common/about_us/files/pdf/Telepresence/CDP_Telepresence_Report_Final.pdf. Accessed 29 Apr 2018
35. O'Toole, K.: Researchers: flexibility may be the key to increased productivity. https://www.gsb.stanford.edu/insights/researchers-flexibility-may-be-key-increased-productivity. Accessed 29 Apr 2018
36. BC.Edu, Bringing work home (2002). https://www.bc.edu/content/dam/files/centers/cwf/research/publications/researchreports/Bringing%20Work%20Home_Telecommuting. Accessed 30 Apr 2018
37. Thomas, D.: How to: avoid burnout. Caterer & Hotelkeeper, vol. 197, no. 44 (2007)
38. Van den Broeck, A., Vansteenkiste, M., De Witte, H., Lens, W.: Explaining the relationships between job characteristics, burnout and engagement: the role of basic psychological need satisfaction. Work Stress **22**(3), 277–294 (2008)
39. Nilles, J.M.: Making Telecommuting Happen. Van Nostrand Reinhold, New York (1994)
40. Shockley, K.: Telecommuting. http://www.siop.org/whitepapers/scientificaffairs/telecommuting/telecommuting.pdf. Accessed 29 Apr 2018
41. Loubier, A.: Benefits of telecommuting for the future of work. https://www.forbes.com/sites/andrealoubier/2017/07/20/benefits-of-telecommuting-for-the-future-of-work/#5864fb3c16c6. Accessed 29 Apr 2018
42. Sullivan, B.: Flexible hours rated as most important perk at work (2015). https://www.nbcnews.com/business/careers/flexible-hours-rated-most-important-perk-work-n444616. Accessed 30 Apr 2018
43. SHRM, Managing Flexible Work Arrangements (2016). https://www.shrm.org/resourcesandtools/tools-and-samples/toolkits/pages/managingflexibleworkarrangements.aspx. Accessed 30 Apr 2018
44. Gallup, America's Coming Workplace: Home Alone (2017). http://news.gallup.com/businessjournal/206033/america-coming-workplace-home-alone.aspx. Accessed 30 Apr 2018

Computing Logic Programming Semantics in Linear Algebra

Hien D. Nguyen[1(✉)], Chiaki Sakama[2], Taisuke Sato[3],
and Katsumi Inoue[4]

[1] University of Information Technology, VNU-HCM,
Ho Chi Minh City, Vietnam
hiennd@uit.edu.vn
[2] Wakayama University, Wakayama, Japan
sakama@sys.wakayama-u.ac.jp
[3] AI Research Center AIST, Tokyo, Japan
satou.taisuke@aist.go.jp
[4] National Institute of Informatics (NII), Tokyo, Japan
inoue@nii.ac.jp

Abstract. Logic programming is a logic-based programming paradigm, and provides languages for declarative problem solving and symbolic reasoning. In this paper, we develop new algorithms for computing logic programming semantics in linear algebra. We first introduce an algorithm for computing the least model of a definite logic program using matrices. Next, we introduce an algorithm for computing stable models of a normal logic program. We also develop optimization techniques for speeding-up those algorithms. Finally, the complexity of them is analyzed and tested in practice.

Keywords: Logic programming · Linear algebra · Definite program
Normal program

1 Introduction

Logic programming provides languages for declarative problem solving and symbolic reasoning, yet symbolic computation often suffers from the difficulty to make it scalable. On the other hand, linear algebra is the core of many applications of scientific computation and has been equipped with several scalable techniques. However, linear algebra has not been used for knowledge representation, since it only handles numbers and does not manipulate symbols. Then, it has recently been recognized that the integration of linear algebraic computation and symbolic computation is one of the promising and challenging topics in AI [1]. Such integration has potential to make symbolic reasoning scalable to real-life datasets. There are some studies for realizing logical reasoning using linear algebra.

In [2], Sato translates the rules of a Datalog program into a set of matrix equations. Based on this, the least model of a Datalog program is computed by solving the matrix equations. Yang *et al.* [3] consider learning representations of entities and relations in knowledge bases using the neural-embedding approach. This method is applied for

© Springer Nature Switzerland AG 2018
M. Kaenampornpan et al. (Eds.): MIWAI 2018, LNAI 11248, pp. 32–48, 2018.
https://doi.org/10.1007/978-3-030-03014-8_3

mining Horn clauses from relational facts represented in a vector space. Real Logic [6] is a framework where learning from numerical data and logical reasoning are integrated using first order logic syntax. Logic tensor networks (LTN) are one of the modern methods for reasoning and learning from the concrete data as real logic. This method has been applied to semantic image interpretation [7].

Logic programming can be represented based on multilinear algebra. In [4, 5], the authors used multilinear maps and tensors to represent predicates, relations, and logical atoms of a predicate calculus. Lin [11] introduces linear algebraic computation of SAT for clausal theories. Besides that, Horn, disjunctive and normal logic programs are also represented by algebraic manipulation of tensors in [8]. The study builds a new theory of logic programming, while implementation and evaluation are left open.

In this paper, we first refine the framework of [8] and present algorithms for finding the least model [9] of a definite program and stable models [12] of a normal program. Some optimization techniques for speeding-up these algorithms are studied. These methods are developed based on the structure of matrices representing logic programs. The complexity of proposed algorithms is evaluated and tested in practice.

The next section presents an algorithm for computing the least model of a definite program and an improved method for this algorithm. Section 3 presents an algorithm for finding stable models of a normal program and its improvement. Section 4 shows experimental results by testing in practice. The last section concludes the paper. Due to space limit, we omit some proofs of propositions and theorems.

2 Definite Programs

We consider a language $\mathfrak{L}$ that contains a finite set of propositional variables and the logical connectives $\neg$, $\wedge$, $\vee$ and $\leftarrow$. Given a logic program P, the set of all propositional variables appearing in P is the *Herband base* of P, denoted B_P.

2.1 Preliminaries

A *definite program* is a finite set of *rules* of the form:

$$h \leftarrow b_1 \wedge \ldots \wedge b_m (m \geq 0) \tag{1}$$

where h and b_i are propositional variables. A rule r is called *d-rule* iff r has the form:

$$h \leftarrow b_1 \vee \ldots \vee b_m (m \geq 0) \tag{2}$$

where h, b_i are propositional variables. A *d-program* is a finite set of rules that are either (1) or (2). Note that the rule (2) is a shorthand of m rules: $h \leftarrow b_1, \ldots, h \leftarrow b_m$, so a d-program is also a definite program. Given a rule r as (1) or (2), define $head(r) = h$ and $body(r) = \{b_1, \ldots, b_m\}$. In particular, the rule is a *fact* if $body(r) = \varnothing$.

A set $I \subseteq B_P$ is an *interpretation* of P. An interpretation I is a *model* of a d-program P if $\{b_1, \ldots, b_m\} \subseteq I$ implies $h \in I$ for every rule (1) in P, and $\{b_1, \ldots, b_m\} \cap I \neq \varnothing$

implies $h \in I$ for every rule (2) in P. A model I is the *least model* of P if $I \subseteq J$ for any model J of P. The T_P - *operator* is a mapping $T_P : 2^{B_P} \rightarrow 2^{B_P}$ which is defined as:

$$T_P(I) = \{h | h \leftarrow b_1 \wedge \ldots \wedge b_m \in P \text{ and } \{b_1, \ldots, b_m\} \subseteq I\} \cup$$
$$\{h | h \leftarrow b_1 \vee \ldots \vee b_n \in P \text{ and } \{b_1, \ldots, b_n\} \cap I \neq \emptyset\}.$$

The powers of T_P are defined as: $T_P^{k+1}(I) = T_P(T_P^k(I))$ and $T_P^0(I) = I$ $(k \geq 0)$.

Given $I \subseteq B_P$, there is a *fixpoint* $T_P^{n+1}(I) = T_P^n(I)(n \geq 0)$. For a definite program P, the fixpoint $T_P^n(\emptyset)$ coincides with the least model of P [9].

2.2   SD-program

We first consider a subclass of definite programs, called SD-programs.

Definition 2.1 (SD-program): A definite program P is called *singly defined* (or SD-program) if $head(r_1) \neq head(r_2)$ for any two rules r_1 and r_2 in $P(r_1 \neq r_2)$.

Definition 2.2 [8] (interpretation vector): Let P be a definite program and $B_P = \{p_1, \ldots, p_n\}$. Then an interpretation I of P is represented by a vector $v = (a_1, \ldots, a_n)^T$ where each element a_i represents the truth value of the proposition p_i such that $a_i = 1$ if $p_i \in I(1 \leq i \leq n)$; otherwise, $a_i = 0$. We write $row_i(v) = p_i$. Given $v = (a_1, \ldots, a_n)^T \in \mathbb{R}^n$, $v[i]$ is the ith element of $v(1 \leq i \leq n)$ and $v[1 \ldots k]$ is a vector $(a_1, \ldots, a_k)^T \in \mathbb{R}^k (k \leq n)$.

Definition 2.3 (matrix representation of a SD-program)[1]: Let P be an SD-program and $B_P = \{p_1, \ldots, p_n\}$. Then P is represented by a matrix $M_P \in \mathbb{R}^{n \times n}$ such that for each element $a_{ij}(1 \leq i, j \leq n)$ in M_P:

1. $a_{ij_k} = \frac{1}{m}$ $(1 \leq k \leq m; 1 \leq i, j_k \leq n)$ if $p_i \leftarrow p_{j_1} \wedge \ldots \wedge p_{j_m}$ is in P.
2. $a_{ii} = 1$ if $p_i \leftarrow$ is in P.
3. $a_{ij} = 0$, otherwise.

M_P is called a *program matrix*. We write $row_i(M_P) = p_i$ and $col_j(M_P) = p_j(1 \leq i, j \leq n)$.

By the condition of an SD-program, there is at most one rule $r \in P$ such that $head(r) = p$ for each $p \in B_P$. Then no two rules are encoded in a single row of M_P.

Definition 2.4 (initial vector): Let P be a definite program and $B_P = \{p_1, \ldots, p_n\}$. Then the *initial vector* is an interpretation $v_o = (a_1, \ldots, a_n)^T$ such that $a_i = 1$ if $row_i(v_o) = p_i$ and a fact $p_i \leftarrow$ is in $P(1 \leq i \leq n)$; otherwise, $a_i = 0$.

---

[1] In [8], the fact is represented by "$p_i \leftarrow T$" and is encoded in a matrix by $a_{ij} = 1$ where $row_i(M_P) = p_i$ and $col_j(M_P) = T$.:

Definition 2.5 [8] (thresholding function):   Given a vector $v = (a_1, \ldots, a_n)^T \in$ $\mathbb{R}^n$, define $\theta(v) = (a'_1, \ldots, a'_n)^T$ where $a'_i = 1 \ (1 \leq i \leq n)$ if $a_i \geq 1$; otherwise, $a'_i = 0$. We call it the θ-*thresholding function* of v.

Given a program matrix $M_p \in \mathbb{R}^{n \times n}$ and an initial vector $v_o \in \mathbb{R}^n$, define:

$$v_{k+1} = \theta(M_P v_k) \quad (k \geq 0).$$

It holds that $v_{k+1} = v_k$ for some $k \geq 0$. When $v_{k+1} = v_k$, we write: $v_k = FP(M_P v_o)$.

Theorem 2.1: Let P be an SD-program and $M_p \in \mathbb{R}^{n \times n}$ its program matrix. Then $m \in \mathbb{R}^n$ is a vector representing the least model of P iff $m = FP(M_P v_o)$ where v_o is the initial vector of P.

Example 2.1: Consider the program $p = \{p \leftarrow q, q \leftarrow p \wedge r, r \leftarrow s, s \leftarrow\}$ with $B_P = \{p, q, r, s\}$ then its program matrix $M_p \in \mathbb{R}^{4 \times 4}$ is the matrix (right). The initial vector of P is $v_o = (0\,0\,0\,1)^T$. Then, $v_1 = q(M_P v_0) = (0\,0\,1\,1)^T$ and $v_2 = \theta(M_P v_1) = (0\,0\,1\,1)^T = v_1$.

$$\begin{array}{cccc} p & q & r & s \\ \end{array}$$
$$\begin{pmatrix} 0 & 1 & 0 & 0 \\ \frac{1}{2} & 0 & \frac{1}{2} & 0 \\ 0 & 0 & 0 & 1 \\ 0 & 0 & 0 & 1 \end{pmatrix} \begin{array}{c} p \\ q \\ r \\ s \end{array}$$

Hence, the vector v_1 represents the least model $\{r, s\}$ of P.

Note that the fact $s \leftarrow$ in P is encoded as the rule $s \leftarrow s$ in M_P. By multiplying M_P and v_0, the 4th element of v_1 represents the truth of s after one-step of deduction.

The study [8] also introduces fixpoint computation of least models. Differently from the current study, [8] works on a program satisfying the MD-condition[2] and sets the empty set as the initial vector for computing fixpoint. In this paper, we work on an SD-program and start with the initial vector representing facts, and facts $p \leftarrow$ in P are encoded by the rule $p \leftarrow p$ rather than $p \leftarrow \top$. This has the effect of reducing non-zero elements in matrices during fixpoint computation. [8] allows the existence of constraints "$\leftarrow q$" in a program while the current study does not. Those constraints are handled as a rule "$p \leftarrow q, \neg p$" in Sect. 3.

2.3   Non-SD Programs

When a definite program P contains two rules: $r_1 : h \leftarrow b_1 \wedge \ldots \wedge b_m$ and $r_2 : h \leftarrow c_1 \wedge \ldots \wedge c_n$, P is transformed to a d-program Q such that:

$$Q = (P \setminus \{r_1, r_2\}) \cup \{r'_1, r'_2, d_1\}$$

where $r'_1 : h_1 \leftarrow b_1 \wedge \ldots \wedge b_m, r'_2 : h_2 \leftarrow c_1 \wedge \ldots \wedge c_n$ and $d_1 : h \leftarrow h_1 \vee h_2$.

Here, h_1 and h_2 are new propositional variables associated with r_1 and r_2, respectively.

Generally, a non-SD program is transformed to a d-program as follows.

---

[2] A definite program P satisfies the *MD-condition* if it satisfies the following condition: For any two rules r_1 and r_2 in P ($r_1 \neq r_2$): $head(r_1) = head(r_2)$ implies $|body(r_1)| \leq 1$ and $|body(r_2)| \leq 1$.

Definition 2.6 (transformation): Let P be a definite program and B_P its Herband base. For each $p \in B_P$, put $P_p = \{r | r \in P \text{ and } head(r) = p\}$ and $R_p = \{r | r \in P_p \text{ and } |P_p| = k > 1\}$. Then define $S_p = \{p_i \leftarrow body(r) | r \in R_p, i = 1, ..., k\}$ and $D_p = \{p \leftarrow p_1 \vee ... \vee p_k\}$. Build a d-program:

$$P' = (P \setminus \underbrace{\bigcup_{p \in B_P} R_p) \cup \bigcup_{p \in B_P} S_p}_{Q} \cup \underbrace{\bigcup_{p \in B_P} D_p}_{D}$$

We have $P' = Q \cup D$ where Q is an SD-program and D is a set of d-rules.

It is easily shown that a d-program P' has the least model M' such that $M' \cap B_P = M$ where M is the least model of P.

Definition 2.7 (matrix representation of a d-program): Let P' be a d-program such that $P' = Q \cup D$ where Q is an SD-program and D is a set of d-rules, and $B_{P'} = \{p_1, ..., p_m\}$ the Herband base of P'. Then P' is represented by a matrix $M_{P'} \in \mathbb{R}^{m \times m}$ such that for each element $a_{ij}(1 \le i, j \le m)$ in $M_{P'}$:

1. $a_{ij_k} = 1 \, (1 \le k \le l; \, 1 \le i, j_k \le m)$ if $p_i \leftarrow p_{j_1} \vee ... \vee p_{j_l}$ is in D.
2. Otherwise, every rule in Q is encoded as in Definition 2.3.

Theorem 2.2: Let P' be a d-program and $M_{P'} \in \mathbb{R}^{m \times m}$ its program matrix. Then $u \in \mathbb{R}^m$ is a vector representing the least model of P' iff $u = FP(M_{P'} v_o)$ where v_o is the initial vector of P'.

2.4   Algorithms for Finding Least Models

Based on Theorem 2.2, we develop an algorithm for computing the least model of a definite program P (Fig. 1).

Example 2.2: Consider $P = \{p \leftarrow q, p \leftarrow r \wedge s, r \leftarrow s, s \leftarrow\}$ and $B_P = \{p, q, r, s\}$. Then P is transformed to a d-program $P' = Q \cup D$ with $B_{P'} = \{p, q, r, s, t, u\}$:

$$Q = \{t \leftarrow q, u \leftarrow r \wedge s, r \leftarrow s, s \leftarrow\}$$
$$D = \{p \leftarrow t \vee u\}.$$

We have the matrix $M_{P'} \in \mathbb{R}^{6 \times 6}$ representing P' (right). Let $v_0 = (0\,0\,0\,1\,0\,0)^T$ be a vector representing facts in P'. Then, $v_1 = \theta(M_{P'} v_0) = (0\,0\,1\,1\,0\,0)^T$, $v_2 = \theta(M_{P'} v_1) = (0\,0\,1\,1\,0\,1)^T, v_3 = \theta(M_{P'} v_2) = (1\,0\,1\,1\,0\,1)^T, v_4 = \theta(M_{P'} v_3) = (1\,0\,1\,1\,0\,1)^T = v_3$. Hence, v_3 is a vector representing the least model of P', and $v_3[1...4]$ is a vector representing the least model of P, that represents $\{p, r, s\}$.

$$M_{P'} = \begin{pmatrix} & p & q & r & s & t & u \\ 0 & 0 & 0 & 0 & 1 & 1 & p \\ 0 & 0 & 0 & 0 & 0 & 0 & q \\ 0 & 0 & 0 & 1 & 0 & 0 & r \\ 0 & 0 & 0 & 1 & 0 & 0 & s \\ 0 & 1 & 0 & 0 & 0 & 0 & t \\ 0 & 0 & \tfrac{1}{2} & \tfrac{1}{2} & 0 & 0 & u \end{pmatrix}$$

Algorithm 2.1:
    Input: a definite program P, and its Herband base $B_P = \{p_1,...,p_n\}$.
    Output: a vector u representing the least model of P.

Step 1: Transform a definite program P to a d-program $P' = Q \cup D$ with $B_{P'} = \{p_1,...,p_m, p_{n+1},...,p_m\}$, where Q is an SD-program and D is a set of d-rules.	**Step 3:** *Compute the least model of P'* $v := v_o$ $u := \theta(M_{P'} \cdot v)$ while $u \neq v$ do
Step 2: - Create the matrix $M_{P'} = (a_{ij})_{1 \leq i,j \leq m}$ representing a d-program P'. - Create the initial vector $v_o = (v_1,...v_m)$ of P'.	$v := u$; $u := \theta(M_{P'} \cdot v)$ end do; #while return $u[1...n]$;

Fig. 1. Computation of least models

In Algorithm 2.1, the complexity of computing $M_{P'}v$ is $O(m^2)$ and computing $\theta(.)$ is $O(m)$. The number of times for iterating $M_{P'}v$ is at most $(m + 1)$ times. So the complexity of Step 3 is $O((m + 1) \times (m + m^2)) = O(m^3)$ in the worst case. Comparing the current study with the previous one [8], the current encoding has an advantage of increasing zero elements in matrices and reducing the number of required iterations in fixpoint computation.

2.5 Column Reduction

This section introduces a method for decreasing the complexity of computing $u = \theta(M_{P'}v)$.

Definition 2.8 (submatrix representation of a d-program): Let P' be a d-program such that $P' = Q \cup D$ where Q is an SD-program and D is a set of d-rules, and $B_{P'} = \{p_1,\ldots, p_m\}$ the Herband base of P'. Then P' is represented by a matrix $N_{P'} \in \mathbb{R}^{m \times n}$ such that each element $b_{ij}(1 \leq i \leq m, 1 \leq j \leq n)$ in $N_{P'}$ is equivalent to the corresponding element $a_{ij}(1 \leq i,j \leq m)$ in $M_{P'}$ of Definition 2.7. $N_{P'}$ is called a *submatrix* of P'.

Note that the size of $M_{P'} \in \mathbb{R}^{m \times m}$ of Definition 2.7 is reduced to $N_{P'} \in \mathbb{R}^{m \times n}$ in Definition 2.8 by $n \leq m$.

Definition 2.9 (θ_D-thresholding): Given a vector $v = (a_1,\ldots, a_m)^T$, define a vector $w = \theta_D(v) = (w_1,\ldots, w_m)^T$ such that (i) $w_i = 1 \, (1 \leq i \leq m)$ if $a_i \geq 1$, (ii) $w_i = 1$ $(1 \leq i \leq n)$ if $\exists j \, w_j = 1 \, (n+1 \leq j \leq m)$ and there is a d-rule $d \in D$ such that $head(d) = p_i$ and $row_j(w) \in body(d)$, and (iii) otherwise, $w_i = 0$. $\theta_D(v)$ is called a θ_D-*thresholding* of v.

Intuitively speaking, the additional condition of Definition 2.9(ii) says "if an element in the body of a d-rule is 1, then the element in the head of the d-rule is set to 1". θ_D adds this condition to θ, in return for reducing columns. By definition, it holds that $\theta_D(v) = \theta_D(\theta(v))$.

$\theta_D(v)$ is computed by checking the value of a_i for $1 \leq i \leq m$ and checking all d-rules for $n+1 \leq j \leq m$. Since the number of d-rules is at most n, the complexity of computing $\theta_D(.)$ is $O(m + (m-n) \times n) = O(m \times n)$.

Theorem 2.3: Let P be a definite program with $B_P = \{p_1, \ldots, p_n\}$, and P' a transformed d-program with $B_{P'} = \{p_1, \ldots, p_n, p_{n+1}, \ldots, p_m\}$. Let $N_{P'} \in \mathbb{R}^{m \times n}$ be a submatrix of P'. Given a vector $v \in \mathbb{R}^n$ representing an interpretation I of P, let $u = \theta_D(N_{P'}v) \in \mathbb{R}^m$.

Then u is a vector representing an interpretation J of P' such that $J \cap B_P = T_P(I)$.

Proof:

Let $v = (v_1, \ldots, v_n)^T$ then $N_{P'}v = (x_1, \ldots, x_n, \ldots, x_m)^T$ with $x_k = a_{k1}v_1 + \ldots + a_{kn}v_n (1 \leq k \leq m)$.

Suppose $\quad w = \theta(N_{P'}v) = (w_1, \ldots, w_m)^T \quad$ and $\quad u = \theta_D(N_{P'}v) = \theta_D(w) = (u_1, \ldots, u_m)^T$.

(I) First, we prove $J \cap B_P \subseteq T_P(I)$.

Let $u_k = 1 (1 \leq k \leq n)$ and $p_k = row_k(u)$. We show $p_k \in T_P(I)$.

(i) Assume $w_k = u_k = 1$. By $w_k = 1, x_k = a_{k1}v_1 + \ldots + a_{kn}v_n \geq 1$.

Let $\{b_1, \ldots, b_r\} \subseteq \{a_{k1}, \ldots, a_{kn}\}$ such that $b_i \neq 0 (1 \leq i \leq r)$. Then, $b_i = 1/r (1 \leq i \leq r)$ and $b_1 v_{b1} + \ldots + b_r v_{br} = 1$ imply $v_{b1} = \ldots = v_{br} = 1$. In this case, there is a rule: $p_k \leftarrow p_{b1} \wedge \ldots \wedge p_{br}$ in P such that $p_{bi} = col_i(N_{P'})$ for $b_i = a_{ki}(1 \leq i \leq r)$ and $\{p_{b1}, \ldots, p_{br}\} \subseteq I$. Hence, $p_k \in T_P(I)$ holds.

(ii) Next assume $u_k \neq w_k$, then $w_k = 0$.

As $w_k = 0$, by definition of $\theta_D(.)$, $\exists j, n + 1 \leq j \leq m$ such that $w_j = 1$. Also, $\exists d_j \in D$ such that $row_j(w) = p_j \in body(d_j)$ and $head(d_j) = p_k$ where d_j has the form: $p_k \leftarrow p_{k1} \vee \ldots \vee p_{kq}$ with $p_j \in \{p_{k1}, \ldots, p_{kq}\} \subseteq B_{P'} \setminus B_P$. By $w_j = 1 (n + 1 \leq j \leq m)$, it holds $x_j = a_{j1}v_1 + \ldots + a_{jn}v_n \geq 1$. Let $\{b_1, \ldots, b_r\} \subseteq \{a_{j1}, \ldots, a_{jn}\}$ such that $b_i \neq 0 (1 \leq i \leq r)$. Then, $b_i = 1/r (1 \leq i \leq r)$ and $b_1 v_{b1} + \ldots + b_r v_{br} = 1$ imply $v_{b1} = \ldots = v_{br} = 1$.

In this case, there is a rule: $p_j \leftarrow p_{b1} \wedge \ldots \wedge p_{br}$ in Q such that $p_{bi} = col_j(N_{P'})$ for $b_i = a_{ki}(1 \leq i \leq r)$ and $\{p_{b1}, \ldots, p_{br}\} \subseteq I$. By transforming a definite program P to a d-program P', we have: $p_k \leftarrow p_{b1} \wedge \ldots \wedge p_{br} \in P$ and $\{p_{b1}, \ldots, p_{br}\} \subseteq I$. Hence, $p_k \in T_P(I)$.

In both (i) and (ii), it holds that $p_k = row_k(u) \in T_P(I)$ if $u_k = 1 (1 \leq k \leq n)$. Then $J \cap B_P \subseteq T_P(I)$.

(II) Next, we prove $T_P(I) \subseteq J \cap B_P$. We show that $p_k \in T_P(I)$ implies $u_k = 1 (1 \leq k \leq n)$.

Let $p_k \in T_P(I)$, then there is $p_k \leftarrow p_{k1} \wedge \ldots \wedge p_{kr} \in P (1 \leq k \leq n)$ such that $\{p_{k1}, \ldots, p_{kr}\} \subseteq I$, so $v_{kj} = 1 (1 \leq j \leq r)$.

(i) If $p_k \leftarrow p_{k1} \wedge \ldots \wedge p_{kr} \in Q$ then $p_{kj} \in B_P$. Then $\exists i, p_{kj} = col_i(N_{P'})(1 \leq i \leq n)$ and $a_{kj} = 1/r$. Hence, $x_k = a_{k1}v_1 + \ldots + a_{kn}v_n = 1$ and $w_k = 1 = u_k$.

(ii) Else if $p_k \leftarrow p_{k1} \wedge \ldots \wedge p_{kr} \notin Q$ then $\exists j, n + 1 \leq j \leq m, p_j \leftarrow p_{j1} \wedge \ldots \wedge p_{jr} \in Q$ and $p_k \leftarrow p_{k1} \vee \ldots \vee p_{kq} \in D$ with $p_j \in \{p_{k1}, \ldots, p_{kq}\}$.

By $p_j \leftarrow p_{j1} \wedge \ldots \wedge p_{jr} \in Q$, it holds $p_{ji} \in B_P$. Then $\exists l, p_{ji} = col_l(N_{P'})$ $(1 \leq l \leq n)$ and $a_{jl} = 1/r$. Thus, $x_j = a_{j1}v_1 + \ldots + a_{jn}v_n = 1$ and $w_j = 1$.

Since $p_k \leftarrow p_{k1} \vee \ldots \vee p_{kq} \in D$ and $row_j(w) = p_j \in \{p_{k1}, \ldots, p_{kq}\}$, it becomes $u_k = 1$(by the definition of θ_D in Definition 2.9(ii)).

By (i) and (ii), $p_k \in T_P(I)$ implies $u_k = 1$ $(1 \leq k \leq n)$, thereby $T_P(I) \in J \cap B_P$

Hence: $J \cap B_P = T_P(I)$ □

Given a matrix $N_{P'} \in \mathbb{R}^{m \times n}$ and the initial vector v_0 of P', define $v_{k+1} = \theta_D(N_{P'}v_k[1\ldots n])(k \geq 0)$. Then it holds that $v_{k+1} = v_k$ for some $k \geq 1$. When $v_{k+1} = v_k$, we write $v_k = FP(N_{P'}v_0[1\ldots n])$. It shows that $FP(N_{P'}v_0[1\ldots n])$ represents the least model of P.

Generally, given a d-program P', the value k of $v_k = FP(N_{P'}v_0[1\ldots n])$ is not greater than the value h of $v_h = FP(M_{P'}v_o)$ in Sect. 2.2.

Example 2.3: For the d-program P' of Example 2.2, we have the submatrix $N_{P'} \in \mathbb{R}^{6 \times 4}$ representing P' (right). Given the initial vector $v_0 = (0\,0\,0\,1\,0\,0)^T$ of P', it becomes $v_1 = \theta_D(N_{P'}v_0[1\ldots 4]) = (0\,0\,1\,1\,0\,0)^T$, $v_2 = \theta_D(N_{P'}v_1[1\ldots 4]) = (1\,0\,1\,1\,0\,1)^T$, $v_3 = \theta_D(N_{P'}v_2[1\ldots 4]) = (1\,0\,1\,1\,0\,1)^T = v_2$.

$$N_{P'} = \begin{pmatrix} & p & q & r & s \\ 0 & 0 & 0 & 0 & p \\ 0 & 0 & 0 & 0 & q \\ 0 & 0 & 0 & 1 & r \\ 0 & 0 & 0 & 1 & s \\ 0 & 1 & 0 & 0 & t \\ 0 & 0 & \tfrac{1}{2} & \tfrac{1}{2} & u \end{pmatrix}$$

Then v_2 is a vector representing the least model of P', and $v_2[1\ldots 4]$ is a vector representing the least model $\{p, r, s\}$ of P. Note that the first element of v_i $(i = 2, 3)$ becomes 1 by Definition 2.9(ii).

By Theorem 2.3, we can replace the computation $u = \theta(M_{P'}v)$ in Step 3 of Algorithm 2.1 by $u = \theta_D(N_{P'}v[1\ldots n])$. In the column reduction method, the complexity of computing $N_{P'}v[1\ldots n]$ is $O(m \times n)$ and computing $\theta_D(.)$ is $O(m \times n)$. The number of times for iterating $N_{P'}v$ is at most $(m + 1)$ times. So the complexity of computing $u = \theta_D(N_{P'}v[1\ldots n])$ is $O((m+1) \times (m \times n + m \times n)) = \mathbf{O(m^2 \times n)}$. Comparing the complexity $O(m^3)$ of Step 3 of Algorithm 2.1, the column reduction reduces the complexity to $O(m^2 \times n)$ as $n < < m$ in general.

3 Normal Programs

In [8], normal programs are converted to disjunctive programs using the transformation by [13], and then encoded in matrices using third-order tensors. In this paper, we first transform normal programs to definite programs using the transformation in [12] and then encode them in matrices as in Sect. 2.

3.1 Computing Stable Models of a Normal Program

A *normal program* P is a finite set of *rules* of the form:

$$h \leftarrow b_1 \wedge \ldots \wedge b_k \wedge \neg b_{k+1} \wedge \ldots \wedge \neg b_m \quad (m \geq 0) \tag{3}$$

where h and b_j are propositional variables. P is transformed to a definite program by rewriting the above rule as:

$$h \leftarrow b_1 \wedge \ldots \wedge b_k \wedge \overline{b_{k+1}} \wedge \ldots \wedge \overline{b_m} \quad (m \geq 0) \tag{4}$$

where $\overline{b_i}$ is a new proposition associated with b_i. We call b_i a positive literal and $\overline{b_j}$ a negative literal.

Given a normal program P and an interpretation $I \subseteq B_P$, the transformed definite program is denoted by P^+, called a *positive form*. As Definition 2.6, we can transform P^+ to a d-program P'. Define $\overline{I} = \{\overline{p} | p \in B_P \backslash I\}$ and $I^+ = I \cup \overline{I}$.

Theorem 3.1 [12]: Let P be a normal program. Then, I is a stable model of P iff I^+ is the least model of $P^+ \cup \overline{I}$.

Definition 3.1 (program matrix for a normal program): Let P be a normal program with $B_P = \{p_1, \ldots, p_k\}$, and P^+ its positive form with $B_{P+} = \{p_1, \ldots, p_k, \overline{q_{n+1}}, \ldots, \overline{q_m}\}$. Also, let P' be a d-program that is obtained from P^+ with $B_{P'} = \{p_1, \ldots, p_k, p_{k+1}, \ldots, p_n, \overline{q_{n+1}}, \ldots, \overline{q_m}\}$. We have $\{q_{n+1}, \ldots, q_m\} \subseteq \{p_1, \ldots, p_k\}$, and P' has n positive literals and $(m-n)$ negative literals. Then P' is represented by a matrix $M_{P'} \in \mathbb{R}^{m \times m}$ such that for each element $a_{ij}(1 \leq i, j \leq m)$ in $M_{P'}$:

1. $a_{ii} = 1$ for $n+1 \leq i \leq m$
2. $a_{ij} = 0$ for $n+1 \leq i \leq m$ and $1 \leq j \leq m$ such that $i \neq j$
3. Otherwise, $a_{ij}(1 \leq i \leq n; \ 1 \leq j \leq m)$ is encoded as in Definition 2.7.

By definition, negative literals are encoded in $M_{P'}$ in the same manner as facts. Intuitively, $a_{ii} = 1$ for $\overline{q_i}$ represents the rule $\overline{q_i} \leftarrow \overline{q_i}$ that means a "guess" for $\overline{q_i}$.

Definition 3.2 (initial matrix): Let P be a normal program and $B_P = \{p_1, \ldots, p_k\}$, P' its transformed d-program (via. P^+) and $B_{P'} = \{p_1, \ldots, p_k, p_{k+1}, \ldots, p_n, \overline{q_{n+1}}, \ldots, \overline{q_m}\}$. The *initial matrix* $M_o \in \mathbb{R}^{m \times h}(1 \leq h \leq 2^{m-n})$ is defined as follows:

- Each row of M_o corresponds to each element of $B_{P'}$ in a way that $\text{row}_i(M_o) = p_i$ for $1 \leq i \leq n$ and $\text{row}_i(M_o) = \overline{q_i}$ for $n+1 \leq i \leq m$.
- $a_{ij} = 1(1 \leq i \leq n, \ 1 \leq j \leq h)$iff a fact $p_i \leftarrow$ is in P; otherwise, $a_{ij} = 0$.
- $a_{ij} = 0(n+1 \leq i \leq m, \ 1 \leq j \leq h)$iff a fact $q_i \leftarrow$ is in P; otherwise, there are two possibilities 0 and 1 for a_{ij}, so it is either 0 or 1.

Each column of M_o corresponds to a potential stable model.

Let P be a normal program and P' its transformed d-program. For the program matrix $M_{P'} \in \mathbb{R}^{m \times m}$ and the initial matrix $M_o \in \mathbb{R}^{m \times h}$. Define: $M_{k+1} = \theta(M_{P'} M_k) \ (k \geq 0)$.

It holds that $M_{k+1} = M_k$ for some $k \geq 0$. When $M_{k+1} = M_k$, we write $M_k = FP(M_{P'} M_o)$.

Suppose $M_k = FP(M_{P'} M_o) \ (k \geq 1)$. Let $u = (a_1 \ldots a_n, a_{n+1} \ldots a_m)^T$ be a column vector in M_k such that $a_j = 1 \ (\text{resp.} a_j = 0) \ (n+1 \leq j \leq m)$ iff $a_i = 0$ (resp. $a_i = 1$) with i such that $1 \leq i \leq n, \text{row}_j(M_o) = \overline{q}_j$ and $\text{row}_i(M_o) = p_i = q_j$. Then we have the next result.

Theorem 3.2: u is a column vector representing the interpretation I of P' iff $I \cap B_P$ is a stable model of P.

3.2   Algorithm for Computing Stable Models

Based on Theorem 3.2, we have an algorithm for finding stable models of a normal program P (Fig. 2).

Example 3.1: Consider $P = \{p \leftarrow q \wedge \neg r \wedge s, q \leftarrow \neg t \wedge q, q \leftarrow s, r \leftarrow \neg t, s \leftarrow, t \leftarrow\}$ with $B_P = \{p, q, r, s, t\}$. First, P is transformed to a positive form P^+ and a d-program P' as follows:

- $P^+ = \{p \leftarrow q \wedge \bar{r} \wedge s, q \leftarrow \bar{t} \wedge q, q \leftarrow s,$
  $r \leftarrow \bar{t}, s \leftarrow, t \leftarrow\}$
- $P' = Q \cup D$ where : $Q = \{p \leftarrow q \wedge \bar{r} \wedge s,$
  $q_1 \leftarrow \bar{t} \wedge q, q_2 \leftarrow s, r \leftarrow \bar{t}, s \leftarrow, t \leftarrow\}$
  $D = \{q \leftarrow q_1 \vee q_2\}$

We have the representing matrix $M_{P'} \in \mathbb{R}^{9 \times 9}$ and the initial matrix $M_o \in \mathbb{R}^{9 \times 2}$:

$$
M_{P'} =
\begin{pmatrix}
 & p & q & r & s & t & q_1 & q_2 & \bar{r} & \bar{t} & \\
0 & 1/3 & 0 & 1/3 & 0 & 0 & 0 & 1/3 & 0 & p \\
0 & 0 & 0 & 0 & 0 & 1 & 1 & 0 & 0 & q \\
0 & 0 & 0 & 0 & 0 & 0 & 0 & 0 & 1 & r \\
0 & 0 & 0 & 1 & 0 & 0 & 0 & 0 & 0 & s \\
0 & 0 & 0 & 0 & 1 & 0 & 0 & 0 & 0 & t \\
0 & \tfrac{1}{2} & 0 & 0 & 0 & 0 & 0 & 0 & \tfrac{1}{2} & q_1 \\
0 & 0 & 0 & 1 & 0 & 0 & 0 & 0 & 0 & q_2 \\
0 & 0 & 0 & 0 & 0 & 0 & 0 & 1 & 0 & \bar{r} \\
0 & 0 & 0 & 0 & 0 & 0 & 0 & 0 & 1 & \bar{t}
\end{pmatrix}
$$

$$
M_0 =
\begin{matrix}
p \\ q \\ r \\ s \\ t \\ q_1 \\ q_2 \\ \bar{r} \\ \bar{t}
\end{matrix}
\begin{pmatrix}
0 & 0 \\
0 & 0 \\
0 & 0 \\
1 & 1 \\
1 & 1 \\
0 & 0 \\
0 & 0 \\
0 & 1 \\
0 & 0
\end{pmatrix}
\quad
M_1 =
\begin{pmatrix}
0 & 0 \\
0 & 0 \\
0 & 0 \\
1 & 1 \\
1 & 1 \\
0 & 0 \\
1 & 1 \\
0 & 1 \\
0 & 0
\end{pmatrix}
\quad
M_2 =
\begin{pmatrix}
0 & 0 \\
1 & 1 \\
0 & 0 \\
1 & 1 \\
1 & 1 \\
0 & 0 \\
1 & 1 \\
0 & 1 \\
0 & 0
\end{pmatrix}
\quad
M_3 =
\begin{pmatrix}
0 & 1 \\
1 & 1 \\
0 & 0 \\
1 & 1 \\
1 & 1 \\
0 & 0 \\
1 & 1 \\
0 & 1 \\
0 & 0
\end{pmatrix}
$$

Then $M_1 = \theta(M_{P'}M_o), M_2 = \theta(M_{P'}M_1), M_3 = \theta(M_{P'}M_2) \cdot M_4 = \theta(M_{P'}M_3) = M_3$ becomes the fixpoint. In this case, the column vector $u = (1\ 1\ 0\ 1\ 1\ 0\ 1\ 1\ 0)^{\mathrm{T}}$ satisfies the condition $u[8] = 1$ iff $u[3] = 0$ where $\text{row}_8(u) = \bar{r}$ and $\text{row}_3(u) = r$. The vector u represents the set $\{p, q, s, t, q_2, \bar{r}\}$ and $\{p, q, s, t, q_2, \bar{r}\} \cap B_P = \{p, q, s, t\}$ is the stable model of P.

In Algorithm 3.1, the complexity of $M_{P'}M$ is $\mathbf{O}(m^2 \times h)$. The number of times for iterating $M_{P'}M$ is at most $(m + 1)$ times. Thus, the complexity of Step 3 is $\mathbf{O}((m+1) \times m^2 \times h) = \mathbf{O}(m^3 \times h)$ in the worst case. In this method, we encode a normal program into a program matrix, while [8] encodes a normal program into a 3rd-order tensor. Since the number of slices in a 3rd-order tensor increases exponentially in general, the current method would have a computational advantage over [8].

Algorithm 3.1:
  Input: a normal program P and the Herband base $B_P = \{p_1,...,p_k\}$
  Output: A set of vectors representing stable models of P.

| Step 1: Transform a normal program P to d-program P' (via P^+) with $B_{P'} = \{p_1,...,p_k,$ $\overline{p_{k+1}},...,\overline{p_n},\overline{q_{n+1}}...,\overline{q_m}\}$ Step 2:
 - Create the matrix $M_{P'} \in \mathbb{R}^{m \times m}$ representing a d-program P'.
 - Create the initial matrix $M_o \in \mathbb{R}^{m \times h}$ of P'.
 Step 3: *Compute a fixpoint* $FP(M_{P'}M_o)$
 $M := M_o$
 $U := \theta(M_{P'}M)$
 while $U \neq M$ do
 $\quad M := U;$
 $\quad U := \theta(M_{P'}M);$
 end do; | Step 4: *Find stable models of P*
 result:=$\{\,\}$;
 for i from 1 to h do
 $\quad v := (a_1...a_n,a_{n+1},...,a_m)^{\mathrm{T}}$ is i^{th}-column of M
 $\quad$ for j from $n+1$ to m do
 $\quad\quad \overline{q_j} := \mathrm{row}_j(M);$
 $\quad\quad$ for l from 1 to n do
 $\quad\quad\quad$ if $\mathrm{row}_l(M) = q_j$ then
 $\quad\quad\quad\quad$ if $a_l + a_j \neq 1$ then break;
 $\quad\quad\quad$ end for; #l
 $\quad\quad\quad$ if $l \leq n$ then break;
 $\quad\quad$ end for; #j
 $\quad\quad$ if $j \leq m$ then break;
 $\quad\quad$ else result := result $\cup \{v\}$;
 $\quad$ end for;
 return result; |

Fig. 2. Computation of stable models

3.3   Column Reduction

We apply the submatrix technique of Definition 2.8 to program matrices for normal programs. That is, instead of considering a program matrix $M_P \in \mathbb{R}^{m \times m}$ of Definition 3.1, we consider a submatrix $N_{P'} \in \mathbb{R}^{m \times r}$ where $r = k + (m-n)$. Note that, $r \ll m$ in general.

Definition 3.4 (initial vector): Let P be a normal program with $B_P = \{p_1,...,p_k\}$, and P^+ its positive form with $B_{P^+} = \{p_1,...,p_k,\overline{q_{n+1}},...\overline{q_m}\}$ where $\{q_{n+1},...,q_m\} \subseteq \{p_1,...,p_k\}$.
  Then the set of initial vectors of a positive form P^+ is defined as follows:
  Let $v_1 \in \mathbb{R}^k$ be a vector representing facts in P where $\mathrm{row}_j(v_1) = p_j$.
  Consider $A \subseteq \mathbb{R}^{r-k}$ where $A = \left\{(1\,0...0)^{\mathrm{T}},(1\,1...0)^{\mathrm{T}},....,(1\,1...1)^{\mathrm{T}}\right\}$ with $\mathrm{card}(A) = 2^{r-k}$, and $B = \{v \in A | \exists i(1 \leq i \leq r-k)$ s.t. $v[i] = 1$ and $\exists j(1 \leq j \leq k)$ s.t. $v_1[j] = 1$ and $\mathrm{row}_j(v_1) = p$ iff $\mathrm{row}_i(v) = \overline{p}$ where v_1 represents facts in $P\}$. Put $v_2 \in \mathbb{R}^{r-k}$s.t. $v_2 \in A \backslash B$. The set of initial vectors V of P^+ is:

$$V = \left\{v \in \mathbb{R}^r | v = \begin{pmatrix} v_1 \\ v_2 \end{pmatrix}, v_2 \in A \backslash B\right\} \text{ and } h = \mathrm{card}(V)$$

Intuitively, the set of initial vectors V represents facts in P together with possible negative literals in P'. By Theorem 2.3, if $v \in \mathbb{R}^r$ is a vector representing an interpretation I of P^+, and $u = \theta_D(N_{P'}v) \in \mathbb{R}^m$, then u is a vector representing an interpretation J of P' and $J \cap B_{P^+} = T_{P^+}(I)$.

For this reason, in Step 3 of Algorithm 3.1, we can replace the computation of a fixpoint $FP(M_{P'}M_o)$ by the computation of a fixpoint $FP(N_{P'}u_o[1\ldots r])$ with the initial vector $u_o \in V$. In the column reduction method, the complexity of computing $N_{P'}u_o[1\ldots n']$ is $O(m \times r)$ and computing $\theta_D(.)$ is $O(m \times r)$. Since the number of times for iterating $N_{P'}u_o[1\ldots r]$ is at most $(m+1)$ times and $|V| = h$, the complexity of step 3 of this algorithm is $O((m+1) \times (m \times r + m \times r) \times h) = O(m^2 \times r \times h)$. Comparing the complexity $O(m^3 \times h)$ of Step 3 of Algorithm 3.1, the column reduction reduces the complexity to $O(m^2 \times r \times h)$ by $r << m$ in general.

Example 3.2: Consider a normal program P and a d-program P' of Example 3.1.

We have the submatrix $N_{P'} \in \mathbb{R}^{9 \times 7}$ representing P':

- $v_1 \in \mathbb{R}^5$ represents the facts in P, $v_1 = (0\,0\,0\,1\,1)^{\mathrm{T}}$
- $A = \left\{ (00)^{\mathrm{T}}, (10)^{\mathrm{T}}, (01)^{\mathrm{T}}, (11)^{\mathrm{T}} \right\}$ with card $(A) = 2^2 = 4$
- $B = \left\{ (01)^{\mathrm{T}}, (11)^{\mathrm{T}} \right\}$, $v_2 \in A \backslash B = \left\{ (00)^{\mathrm{T}}, (10)^{\mathrm{T}} \right\}$
- $V = \left\{ (0\,0\,0\,1\,1\,0\,0)^{\mathrm{T}}, (0\,0\,0\,1\,1\,1\,0)^{\mathrm{T}} \right\}$
  with $h = \mathrm{card}(V) = 2$

$$N_{P'} = \begin{pmatrix} 0 & 1/3 & 0 & 1/3 & 0 & 1/3 & 0 \\ 0 & 0 & 0 & 0 & 0 & 0 & 0 \\ 0 & 0 & 0 & 0 & 0 & 0 & 1 \\ 0 & 0 & 0 & 1 & 0 & 0 & 0 \\ 0 & 0 & 0 & 0 & 1 & 0 & 0 \\ 0 & 0 & 0 & 0 & 0 & 1 & 0 \\ 0 & 0 & 0 & 1 & 0 & 0 & 1 \\ 0 & \tfrac{1}{2} & 0 & 0 & 0 & 0 & \tfrac{1}{2} \\ 0 & 0 & 0 & 1 & 0 & 0 & 0 \end{pmatrix} \begin{matrix} p \\ q \\ r \\ s \\ t \\ \bar{r} \\ \bar{t} \\ q_1 \\ q_2 \end{matrix}$$

with column headers $p \quad q \quad r \quad s \quad t \quad \bar{r} \quad \bar{t}$

Compute a fixpoint $FP(N_{P'}u_o)$ $(u_o \in V)$:

(i) For $u_o = (0\,0\,0\,1\,1\,0\,0)^{\mathrm{T}}$:

$$u_1 = \theta_D(N_{P'}u_o) = (0\,1\,0\,1\,1\,0\,0\,0\,1)^{\mathrm{T}}$$
$$u_2 = \theta_D(N_{P'}u_1[1\ldots 7]) = (0\,1\,0\,1\,1\,0\,0\,0\,1)^{\mathrm{T}} = u_1.$$

$\mathrm{row}_3(u_1) = r$ and $\mathrm{row}_6(u_1) = \bar{r}$ then $u_1[3] + u_1[6] = 0$, so u_1 does not represent a stable model of P.

(ii) For $u_o = (0\,0\,0\,1\,1\,1\,0)^{\mathrm{T}}$: $u_1 = \theta_D(N_{P'}u_o) = (0\,1\,0\,1\,1\,1\,0\,0\,1)^{\mathrm{T}}$, $u_2 = \theta_D(N_{P'}u_1[1\ldots 7]) = (1\,1\,0\,1\,1\,1\,0\,0\,1)^{\mathrm{T}}$, $u_3 = \theta_D(N_{P'}u_2[1\ldots 7]) = (1\,1\,0\,1\,1\,1\,0\,0\,1)^{\mathrm{T}} = u_2$.

$$\mathrm{row}_3(u_2) = r \text{ and } \mathrm{row}_6(u_2) = \bar{r} \text{ then } u_2[3] + u_2[6] = 1$$
$$\mathrm{row}_5(u_2) = t \text{ and } \mathrm{row}_7(u_2) = \bar{t} \text{ then } u_2[5] + u_2[7] = 1$$

u_2 represents the set $\{p, q, s, t, \bar{r}, q_2\}$ and $\{p, q, s, t, \bar{r}\} \cap B_P = \{p, q, s, t\}$ is the stable model of P.

4   Experimental Results

In this section, we compare runtime for finding the least model of a definite program and the set of stable models of a normal program by the following three algorithms: (i) computing the fixpoint of the T_P-operator; (ii) matrix computation; (iii) column reduction computation. The testing is run on a GPU that has configuration as follows:

- Operating system: Linux Ubuntu 16.04 LTS 64bit.
- CPU: Intel® Core™ i7-6800 K <3.4 GHz/14 nm/ Cores = 6/ Threads = 12/ Cache = 15 MB>, Memory 32 GB, DDR-2400
- GPU: GeForce GTX1070TI GDDR5 8 GB
- Implementation language: Maple 2017, 64 bit [14].

GPU speeds up the computing and further speed-up would be gained by using CUDA package in Maple.

4.1   Testing on Definite Programs

In this testing, given the size $n = |B_P|$ of the Herband base B_P and the number $m = |P|$ of rules in P, rules are created randomly as in Table 1:

Table 1. Proportion of rules in P based on the number of propositional variables in their bodies

Number of elements in body	0	1	2	3	4	5	6	7	8
Number of rules (proportion)	x, where x < n/3	4%	4%	10%	40%	35%	4%	2%	~1%

Based on (n, m), generate a definite program P randomly. After that, we transform P to a d-program $P' = Q \cup D$ where Q is an SD-program and D is a set of d-rules. The program P' will have n' variables and m' rules. Table 2 shows the results of testing Algorithm 2.1 on P' and computation by the T_P-operator [9] for constructing the least model of a program P. There are two important steps in Algorithm 2.1: Step 2 for creating a program matrix $M_{P'}$ to represent a definite program P', and step 3 for computing the fixpoint. We compare three cases—**(Case 1):** Use the T_P-operator on a program P; **(Case 2):** naive computation on a program P' by Algorithm 2.1; **(Case 3):** computation by column reduction on a program P' as Sect. 2.5.

Note that in some cases the number of rules in P' is smaller than those of $P(m' < m)$. This is because we eliminate every rule r in P' such that $head(r) = p$ and the fact $p \leftarrow$ is in P. Comparison of fixpoint computation is shown in Fig. 3. We can observe the following facts: The naive method is slower than the T_P-operator while the column reduction technique significantly reduces runtime and is fastest among three algorithms. The runtime efficiency of column reduction comes from the fact $n < < n'$.

Table 2. Results of testing on definite programs

n	m	T_P - operator (sec.)	n'	m'	Matrix Fixpoint/All (sec.)	Column reduction Fixpoint/All (sec.)
20	200	0.066	173	173	0.277/0.288	0.009/0.018
20	400	0.07	396	396	0.225/0.238	0.019/0.034
20	8,000	0.628	6,047	6,047	6.491/6.709	0.103/0.251
50	2,500	0.499	2,430	2,430	3.797/3.925	0.114/0.205
50	12,500	1.952	8,858	8,858	8.709/9.023	0.377/0.812
100	5,000	2.056	4,707	4,707	13.23/13.326	0.661/0.978
100	10,000	1.935	7,000	7,000	11.166/11.479	0.79/1.27
200	400	0.037	451	428	0.059/0.073	0.012/0.06
200	20,000	5.846	16,052	16,052	25.093/25.945	3.973/6.73

"All" means the time for creating a program matrix and computing the fixpoint.

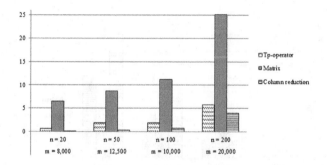

Fig. 3. Results of testing about fixpoint computing on definite programs

4.2   Testing on Normal Programs

In this testing, given the size $n = |B_P|$ of the Herband base B_P and the number $m = |P|$ of rules in P, rules are created randomly as before (Table 1).

Based on (n, m), generate a normal program P randomly. After that, we transform P to a d-program P' with k negative literals in a program P.

Table 3 is the results of testing Algorithm 3.1 on P' and computation by the T_P-operator (using Theorem 3.1) on P [12] for computing the stable models of a program P. There are three important steps in Algorithm 3.1: Step 2 for creating a program matrix for representing a d-program P', Step 3 for computing the fixpoint and Step 4 for finding the set of vectors which represent stable models. We compare three cases— **(Case 1):** Computation by the T_P-operator (using Theorem 3.1) for computing stable models of on P; **(Case 2):** the naive computation on a program P' by Algorithm 3.1; **(Case 3):** the column reduction computation on a program P' as presented in Sect. 3.2 of Step 3. Comparison of fixpoint computation is shown in Fig. 4.

Table 3. Results of testing on normal programs

n	m	k	T_P-operator (sec.)	Matrix Fixpoint/All (sec.)	Column reduction Fixpoint/All (sec.)
20	400	8	2.432	19.603/19.714	3.338/3.362
20	8,000	6	5.531	12.368/12.696	4.502/4.603
50	100	8	0.221	1.155/1.224	0.278/0.291
50	2,500	8	36.574	37.863/38.463	29.582/29.786
50	12,500	7	49.485	30.819/32.00	48.883/49.32
100	5,000	8	103.586	31.68/32.338	69.579/69.851
100	10,000	8	264.547	84.899/87.142	192.981/194.003
200	400	6	0.429	1.928/2.021	1.222/1.342
200	13,300	6	185.778	48.185/49.185	124.119/126.255

"All" means the time for creating a program matrix and computing the fixpoint.

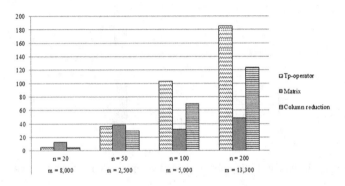

Fig. 4. Results of testing about fixpoint computing on normal programs

By the table we can observe the following fact: matrix computation is effective when the size of n is large (n =100 or 200). Computation by column reduction is faster than computation by the T_P-operator, while it is slower than the naive method in case of n = 100 or 200. To see the effect of computation by column reduction, we would need further environment that realizes efficient computation of matrices.

5   Conclusion

In this paper, we proposed methods for representing logic programming based on linear algebra. We develop new algorithms for computing logic programming semantics in linear algebra and the improvement methods for speeding-up those algorithms.

The results of testing show that the computation by column reduction is fastest in computing least models, while the naive matrix computation on a d-program is often better than column reduction in computing stable models. It is known that the least model of a definite program is computed in $O(N)$ [15] where N is the size (number of literals) of a program. Since the column reduction computation takes $O(m^2 \times n)$ time, it would be effective when $m^2 \times n < N$, i.e., the size of a program is large with a relatively small number of atoms. For computation of stable models of a normal program, although the size of the program matrix and the initial matrix are large, they have many zero elements. We can improve the method for representing matrices in sparse forms which also brings storage advantages with a good matrix library. Introducing partial evaluation [18] would also help to reduce runtime. We need further optimization and comparison with existing answer set solvers such as clasp [16], DLV [17].

The performance of our linear algebraic implementation heavily depends on the manipulation of matrices. We have used Maple for implementation, but our methods can be realized by other computer languages and architectures. It is now expected that more powerful platforms are developed for linear algebraic computation in the near future. Our methods would have the merits when such advanced technologies become available. Yet, linear algebraic computation for logic programming has just started, so there will be a lot of rooms for improvement and optimization.

Acknowledgment. This work was supported by JSPS KAKENHI Grant Numbers JP17H00763 and JP18H03288.

References

1. Saraswat, V.: Reasoning 2.0 or machine learning and logic–the beginnings of a new computer science. Data Science Day, Kista Sweden (2016)
2. Sato, T.: A linear algebraic approach to Datalog evaluation. Theory Pract. Log. Program. **17**(3), 244–265 (2017)
3. Yang, B., Yih, W., He, X., Gao, J., Deng, L.: Embedding entities and relations for learning and inference in knowledge bases. In: Third International Conference on Learning Representations (ICLR 2015), San Diego, USA (2015)
4. Grefensette, E.: Towards a formal distributional semantics: simulating logical calculi with tensors. In: Proceedings of Second Joint Conference on Lexical and Computational Semantics (*SEM), vol. 1, pp. 1–10, Atlanta, USA (2013)
5. Coecke, B., Sadrzadeh, M., Clarky, S.: Mathematical foundations for a compositional distributional model of meaning. Linguist. Anal. **36**, 345–384 (2011)
6. Serafini, L., d'Avila Garcez, A.S.: Learning and reasoning with logic tensor networks. In: Adorni, G., Cagnoni, S., Gori, M., Maratea, M. (eds.) AI*IA 2016. LNCS (LNAI), vol. 10037, pp. 334–348. Springer, Cham (2016). https://doi.org/10.1007/978-3-319-49130-1_25
7. Serafini, L., Donadello, I., Garcez, A.: Learning and reasoning with logic tensor networks: theory and application to semantic image interpretation. In: Proceedings of 32nd ACM SIGAPP Symposium on Applied Computing (SAC 2017), pp. 125–130, Marrakech, Morocco (2017)
8. Sakama, C., Inoue, K., Sato, T.: Linear algebraic characterization of logic programs. In: Li, G., Ge, Y., Zhang, Z., Jin, Z., Blumenstein, M. (eds.) KSEM 2017. LNCS (LNAI), vol. 10412, pp. 520–533. Springer, Cham (2017). https://doi.org/10.1007/978-3-319-63558-3_44
9. van Emden, M.H., Kowalski, R.A.: The semantics of predicate logic as a programming language. J. ACM **23**(4), 733–742 (1976)

10. Kolda, T., Bader, B.: Tensor decompositions and applications. SIAM Rev. **51**(3), 455–500 (2009)
11. Lin, F.: From satisfiability to linear algebra. In: Invited Talk, 26th Australian Joint Conference on Artificial Intelligence (2013)
12. Alferes, J.J., Leite, J.A., Pereira, L.M., Przymusinska, H., Przymusinski, T.: Dynamic updates of non-monotonic knowledge bases. J. Logic Program. **45**(1–3), 43–70 (2000)
13. Fernandez, J.A., Lobo, J., Minker, J., Subrahmanian, V.S.: Disjunctive LP + integrity constraints = stable model semantics. AMAI **8**(3–4), 449–474 (1993)
14. Maple. https://www.maplesoft.com/support/install/maple2017_install.html
15. Dowling, W.F., Gallier, J.H.: Linear-time algorithms for testing the satisfiability of propositional Horn formulae. J. Logic Program. **1**(3), 267–284 (1984)
16. Clasp. https://potassco.org/clasp/
17. DLV system. http://www.dlvsystem.com/dlv/
18. Sakama, C., Nguyen, H.D., Sato, T., Inoue, K.: Partial evaluation of logic programs in vector space. In: 11th Workshop on Answer Set Programming and Other Computing Paradigms (ASPOCP 2018), Oxford, UK, July 2018

Progressively Improving Supervised Emotion Classification Through Active Learning

Xin Kang$^{(\boxtimes)}$, Yunong Wu, and Fuji Ren

Tokushima University, Tokushima 7708506, Japan
{kang-xin,ren}@is.tokushima-u.ac.jp, wuyunong@tokushima-u.ac.jp

Abstract. Recognizing human emotions from pieces of natural language has been a challenging task in artificial intelligence, for the difficulty of acquiring high-quality training examples. In this paper, we propose a novel method based on active learning to progressively improve the performance of supervised text emotion classification models, with as few human labor as possible in annotating the training examples. Specifically, the active learning algorithm interactively communicates with the supervised emotion classification model to find the potentially most effective training examples from a huge set of unlabeled data and increases the training data by acquiring emotion labels for these examples from the human experts. Our experiment of multi-label emotion classification on Japanese tweets suggests that the proposed method is effective in steadily improving the supervised classification results by incrementally feeding a classification model with the new tweets of well-balanced emotion labels.

Keywords: Text emotion classification · Active learning
Label balancing

1 Introduction

The recognition of human emotions has been a popular research in human computer interaction [5,11,19], mental disease diagnosis [2,3,14,18], as well as cognitive neuroscience [1,12]. Among these researches, interpreting emotions from the natural language has been challenging the natural language processing studies, for the nature of difficulty in human beings to understand and to annotate the emotion labels to natural language pieces [8,16] and the nature of extremely high bias in the observation of different emotion labels in the real world texts [9]. These problems have limited the development of many supervised text emotion classification models [7,9,10,15,17,21,22] and have pushed the semi-supervised models to the extremely biased regions for emotion classification [8,20,24].

In this paper, we propose a novel method based on active learning to progressively improve the learning of a supervised text emotion classification model, by incrementally feeding the model with the potentially most effective training

© Springer Nature Switzerland AG 2018
M. Kaenampornpan et al. (Eds.): MIWAI 2018, LNAI 11248, pp. 49–57, 2018.
https://doi.org/10.1007/978-3-030-03014-8_4

examples. A multi-label logistic regression classifier is learned to predict multiple emotion labels in Joy, Love, Expectation, Surprise, Hate, Sorrow, Anger, Anxiety, and Neutral [16] for each tweet. The classifier then is progressively improved with the carefully selected high-quality training examples by an active learning algorithm. Specifically, the algorithm firstly evaluates the effectiveness of large number of unlabeled tweets with four distinct criteria, e.g. complementariness, informativeness, representativeness, and diverseness, based on the model prediction and their linguistic similarity to each other. It then integrates an effective priority for all candidates, acquires emotion labels from human experts for a specified few of the prioritized examples, and updates the supervised classification model with these examples. The progress continues until a promising emotion classifier is learned. Our experiment on Japanese tweet emotion classification suggests that the proposed method could steadily improve a supervised learning process by incrementally acquiring high-quality and well-balanced training examples.

The rest of this paper is arranged as follows: Sect. 2 briefly reviews the related work of the supervised and semi-supervised learning methods for text emotion classification; Sect. 3 illustrates our active learning algorithm for progressively improving a supervised emotion classification model; Sect. 4 shows the experiment of Japanese tweet emotion classification with active learning and compares the results to those of an emotion classification with randomly sampled training examples; finally Sect. 5 concludes this paper.

2   Related Work

The text emotion classification problem was firstly proposed in the study of Liu et al. [13], in which the authors built an affect model of English sentences based on the common-sense knowledge and emotion lexicons. A sentence was classified into one of the six Ekman emotion categories [4], i.e. Anger, Disgust, Fear, Happiness, Sadness, and Surprise. Later studies of text emotion classification employed supervised learning models, such as the Support Vector Machines [7,9,10,15,17,22], Naive Bayes [9,15,17], and K-Nearest-Neighbor [15,21]. Kang et al. [6] firstly studied the multi-label emotion classification problem in Blog articles, by integrating separate emotion labels as binary random variables into a graphical model. Wu et al. [23] employed the conditional random fields model for the multi-label word emotion classification and a transformed logistic regression model for the multi-label sentence emotion classification. The studies of [9,17] further developed the collapsed Gibbs sampling algorithm for inferring the multi-label word emotions and document emotions in Blog articles based on the Bayesian network models.

Because supervised learning models required large amount of labeled emotion corpus for training, which were usually expensive to acquire, semi-supervised learning models, such as the hierarchical Bayesian networks [8], modified adsorption label-propagation [20], semi-supervised SVM [24], were also employed for text emotion classification. However, because emotion labels were complicatedly correlated in all granularities of texts [8,17], it was very difficult for a semi-supervised learning model to associate the unlabeled training examples correctly to different emotion labels. More importantly, because the distribution of different emotion labels was highly-biased [9], the semi-supervised models were more likely to observe the statistically frequent emotions such as Joy and Love than to observe the statistically rare emotions such as Surprise and Hate. This made the semi-supervised models even harder to recognize the essentially rare emotions in the text. In this paper, we proposed a novel method based on active learning to solve these problems, by incrementally acquiring the multi-labeled emotional samples from a huge set of unlabeled data and constructing an emotion learning corpus with well-balanced emotional labels.

3   Learning an Emotion Classifier Actively

3.1   Supervised Emotion Classification

A supervised multi-label classification model is constructed with a series of logistic regression classifiers σ_k, each of which learns to predict a probability $y_k \in [0,1]$ for observing an emotion label k in a piece of tweet x by

$$y_k = \sigma_k(x). \tag{1}$$

To simplify the learning process of supervised emotion classification, we employ the bag-of-words features of tweet texts. All training and testing tweets are split into word lists with the Japanese morphological analysis engine Janome[1], and a vocabulary is constructed by collecting a maximum of 10^5 of the distinct training set words. Based on this vocabulary each tweet is mapped into a binary vector x, with the 1's reflecting the observation of each word in the tweet.

3.2   Active Learning Progress

For the above supervised emotion classification model, the quality of training data could greatly affect its performance. In this paper, we propose an active learning algorithm to incrementally generate a high-quality training data for learning the emotion classifier. With an initially constructed small training data set $\mathcal{X}$, the active learning algorithm iteratively moves m of the potentially most effective training examples from an unlabeled tweet data set $\mathcal{U}$ to the training data set $\mathcal{X}$ every time with emotion annotations from the human experts, by integrating an effective priority score based on the following four priority criteria.

The **complementariness** criterion employs the distribution of emotion labels in a candidate example x

$$p_k = \frac{y_k}{\sum_{k'=1}^{K} y_{k'}} \tag{2}$$

---

[1] https://mocobeta.github.io/janome/en/.

and the distribution of emotion labels in the training set $\mathcal{X}$ of N examples

$$q_k = \frac{\sum_{i=1}^{N} \mathbb{1}\{y_k^{(i)} \geq 0.5\}}{\sum_{k'=1}^{K} \sum_{i=1}^{N} \mathbb{1}\{y_k^{(i)} \geq 0.5\}}, \tag{3}$$

and evaluates the complementariness priority of x as the difference of these two distributions with the Kullback-Leibler divergence

$$\begin{aligned} c(x) &= D_{\mathrm{KL}}(p\|q) \\ &= \sum_{k=1}^{K} p_k \left(\log p_k - \log q_k\right). \end{aligned} \tag{4}$$

Intuitively, the complementariness priority $c(x)$ is large if x is emotionally very different from the current training examples in $\mathcal{X}$. This criterion allows the active learning algorithm to complement a training set of well-balanced emotion labels.

The **informativeness** criterion employs the entropy of the predicted probability y_k to evaluate the information (or uncertainty) in emotion prediction k for a candidate example x

$$\mathrm{H}(y_k) = -y_k \log y_k - (1 - y_k) \log(1 - y_k) \tag{5}$$

and evaluates the informativeness priority of x by taking the average of $\mathrm{H}(y_k)$ among all emotion categories

$$i(x) = \frac{1}{K} \sum_{k=1}^{K} \mathrm{H}(y_k). \tag{6}$$

Intuitively, the informativeness priority $i(x)$ is large if the classification model gives very blurry emotion predictions for x. This criterion allows the active learning algorithm to add examples with the maximum information to the current training set.

The **representativeness** criterion employs the cosine similarity on the bag-of-words features for two tweet examples x and x'

$$sim(x, x') = \frac{x \cdot x'}{\|x\| \times \|x'\|} \tag{7}$$

and evaluates the representativeness priority $r(x)$ of a candidate example x by taking the average of cosine similarities of x to all other examples x' in the unlabeled data set $\mathcal{U}$

$$r(x) = \frac{1}{|\mathcal{U}|} \sum_{x' \in \mathcal{U}} sim(x, x'). \tag{8}$$

Intuitively, the representativeness priority $r(x)$ is large if the candidate example x is linguistically similar to many other candidate examples x', i.e. learning emotions with x would be similar to many other examples x'. This criterion allows the active learning algorithm to acquire as few human labor as possible in annotating the training examples incrementally.

The **diverseness** criterion employs the opposite of cosine similarity on bag-of-words features as the distinction for two tweet examples x and x'

$$\overline{sim}(x, x') = -sim(x, x') \tag{9}$$

and evaluates the diverseness priority $d(x)$ of a candidate example x by taking the minimum of the distinctions of x to all other examples x' in the training set $\mathcal{X}$

$$d(x) = \min_{x' \in \mathcal{X}} \overline{sim}(x, x'). \tag{10}$$

Intuitively, the diverseness priority $d(x)$ is large if the candidate example x is linguistically distinct to all training examples $x' \in \mathcal{X}$. This criterion allows the active learning algorithm to avoid taking similar examples to those already labeled in the training data, and therefore saves the human labor in manual annotation.

The algorithm for the active learning progress is shown in Algorithm 1. Given a weak emotion classifier σ learned with limited training examples in $\mathcal{X}$, for each learning step i the active learning algorithm takes n of the potentially most effective examples x from a folder of unlabeled data $\mathcal{U}$, acquires their emotion annotations e, and appends these labeled data to the current training set $\mathcal{X}$. This process is repeated for m times until a promising supervised emotion classifier σ is learned.

Algorithm 1. Actively learning an emotion classifier

Initialize $\mathcal{X}$ with labeled tweets
  for $i = 1 \rightarrow m$ **do**
    Learn emotion classifier σ with $\mathcal{X}$
    Initialize $\mathcal{U}$ with new unlabeled tweets
    for $j = 1 \rightarrow n$ **do**
      $x = \arg\max_{x \in \mathcal{U}} c(x) + i(x) + r(x) + d(x)$
      Acquire emotion annotation e for x
      Append (x, e) to $\mathcal{X}$ and remove x from $\mathcal{U}$
    end for
  end for

---

4 Experiment

We examine the effectiveness of the proposed method through a multi-label emotion classification experiment with Japanese tweets. Each tweet is associated with one or more emotion labels from Joy, Love, Expectation, Surprise, Hate, Sorrow, Anger, Anxiety, and Neutral [16]. As a general supervised classification model, the multi-label logistic regression classifier is employed for tweet emotion classification. Comparison with the other supervised classification models except multi-label logistic regression under active learning is beyond the scope of this article. We analyses the progressive improvements of emotion classification by generating high-quality training data based on active learning and compare them to the improvements based on a randomly sampled training data.

The experiment data consists of an initial training data of 600 labeled tweets, an unlabeled training data of 2×10^5 tweets, and a testing data of 675 tweets. All emotion labels have been manually annotated by three human experts. The tweet data was randomly extracted from the Twitter stream from 2017–10–20 to 2018–01–15, with those extremely short (e.g. fewer than 10 characters) and extremely long (e.g. more than 140 characters) filtered out.

As depicted in the active learning progress of Algorithm 1, the initial training data $\mathcal{X}$ consists of 600 labeled tweets, and the unlabeled data is split into $m = 20$ folders, with each folder $\mathcal{U}$ consisting of 10^4 tweets. For each learning step the algorithm gets $n = 50$ tweets from a new $\mathcal{U}$, acquires emotion annotations from three human experts, and appends these labeled tweets to the current training data $\mathcal{X}$. The supervised emotion classification model σ is progressively improved by learning with this incrementally constructed training data $\mathcal{X}$.

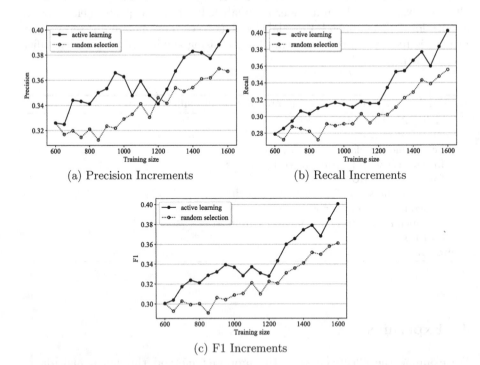

(a) Precision Increments

(b) Recall Increments

(c) F1 Increments

Fig. 1. Improvement of emotion classification with respect to the incrementally increased training data

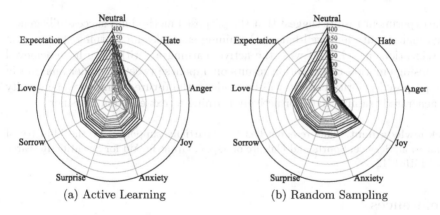

(a) Active Learning   (b) Random Sampling

Fig. 2. The number of different emotion labels in increased training data

To find the improvement of supervised emotion classification through active learning, we made a comparative experiment by randomly sampling $n = 50$ tweets for $m = 20$ folders and append these data with manually annotated emotion labels to the training data $\mathcal{X}'$, to progressively learn a classifier σ'. The emotion classification results from σ and σ' are shown in Fig. 1, with the micro-averaged precision, recall, and F1 scores plotted for each learning step.

The results suggest that active learning algorithm has generated high-quality training examples for learning a supervised emotion classification model, with the classification results steadily improved. And these improvements are significantly higher than those brought by the randomly sampled training examples. With actively selected 10^3 training examples, the supervised emotion classification model has achieved promising micro-averaged precision, recall, and F1 scores of 39.91, 40.22, and 40.07, respectively.

Because the bias of emotion labels has been proved to the one of the major causes of emotion classification error, we further count the emotion labels in the incrementally constructed training data. Figure 2 shows the numbers of annotated emotion labels to tweets at each learning step for active learning and for random sampling, respectively. The active learning algorithm has significantly found many statistically rare emotion labels such as Hate and Anger and has considerably suppressed the selection of the statistically frequent emotion labels such as Joy, Love, and Neutral. These results suggest that active learning algorithm could generated well-balanced examples for learning a supervised emotion classification model.

5   Conclusion

In this paper, we propose a novel method based on active learning to progressively improve the performance of supervised text emotion classification models, with as few human labor as possible in annotating the training examples.

The experiment results suggest that the proposed method has successfully generated high-quality and well-balanced training examples for learning the emotion classification model. And with the active learning algorithm we have achieved promising emotion classification results on Japanese tweets. Further analyses of the proposed priority criteria will be made in the future to improve the quality of generated training data for actively learning a text emotion classifier.

Acknowledgment. This research has been partially supported by the Ministry of Education, Science, Sports and Culture of Japan, Grant-in-Aid for Scientific Research (A), 15H01712.

References

1. Buhle, J.T., et al.: Cognitive reappraisal of emotion: a meta-analysis of human neuroimaging studies. Cereb. Cortex **24**(11), 2981–2990 (2014)
2. Bylsma, L., Morris, B., Rottenberg, J.: A meta-analysis of emotional reactivity in major depressive disorder. Clin. Psychol. Rev. **28**(4), 676–691 (2008)
3. Domes, G., Schulze, L., Herpertz, S.: Emotion recognition in borderline personality disorder-a review of the literature. J. Pers. Disord. **23**(1), 6–19 (2009)
4. Ekman, P.: Facial expression and emotion. Am. Psychol. **48**(4), 384 (1993)
5. Gunes, H., Schuller, B.: Categorical and dimensional affect analysis in continuous input: current trends and future directions. Image Vis. Comput. **31**(2), 120–136 (2013)
6. Kang, X., Ren, F.: Sampling latent emotions and topics in a hierarchical Bayesian network. In: 2011 7th International Conference on Natural Language Processing and Knowledge Engineering (NLP-KE), pp. 37–42. IEEE (2011)
7. Kang, X., Ren, F., Wu, Y.: Bottom up: exploring word emotions for Chinese sentence chief sentiment classification. In: 2010 International Conference on Natural Language Processing and Knowledge Engineering (NLP-KE), pp. 1–5. IEEE (2010)
8. Kang, X., Ren, F., Wu, Y.: Semisupervised learning of author-specific emotions in micro-blogs. IEEJ Trans. Electr. Electron. Eng. **11**(6), 768–775 (2016)
9. Kang, X., Ren, F., Wu, Y.: Exploring latent semantic information for textual emotion recognition in blog articles. IEEE/CAA J. Automatica Sinica **5**(1), 204–216 (2018)
10. Li, W., Xu, H.: Text-based emotion classification using emotion cause extraction. Expert. Syst. Appl. **41**(4), 1742–1749 (2014)
11. Lin, J.C., Wu, C.H., Wei, W.L.: Error weighted semi-coupled hidden Markov model for audio-visual emotion recognition. IEEE Trans. Multimed. **14**(1), 142–156 (2012)
12. Lindquist, K.A., Wager, T.D., Kober, H., Bliss-Moreau, E., Barrett, L.F.: The brain basis of emotion: a meta-analytic review. Behav. Brain Sci. **35**(03), 121–143 (2012)
13. Liu, H., Lieberman, H., Selker, T.: A model of textual affect sensing using real-world knowledge. In: Proceedings of the 8th International Conference on Intelligent User Interfaces, pp. 125–132. ACM (2003)
14. Mo, H., Wang, J., Li, X., Wu, Z.: Linguistic dynamic modeling and analysis of psychological health state using interval type-2 fuzzy sets. IEEE/CAA J. Automatica Sinica **2**(4), 366–373 (2015)

15. Pratama, B.Y., Sarno, R.: Personality classification based on twitter text using Naive Bayes, KNN and SVM. In: 2015 International Conference on Data and Software Engineering (ICoDSE), pp. 170–174. IEEE (2015)
16. Quan, C., Ren, F.: A blog emotion corpus for emotional expression analysis in Chinese. Comput. Speech Lang. **24**(4), 726–749 (2010)
17. Ren, F., Kang, X.: Employing hierarchical Bayesian networks in simple and complex emotion topic analysis. Comput. Speech Lang. **27**(4), 943–968 (2013)
18. Ren, F., Kang, X., Quan, C.: Examining accumulated emotional traits in suicide blogs with an emotion topic model. IEEE J. Biomed. Health Inform. **20**(5), 1384–1396 (2015)
19. Scherer, S., et al.: A generic framework for the inference of user states in human computer interaction. J. Multimodal User Interfaces **6**(3–4), 117–141 (2012)
20. Summa, A., Resch, B., Strube, M.: Microblog emotion classification by computing similarity in text, time, and space. In: Proceedings of the Workshop on Computational Modeling of People's Opinions, Personality, and Emotions in Social Media (PEOPLES), pp. 153–162 (2016)
21. Tokuhisa, R., Inui, K., Matsumoto, Y.: Emotion classification using massive examples extracted from the web. In: Proceedings of the 22nd International Conference on Computational Linguistics-Volume 1, pp. 881–888. Association for Computational Linguistics (2008)
22. Wen, S., Wan, X.: Emotion classification in microblog texts using class sequential rules. In: AAAI, pp. 187–193 (2014)
23. Wu, Y., Kita, K., Matsumoto, K., Kang, X.: A joint prediction model for multiple emotions analysis in sentences. In: Gelbukh, A. (ed.) CICLing 2013. LNCS, vol. 7817, pp. 149–160. Springer, Heidelberg (2013). https://doi.org/10.1007/978-3-642-37256-8_13
24. Yin, C., Xiang, J., Zhang, H., Wang, J., Yin, Z., Kim, J.U.: A new SVM method for short text classification based on semi-supervised learning. In: 2015 4th International Conference on Advanced Information Technology and Sensor Application (AITS), pp. 100–103. IEEE (2015)

Regularizing Feature Distribution Using Sliced Wasserstein Distance for Semi-supervised Learning

Jinhyung Kim[(✉)], Chanho Lee, and Junmo Kim

Korea Advanced Institute of Science and Technology, Daejeon, South Korea
{kkjh0723,yiwan99,junmo.kim}@kaist.ac.kr

Abstract. We propose a novel consistency based regularization method for semi-supervised image classification, called feature distribution matching (FDM), which is designed to induce smoothness of feature space by reducing sliced Wasserstein distance between feature distributions of labeled and unlabeled set. Unlike previous perturbation based methods, FDM does not require extra computational cost except one regularization loss. Our result shows that FDM combined with entropy minimization improves classification accuracy compared to supervised-only baseline and some previous methods. We also analyze our method by visualizing feature embeddings which shows that FDM lead smooth data manifold on feature space.

Keywords: Semi-supervised learning · Deep neural network
Image classification

1 Introduction

Deep learning has been advanced and keeps updating its record on image classification benchmarks though there is a limitation that it requires a large dataset with labels for supervised learning. Obtaining reliable labels for large sets of images often needs a lot of human effort. Semi-supervised learning recently has received considerable attention since it alleviates the need of labels for all samples. Semi-supervised learning tries to solve the problem when there is a large collection of data but only a small subset of it has labels. Therefore the main concern of semi-supervised learning algorithms is how to exploit information of unlabeled data to keep the model from overfitting to small labeled data and to enhance the performance. Semi-supervised learning also has great potential to be used in real world applications since there are tremendous data available on Web but all cannot possibly be labeled.

Recently, there are two mainstreams of deep learning based approaches for semi-supervised image classification. First is generative model based approaches, such as [2,11,21], which utilize deep generative models to extract rich representation from an image or to generate samples which are of use to training. However,

© Springer Nature Switzerland AG 2018
M. Kaenampornpan et al. (Eds.): MIWAI 2018, LNAI 11248, pp. 58–68, 2018.
https://doi.org/10.1007/978-3-030-03014-8_5

these methods usually require additional efforts to design and train the complex generative model. Second is consistency loss based approaches [15,17,18,23]. These methods train a classifier with an additional loss which induces consistent prediction by minimizing output distance between the student network and the teacher network. These methods reported cutting-edge performance on several benchmarks though one major drawback is that those algorithms need to calculate multiple forward passes in most cases and sometimes need to backpropagate multiple times.

We propose a novel consistency regularization method, Feature Distribution Matching (FDM), which is assumed to smooth data manifold indirectly by reducing the distance between feature distribution of labeled set and that of unlabeled set. We utilize Wasserstein distance as our distance metric which recently draws large attention of machine learning community [1,3,12,24]. Our method can be applied to any existing deep classifier by adding a relatively simple loss function without multiple forward computations. We will present quantitative and qualitative results on SVHN and CIFAR-10 dataset which show effectiveness of our proposed method. FDM combined with Entropy Minimization (EM) shows performance improvement over our supervised-only baseline and comparable accuracy with some previous consistency based algorithms. Although our method is not as good as some state-of-the-art methods, it has some advantages that it does not need multiple forward-backward computations. We will also present visualization of feature embeddings to show that FDM affects organization of feature space consistent with our assumption.

2   Related Works

Several recent studies on semi-supervised learning focused on regularization techniques which assure consistency or smoothness of output distribution of the classifier. Because our proposed method is based on encouraging consistency of domain between labeled and unlabeled data, we will concentrate more on recent consistency based methods.

Laine and Aila suggested Π-model [15] and showed that teacher with random perturbation can give more robust prediction by self-ensembling. Temporal Ensembling [15] keeps exponential moving average of previous network predictions over training epochs and use it as a target vector, rather than use predictions of current teacher network. Temporal Ensembling alleviates the computational burden of Π-model caused by computing forward pass twice for self-ensembling via taking more memory space for saving estimated target vectors of each training sample. This modified technique helps not only reduce the training time but improve performance due to more accurate target.

Mean Teacher [23] could obtain better target by averaging model parameters, rather than averaging output predictions as in Temporal Ensembling. The teacher model of Mean Teacher predicts target using exponential moving average of model parameters. Consistency loss between teacher and student model induces more accurate model parameters, result in better test accuracy.

While most self-ensembling based methods induce smoothness by reducing the distance from the model prediction to the prediction of the teacher network with heuristic and random input perturbation, Virtual Adversarial Training (VAT) [18] utilizes a specific perturbation to the input, which modifies the output most. They proposed a method to obtain the perturbation by calculating gradient of input perturbation with respect to the dissimilarity between the prediction with perturbation and prediction without perturbation.

According to Luo and others [17], most semi-supervised learning methods based on self-ensembling have considered only perturbation of single data point for consistency. Smooth Neighbors on Teacher Graphs (SNTG) [17] guides the student model to learn similar neighboring points on graph constructed based on the prediction of the teacher model to achieve smooth low-dimensional manifold by consistency loss. SNTG has an advantage that it can be easily combined with other local consistency losses above and showed that classification accuracy increased.

Entropy Minimization (EM) [4] and Pseudo-Label [16] are not consistency-based method but often used in semi-supervised learning because of their simplicity. Both methods are similar in that they provide losses to increase the confidence of the model prediction. However, EM regularizes entropy of the model prediction while Pseudo-Labeling provides additional supervised loss for unlabeled samples when their maximum predicted probability exceeds a certain threshold.

Many consistency-based methods showed state-of-the-art performance in semi-supervised image classification task, but they suffer from the trade-off between computation and memory. We propose a novel regularization method which induces consistency between labeled and unlabeled data distribution with single forward and backward computation.

3 Method

In this section, we will describe our proposed regularization method, Feature Distribution Matching (FDM), along with the entropy regularization which is also used in our semi-supervised learning experiments. First, we will define common notations and then introduce sliced Wasserstein distance briefly followed by each regularization loss in following subsections. Let $x \in \mathbb{R}^I$ denotes an input image where I is the size of the image and $y \in \mathbb{R}^C$ denotes a label vector where C is the number of classes. Let $f_\phi(x)$ be the classifier parameterized by ϕ, i.e. a deep neural network in our case. $f_\phi(x)$ can be decomposed into $g \circ h$ where h transforms an input x to a feature vector using a deep network and g maps the feature vector to the output prediction by a linear transform followed by a softmax layer. Let $\mathcal{D}_L = \{x^{(n)}, y^{(n)} | n = 1, ..., N_l\}$ and $\mathcal{D}_{UL} = \{x^{(n)} | n = 1, ..., N_{ul}\}$ are labeled and unlabeled dataset respectively. The entire set of image samples from both labeled and unlabeled datasets is denoted by $\mathcal{D}_T$. The model is trained by a supervised loss for $\mathcal{D}_L$ and regularization losses for $\mathcal{D}_T$. Additionally, $\mathcal{M}$ indicates mini-batch which is composed of two subsets $\mathcal{M}_L = \mathcal{M} \cap \mathcal{D}_L$ and

$\mathcal{M}_T = \mathcal{M} \cap \mathcal{D}_T$, and Θ indicates set of samples θ_l from unit sphere $\mathbb{S}^{d-1}$ for approximating sliced Wasserstein distance.

3.1 Sliced Wasserstein Distance

To match feature distribution of labeled and unlabeled data, we propose a loss function with distance metric of probability distribution, called Wasserstein distance. Wasserstein distance between two probability measures ρ_X and ρ_Y is defined as below.

$$W_c(p_X, p_Y) = \inf_{\gamma \in \Gamma(\rho_X, \rho_Y)} \int_{X \times Y} c(x, y) d\gamma(x, y) \tag{1}$$

where $d\rho_X = p_X(x)dx$ and $d\rho_Y = p_Y(y)dy$, and γ is joint probability distribution of ρ_X and ρ_Y, and $c : X \times Y \to \mathbb{R}+$ is transportation cost function. i.e. Euclidean distance. However, our feature distribution is not a continuous probability function but a set of feature embeddings. Following Deshpande et al. [3], quadratic Wasserstein distance between two sets of samples $\mathcal{X}$ and $\mathcal{Y}$ can be expressed as below,

$$W_2^2(\mathcal{X}, \mathcal{Y}) = \frac{1}{|\mathcal{Y}|} \min_{\sigma \in \Sigma_{|\mathcal{Y}|}} \sum_{i=1}^{|\mathcal{Y}|} \|\mathcal{X}_{\sigma(i)} - \mathcal{Y}_i\|_2^2 \tag{2}$$

where σ is the set of all possible permutations of $\mathcal{Y}$. Equation (2) derives the sum of one-to-one distance between two sets and permutation σ minimizes the sum of distance. However, it is still hard to utilize because the derivation of minimum distance permutation has high computational complexity. To simplify this problem, we now consider the Wasserstein distance of one-dimensional data where $\mathcal{X}, \mathcal{Y} \in \mathbb{R}^1$. Then permutation σ_X, σ_Y simply can be derived by just sorting the samples. Following Kolouri et al. [12], these one-dimensional Wasserstein distance can be utilized by slicing high-dimensional probability to one-dimensional probability via Radon transform. Intuitively, we slice d-dimensional probability distribution to one-dimensional probability distribution by projecting on $d - 1$ unit vector. This is the main idea of sliced Wasserstein distance and it can be defined as closed form:

$$SW_2(\mathcal{X}, \mathcal{Y}) = \int_{\theta \in \Theta} W_2^2(\theta \cdot \mathcal{X}, \theta \cdot \mathcal{Y}) d\theta \tag{3}$$

From the notation above, θ is all possible unit vector for projection on d-dimension and Θ is unit sphere $\mathbb{S}^{d-1}$. For our implementation, unit sphere Θ is approximated as a set of randomly sampled unit vectors as in [12]. For readers who want more rigorous description of Wasserstein distance and its application to machine learning, we recommend referring to [3,12,13].

3.2 Feature Distribution Matching

Most existing consistency-based methods induce output smoothness of neighboring input data by explicitly minimizing the discrepancy between the predictions of the teacher and the student. Although those methods have shown state-of-the-art performances on several semi-supervised image classification tasks, it requires either multiple forward computation or additional memory. Our proposed method is designed to lead feature smoothness by matching feature distributions of samples from $\mathcal{D}_L$ and $\mathcal{D}_T$ with only additional loss term. The idea is that by regularizing two distributions to lie on a same bounded feature space, feature points of the unlabeled set can fill the empty space between sparse feature points of the labeled set. Rather than making $\mathcal{D}_T$ distribution follow $\mathcal{D}_L$ distribution, we force both distributions follow same prior distribution p_z by minimizing approximated sliced Wasserstein distance loss L_f as,

$$L_{fl} = \frac{1}{|\Theta|} \frac{1}{|\mathcal{M}_L|} \sum_{l=1}^{|\Theta|} \sum_{m=1}^{|\mathcal{M}_L|} c(\theta_l \cdot z_{i[m]}, \theta_l \cdot h(x_{j[m]}^L)) \tag{4}$$

$$L_{ft} = \frac{1}{|\Theta|} \frac{1}{|\mathcal{M}_T|} \sum_{l=1}^{|\Theta|} \sum_{m=1}^{|\mathcal{M}_T|} c(\theta_l \cdot z_{i[m]}, \theta_l \cdot h(x_{k[m]}^T)) \tag{5}$$

$$L_f = L_{fl} + L_{ft} \tag{6}$$

where c is the cost, in our case Euclidean distance, $z_i \sim p_z$ are the samples from prior distribution, x^L and x^T are samples from $\mathcal{D}_L$ and $\mathcal{D}_T$ in a mini-batch respectively. $i[m]$, $j[m]$, and $k[m]$ are the sorted indices according to $\theta_l \cdot z_m$, $\theta_l \cdot h(x_m^L)$, and $\theta_l \cdot h(x_m^T)$ respectively.

3.3 Entropy Regularization

Entropy Minimization (EM) [4] is one of the simple regularization techniques for semi-supervised learning which makes the model predict with more confidence by minimizing the entropy of predicted class probability. This regularization is proposed to be used in our model as,

$$L_e = \frac{1}{|\mathcal{M}_T|} \sum_{m=1}^{|\mathcal{M}_T|} \sum_{i=1}^{C} -f_\phi(x_m)_i \log f_\phi(x_m)_i \tag{7}$$

where C is the number of classes and $f_\phi(x_m)_i$ is the predicted probability of ith class when input is x_m. In [4], it is reported that EM can improve the classification performance by encouraging the decision boundary positioned in the low density area. However, it is known to be advantageous only when classes can be separated easily. We found that the EM loss is quite effective empirically so we utilize it along with our proposed methods.

3.4 Final Objective Function

Our final objective function is a combination of the cross-entropy loss L_{ce} for labeled samples and regularization terms above as,

$$L = L_{ce} + \lambda_e L_e + \lambda_f L_f \tag{8}$$

where λ_e and λ_f are constant and non-negative coefficients for two regularization losses. Stochastic gradient descent with mini-batch is used to optimize the objective function. The mini-batch is composed of equal number of samples from $\mathcal{D}_L$ and $\mathcal{D}_T$ in our experiments.

4 Experiments

In this section, experimental results of our proposed method on several benchmark datasets will be reported, compared to our baseline model and the previous work [20] which tested several consistency-based methods in a unified framework. However, it is noted that the result cannot be directly comparable with ours since the training setting is quite different. For the clarity of our experiment, we first describe detailed experimental settings followed by the quantitative and qualitative results.

4.1 Dataset Specification and Data Augmentation

SVHN [19], street house number dataset, is one of the popular image classification benchmarks for semi-supervised learning. SVHN contains digit images from real world and the image size is 32×32. For semi-supervised learning setting, only 1000 labels are assumed to be observable among 65,937 training set and 7,320 samples are used for the validation. Test set is composed of 26,032 samples as originally provided. For SVHN, we only apply random translation as data augmentation.

CIFAR-10 [14] is another widely used image classification benchmark for semi-supervised learning. CIFAR-10 is a set of small images (32×32) grouped into 10 different classes and composed of 50,000 and 10,000 samples for training and testing respectively. For semi-supervised learning, conventionally 4,000 labels of the entire training set are assumed to be observable for the training and 5,000 image-label pairs are used for the validation. We follow this training convention though it has some critics about large validation set size [20]. Consequently, 41,000 images remain trainable without label. We normalized the image with the mean and standard deviation of the dataset and applied standard data augmentations which are random horizontal flipping and translation. It is known that data augmentation can affect performance of CIFAR-10 significantly in semi-supervised learning setting. Note that our data augmentation is relatively simple compared to previous semi-supervised learning studies.

4.2   Training Setting

For the experiment, we considered several recent and widely used network architectures for image classification. Pre-activation Residual Network (PreResNet) [6], a variant of typical ResNet [5], is one of the good options because of its reasonable performance and availability. PreResNet shows performance improvement over original ResNet in several image classification benchmarks by changing the order of operations (convolution, non-linear activation and batch normalization [9]) inside residual blocks. Therefore PreResNet can be easily implemented by modifying ResNet architecture provided by most modern deep learning frameworks. Our implementation follows the original PreResNet except that we downsample (when it is needed) the input signal of the block while downsampling is done after the first ReLU activation of the block in the original form. Also, there is one linear feature layer added between average pooling and output layer for the proposed regularization. We used moderate 32 layer PreResNet with 16 feature dimensions in our entire experiments. Our supervised-only baseline experiment shows compatible performance with that of recent work on evaluating several semi-supervised methods in a common setting [20].

Several previous works on semi-supervised image classification with consistency regularization [15,18,23], Dropout [22] is applied to add stochastic perturbation to the network. Stochastic Depth [8], which was originally proposed to help training deep networks is another possible choice to add random perturbation and is suitable for our network structure. We follow the linearly decaying survival rate toward 0.5 in the paper.

For optimization, although lots of adaptive learning rate techniques, such as Adam [10], have been proposed, we used simple stochastic gradient descent (SGD) with momentum and learning rate schedule. We believe this simple optimizer is still commonly used and effective in image classification tasks as shown in other works [5–7]. The learning rate starts from 0.1 and is multiplied by 0.1 at half and three-quarters of total training epochs. The momentum and weight decay are set to 0.9 and 0.0001 respectively. For regularization losses, constant coefficients λ_e and λ_f are both set to 1 and the number of samples in Θ is set to 50. We decide to use unit sphere distribution for prior distribution p_z since it is bounded and may be advantageous for the linear classifier.

For the supervised only baseline, mini-batch size is set to 256. For the semi-supervised setting, mini-batch size is same but made up of equal number of samples from $\mathcal{D}_L$ and $\mathcal{D}_T$. We redefine an epoch as one iteration of $\mathcal{D}_T$, so unlabeled samples are trained once in an epoch while labeled examples are shown multiple times since $|\mathcal{D}_L| < |\mathcal{D}_T|$. It naturally emphasizes the influence of labeled examples on training. We consider this setting in order to prevent the regularization loss from affecting too much on learning especially in early phase of the training.

4.3   Quantitative Results on SVHN and CIFAR-10

The test error rates of our proposed method and baselines are presented in Table 1 along with that of several semi-supervised learning methods reported

Table 1. Test error rates on SVHN (1k labels) and CIFAR-10 (4k labels).

Method	SVHN	CIFAR-10
Results from [20]		
Supervised	12.83 (0.47)	20.26 (0.38)
Π-Model	7.19 (0.27)	16.37 (0.63)
Mean Teacher	5.65 (0.47)	15.87 (0.28)
VAT	5.63 (0.20)	13.86 (0.27)
VAT+EM	5.35 (0.19)	13.13 (0.39)
Pseudo-Label	7.62 (0.29)	17.78 (0.57)
Ours		
Supervised	12.82 (0.79)	20.48 (0.53)
FDM	12.96 (0.70)	19.25 (0.97)
EM	8.53 (0.33)	17.46 (0.52)
FDM + EM	6.92 (0.39)	15.9 (0.33)

in [20]. Following evaluation setting in [20], the test error is obtained at the point when the validation error is lowest through each training, and all methods are evaluated under 10 different label/unlabel divisions. The mean and standard deviation of the error rate over 10 runs are presented.

First, we compare our proposed method with our baseline experiments. We found that simple Entropy Minimization (EM) method improves performance substantially over supervised-only training on both benchmarks. Our proposed method, which is a combination of Feature Distribution Matching (FDM) and EM, shows performance improvement over both supervised-only baseline and EM-only method. One could find that error rate of FDM-only method is reduced little on CIFAR-10 and even increased on SVHN over supervised-only method. However, when FDM is combined with EM, the error rate is reduced even further than both FDM-only and EM-only methods, especially on SVHN. The reason is not clear but FDM may require additional guidance signal which tells how the feature space should be organized. For example, in our case, distributions of both labeled samples and entire training samples are forced to follow the bounded distribution (unit sphere) by FDM which causes the unlabeled samples to fill the empty feature spaces between labeled sample. However, FDM regularization itself does not tell the policy of filling the space to the unlabeled samples. When EM loss is additionally provided, the feature distribution of the unlabeled samples may be organized to minimize the entropy and boost the effect on the performance.

Second, we compare our results to other methods in [20]. Our supervised-only baseline shows similar error rates to that of [20] on both SVHN and CIFAR-10 though the network architecture and training details are different. Our FDM+EM method shows better performance than pseudo-labeling method and Π-model on both benchmarks. Though our method shows comparable performance with Mean Teacher methods on CIFAR-10, there is still a gap from state-of-the-art consistency-based methods. However, our method has an advantage that it requires only one forward and backward computation while most consistency-based methods require multiple forward (and sometimes multiple backward) computations in training phase which makes them hard to scale.

4.4 Visualization of Feature Space

For analyzing the model, we visualize its feature vectors by projecting to 2-D space using PCA. Figure 1 shows the feature embeddings on three different data divisions (labeled, unlabeled, and test), and of three different models (supervised-only, EM, and FDM+EM). For unlabeled and test dataset which contain 41 k and 10 k samples, we draw 4k samples for the more clear figure. It is clear in the left column of the Fig. 1 that feature vectors from same class (same color) are more tightly clustered in case of FDM+EM than other two, though it is more vague on unlabeled (middle) and test (right) sets. It means samples from the same classes are closer in feature space and feature space is more smooth within a class which fit our assumption. As shown in the figure, the fact that features of

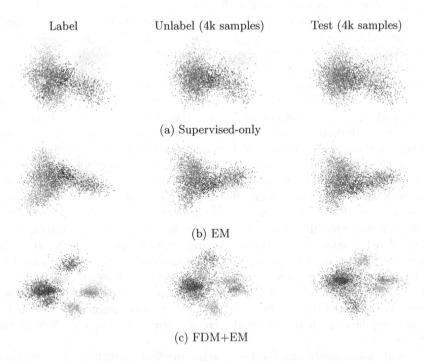

Fig. 1. Visualization of feature embeddings on CIFAR-10 train-label (left), train-unlabel (middle) and test (right) data using PCA. Only 4k samples are selected for better visualization. Feature embeddings of (a) supervised-only, (b) EM, and (c) FDM+EM models are presented in each row. Colors set depending on their true label.

FDM+EM are less overlapped between classes can explain better classification accuracy compared to others because of better separability for the classifier.

5 Conclusion

The quantitative result on SVHN and CIFAR-10 shows that our proposed method, FDM combined with EM, improves classification accuracy considerably on semi-supervised setting over supervised learning using only labeled samples. It is hard to compare directly because of different setting, our method outperforms Psuedo-label and Π-model, and showed comparable performance to Mean Teacher on CIFAR-10. Although FDM cannot achieve state-of-the-art classification accuracy on the benchmarks, our objective is developing an algorithm of reasonable performance with less computation which can be scalable to larger dataset for the future. Additionally, we do not use complex scheduling (e.g. ramp-up/ramp-down) and optimization algorithm (e.g. Adam) which is typically utilized in previous works. Therefore it is expected that our method can be more scalable to larger datasets which is our future direction. It will be also interesting to combine FDM with other consistency-based methods.

The qualitative result showed that our algorithm affects feature organization as we expected. The FDM regularization along with EM induces feature-level smoothness and less overlap between classes. We expect that the regularized feature let linear classifier to set decision boundary better. However it is noted that the FDM loss does not minimize smoothness loss directly but makes labeled and unlabeled distributions are placed on a same, bounded subspace of entire feature space. We intuitively come up with this idea so current work is limited in rigorous mathematical or logical explanation for the behavior. Also, it is required to explore the effect of several designing choices such as prior distribution both quantitatively and qualitatively.

Acknowledgments. This work was supported by Institute for Information & communications Technology Promotion(IITP) grant funded by the Korea government(MSIT) (2017-0-01780, The technology development for event recognition/relational reasoning and learning knowledge based system for video understanding).

References

1. Arjovsky, M., Chintala, S., Bottou, L.: Wasserstein generative adversarial networks. In: ICML, Proceedings of Machine Learning Research, vol. 70, pp. 214–223. PMLR (2017)
2. Dai, Z., Yang, Z., Yang, F., Cohen, W.W., Salakhutdinov, R.: Good semi-supervised learning that requires a bad GAN. In: NIPS, pp. 6513–6523 (2017)
3. Deshpande, I., Zhang, Z., Schwing, A.G.: Generative modeling using the sliced Wasserstein distance. CoRR abs/1803.11188 (2018)
4. Grandvalet, Y., Bengio, Y.: Semi-supervised learning by entropy minimization. In: Saul, L.K., Weiss, Y., Bottou, L. (eds.) Advances in Neural Information Processing Systems, vol. 17, pp. 529–536. MIT Press (2005)

5. He, K., Zhang, X., Ren, S., Sun, J.: Deep residual learning for image recognition. In: CVPR, pp. 770–778. IEEE Computer Society (2016)
6. He, K., Zhang, X., Ren, S., Sun, J.: Identity mappings in deep residual networks. In: Leibe, B., Matas, J., Sebe, N., Welling, M. (eds.) ECCV 2016. LNCS, vol. 9908, pp. 630–645. Springer, Cham (2016). https://doi.org/10.1007/978-3-319-46493-0_38
7. Huang, G., Liu, Z., van der Maaten, L., Weinberger, K.Q.: Densely connected convolutional networks. In: CVPR, pp. 2261–2269. IEEE Computer Society (2017)
8. Huang, G., Sun, Y., Liu, Z., Sedra, D., Weinberger, K.Q.: Deep networks with stochastic depth. In: Leibe, B., Matas, J., Sebe, N., Welling, M. (eds.) ECCV 2016. LNCS, vol. 9908, pp. 646–661. Springer, Cham (2016). https://doi.org/10.1007/978-3-319-46493-0_39
9. Ioffe, S., Szegedy, C.: Batch normalization: accelerating deep network training by reducing internal covariate shift. In: ICML, JMLR Workshop and Conference Proceedings, vol. 37, pp. 448–456 (2015). JMLR.org
10. Kingma, D.P., Ba, J.: Adam: a method for stochastic optimization. CoRR abs/1412.6980 (2014)
11. Kingma, D.P., Mohamed, S., Rezende, D.J., Welling, M.: Semi-supervised learning with deep generative models. In: NIPS, pp. 3581–3589 (2014)
12. Kolouri, S., Martin, C.E., Rohde, G.K.: Sliced-Wasserstein autoencoder: an embarrassingly simple generative model. CoRR abs/1804.01947 (2018)
13. Kolouri, S., Park, S.R., Thorpe, M., Slepcev, D., Rohde, G.K.: Optimal mass transport: signal processing and machine-learning applications. IEEE Signal Process. Mag. **34**(4), 43–59 (2017)
14. Krizhevsky, A., Hinton, G.: Learning multiple layers of features from tiny images. Master's thesis, Department of Computer Science, University of Toronto (2009)
15. Laine, S., Aila, T.: Temporal ensembling for semi-supervised learning. CoRR abs/1610.02242 (2016)
16. Lee, D.H.: Pseudo-label: the simple and efficient semi-supervised learning method for deep neural networks, July 2013
17. Luo, Y., Zhu, J., Li, M., Ren, Y., Zhang, B.: Smooth neighbors on teacher graphs for semi-supervised learning. CoRR abs/1711.00258 (2017)
18. Miyato, T., Maeda, S., Koyama, M., Ishii, S.: Virtual adversarial training: a regularization method for supervised and semi-supervised learning. CoRR abs/1704.03976 (2017)
19. Netzer, Y., Wang, T., Coates, A., Bissacco, A., Wu, B., Ng, A.Y.: Reading digits in natural images with unsupervised feature learning. In: NIPS Workshop on Deep Learning and Unsupervised Feature Learning (2011)
20. Oliver, A., Odena, A., Raffel, C., Cubuk, E.D., Goodfellow, I.J.: Realistic evaluation of deep semi-supervised learning algorithms. CoRR abs/1804.09170 (2018). http://arxiv.org/abs/1804.09170
21. Salimans, T., Goodfellow, I.J., Zaremba, W., Cheung, V., Radford, A., Chen, X.: Improved techniques for training GANs. In: NIPS, pp. 2226–2234 (2016)
22. Srivastava, N., Hinton, G.E., Krizhevsky, A., Sutskever, I., Salakhutdinov, R.: Dropout: a simple way to prevent neural networks from overfitting. J. Mach. Learn. Res. **15**(1), 1929–1958 (2014)
23. Tarvainen, A., Valpola, H.: Mean teachers are better role models: weight-averaged consistency targets improve semi-supervised deep learning results. In: Guyon, I., et al. (eds.) Advances in Neural Information Processing Systems, vol. 30, pp. 1195–1204 (2017)
24. Tolstikhin, I.O., Bousquet, O., Gelly, S., Schölkopf, B.: Wasserstein auto-encoders. CoRR abs/1711.01558 (2017)

Automated Pixel-Level Surface Crack Detection Using U-Net

Jinshu Ji, Lijun Wu[✉], Zhicong Chen, Jinling Yu, Peijie Lin,
and Shuying Cheng

College of Physics and Information Engineering, Fuzhou University,
Fuzhou 350116, China
lijun.wu@fzu.edu.cn

Abstract. Crack detection is significant for the inspection and diagnosis of concrete structures. Various automated approaches have been developed to replace human-conducted inspection, many of which are not adaptive to various conditions and unable to provide localization information. In this paper, an end-to-end semantic segmentation neural network based on U-net is employed to detect crack. Due to the limited number of available annotated samples, data augmentation is employed to avoid overfitting. The adopted network is trained by only 200 images of 512×512 pixels resolutions and achieves a satisfactory accuracy of 99.56% after 37 epochs. The output is an image of the same size as the input image where each pixel is assigned a class label, i.e. crack or not crack. It takes about 7 s to process an image of designed size on CPU. Combined with sliding window technique, our model can cope with any image of larger size. Comparative experiment results show that our model outperforms traditional Canny and Sobel edge detection methods in a variety of complex environment without extracting features manually.

Keywords: Computer vision · Deep learning · Crack detection
Semantic segmentation

1 Introduction

It is significant to detect defects of civil infrastructures at fixed periods to minimize economic damage, future deterioration and even the loss of human life in some severe cases. Cracks on structure surfaces are major indicators that show the degradation of concrete structures. Crack detection used to be performed manually by practiced human inspectors in the past. However, the human-conducted crack detection methods are likely to be subjective, inefficient and expensive. Moreover, it is hard to inspect all corners of the civil infrastructures by manual methods due to the safety issue. Therefore, a number of automated crack detection methods that primarily employ image processing techniques have been proposed to replace human-conducted methods for defect detection. For

© Springer Nature Switzerland AG 2018
M. Kaenampornpan et al. (Eds.): MIWAI 2018, LNAI 11248, pp. 69–78, 2018.
https://doi.org/10.1007/978-3-030-03014-8_6

normal sensory system, i.e. optical fiber sensor system, it is difficult to ensure the data obtained through numerous sensors actually indicate structural defects because noisy signals or sensory system fault may cause misdetection, no mention its requirement of dense deployment in order to catch the defects. Compared with the normal sensory system, the vision-based methods are able to identify almost all apparent defects without a large number of sensors, thus reducing costs significantly and getting remarkable results.

According to the review on the existing computer vision based defect detection methods in [1,2], the relevant methods can be roughly classified as edge detection algorithms, morphological methods, threshold-based approaches, percolation, machine learning methods and other approaches. Sorts of edge detection methods are compared in [3] and the Haar Wavelet transformation performs better among them for crack detection. However, simple edge detection algorithms are only robust to high-contrast images and vulnerable to the noises, which are likely to generate discontinued cracks. Morphological methods [4] are in similar conditions. Threshold-based approaches [5,6] are developed to detect cracks by setting local or global thresholds with limitations for images under complex illuminations. Percolation-based image processing techniques [7,8] start by initializing a seed region and then label the neighboring regions as crack regions through the percolation process. However, fine cracks may be undetected because these methods strongly depend on user input to initialize the seed pixels. Machine learning methods, such as principal component analysis (PCA), Support Vector Machine (SVM), K-Means and Back Propagation neural network (BP), are employed to detect structural defects and achieve good results [9–12], but many cannot yet provide practical application under various environmental conditions since they still require different manual setting to adapt to different illuminations, shooting angle, etc.

In recent years, deep convolutional neural networks (CNN) have achieved great success in the field of image classification and attracted many research groups. It is worth noting that Cha et al. developed a CNN for piecewise classification on concrete cracks using sliding window techniques without the application of conventional image processing techniques for extracting the defect features [13]. Their method achieved about 98% accuracy in classifying a small image patch as intact or cracked in relatively complex environments. However, the study is implemented at block level rather than pixel level and therefore incapable of finding the exact location of cracks in the images.

To exactly locate the cracks, image segmentation [14], which outputs a label to each pixel in an image, can be a good solution. The visible geometric features i.e. length, width, shape, etc., are critical indicators to identify crack type and severity level, which can be identified after a pixel level class label. Therefore, it can replace human-conducted inspection in some application scenarios for its accurate measurements.

In this study, instead of constructing a new model, we utilize a modified U-net [15] for the crack extraction task. The U-net is originally proposed for biomedical image segmentation and then becomes popular for binary image segmentation tasks such as road extraction [16], building detection [17] and retinal blood vessel segmentation [18]. This architecture requires no feature extraction and obtains an improvement in segmentation accuracy with small dataset over common methods.

2   Network Architecture

As shown in Fig. 1, an U-net architecture includes a contractive path to capture context and an expansive path to improve localization accuracy. The contractive path follows the typical architecture of CNN with a series of convolutions, Rectified Linear Unit (ReLU) activations and max poolings, which extracts features of different levels and increases the number of feature channels at each downsampling step. The symmetric expansive path upsamples the feature maps to progressively increase the resolution of the detected features. Concatenations (skip-connections) are employed between the both paths to merge the upsampled outputs with high-level representation from the contractive path, which ensure both global information and localization accuracy. In order to reduce the number of feature maps to the desired number of classes, a 1 × 1 convolutional layer is added at the last layer. The kernel size in other convolutional layers is 3 × 3. To generate nonlinearity, each convolution is followed by a ReLU activation function except the last layer where sigmoid function is used in binary-label problem while softmax in multi-label problem. 2 × 2 max-pooling operation and 2 × 2 up-convolution operation are employed in the whole model. The final output of the network is a pixel level mask which shows the class of each pixel.

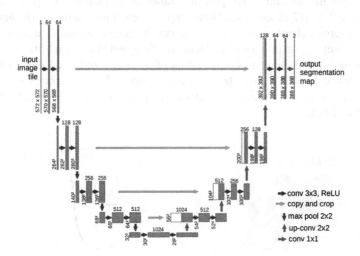

Fig. 1. U-net architecture.

For this surface crack detection problem, there are a few modifications from the original U-net architecture. First, input size is set to 512 × 512 pixels instead of 572 × 572 pixels that is designed in original U-net. Secondly, we use zero padding to avoid shrinking for all the convolutional layers of both contractive and expansive path. Moreover, we choose to adopt Adam optimizer instead of the stochastic gradient descent (SGD) because of its faster convergence speed. Finally, two dropout layers are used to avoid overfitting, which temporarily disconnect the neural connections between connected layers with a certain probability during training phase.

3 Dataset and Data Augmentation

3.1 Image Acquisition and Preprocessing

Refer to [15], the U-net achieves excellent performance using only 30 annotated images for training. Since there is no public dataset for crack detection, image acquisition, image annotation and image preprocessing are conducted to generate a primary small dataset. To build a dataset containing different types of cracking patterns, 30 raw images (with a resolution of 3024 × 4032 pixels or 3456 × 4608 pixels) are collected using iPhone 7 camera and unmanned aerial vehicle. The images are taken from three college buildings under different complex conditions at a distance of 1.0–1.5 m from camera.

We use LabelMe, a graphical image annotation tool that supports for semantic and instance segmentation, to mark the crack area in each raw image and save the annotations as a JSON file. These JSON files are then converted to PNG files and eventually act as masks where 1 represents crack, 0 otherwise.

Each raw image and corresponding label is randomly cropped into 100 patches of 512 × 512 pixels resolutions respectively. The reason for the adoption of small cropping size is that a neural network trained on small images allows scanning of any input images lager than the designed size. In addition, because the U-net architecture consists of 5 max pooling layers, only an image with side length divisible by $32(2^5)$ can be used as an input. Figure 2 shows one of the cropped images from our dataset with corresponding mask in which crack is identified in black.

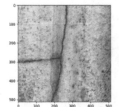 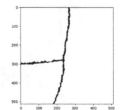

Fig. 2. Image and corresponding mask with crack identified in black.

Though the images of our dataset are manually annotated with two-round inspection to guarantee the ground truths as accurate as possible at pixel level, mislabeling is unavoidable due to crack boundary blur. It reduces the performance of the model to some extent, resulting in a suboptimal performance at testing phase. Another problem is class imbalance that there are much more not-crack pixels than crack pixels in most of our images. To solve this issue, we further removed the images with few crack pixels from our dataset and finally used 200 images as our preliminary dataset. 70% of the dataset patches are applied to train, 15% of the dataset is used for validation and the remaining 15% is used for test.

3.2 Data Augmentation

Data augmentation is adopted to avoid overfitting and hence ensure the robustness and invariance of the network on small databases. The data augmentation methods applied in this study are shown in Table 1. We transform the images with a certain probability by custom functions and use Keras framework to achieve powerful real time data augmentation when feeding the network at each batch with a few lines of code. Among these methods, rotation, flipping, zoom and shift lead to displacement of images. Shear operation result in slightly distortion of cracks. Gamma transformation changes the brightness. We blur the images and add some noise to strengthen the generalization ability of network.

Table 1. Data augmentation methods applied in this study.

Methods	Range
Rotation	$90°, 180°, 270°$ with 25% probability
Flip horizontally	25% probability
Flip vertically	25% probability
Zoom	$\pm 5\%$
Shift	10% on both horizontal and vertical direction
Shear	10% on horizontal direction
Blur	25% probability
Gamma	25% probability
Noise	25% probability

4 Experiments

4.1 Loss Function

Seeing that image segmentation task can be considered as a pixel-level classification problem, we apply the binary cross entropy that is commonly used as a cost function in binary classification tasks. The binary cross entropy loss function is defined as

$$L = -\frac{1}{n}\sum_{i=1}^{n}(y_i \log \hat{y}_i + (1 - y_i)\log(1 - \hat{y}_i)) \tag{1}$$

where n is the number of training samples, y_i is the ground truth of pixel i and $\hat{y}_i$ is the predicted probability for the corresponding pixel.

4.2 Metric

Although precision and recall are commonly used as the major metrics in binary-category problems, they may conflict in some cases. Therefore, a harmonic average of the both metrics called Dice Coefficient or F1 score is also widely applied to measure the similarity between the predict result and ground truth. It is can be written as

$$Dice = \frac{2 \times |X \cap Y|}{|X| + |Y|} = \frac{2 \times precision \times recall}{precision + recall} \tag{2}$$

where X is the predict result and Y is the true mask. It reaches its best value at 1 and worst at 0. To prevent the denominator from being zero, we modify the above formula by adding a factor of 1.

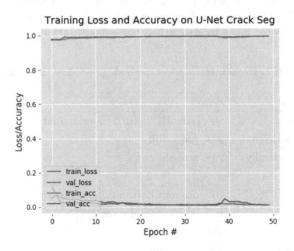

Fig. 3. Accuracies and losses for each epoch.

4.3 Training Details

We implement the explained network using Anaconda science platform and Keras framework(use TensorFlow as backend) in the computer of Intel Core i5-4430 CPU. Because of the memory limitation, we train the model with a batch size of 2. At the convolutional layers, He normal initializer [19] is used to speed up the training process. It draws samples from a truncated normal distribution centered on 0 with standard deviation of $\sqrt{2/fan_{in}}$, where fan_{in} is the number of input units in the weight tensor. The dropout rate at the two dropout layers of our model is both 0.5. Adam optimizer is used in our architecture with a learning rate of 0.0001. Each image is normalized before feeding into the network. It takes about 30 hours for training of 50 epochs. We saved the latest best model according to the quantity monitored using the Keras ModelCheckpoint. Figure 3 shows the learning curve of our network. The loss of training phase reaches the minimum (0.01025) at 37th epoch and the corresponding accuracy is 99.56%. The Dice coefficient on validation set is about 82.3%.

5   Results and Discussion

The output of this modified U-net is an image of the same size as the input image where each pixel value is in the range (0, 1) and represents a probability of crack or background. Segmentation of a 512 × 512 pixels image takes about 7 s on the CPU. We then convert it to a binary image by a threshold 0.5. We set the pixel values which are less than the threshold to be 0. Otherwise, set the pixel values to be 1. All pixel values are multiplied by 255 to obtain a visible predicted mask. Some predicted results from our test set are showed in Fig. 4. The test results demonstrate that our method can successfully cope with crack detection in various complex background scene such as fine cracks, cracks in shadowed images and cracks with disturbing noise. It should be mentioned that our model did not get satisfactory result at the beginning for the poor performance in certain types of features due to the limited number of corresponding training samples. It is necessary to augment training data of corresponding type and put a portion of hard samples into training set and then retrain the network.

Other raw images are used to test the performance of our model, compared with Canny and Sobel edge detection methods. We make a discussion by two examples given in Figs. 5 and 6. As shown in Fig. 5, Canny and Sobel edge detection methods are incapable of distinguishing cracks from stains, pits and scratches, while our method outperforms the both methods with acceptable detection result. As shown in Fig. 6, the blurred boundary between cracks and textures caused by moss and rough surface of the cement wall makes it much difficult for automated crack extracting. Canny and Sobel edge detection methods have a poor performance under this kind of condition. Our method is able to provide almost all of crack information without post-processing in spite of some misclassification on the moss area and image edge.

Although our model achieves high accuracy and has robust performance in crack extraction task, there is still room for improvement in this work. Since 2D image provides no depth information of cracks, 3D image can be used to replace 2D image to extract internal information or improve the reliability of severity level evaluation. Moreover, a large scale image dataset containing more different types of cracking patterns is necessary to train a powerful network for automated defect detection.

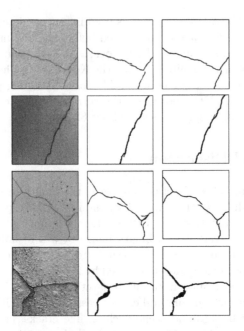

Fig. 4. Original images, ground-truth label and predicted masks from our test set.

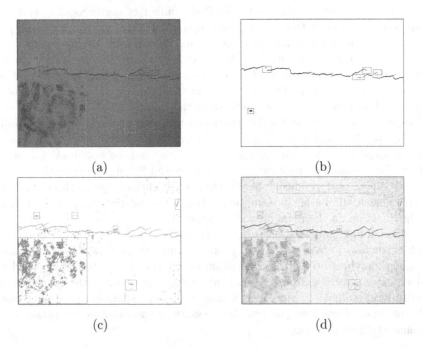

Fig. 5. Cracks with stains, pits and scratches: (a) raw image, (b) our method, (c) Canny edge detection, and (d) Sobel edge detection.

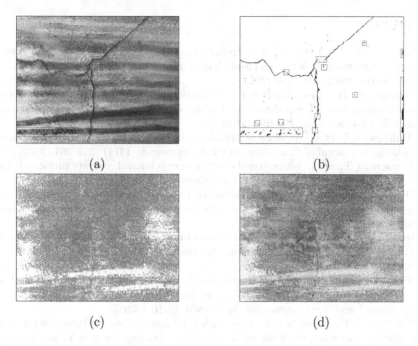

Fig. 6. Cracks with moss on the rough surface of cement wall: (a) raw image, (b) our method, (c) Canny edge detection, and (d) Sobel edge detection.

6 Conclusion

In this work, we first build a small dataset. A total of 30 raw images containing different types of cracks were obtained under various conditions to enhance adaptability of the neural network. The raw images were annotated and then cropped into small patch images with 512 × 512 pixels resolution for training, validation and test processes. We developed a robust network based on U-net architecture to detect crack on structure surfaces. 512 × 512 pixels is adopted as input size of our network and the output is a mask image that shows the class of each pixel. Using sliding window techniques, the model can cope with the larger size images. Our proposed method without post-processing achieves an acceptable accuracy in various complex background and outperforms traditional edge detection methods.

Acknowledgements. The authors would like to acknowledge the supports by the National Natural Science Foundation of China (Grant No. 61601127, 51508105, and 61574038), the Fujian Provincial Department of Science and Technology of China (Grant No. 2016H6012, and 2018J0106), the Fujian Provincial Economic and Information Technology Commission of China (Grant No. 830020, 83016006), and the Science Foundation of Fujian Education Department of China (Grant No. JAT160073).

References

1. Koch, C., et al.: A review on computer vision based defect detection and condition assessment of concrete and asphalt civil infrastructure. Advanced Engineering Informatics **29**(2), 196–210 (2015)
2. Mohammad, R., et al.: A survey and evaluation of promising approaches for automatic image-based defect detection of bridge structures. Structure and Infrastructure Engineering **5**(6), 455–486 (2009)
3. Abdelqader, I., et al.: Analysis of edge-detection techniques for crack identification in bridges. Journal of Computing in Civil Engineering **17**(4), 255–263 (2015)
4. Yamaguchi, T., et al.: Image-based crack detection for real concrete surfaces. IEEE Transactions on Electrical & Electronic Engineering **3**(1), 128–135 (2010)
5. Oliveira, H., Lobato Correia, P.: Automatic road crack segmentation using entropy and image dynamic thresholding. In: 17th European Signal Processing Conference, pp. 622–626. IEEE (2009)
6. Hu, D., et al.: Wall crack detection based on image processing. In: 3rd International Conference on Intelligent Control and Information Processing, pp. 597–600. IEEE (2012)
7. Yamaguchi, T., Nakamura, S., Hashimoto, S.: An efficient crack detection method using percolation-based image processing. In: 3rd IEEE Conference on Industrial Electronics and Applications, pp. 1875–1880. IEEE (2008)
8. Yamaguchi, T., Hashimoto, S.: Fast crack detection method for large-size concrete surface images using percolation-based image processing. Machine Vision & Applications **21**(5), 797–809 (2010)
9. Abdel-Qader, I., et al.: PCA-based algorithm for unsupervised bridge crack detection. Advances in Engineering Software **37**(12), 771–778 (2006)
10. Hutchinson, T., et al.: Improved image analysis for evaluating concrete damage. Journal of Computing in Civil Engineering **20**(3), 210–216 (2006)
11. Cui, F., et al.: Images crack detection technology based on improved K-means algorithm. Journal of Multimedia **9**(6), 67–73 (2014)
12. Moon, H., Kim, J., et al.: Inteligent crack detecting algorithm on the concrete crack image using neural network. In: International Symposium on Automation and Robotics in Construction, (2011). 10.22260/ISARC2011/0279
13. Cha, Y., et al.: Deep learning-based crack damage detection using convolutional neural networks. Computer-aided Civil & Infrastructure Engineering **32**(5), 361–378 (2017)
14. Hao, M., et al.: An improved neuron segmentation model for crack detection C Image Segmentation Model. Cybernetics & Information Technologies **17**(2), 119–133 (2017)
15. Ronneberger, O., et al.: U-net: convolutional networks for biomedical image segmentation. In: Medical Image Computing and Computer-Assisted Intervention, pp. 234–241. Springer (2015)
16. Zhang, Z., Liu, Q., Wang, Y.: Road extraction by deep residual U-net. IEEE Geoscience and Remote Sensing Letters **15**(5), 749–753 (2018)
17. Vladimir, I., et al.: Satellite imagery feature detection using deep convolutional neural network: a Kaggle competition. ArXiv:1706.06169 CS. (2017)
18. Gao, X., et al.: Retinal blood vessel segmentation based on the Gaussian matched filter and U-net. In: 10th International Congress on Image and Signal Processing, BioMedical Engineering and Informatics. IEEE (2017)
19. He, K., et al.: Delving deep into rectifiers: surpassing human-level performance on ImageNet classification. In: IEEE International Conference on Computer Vision, pp. 1026–1034. (2015)

A Novel Method of Automatic Crack Detection Utilizing Non-linear Relaxation Method and Crack Geometric Features for Safety Evaluation of Concrete Structure

Hoang Nam Nguyen$^{(\boxtimes)}$, Van Duc Phan, and Van Binh Nguyen

Faculty of Mechanical, Electrical, Electronic and Automotive Engineering,
Nguyen Tat Thanh University, Ho Chi Minh City, Vietnam
nhnam@ntt.edu.vn

Abstract. Traditionally, surface cracks of concrete structures are manually measured and recorded by experienced inspectors. Recently, many crack detection techniques utilizing image processing have been proposed to detect cracks in 2D piecewise constant image. However, crack images in real applications such as building safety evaluation and bridge maintenance are usually 2D multiple-phase piecewise constant images. Furthermore, these methods require the user to choose appropriate parameters, especially the threshold in image segmentation step, for a certain set of images with similar contrast. This paper presents a novel automatic method for the efficient detection of cracks in 2D multiple-phase piecewise constant crack image without predefined thresholds in image binarization step. Firstly, cracks are enhanced utilizing 2 geometric features of crack including tubular and symmetric properties. In the second step, we proposed a crack-feature based non-linear relaxation method to detect crack from the enhanced images. Finally, we proposed a crack probability based binarization method to extract the binary crack map. The robustness of our proposed method are demonstrated in various crack images of building concrete structures.

Keywords: Automatic crack detection · Non-linear relaxation
Phase symmetry · Frangi's filter · Image segmentation · Local thresholding

1 Introduction

Image-based crack detection is highly desirable for automatic and objective crack assessment in building safety evaluation or maintenance of concrete structures, which suffer high loads such as columns of buildings and bridges. Traditionally, experienced humans detect and measure cracks using conventional visual and manual approaches, which are very costly, time-consuming, labor-intensive, and subjective [1]. Recently, many image processing techniques have been proposed to achieve automatic crack detection. However, accurate detection and localization of cracks from real images of building or bridge is difficult because these images usually contain various blebs,

© Springer Nature Switzerland AG 2018
M. Kaenampornpan et al. (Eds.): MIWAI 2018, LNAI 11248, pp. 79–91, 2018.
https://doi.org/10.1007/978-3-030-03014-8_7

irregularities in crack shape and size, and other unintended objects of non-concrete structures.

Available techniques of automatic crack detection in still images typically work by preprocessing the image to enhance the contrast between cracks and background before a binarization step (e.g. thresholding) is applied. Hutchinson and Chen [2] used the Canny filter and wavelet transformation for crack detection. Ito et al. [3] combined some image processing techniques such as wavelet transform, shading correction, and binarization to detect cracks. Yamaguchi et al. [4] proposed a crack-detection method based on the percolation model in which binarization is included after the percolation processing. Abdel-Qader et al. [5] compared the effectiveness of crack detection among wavelet transform, Fourier transform, Sobel filter, and Canny filter. All of these methods require the user to choose appropriate binarization thresholds for each set of images.

Lee [6] proposed a system for automatic inspection of bridges but including a post-processing supervised manipulation. This method is claimed to be able to detect crack automatically by using some techniques such as median filter, morphological image processing. On the other hand, those techniques can only be applied for two-phase piecewise constant image and are not applicable for crack image with clear step edge.

Shan et al. [7] used stereo-vision camera to detect edges of cracks. This method proposed a novel Canny-Zernike combination algorithm, which can obtain the image coordinates of crack edge in the image accurately. However, this method can not discriminate between edge of cracks and edge of other non-crack objects in the images.

Chen et al. [8] developed a crack detection system using multi-temporal images by utilizing the first derivative of a Gaussian filter. This method can compute the crack width in a controlled environment but requiring users to put nodes along the crack, and thus is not automatic.

Fujita and Hamamoto [9] used Frangi's filter [11] and probabilistic relaxation to automatically segment cracks from noisy real concrete surface images. However, Frangi's filter also enhances the step edges in the image so this method failed to detect crack from 2D multiple-phase images that have clear step edges.

Wang et al. [10] proposed an algorithm that integrates morphological approach, percolation approach and practical technique. This technique can detect crack accurately but needs user intervention. Nguyen et al. [12] used B-spline level set method to detect crack in 2D images but it takes a lot of computing resources for the level set model to converge.

In this paper, we proposed a novel automatic crack detection method for localizing cracks from images of buildings, bridges or other civil engineering infrastructure that contains concrete structures and unintended objects. To classify between step edges and cracks in images, we assumed that cracks possesses two geometric properties including tubular and symmetric properties. Generally, we proposed 3 main steps for automatic crack detection. In the first step, we need to enhance crack and remove other unintended objects in the images by utilizing 2 geometric features of crack. In the second step, we adapt a non-linear relaxation method to segment crack automatically from the enhanced crack images. In the final step, a proposed crack probability based binarization method is used to extract the binary crack map.

2 Proposed Method

2.1 Two and Multiple Phases Piece-Wise Constant Image

Images of surface concrete structures, which are demonstrated in available automatic crack detection techniques [1–10], are usually 2D piecewise constant images. However, in our work, we try to detect cracks from 2D multiple-phase piecewise constant images of civil infrastructures such as building, bridges… that contain surface cracks. To understand the differences between two-phase piecewise constant image and multiple-phase piece-wise constant image, we can look at the Fig. 1. The right image is the 2D multiple-phase piecewise constant image, which has more than two phases of intensities including "bright phase" of the background, "dark phase" of crack and some phases of other objects in building. The left image, which is called as a two-phase piecewise constant image, contains only two phases, "bright phase" and "dark phase".

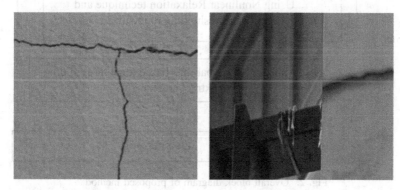

Fig. 1. Examples of two-phase and multiple phase piece-wise constant images

2.2 Block Diagram of the Proposed Algorithm

The proposed algorithm is shown in Fig. 2. Generally, we proposed 3 main steps for crack enhancement and detection.

Let $I(\mathbf{x})$ be the input crack image. In the first step, we enhance crack and remove other unintended objects in the image by computing the tubular and symmetric feature. In the second step, we adapt a non-linear relaxation method to segment crack from the crack feature image to obtain the crack map, which is a binary image where "1" pixel represent the crack pixel and "0" pixel belongs to background. In the third step, we extract the binary crack map using crack probability-based local thresholding.

2.3 Crack Feature Image

In our previous work [12], we consider cracks are elongated dark objects which are tubular (line-like). In addition, crack also has a symmetric property since the pixel intensity profile of the cross-section across the crack center-line resembles an inversed Gaussian curve as shown in Fig. 2. In this paper, we utilize the crack tubular and

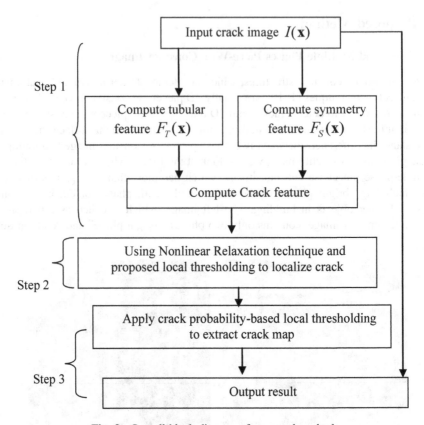

Fig. 2. Overall block diagram of proposed method

symmetric features to enhance crack and remove unintended objects. Let $I(\mathbf{x})$ be the input image, the crack feature image $C_{TS}(\mathbf{x})$, which represents the possibility of a pixel $\mathbf{x}(x, y)$ to be inside a crack, is defined as:

$$C_{TS}(\mathbf{x}) = C_T(\mathbf{x}) \cdot C_S(\mathbf{x}) \tag{1}$$

where $C_T(\mathbf{x})$ and $C_s(\mathbf{x})$ are tubular and symmetric feature values at pixel $\mathbf{x}(x, y)$, respectively. We aim to divide crack image into regions of high crack feature value and a region of low crack feature value (background and other non-crack objects) (Fig. 3).

2.3.1 Tubular Feature
Frangi et al. [10] proposed to compute the vesselness measure of vessels using a multi-scale method. We assumed that the tubular feature of cracks is equal with vesselness measure of vessels and utilize the Frangi's filter to obtain tubular feature of cracks.

The two eigenvectors e_1, e_2 and their corresponding eigenvalues λ_1, λ_2 of the Hessian matrix $\nabla^2 I(\mathbf{x})$ can be used as shape directors for $I(\mathbf{x})$. The tubular feature $C_{T,\sigma}(\mathbf{x}, \sigma)$ for a point $\mathbf{x}$ at a single scale σ is computed as [10]

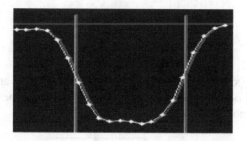

Fig. 3. Pixel intensity profile of a cross-section across the crack-centerline

$$C_{T,\sigma}(\mathbf{x}, \sigma) = \begin{cases} 0, & \text{if } \lambda_2 \leq 0 \\ e^{\frac{-A_\alpha^2}{2a^2}}\left(1 - e^{\frac{-S^2}{2b^2}}\right), & \text{otherwise} \end{cases} \tag{2}$$

where $A_\alpha = \left|\frac{\lambda_1}{\lambda_2}\right|$; $S = (\lambda_1^2 + \lambda_2^2)^{1/2}$; α, b are the thresholds that control the sensitivity of $C_{T,\sigma}(\mathbf{x}, \sigma)$ to the measures A_α, S. The normalized derivatives proposed by Lindeberg [13] were used to compute the derivatives in the Hessian matrix.

From (2), we attain the tubular feature for 1 single scale σ. For a given set of scales Ω_σ, the maximum tubular feature of different scales Ω_σ was chosen to be the unique multi-scale tubular feature of the image:

$$C_T(\mathbf{x}) = \max_{\sigma \in \Omega_\sigma} \{C_{T,\sigma}(\mathbf{x}, \sigma)\} \tag{3}$$

where $\max\{.\}$ is the maximum value of a set of $C_{T,\sigma}(\mathbf{x}, \sigma)$.

2.3.2 Symmetric Feature

The symmetric feature can be extracted using the local phase information [14–16]. We combine the phase symmetry concept [11] and the monogenic signal framework [17] to compute the symmetric feature of cracks. Let $LG(\mathbf{x})$ be the isotropic log-Gabor filter given as

$$LG(\mathbf{x}) = F^{-1}\left\{\exp\left(-\frac{(\log(\theta/\theta_0))^2}{2(\log(k/\theta_0))^2}\right)\right\} \tag{4}$$

where θ is the spherical co-ordinate of the image in the frequency domain, θ_0 is the center frequency of each sale. We choose 6 scales so $\theta_0 = 1/2 * 2.1^{h-1}$, $h = \{1, 2, 3, 4, 5, 6\}$, $k/\theta_0 = 0.65$.

From the log-Gabor filter, we can build the monogenic signal $G(\mathbf{x})$ at $\mathbf{x} = (x, y)$ pixel as a three dimensional vector [17]:

$$G(\mathbf{x}) = [G^1(\mathbf{x}), G^2(\mathbf{x}), G^3(\mathbf{x})] \tag{5}$$

$$G^1(\mathbf{x}) = I(\mathbf{x}) * LG(\mathbf{x}) * m_1(\mathbf{x}) \tag{6}$$

$$G^2(\mathbf{x}) = I(\mathbf{x}) * LG(\mathbf{x}) * m_2(\mathbf{x}) \tag{7}$$

$$G^3(\mathbf{x}) = I(\mathbf{x}) * LG(\mathbf{x}) \tag{8}$$

where $m_1(\mathbf{x})$ and $m_2(\mathbf{x})$ are two monogenic signal filters. $G_{odd}(\mathbf{x})$ and $G_{even}(\mathbf{x})$ are two even symmetric and odd symmetric filter responses, which can be represented by the components of the monogenic signal as

$$G_{odd}(\mathbf{x}) = \sqrt{(G^1(\mathbf{x}))^2 + (G^2(\mathbf{x}))^2} \tag{9}$$

$$G_{even}(\mathbf{x}) = G^3(\mathbf{x}) \tag{10}$$

The phase symmetry then can be formulated from the monogenic signal as

$$P_S(\mathbf{x}) = \frac{Max\left\{\sum_h \left(-G_{even}^h(\mathbf{x}) - |G_{odd}^h(\mathbf{x})|\right) - T_{noise}, 0\right\}}{\sum_h \sqrt{\left(G_{even}^h(\mathbf{x})\right)^2 + \left(G_{odd}^h(\mathbf{x})\right)^2} + \zeta} \tag{11}$$

where T_{noise} is a noise threshold, ζ is a small constant to prevent division by zero.

The shortcoming of phase symmetry in crack detection application is that it also has high values for round dots. To overcome this, we used the symmetric feature as the average value of the phase symmetry along the crack direction as follows [12]:

$$C_S(\mathbf{x}) = \max_o \left\{ \frac{\sum_{p=1}^{M} P_S(\mathbf{x}_p^o)}{N} \right\} \tag{12}$$

where $P_S(\mathbf{x}_p^o)$ is the phase symmetry of the pth pixel on the virtual line segment passing through $\mathbf{x}$ in o^{th} direction. N is the total number of each virtual line segment passing through $\mathbf{x}$ and M is the total number of pixels on each virtual line segment.

2.4   Nonlinear Relaxation Method for Crack Detection

From the crack feature image $C(\mathbf{x})$, we can apply B-spline level set method to extract crack regions. This method requires to build a matrix of B-spline radial basis functions that is half the size of the input images. For image of sizes lager than 1000×1000, a lot of computing resources and memory must be used for computation of the convolution task between this matrix and the input image until the convergence. Therefore, we utilize Nonlinear relaxation method, which does not requires convolution between large matrixes for crack detection. Nonlinear relaxation labeling is mainly used to label objects from noisy data [9, 18]. For a focal pixel, the probability of $\mathbf{x}$ to belong to a crack segment is defined as

$$P_C(\mathbf{x}) = \frac{\log(C(\mathbf{x})+1)}{\log(C_{\max}(\mathbf{x})+1)} \tag{13}$$

where $C_{\max}(\mathbf{x})$ is the maximum crack feature value. On the other hand, the probability of $\mathbf{x}$ to belong to background is $P_B(\mathbf{x}) = 1 - P_C(\mathbf{x})$. $P_C(\mathbf{x})$ can be updated by the rule proposed by Peleg [19] as

$$P'_C(\mathbf{x}) = \frac{P_C(\mathbf{x})Q_C(\mathbf{x})}{P_C(\mathbf{x})Q_C(\mathbf{x}) + P_B(\mathbf{x})Q_B(\mathbf{x})} \tag{14}$$

where $Q_C(\mathbf{x})$, $Q_B(\mathbf{x})$ are the strengths of support that $\mathbf{x}$ belonging to crack and background, respectively, from all the neighbor pixels $\mathbf{x}_i$ belongs to $R_{\mathbf{x}}$

$$Q_C(\mathbf{x}) = \frac{1}{N(R_{\mathbf{x}})} \sum_{\mathbf{x} \in R_{\mathbf{x}}} P_C(\mathbf{x}) \tag{15}$$

where $N(R_{\mathbf{x}})$ is the total number of pixels in the supporting region $R_{\mathbf{x}}$. In this paper, we observe that the neighboring crack pixels of $\mathbf{x}$, which have high crack feature values, should lie in a line segment passing through $\mathbf{x}$. Therefore, we choose $R_{\mathbf{x}}$ to be one of a set of line segments passing through $\mathbf{x}$ defined as $\{R_1, R_2, \ldots, R_o\}$. In this paper, we choose 4 regions as 4 line segments along 4 angular directions $\{0, \pi/4, \pi/2, 3\pi/4\}$. The chosen region is the one that gives the maximum $P_C(\mathbf{x})$. We update $P_C(\mathbf{x})$ by the following rule:

$$P'_C(\mathbf{x}) = \max_i \frac{P_C(\mathbf{x})Q^i_C(\mathbf{x})}{P_C(\mathbf{x})Q^i_C(\mathbf{x}) + P_B(\mathbf{x})Q^i_B(\mathbf{x})} \tag{16}$$

$$Q^i_C(\mathbf{x}) = \frac{1}{N(R_i)} \sum_{\mathbf{x} \in R_i} P_C(\mathbf{x}) \tag{17}$$

The updating process for all pixels is repeated until $P_C(\mathbf{x})$ converges or stabilizes. The converged or stabilized $P_C(\mathbf{x})$ is called as $\bar{P}_C(\mathbf{x})$.

2.5 Crack Probability Based Binarization Method for Crack Localization

From the converged probability $P_C(\mathbf{x})$, we proposed to use crack probability based binarization method to localize crack:

Step 1: Apply locally thresholding to $C(\mathbf{x})$ to achieve $TH(\mathbf{x})$.
Step 2: Choose the binary crack map as

$$B(\mathbf{x}) = \begin{cases} 1, & \bar{P}(\mathbf{x})_C > 0.5 \\ 0, & otherwise \end{cases} \tag{18}$$

Step 3: Create a new binary crack map $B(\mathbf{x})$ by setting all the neighbor pixels of '1' pixels in $B(\mathbf{x})$ to be '1'.

Step 4: Create a new binary crack map $B(\mathbf{x})$ by implementing an "AND" operation between $B(\mathbf{x})$ and $TH(\mathbf{x})$

$$B(\mathbf{x}) = B(\mathbf{x}) \,\&\, TH(\mathbf{x}) \tag{19}$$

Step 5: Repeat step 3 and 4 until $B(\mathbf{x})$ converges or stabilizes. The converged $B(\mathbf{x})$ is the final result.

3   Results

The proposed method was implemented in Matlab 7.10 and tested on a computer with Intel Core I3 2.1 GHz CPU and 8 GB RAM. The following settings are applied:

- The image has an eight-bit dynamics and 2 dimensions.
- $\alpha = 0.5, b = 15, \Omega_\sigma = \{0.5, 1, 1.5, 2, 2.5, 3\}$.
- $C_S(\mathbf{x})$ are computed over 6 scales with following parameters $K/\theta_0 = 0.65$, $\zeta = 0.0001, M = 15, N = 12$. These parameters are empirically tuned based on our experiments on a dataset of 50 crack images.

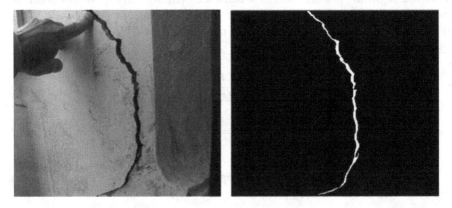

Fig. 4. Automatic crack detection in a concrete column. Left image is the input crack image, right image is the detected binary crack map

Figure 4 shows the results of automatic crack detection in 2D multiple-phase image of a concrete column. Although there's a human hand in the crack image, our method can successfully detect the crack. To further demonstrate the capability of automatic crack detection in a real scene of building, Fig. 5 shows another successful example of detecting crack in an image of wall and ground. These two examples proved that our proposed method is effective in automatically detecting crack in 2D multiple-phase image.

Figure 6 shows another experiment in which we detect crack from image of a scene in building. There's a steel tube and some other non-crack objects in the 2D multiple-

Fig. 5. Automatic crack detection in a image of wall and ground. Left image is the input crack image, right image is the detected binary crack map

phase image. However, the proposed method can accurately detect the crack while ignoring all the non-crack objects.

In the next experiment, we make a comparison between our proposed method and Hutchinson's method [20], Fujita's method [9] which is claimed to be able to detect crack in noisy images of concrete surface. We use the robust set of parameters for Fujita's method as described in [9]. Parameters for Hutchinson's method is referenced from [20]. From the results in Fig. 8, we can observe that our proposed method detect crack correctly in the images of buildings. In contrast to our method, Fujita's method, have considered many step edges as crack. Hutchinson's method failed to detect crack as it only can work in two phase piece wise constant images.

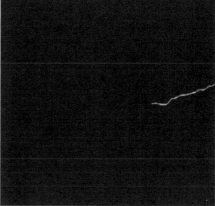

Fig. 6. Automatic crack detection in an image of a scene in building. Left image is the input crack image, right image is the detected binary crack map

To build a metrics for comparing our method and other methods, similar with [21], we need to build the ground truth of images in our experiment by asking the volunteers to observe and select the cracked regions in images. Adapting the formulation of precision and recall concepts from [21], we use two following metrics to compute the accuracy of all the methods:

$$Precision = \frac{|GA_{conn}|}{|CD|} \tag{20}$$

$$Recall = \frac{|GA \cap CD|}{|GA|} \tag{21}$$

where GA are the pixels volunteers chose to be inside the cracks. CD are the pixels detected by the level set models. GA_{conn} are those pixels detected in CD which are connected to cracks in GT. High value of Recall proves that a large portion of pixels inside crack have been detected. Concurrently, high value of Precision shows that a large number of pixels detected by the level set model really belong to true cracks. As Hutchinson method cannot converge to detect crack in image with many clear step edge as in our experiments shown in Fig. 8, in the Table 1, we only make a comparison between our method and Fujita's method. We can see that our method have high precisions and recalls in all three experiments while Fujita's method only can obtain very low precisions as it detect many non-crack objects in the image. This shows that our method is more precise than Fujita's method in detecting crack in images with many clear step edges.

In Fig. 7, we add 2 more experiments to demonstrate the effectiveness of our method in the surfaces of other materials. Our method can extract crack effectively although there are many clear step edges in the image. This show the high probability for the proposed method to be applied in crack detection in multiple-phase intensity inhomogeneous images.

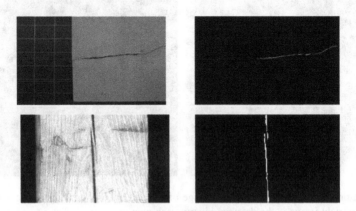

Fig. 7. Automatic crack detection in an image of different materials. Left image is the input crack image, right image is the detected binary crack map

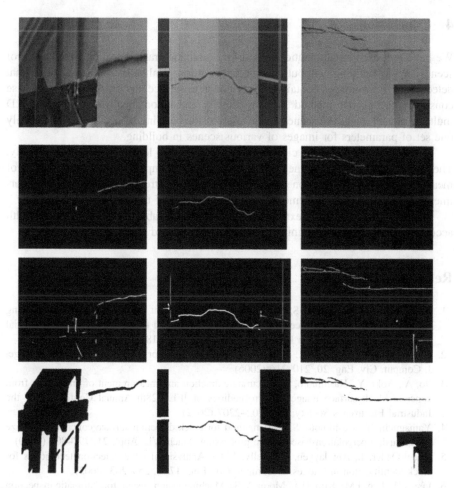

Fig. 8. Comparison between proposed method, Fujita's method [9] and Hutchinson's method [20]. From first to fourth row: input image, binary image result from the proposed method, result of Fujita's method, result of Hutchinson's method.

Table 1. Comparing precision and recall of our method and Fujita's method

Image no.	Proposed method		Fujita's method	
	Precision	Recall	Precision	Recall
1	0.9616	0.9565	0.3056	0.9129
2	0.9618	0.9600	0.2390	0.9963
3	0.9310	0.9848	0.3808	0.9795

4 Conclusions

We have proposed an automatic method for automatic crack detection from image of scenes in the building without human intervention. Unlike available methods that detect crack from images containing only concrete surface and cracks (2D piece-wise constant images), our method localize directly and automatically the cracks in 2D multiple-phases images of scenes inside and outside building. Especially, we used only one set of parameters for images of various scenes in building.

Our method can assist the civil engineering experts to localize crack automatically. The output of this advanced method can be used as the input for automatic method of measuring widths of cracks on the surface of concrete structure. A number of experiments have been given to demonstrate the robustness of the proposed method.

In the near future, we will extend our method to be capable of measuring crack width accurately from images containing concrete structures and other non-crack objects.

References

1. Yamaguchi, T., Nakamura, S., Hashimoto, S.: An efficient crack detection method using percolation-based image processing. In: Proceedings of 3rd IEEE Conference on Industrial Electronics and Applications ICIEA 2018, Singapore, pp. 1875–1880 (2008)
2. Hutchinson, T.C., Chen, Z.: Improved image analysis for evaluating concrete damage. J. Comput. Civ. Eng. **20**, 210–216 (2006)
3. Ito, A., Aoki, Y., Hashimoto, S.: Accurate extraction and measurement of fine cracks from concrete block surface image. In: Proceedings of IEEE 28th Annual Conference of the Industrial Electronics Society, pp. 2202–2207 (2002)
4. Yamaguchi, T., Hashimoto, S.: Fast method for crack detection surface concrete large-size images using percolation-based image processing. Mach. Vis. Appl. **21**, 797–809 (2010)
5. Abdel-Qader, I., Abudayyeh, O., Kelly, M.E.: Analysis of edge detection techniques for crack identification in bridges. J. Comput. Civ. Eng. **17**(3), 255–263 (2003)
6. Lee, J.H., Lee, J.M., Kim, H.J., Moon, Y.S.: Machine vision system for automatic inspection of bridges. In: Congress Image Signal Process, vol. 3, pp. 363–366 (2008)
7. Shan, B., Zheng, S., Jinping, O.: A stereovision-based crack width detection approach for concrete surface assessment. KSCE J. Civ. Eng. **20**(2), 803–812 (2016)
8. Chen, L., Shao, Y., Jan, H., Huang, C., Tien, Y.: Measuring system for cracks in concrete using multi-temporal images. J. Surv. Eng. **132**, 77–82 (2006)
9. Fujita, Y., Hamamoto, Y.: A robust automatic crack detection method from noisy concrete surfaces. Mach. Vis. Appl. **22**, 245–254 (2011)
10. Frangi, A.F., Niessen, W.J., Vincken, K.L., Viergever, M.A.: Multiscale vessel enhancement filtering. In: Wells, W.M., Colchester, A., Delp, S. (eds.) MICCAI 1998. LNCS, vol. 1496, pp. 130–137. Springer, Heidelberg (1998). https://doi.org/10.1007/BFb0056195
11. Wang, P., Huang, H.: Comparison analysis on present image-based crack detection methods in concrete structures. In: Proceedings of 2010 3rd International Congress on Image and Signal Processing (CISP 2010), vol. 5, pp. 2530–2533 (2010)
12. Nguyen, H.N., Nguyen, T.Y., Pham, D.L.: Automatic measurement of concrete crack width in 2D multiple-phase images for building safety evaluation. In: Nguyen, N.T., Hoang, D.H., Hong, T.-P., Pham, H., Trawiński, B. (eds.) ACIIDS 2018. LNCS (LNAI), vol. 10752, pp. 638–648. Springer, Cham (2018). https://doi.org/10.1007/978-3-319-75420-8_60

13. Lindeberg, T.: Edge detection and ridge detection with automatic scale selection. Int. J. Comput. Vis. **30**, 117–156 (1998)
14. Kovesi, P.: Symmetry and asymmetry from local phase. In: Tenth Australian Joint Conference on Artificial Intelligence, Australia, pp. 185–190 (1997)
15. Kovesi, P.: Image features from phase congruency. Videre J. Comput. Vis. Res. **1**, 1–26 (1999)
16. Nguyen, H.N., Kam, T.Y., Cheng, P.Y.: Automatic crack detection from 2D images using a crack measure-based B-spline level set model. Multidimens. Syst. Signal Process. **29**, 213–244 (2016)
17. Felsberg, M., Sommer, G.: The monogenic signal. IEEE Trans. Signal Process. **49**, 3136–3144 (2001)
18. Eklundh, J.O., Yamamoto, H., Rosenfeld, A.: A relaxation method for multispectral pixel classification. IEEE Trans. Pattern Anal. Mach. Intell. **PAMI-2**, 72–75 (1980)
19. Peleg, S.: A new probabilistic relaxation scheme. IEEE Trans. Pattern Anal. Mach. Intell. **PAMI-2**(4), 362–369 (1980)
20. Chen, Z.Q., Hutchinson, T.C.: Image-based framework for concrete surface crack monitoring and quantification. In: Advances in Civil Engineering 2010 (2010)
21. Padalkar, M.G., Joshi, M.V.: Auto-inpainting heritage scenes: a complete framework for detecting and infilling cracks in images and videos with quantitative assessment. Mach. Vis. Appl. **26**, 317–337 (2015)

Optimal Data Collection of MP-MR-MC Wireless Sensors Network for Structural Monitoring

Qinghua Li, Zhicong Chen(✉), Lijun Wu, Shuying Cheng, and Peijie Lin

College of Physics and Information Engineering, Fuzhou University,
Fuzhou 350116, China
zhicong.chen@fzu.edu.cn

Abstract. Structural health monitoring (SHM) is a kind of data-intensive applications for wireless sensors networks, which usually requires high network bandwidth. However, the bandwidth of traditional single-radio single-channel (SR-SC) WSN is quite limited. In order to meet the requirement of structural monitoring, multi-radio multi-channel (MR-MC) WSN is emerging. In this paper, we address the optimal data collection problem in MR-MC WSN by modelling it as an integer linear programming problem. Combining the advantages of the particle swarm optimization (PSO) algorithm and flower pollination optimization (FPA) algorithm, we propose a new hybrid algorithm BFPA-PSO to solve the optimization problem under the constraint of time slot and multi-power multi-radio multi-channel (MP-MR-MC). Theoretical analysis and simulation experiments are carried out and the results show that the proposed method has good performance in improving network capacity as well as reducing energy consumption.

Keywords: Structural health monitoring · Data collection · MR-MC
BFPA-PSO

1 Introduction

Structural health monitoring (SHM) is widely used in large civil infrastructures (especially in long-span bridges and high-rise buildings), which is used to detect damages and thus improve public safety [1–3]. For instance [4], 64 sensor nodes were installed on the Golden Gate Bridge, the network topology can be abstracted as the complex three-dimensional long chain structure shown in Fig. 1, most data collection needs to be forwarded by multiple routers. In [5], the maximization problem of throughput in single-hop network is considered, and two algorithms, named as ODSAA and ODAA, are running centrally by the mobile sink, which are used to find the sub-optimal solutions in a reasonable computation time. While [6] discuss the influence of network deployment on capacity, and proposed a non-uniform sensor distribution strategy to increase the

© Springer Nature Switzerland AG 2018
M. Kaenampornpan et al. (Eds.): MIWAI 2018, LNAI 11248, pp. 92–103, 2018.
https://doi.org/10.1007/978-3-030-03014-8_8

total data capacity. As mentioned above, most existing data collection strategies are for single-radio single-channel (SR-SC) or single-radio multi-channel (SR-MC) WSNs, which severely limits the improvement of network capacity [7]. For meeting the high network bandwidth of SHM WSN, multi-radio multi-channel (MR-MC) gradually attracts the attention of researchers [8,9]. Fan et al. [9] proposed MMDC algorithm to solve the link scheduling of WSN network with the communication of multi-power multi-radio multi-channel (MP-MR-MC).

This work is motivated by the advantage of MP-MR-MC communication, and propose a new hybrid algorithm BFPA-PSO to solve the joint problem of scheduling, channel assignment and routing in MP-MR-MC network. The aim of this work is to improve network capacity as well as reduce energy consumption. Our propose algorithm has obvious advantage in solving the problem of MP-MR-MC by comparing it with the well-known algorithms, Genetic Algorithm (GA) [10], Binary Bat Algorithm (BBA) [11], Binary Flower Pollination Algorithm (BFPA) [12], Binary Gravitational Search Algorithm (BGSA) [13], Binary Particle Swarm Optimization (BPSO) [14].

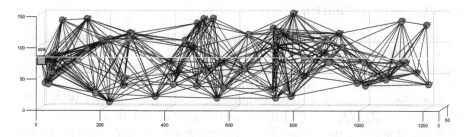

Fig. 1. Three-dimensional long chain network topology of 64 sensor nodes.

2   System Model

2.1   Network Model

We consider a network with sensor nodes and one sink deployed in appropriate location, which is denoted as $G = (V, E)$, where $V = \{v_1, v_2, \cdots, v_n\}$, and $L = \{l_{uv} = (u, v) | u \in V, v \in V\}$ correspond to the set of sensor nodes and links, respectively. Here, $\Re_u = \{\gamma_1, \gamma_2, \cdots, \gamma_H\} (u \in V)$ represents the identification of the H radios equipped on sensor u. $C = \{c_1, c_2, \cdots, c_K\}$ holds the set of non-overlap channels to be used by radios. Furthermore, λ transmission power levels are adopted in this paper, denoted as $P = \{p_1, p_2, \cdots, p_\lambda\}(p_i < p_{i+1}, i = 1, 2, \cdots, \lambda - 1)$. Which also means every node has λ corresponding transmission radius $R = \{r_1, r_2, \cdots, r_\lambda\}(r_i < r_{i+1}, i = 1, 2, \cdots, \lambda - 1)$.

2.2   Energy Model

We take node residual energy into account, because energy is inevitably consumed when sending and receiving data between nodes [15]. Assume that residual energy of node v is $E_v(\tau)$, $v \in V$ and τ denotes τ^{th} time slot. e^o represents the energy consumed to receive a packet, it is a constant. t_{uv} represents link l_{uv} transmission time and $p(uv) \in P$ denotes the power level assigned for link l_{uv} then the transmission energy consumption e_u can be calculated as:

$$e_u = p(uv)t_{uv} \tag{1}$$

And then residual energy of sender u and receiver v in time slot $\tau + 1$ can be updated as following respectively:

$$E_u(\tau + 1) = E_u(\tau) - e_u \tag{2}$$

$$E_v(\tau + 1) = E_v(\tau) - e^o \tag{3}$$

2.3   Capacity Definition

Network capacity is an important measurement to evaluate network performance, particularly for SHM WSN. For simplicity, we use the data receiving rate at the sink in one round to measure its achievable network capacity, which has also been adopted by [7].

Considering the data packets produced by sensor nodes in SHM WSN is different, we use $\{Q_1, Q_2, \cdots, Q_n\}$ to denote the number of data packets produced by n sensor nodes at one round. Furthermore, we assume that every packet can be transmitted within one time slot. If the size of one packet is set to be b bits, then the capacity can be formulated as:

$$\omega = \frac{b * \sum_{i=1}^{n} Q_i}{\sum \tau} \tag{4}$$

where $\sum \tau$ represents the total number of time slots required for the sink to collect all the data in one round.

3   MP-MR-MC Problem

We consider MP-MR-MC network link scheduling problem under the physical interference model with the goal of achieving maximum network capacity and minimizing the total energy consumption in SHM applications. For solving that, we first formulate corresponding constraint conditions. Then use the hybrid algorithm BFPA-PSO proposed in this paper to find the optimal link scheduling solution for joint power selection, radio and channel allocation.

3.1   Concurrent Transmission Link

We use $CTLS = \{\varphi_\tau | \tau = 1, 2, \cdots, s\}$ to denote the Concurrent Transmission Link Set ($CTLS$), which is also defined in [16], φ_τ represents a set of links that can be transmitted without interference in the τth time slot, s denotes the total number of time slots required for the sink to collect all data in the network.

Let, for each link l_{uv}, the tuple $(l_{uv}, (\Re_u^i, \Re_v^j), c(uv), p(uv))$ represents the activation status, power, channel and radio allocation over l_{uv} at any given time slot, which can be abbreviated as $l_{uv}^{i,j,c,p}$. The variables can be defined in detail as follows:

$$X(l_{uv}^{i,j,c,p}, \tau) = \begin{cases} 1 & \text{tuple is activated at } \tau \text{ time slot} \\ 0 & \text{otherwise} \end{cases} \tag{5}$$

$$\Re_u^i = \begin{cases} 1 & \text{radio } \gamma_i \text{ is occupied on node } u \\ 0 & \text{otherwise} \end{cases} \tag{6}$$

here, $l_{uv}^{i,j,c,p}$ and $\Re_u^i$ are binary variables, $\Re_u^i$ indicates radio γ_i on node u is occupied. At one time slot, however, the radio can only be used at most once, which is expressed as:

$$\sum_{l_{uv}^{\Re^*} \in \varphi_\tau} \Re_u^i + \sum_{l_{wu}^{\Re^*} \in \varphi_\tau} \Re_u^i \leq 1 (u \in V, v \in V, w \in V) \tag{7}$$

where l_{uv} and l_{wu} represent $u - related$ links. $l_{uv}^{\Re^*}$ indicates that only the radio allocation is considered. To avoid channel-conflict, the same channel can only be used once by one node at a given time slot, which can be expressed as follows:

$$\sum_{l_{uv}^{C^*} \in \varphi_\tau} c_i(uv) + \sum_{l_{wu}^{C^*} \in \varphi_\tau} c_i(wu) \leq 1 (u \in V, v \in V, w \in V) \tag{8}$$

$$c_i(uv) = \begin{cases} 1 & \text{channel } i \text{ is assigned to } l_{uv} \\ 0 & \text{otherwise} \end{cases} \tag{9}$$

Each radio on the sensor node can only be tuned to a specific channel in a time slot. To ensure that the number of channels used by a sensor node at τ^{th} time slot does not exceed the number of radios, the scheduled links should satisfy the following inequality:

$$\sum_{l_{uv}^{C^*} \in \varphi_\tau, i=1}^{K} c_i(uv) + \sum_{l_{wu}^{C^*} \in \varphi_\tau, i=1}^{K} c_i(wu) \leq \sum_{l_{uv}^{\Re^*} \in \varphi_\tau, j=1}^{H} \Re_u^j + \sum_{l_{wu}^{\Re^*} \in \varphi_\tau, j=1}^{H} \Re_u^j \tag{10}$$

where K and H are constants representing the number of channels and the number of radios, respectively.

3.2 Physical Interference Model

In WSN, the most popular interference models are protocol interference model and physical interference model [17]. In this paper, we adopt physical interference model to reflect the physical reality, which is known as more precise than protocol interference model. Under the physical interference model, the signal-to-interference-plus-noise-ratio $(SINR)$ can be formulated mathematically as follows:

$$SINR_{uv} \triangleq \frac{p(uv) \cdot \eta \cdot d(u,v)^{-\kappa}}{\sum_{l_{ij}^{P^*} \in \varphi_\tau} p(ij) \cdot \eta \cdot d(i,v)^{-\kappa} + N_0} \geq \delta \qquad (11)$$

where φ_τ denotes a set of $CTLS$ in τ^{th} time slot. $l_{ij}^{P^*}$ means that only the power selection of the link is considered. $i \in V, u \in V, i \neq u$, $p(ij)$ is the transmission power assigned to link l_{ij}. $d(u,v)$ represents the Euclidean distance between node u and node v. The constant η denotes the reference loss factor, and κ is path-loss exponent between 2 and 5. $N_0 \geq 0$ denotes ambient noise and $\delta \geq 1$ represents node V threshold for successfully receiving data packets through link l_{uv}.

3.3 Routing Tree

One of the most important steps for solving MP-MR-MC problem concerns the link extraction, target at finding the most important subset of links that leads to the best fitness. Hence, after all solutions are initialized, we use the selected links to construct a routing tree, in which data can be transmitted concurrently without interference.

In this paper, we use the data receiving rate at the sink to measure its achievable network capacity. In order to get better capacity, all the radios equipped on sink should be fully utilized at each time slot. We follow the steps below to build a routing tree.

Step1: We first choose sink as the starting node to build the routing tree, as long as any *sink − related* links are activated. Otherwise, randomly choose a node with any activated links. The first chosen node is called the root of the routing tree and is denoted as Γ.

Step2: In most cases, multiple related links are activated at the same time, we greedily choose the link with the smallest ratio of residual energy to packet size, also refer as major link $l^{major} = min\{\frac{E_{u^*}(t)}{Q_{u^*}(t)}|l(u^*, \Gamma) \in L_\Gamma^{active}\}$, where L_Γ^{active} is a set containing all $\Gamma − related$ activated links, $E_{u^*}(t)$ and $Q_{u^*}(t)$ represent the residual energy and the packet size at node u^* respectively.

Step3: Store u^* in the children set $CID = u^*$. If there are available links, continue to search L_Γ^{active} for other major links, and save the corresponding children in CID.

Step4: Assign major links for the nodes in CID separately and save all sending nodes of major links. Repeat until CID is empty.

Step5: Perform $Step1 \sim Step4$ until all sensor data are collected by sink.

All the major links are stored in the φ_τ. According to $Step1 \sim Step4$, one optimal set of concurrent transmission links at one time slot can be found. And $Step1 \sim Step5$ complete a round data collection by scheduling optimal links slot by slot.

4   The Hybrid Algorithm BFPA-PSO for MP-MR-MC Scheduling Problem

4.1   Flower Pollination Optimization Algorithm

Flower pollination algorithm (FPA) was proposed in [18], is known for its superiority in controlling the balance between global search and local search. In global pollination, if we represented the best solution at the current generation as G_{best}, then pollinators' behavior can be mathematically formulated as follows:

$$x_i^{t+1} = x_i^t + \alpha L(G_{best} - x_i^t) \tag{12}$$

$$L \sim \frac{\partial \Phi(\partial) \sin(\pi \partial / 2)}{\pi} \frac{1}{\xi^{1+\partial}} (\xi \geq \xi_0 > 0) \tag{13}$$

where x_i^t and x_i^{t+1} represent the ith solution at generation t and $t+1$ respectively. L denotes the step size, α is a scale factor for controlling step size. $\bar{\Phi}(\partial)$ is the standard gamma function. The local pollination can be mathematically formulated as:

$$x_i^{t+1} = x_i^t + \varepsilon(x_m^t - x_n^t) \tag{14}$$

x_m^t and x_n^t respectively represent m solution and n solution at generation t. ε is a uniform distribution variable whose range is $[0, 1]$.

4.2   BFPA-PSO Algorithm

The problem jointly solving the power assignment, radio assignment, channel assignment and scheduling in WSN can be succinctly stated as finding all the concurrent transmission links at every time slot until all packets in G are received by sink. In this section, we introduce how to use the hybrid algorithm BFPA-PSO to improve the capacity of MP-MR-MC WSN, the general principle of BFPA-PSO is shown in Fig. 2.

BFPA was first mentioned in [12] and is used to solve the problem of feature selection. Similarly to [12], the solutions in our implementation are modeled as $d-dimensional$ array with M elements, and a binary solution vector is used to denote whether a given link is activated.

PSO is a meta-heuristic optimization technique based on the simulation of social behavior of flocks [19]. The updating formula are shown in Eqs. (15) and (16).

$$v_i^{t+1} = wv_i^t - c1r1(Z_i^{best} - x_i^t) - c2r2(G_{best} - x_i^t) \tag{15}$$

$$x_i^{t+1} = x_i^t + v_i^{t+1} \tag{16}$$

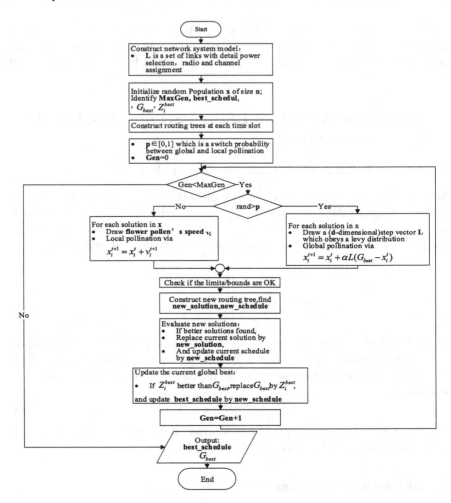

Fig. 2. General principle of BFPA-PSO.

where v_i denotes the particle's speed, $c1$ and $c2$ are acceleration factors, $r1$ and $r2$ represent random values between 0 and 1. w is weighting coefficient. Z_i^{best} and G_{best} represent the best local position and global position respectively. The PSO has many benefits, such as greater convergence and directing an early converging towards a local optima via the search velocity [20]. The FPA has good exploration characteristics via Levy flight. In the proposed algorithm, we gathered the characteristics of PSO and FPA to compose a new hybrid algorithm to solve the issue of MP-MR-MC. The BFPA local pollination is improved as:

$$v_i^{t+1} = v_i^t - c1r1(Z_i^{best} - x_i^t) - c2r2(G_{best} - x_i^t) \tag{17}$$

$$x_i^{t+1} = x_i^t + v_i^{t+1} \tag{18}$$

4.3   Fitness Function

The fitness function is used to find the best link scheduling for achieving optimal data collection. In our research, the fitness function is two-objective. The first objective aims at improving the network capacity, and the second is used to reduce total energy consumption. The fitness function is given by Eq. (19):

$$Fitness = \frac{w1}{\omega} + w2 * \vartheta \tag{19}$$

here, ω denotes the capacity of the network, and ϑ denotes the energy consumed to complete a round of data collection. $w1$, $w2$ represent the weights for ω and ϑ respectively. Assume that the initial energy of the node is $E_i^{init}(i \in V)$, then ϑ can be formulated as:

$$\vartheta = \sum_{i=1}^{n} E_i^{init} - E_i \tag{20}$$

5   Performance Evaluation

In this section, we summarize and discuss the experimental results regarding the proposed algorithm BFPA-PSO for solving the problem of MP-MR-MC. The experiments were carried out using MATLAB R2014a. In the simulation, we consider a network with 10, 20, 30 nodes, respectively. Simulation settings are detailed in the Table 1, each data packet size is set to be 512 bits. Considering the requirement of real applications and the implementation limitation, each node in WSN is equipped with up to 2 radios. We consider the communication modes of single-power single-radio single-channel (SP-SR-SC), single-power single-radio multi-channel (SP-SR-MC) and multi-power multi-radio multi-channel (MP-MR-MC), the detailed configuration of power level, radio and channel is shown in Table 2.

Table 1. Network model parameter settings.

Node number	$P(W)$	H	K	$Field(m^3)$	$R(m)$
10	0.1/0.2	2	5	40 * 50 * 300	100/200
20	0.1/0.2	2	5	40 * 50 * 1000	100/200
30	0.1/0.2	2	5	40 * 50 * 1000	100/200

In order to assess the performance of the proposed algorithm, we conduct a comparison study with the well-known algorithm, i.e. GA, BBA, BFPA, BGSA, and BPSO. The used parameters for each algorithm are illustrated in Table 3. Each algorithm is executed 10 times and its average value is plotted as Fig. 3 shown. As the Fig. 3 shown, GA, BFPA and BGSA are not suitable for our MP-MR-MC network scheduling problem. The algorithm of BBA find the best

Table 2. The setting of communication mode.

Communication mode	H	K	$P(W)$	$R(m)$	E^{init}	Q
SP-SR-SC	1	1	0.2	200	10	1/2/3
SP-SR-MC	1	5	0.2	200	10	1/2/3
MP-MR-MC	2	5	0.2	100/200	10	1/2/3

Table 3. Parameters used for each algorithm.

Algorithm	Parameters
GA	$P_c = 0.6, P_m = 0.01$
BBA	$A = 0.25, r = 0.1, f_{min} = 0, f_{max} = 1$
BFPA	$\alpha = 0.01, p = 0.8$
BGSA	$G_0 = 1, \varepsilon = 0.0007$
BPSO	$c1 = c2 = 1.49445$
BFPA-PSO	$c1 = c2 = 1.49445, \alpha = 0.01, p = 0.85$

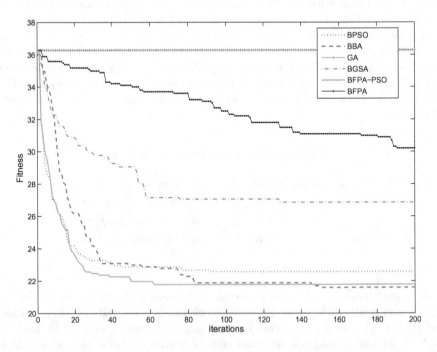

Fig. 3. Comparison between BPSO, BBA, GA, BGSA, BFPA and BFPA-PSO.

fitness at last, but it has slower convergence than BPSO and BFPA-PSO. By comparison, our proposed hybrid algorithm BFPA-PSO has obvious advantages in convergence and global optimization.

Most applications of SHM data collection are based on SP-SR-SC and SP-SR-MC, Fig. 4(a) shows that communication of SP-SR-SC and SP-SR-MC greatly limit the network capacity. However, MP-MR-MC communication performs well in improving of network capacity, as well as effectively reducing the overall network energy consumption, as Fig. 4(b) shown.

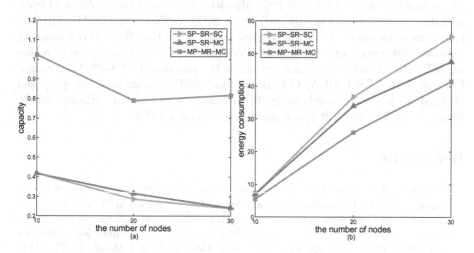

Fig. 4. (a) Comparison the capacity, and (b) total energy consumption among the communication of SP-SR-SC, SP-SR-MC and MP-MR-MC.

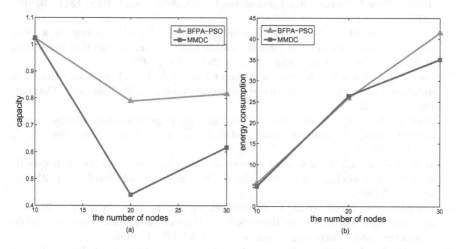

Fig. 5. Comparison the (a) capacity and (b) total energy consumption between MMDC and BFPA-PSO

Then, we compare BFPA-PSO with the MMDC algorithm. As Fig. 5 shown, MMDC can control the total energy consumption of the network to some extent. As network nodes increase, our proposed algorithm BFPA-PSO has obvious advantages in improving network capacity and reducing energy consumption.

6   Conclusions

In this study, we propose a new hybrid algorithm BFPA-PSO, which combines the advantage of the FPA and PSO algorithms, to solve the problem of optimal data collection in the applications of SHM WSN under the MP-MR-MC communication mode. The experimental results show that the network capacity improvement and energy consumption decrease in SHM can be achieved by utilizing MP-MR-MC communication optimized the proposed BFPA-PSO algorithm. Compared to BPSO, BBA, GA, BGSA and BFPA algorithms, the proposed BFPA-PSO has obvious advantage in convergence and global optimization. In future, we will implement this algorithm in the actual WSN.

References

1. Risodkar, Y.R., Pawar, A.S.: A survey: structural health monitoring of bridge using WSN. In: International Conference on Global Trends in Signal Processing. Information Computing and Communication, Jalgaon, pp. 615–618. IEEE (2017)
2. Chen, Z., Casciati, F.: A low-noise, real-time, wireless data acquisition system for structural monitoring applications. Struct. Control. Health Monit. 21(7), 1118–1136 (2014)
3. Chen, Z.C., Casciati, S., Faravelli, L.: In-situ validation of a wireless data acquisition system by monitoring a pedestrian bridge. Adv. Struct. Eng. 18(1), 97–106 (2014)
4. Kim, S., Pakzad, S., Culler, D.: Health monitoring of civil infrastructures using wireless sensor networks. In: International Symposium on Information Processing in Sensor Networks, Cambridge, pp. 254–263. IEEE (2007)
5. Mehrabi, A., Kim, K.: General framework for network throughput maximization in sink-based energy harvesting wireless sensor networks. IEEE Trans. Mob. Comput. 16(7), 1881–1896 (2017)
6. Lian, J., Naik, K., Agnew, G.B.: Data capacity improvement of wireless sensor networks using non-uniform sensor distribution. Int. J. Distrib. Sens. Netw. 2(2), 121–145 (2006)
7. Ji, S., Cai, Z., Li, Y., Jia, X.: Continuous data collection capacity of dual-radio multi-channel wireless sensor networks. IEEE Trans. Parallel Distrib. Syst. 23(10), 1844–1855 (2012)
8. Kodialam, M., Nandagopal, T.: Characterizing the capacity region in multi-radio multi-channel wireless mesh networks. In: International Conference on Mobile Computing and Networking, Cologne, pp. 73–87. DBLP (2005)
9. Fan, B., Li, J., Guo, L., Liu, X.: A multi-power multi-channel data collection scheduling algorithm in dual-radio sensor networks. Telecommun. Sci. 28(2), 36–45 (2012)

10. Babatunde, O., Armstrong, L., Leng, J., Diepeveen, D.: A genetic algorithm-based feature selection. Br. J. Math. Comput. Sci. 5(4), 889–905 (2014)

11. Mirjalili, S., Mirjalili, S.M., Yang, X.S.: Binary bat algorithm. Neural Comput. Appl. 25(3–4), 663–681 (2014)

12. Rodrigues, D., Yang, X.-S., de Souza, A.N., Papa, J.P.: Binary flower pollination algorithm and its application to feature selection. In: Yang, X.-S. (ed.) Recent Advances in Swarm Intelligence and Evolutionary Computation. SCI, vol. 585, pp. 85–100. Springer, Cham (2015). https://doi.org/10.1007/978-3-319-13826-8_5

13. Rashedi, E., Nezamabadi-Pour, H., Saryazdi, S.: BGSA: binary gravitational search algorithm. Natural Comput. 9(3), 727–745 (2010)

14. Kennedy, J., Eberhart, R.C.: A discrete binary version of the particle swarm algorithm. In: IEEE International Conference on Systems. Man, and Cybernetics, Orlando, pp. 4104–4108. IEEE (1997)

15. Chen, Z.C.: Energy efficiency strategy for a general real-time wireless sensor platform. Smart Struct. Syst. 14(4), 617–641 (2014)

16. Li, J., Guo, X., Guo, L.: Joint routing, scheduling and channel assignment in multi-power multi-radio wireless sensor networks. In: IEEE International Performance Computing and Communications Conference, Orlando, pp. 1–8. IEEE (2011)

17. Gupta, P., Kumar, P.R.: The capacity of wireless networks. IEEE Trans. Inf. Theory 46(2), 388–404 (2002)

18. Yang, X.-S.: Flower pollination algorithm for global optimization. In: Durand-Lose, J., Jonoska, N. (eds.) UCNC 2012. LNCS, vol. 7445, pp. 240–249. Springer, Heidelberg (2012). https://doi.org/10.1007/978-3-642-32894-7_27

19. Kennedy, J., Eberhart, R.: Particle swarm optimization. In: Sammut, C., Webb, G.I. (eds.) Encyclopedia of Machine Learning, vol. 4, pp. 1942–1948. Springer, Boston (2011). https://doi.org/10.1007/978-1-4419-1153-7_200581

20. Vijayalakshmi, K., Anandan, P.: A multi objective Tabu particle swarm optimization for effective cluster head selection in WSN. Cluster Comput. 6, 1–8 (2018)

Emoticon-Based Emotion Analysis for Weibo Articles in Sentence Level

Yunong Wu$^{(\boxtimes)}$, Xin Kang, Kazuyuki Matsumoto, Minoru Yoshida,
and Kenji Kita

Faculty of Engineering, Tokushima University, Tokushima, Japan
wuyunong@tokushima.ac.jp,
{kang-xin,matumoto,mino,kita}@is.tokushima.ac.jp

Abstract. In this study, we propose a multi-label emotion study for Weibo articles in sentence level based on word and emoticon feature. We crawl articles from Weibo randomly, and extract sample sentences based on word emotion lexicon which has been constructed from a Chinese emotion corpus (Ren-CECps). Two machine learning methods including Support Vector Machine and Logistic Regression are employed to conduct the emotion classification experiments with the word feature and the combination feature of words and emoticons respectively. The significantly improved results given by classification experiments with the emoticon feature prove the effectiveness of taking emoticons in emotion analysis.

Keywords: Emotion analysis · Multi-label · Emoticons

1 Introduction

In recent years, with the growing popularity development of smart phones, more and more people have started the social network lives. They share information with friends, record wonderful moment stayed with families, and show their attitude towards some hot events in written texts on the website like Twitter, Weibo and so on. Rather than story, news or other textual information, the articles on social network are rich in emotions. In other words, these articles are able to reflect the real emotion states of the authors at most of the time. However, emotion analysis is a complex issue, since human emotions are the private states which are difficult to access. Nowadays, many researchers pay much attention to the text emotion analysis by using the semantic or syntactic information involved in texts.

In general, emotion analysis is conducted based on a coarse-to-fine procedure. Previous researches concentrated on the polarity classification to recognize the positive, negative, and sometimes neutral emotions. Coarse-grained emotion analysis has been applied in the product comments [1] and movie reviews issues [2, 3]. However, because emotions are complex and private states of human, researchers usually need to conduct the fine-grained emotion analysis to capture the real states. Aman proposed an emotion annotation study to identify the six emotion categories and emotion intensity [4]. Wu built a joint prediction mode consisted of three different machine learning

© Springer Nature Switzerland AG 2018
M. Kaenampornpan et al. (Eds.): MIWAI 2018, LNAI 11248, pp. 104–112, 2018.
https://doi.org/10.1007/978-3-030-03014-8_9

methods for document emotion analysis [5]. Roberts analyzed the emotion distribution for seven emotions and proposed a method to discover emotions automatically [6].

We find that many social network websites supply the emoticon function for the users to write the posts or to give the comments on others' posts. Popular social network sites like Facebook, Twitter, and Weibo supply hundreds of emoticons for users to express emotional information vividly instead of words. For examples, can convey positive emotion Joy, can convey negative emotion Sorrow, can convey Anger. In many researches, emoticons were filtered out with stop words in the preprocessing procedure, since emoticons were regarded as noisy components in the data. In these researches the emotional information taken by emoticons were ignored, which caused the reduction of emotion recognition rate. Table 1 shows the example sentences with emoticons and the corresponding emotions in pure words and sentences, respectively.

Table 1. Sample sentences containing emoticons.

Sentence	Word emotion	Sentence emotion
又是一个地域的问题。 It's still an area phenomenon.	Neutral	Sorrow
夕阳看着好像咸蛋黄啊。 The setting sun looks like salted egg yolk.	Neutral	Love
塑料姐妹花。 Plastic flower of girls	Neutral	Joy Hate-Anger

The above sentences don't contain any emotional word, however, they can convey emotions through the emoticons. Sentence 1 conveys the negative emotion Sorrow because of the regional discrimination problem, Sentence 2 conveys the positive emotion Love, and Sentence 3 conveys two emotions of Joy and Hate-Anger in describing the hypocritical friendship between girls.

In this study, we implement experiments of emotion analysis for Weibo articles including posts and comments on the sentence level. We crawl 222,000 articles from Weibo, and select articles, which contain emoticons and have the length of 20 to 40 Chinese characters. We have annotated sentences with multiple emotion labels that would be much closer to the real human emotions. And because that Hate and Anger are found together in the same sentences at the most of the time, we treat them as a compound emotion Hate-Anger in this study. Six emotions <Joy, Love, Hate-Anger, Anxiety, Sorrow, Expect> are chosen as the basic emotions for the analysis scheme. Two machine learning methods, which are Support Vector Machine (SVM) [7] and Logistic Regression (LGR) [8], are employed based on the word and emoticon feature for the emotion analysis experiment. The significantly improved emotion analysis results based on the combination of word and emoticon features suggest that emoticons in sentences could make the significant contribution to emotion expression. The results also suggest that we can use emoticons as feature to improve the emotion analysis.

The remainder of this paper is organized as follows: In Sect. 2, we introduce related work on coarse-grained sentiment classification and fine-grained multi-emotion analysis; we describe the method of emotion analysis for Weibo articles on sentence level with two machine learning methods based on the word feature and the emoticon feature in Sect. 3; We conduct four sentence emotion analysis experiments based on the word features and the combination of word and emoticon features, and evaluate results in Sect. 4; Finally, we conclude our work in Sect. 5.

2   Related Work

Affective information computing in natural language processing has been attracting significant attentions in recent years. Emotion analysis has been divided into two levels including the coarse-grained level and the fine-grained level. The coarse-grained level emotion analysis, which is named sentiment analysis sometimes, aims at the polarity classification with the positive and negative polarity classes. Kennedy presented two methods for the movie review polarity classification based on the valence shifters in sentences, which included negations, intensifiers and diminishers [9]. Wei employed a sentiment ontology tree to learn the sentiments from comments of digital camera [10]. Kouloumpis trained an AdaBoost.MH classifier by using three different corpora of Twitter messages with the n-gram feature, the lexicon feature, the part-of-speech feature and the micro-blogging feature [11]. However, searchers have gradually realized that only positive and negative polarities cannot describe the real emotions of people, because words are capable of conveying more complicated emotions. Li carried out the experiment on text-based emotion classification with six emotion categories by using emotion cause extraction [12]. Balabantaray showed how to collect an emotion corpus automatically from Twitter and built a multi-class emotion classifier to determine people's emotion [13]. We notice that almost all social network websites provide various emoticons, which can convey the users' emotions more directly than words. We count the sentences containing emoticons from all the sentences we crawled randomly from Weibo, and find out that more than 10% of sentences contain at least one emoticon. Aoki calculated the co-occurrence value between words and emotions to build the emoticons lexicon [14]. Zheng recognized the emoticons and smilies in high frequency and assigned them with six emotion labels [15]. Song employed the Bayesian rule to calculate the emoticon emotion distributions for building a word emotion lexicon [16]. Tang proposed a method to gather pseudo-labeled corpus from Weibo via emoticons [17]. However, they only analyzed the emoticons or used them to collect sentences but ignored the emotional information taken by the emotions.

In this study, we propose to use emoticons as feature for sentence emotion analysis. Two machine leaning methods, which are Support Vector Machine and Logistic Regression, are used to examine the effectiveness of the emoticon features for emotion classification. The significantly improved results in emotion classification based on the combination feature of words and emoticons prove the effectiveness of employing emoticons for text emotion analysis.

3   Emotion Analysis Based on Emoticons

In this study, we propose two machine learning methods including Support Vector Machine and Logistic Regression to examine the effectiveness of emoticons as features for sentence emotion classification from different perspectives.

3.1   Classifier Trained by Support Vector Machine

Support Vector Machine is a popular model for the binary classification problem. The SVM model fits a function that attempts to separate two classes of data by a hyperplane and maximizes the margin around the separating hyperplane, so that the model can get a local optimum.

There are six emotion categories <Joy, Love, Hate-Anger, Anxiety, Sorrow, Expect> chosen for emotion analysis, and most of the sentences are annotated with more than one emotion labels. Therefore, we have to preprocess the data before feeding them to the binary classification models. For the multi-class classification problem, we train K classifiers (K = 6) by the one-vs-rest strategy. As most of sentences are annotated with multiple labels, we convert the multi-label classification problem to multiple single-label classification problems. If a sentence contains multiple emotion labels, we replicate this sentence into multiple sentences with each sentence only has a single emotion label. Specifically, the sentence is preprocessed in the form as below:

$$\text{sent}_i = [\{w_1, w_2, \ldots, w_m\}, \{emot_1, emot_2, \ldots, emot_n\}, \text{emo}_k] \tag{1}$$

in which, $\{w_m\}$ are the words contained in sentence, $\{emot_n\}$ are the emoticons in the sentence, and emo_k is the k_{th} emotion conveyed by the sentence.

3.2   Classifier Trained by Logistic Regression

Logistic Regression is a statistical probability model for the binary classification problem, which uses all class data in the dataset and computes the probability of each feature belonging to each class. Therefore, the logistic regression model can be sensitive to outliers and can get a global optimum.

To solve the multi-label sentence emotion classification problem, we also need to train K binary classifiers for K emotions with the one-vs-rest strategy. The k_{th} classifier generates a probability p_k which represents the possibility of k_{th} emotion conveyed by sentence.

$$y_k = h_k(x_i) = p_k(y_i | x_i) \tag{2}$$

3.3   Extract Sample Sentences by Word Emotion Lexicon

Because our emotion classification is conducted on Weibo articles crawled randomly, we have to build a labeled set of Weibo sentences by extracting the Weibo sample and by annotating the emotion labels. Under the consideration that the imbalance problem in emotional labels could greatly influence the emotion classification results, we try to maintain the balance of emotion labels in the labeled set, by extracting approximately the same number of sample sentences for each emotion category. Based on a strong assumption that sentences can express the same emotion as the words contained in the sentences at most of the time, we plan to extract the sentences which contain the high frequency emotional words in word our emotion lexicon for each emotion category. We use Ren-CECps[1], which is well manually annotated Chinese emotion corpus with eight emotion categories <Joy, Love, Hate, Anger, Anxiety, Sorrow, Surprise, Expect>, for constructing the emotion lexicon. The detailed algorithm for extracting the sample sentences is shown as follows:

Algorithm 1: Sample sentence extraction

```
1:   word_dict <- frequent emotional words in Ren-CECps
2:   sent_list <- sentences crawled from Weibo
3:   for k in {1 ... K}: #K is emotion category
4:       emoSent[k] = [] #empty list
5:   for sent in sent_list:
6:       if sent has emoWord:
7:           word <- first emoWord
8:           emo  <- word_dict[word]
9:           if length(emoSent[emo]) <= 700:
10:              add sent to emoSent[emo]
11:  return emoSent
12:  end for
```

Because there may be multiple emotional words in one sentence, when we extract sentences containing emotional word for each emotion category, we only consider the first emotional word in that sentence. There are inevitably small quantitative difference for each emotion category.

4 Experiment

In this study, we perform experiments of emotion analysis for Weibo articles on the sentence level. We crawl articles randomly including posts and comments with the Weibo api[2], and select articles by two conditions: (1) each article has at least one emoticon; (2) without emoticons the pure text of each article should contain 20 to 40 Chinese characters. There are totally 222,000 sentences crawled by using the Weibo api, and we extract 4,200 training sentences by using the Algorithm 1, and manually annotate emotions to these sentences.

---

[1] http://a1-www.is.tokushima-u.ac.jp/member/ren/Ren-CECps1.0/DocumentforRen-CECps1.0.html.

[2] http://open.Weibo.com/wiki/API.

We carry out two groups of experiments with the pure words feature and the combination feature of words and emoticons based on the Support Vector Machine classification and the Logistic Regression classification respectively.

4.1 Evaluation Methods

We adopt the most popular Macro Metrics to evaluate multi-class and multi-label sentence analysis with $K = 6$ emotion categories and measure the effectiveness of emoticon feature.

- **Macro Precision:**

$$MacP = \frac{1}{K} \sum_k \frac{TP_k}{TP_k + FP_k} \tag{3}$$

- **Macro Recall:**

$$MacR = \frac{1}{K} \sum_k \frac{TP_k}{TP_k + FN_k} \tag{4}$$

- **Macro F-score:**

$$MacF = \frac{2 * MacP * MacR}{MacP + MacR} \tag{5}$$

- **Accuracy:**

$$Accuracy_k = \frac{TP_k + TN_k}{TP_k + TN_k + FP_k + FN_k} \tag{6}$$

In (3), TP_k denotes the count of k_{th} emotion predicted correctly, FP_k denotes the count of k_{th} emotion predicted incorrectly. In (4), FN_k denotes the counts of k_{th} emotion

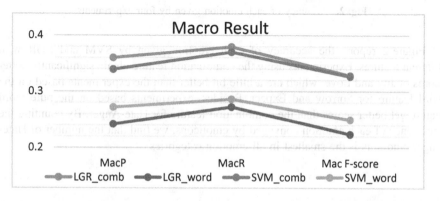

Fig. 1. Macro precession, Macro recall and Mac F-score given by four experiments with different features.

which can't be predicted. (5) evaluates the mean values of *F-score* which can measure the overall effectiveness comprehensively.

4.2 Result and Discussion

We have carried totally four experiments by the pure words feature and the combination feature of words and emoticons based on the Support Vector Machine classification and the Logistic Regression classification, respectively. Macro metrics and Accuracy are adopted for measuring the performance given by different experiments.

As shown in Fig. 1, both experiments using the combination feature of words and emoticons get the best scores in macro precession, macro recall and macro F-score compared to experiments only using pure words feature. When only using words feature, the SVM classification gets better score than the LGR classification, while using the combination feature, the LGR classification gets better score than the SVM classification. The LGR model is sensitive to all the feature, since it calculates all the feature in dataset, while the SVM model is only sensitive to the point data near the hyperplane, because the count of emotions is less than the count of words.

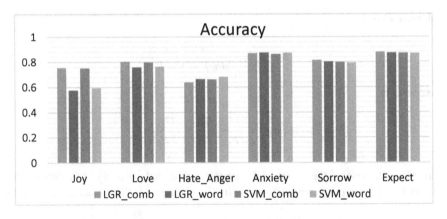

Fig. 2. Accuracy of each emotion given by four experiments

Figure 2 reports the accuracy of each emotion given by SVM and LGR with different features. Experiments using the combination feature obtain significantly better scores of Joy and Love, which are a little bit better than the experiments based on the word feature for Sorrow and Expect. Besides, experiments based on the pure word feature get better scores than the combination feature for Hate-Anger. By counting the occurrence of each emotion conveyed by emoticons, we find that the number of Hate-Anger emotions is the smallest in all emotion categories.

5   Conclusions

In this study, we propose a study on multi-label emotion analysis for Weibo articles in sentence level. We crawl articles including posts and comments randomly and extract label-balanced sample sentences from Weibo articles based on word emotion lexicon constructed from Ren-CECps. We examine the effectiveness of emoticons from two perspectives, which are local optimum and global optimum, based on Support Vector Machine classification and Logistic regression classification, with the word feature and the combination feature of words and emoticons respectively. Both classification model adopting the combination feature achieve the best results in macro precession, macro recall, macro F-score and accuracy for each emotion. These results demonstrate that emoticons in sentence make a significant contribution to the sentence emotion expression.

References

1. Zhang, D., Xu, H., Su, Z., et al.: Chinese comments sentiment classification based on word2vec and SVMperf. Expert Syst. Appl. **42**(4), 1857–1863 (2015)
2. Turney, P.D.: Thumbs up or thumbs down?: semantic orientation applied to unsupervised classification of reviews. In: Proceedings of the 40th Annual Meeting on Association for Computational Linguistics, pp. 417–424. Association for Computational Linguistics (2002)
3. Pang, B., Lee, L., Vaithyanathan, S.: Thumbs up?: sentiment classification using machine learning techniques. In: Proceedings of the ACL 2002 Conference on Empirical Methods in Natural Language Processing, vol. 10, pp. 79–86. Association for Computational Linguistics (2002)
4. Aman, S., Szpakowicz, S.: Identifying expressions of emotion in text. In: Matoušek, V., Mautner, P. (eds.) TSD 2007. LNCS (LNAI), vol. 4629, pp. 196–205. Springer, Heidelberg (2007). https://doi.org/10.1007/978-3-540-74628-7_27
5. Wu, Y., Kita, K., Matsumoto, K.: Three predictions are better than one: Sentence multi-emotion analysis from different perspectives. IEEJ Trans. Electr. Electron. Eng. **9**(6), 642–649 (2014)
6. Roberts, K., Roach, M.A., Johnson, J, et al.: EmpaTweet: annotating and detecting emotions on Twitter. In: LREC, vol. 12, pp. 3806–3813 (2012)
7. Hearst, M.A., Dumais, S.T., Osuna, E., et al.: Support vector machines. IEEE Intell. Syst. Their Appl. **13**(4), 18–28 (1998)
8. Peng, C.Y.J., Lee, K.L., Ingersoll, G.M.: An introduction to logistic regression analysis and reporting. J. Educ. Res. **96**(1), 3–14 (2002)
9. Kennedy, A., Inkpen, D.: Sentiment classification of movie reviews using contextual valence shifters. Comput. Intell. **22**(2), 110–125 (2006)
10. Wei, W., Gulla, J.A.: Sentiment learning on product reviews via sentiment ontology tree. In: Proceedings of the 48th Annual Meeting of the Association for Computational Linguistics, pp. 404–413. Association for Computational Linguistics (2010)
11. Kouloumpis, E., Wilson, T., Moore, J.D.: Twitter sentiment analysis: the good the bad and the OMG! In: ICWSM, vol. 11, pp. 538–541 (2011)
12. Li, W., Xu, H.: Text-based emotion classification using emotion cause extraction. Expert Syst. Appl. **41**(4), 1742–1749 (2014)

13. Balabantaray, R.C., Mohammad, M., Sharma, N.: Multi-class Twitter emotion classification: a new approach. Int. J. Appl. Inf. Syst. **4**(1), 48–53 (2012)
14. Aoki, S., Uchida, O.: A method for automatically generating the emotional vectors of emoticons using weblog articles. In: Proceedings of 10th WSEAS International Conference on Applied Computer and Applied Computational Science, Stevens Point, Wisconsin, USA, pp. 132–136 (2011)
15. Yuan, Z., Purver, M.: Predicting emotion labels for Chinese microblog texts. In: Gaber, M. M., Cocea, M., Wiratunga, N., Goker, A. (eds.) Advances in Social Media Analysis. SCI, vol. 602, pp. 129–149. Springer, Cham (2015). https://doi.org/10.1007/978-3-319-18458-6_7
16. Song, K., Feng, S., Gao, W., et al.: Build emotion lexicon from microblogs by combining effects of seed words and emoticons in a heterogeneous graph. In: Proceedings of the 26th ACM Conference on Hypertext and Social Media, pp. 283–292. ACM (2015)
17. Tang, D., Qin, B., Liu, T., Li, Z.: Learning Sentence Representation for Emotion Classification on Microblogs. In: Zhou, G., Li, J., Zhao, D., Feng, Y. (eds.) NLPCC 2013. CCIS, vol. 400, pp. 212–223. Springer, Heidelberg (2013). https://doi.org/10.1007/978-3-642-41644-6_20

Aerial Image Semantic Segmentation Using Neural Search Network Architecture

Duc-Thinh Bui[1], Trong-Dat Tran[1], Thi-Thuy Nguyen[2,3], Quoc-Long Tran[1], and Do-Van Nguyen[1,3](✉) (iD)

[1] UET, Vietnam National University, Hanoi, Vietnam
thinh.ducbui@gmail.com, trantrongdat1@gmail.com, tqlong@gmail.com,
ngdovan@gmail.com
[2] Vietnam National University of Agriculture, Hanoi, Vietnam
myngthuy@gmail.com
[3] Institute of Artificial Intelligence, Hanoi, Vietnam

Abstract. In remote sensing data analysis and computer vision, aerial image segmentation is a crucial research topic, which has many applications in environmental and urban planning. Recently, deep learning is using to tackle many computer vision problem, including aerial image segmentation. Results have shown that deep learning gains much higher accuracy than other methods on many benchmark data sets. In this work, we propose a neural network called NASNet-FCN, which based on Fully Convolutional Network - a frame work for solving semantic segmentation problem and image feature extractor derived from state-of-the-art object recognition network called Neural Search Network Architecture. Our networks are trained and judged by using benchmark dataset from ISPRS Vaihingen challenge. Results show that our methods achieved state-of-the-art accuracy with potential improvements.

Keywords: Aerial image · Semantic segmentation
Neural Search Network Architecture

1 Introduction

Semantic segmentation is a task of predicting dense-pixel maps from original input images. Each pixel is mapping with predefined classes such as car, tree, building. This is the fundamental research topic in remote sensing data analysis and has many applications in real-life for example urban planning, forest management and environmental modelling. Although having been extensively researched for about two decades, there is still no fully automated method used in practice. The main challenge of this task is the heterogeneous appearance and high intra-class variances of objects e.g. buildings, streets and cars on very high resolution images [1].

© Springer Nature Switzerland AG 2018
M. Kaenampornpan et al. (Eds.): MIWAI 2018, LNAI 11248, pp. 113–124, 2018.
https://doi.org/10.1007/978-3-030-03014-8_10

In the past, [2–5] used the hand-crafted feature extracted from one pixel or a window of small size of aerial image as the input feature for classification algorithm e.g. Support Vector Machine, Random Forest, AdaBoost to learn the non-linear decision boundary between classes. Other researches [6,7] used unsupervised feature learning algorithm to create input feature for neural network learning on road detection task. The unsupervised feature learning algorithm is proved that it can learn filters similar like oriented edge detectors and Gabor wavelets and possibility choose the right filters for given task.

Recently, deep learning, especially deep convolutional neural network (CNN), has been used to tackle many problems in computer vision and boost the accuracy of these problems and achieved state-of-the-art results compared with other methods. For semantic segmentation task, Fully Convolutional Network (FCN) [8] is the first works try to use CNN to build pixel-to-pixel prediction. FCN used object recognition neural network architectures as feature extraction step and the feature map is upsampled by using fractional stride convolution or deconvolution layer.

In this work, we build up our semantic segmentation network based on the state-of-the-art object recognition network called Neural Architecture Search Network (NASNet) [9] and FCN framework. We evaluate our model performance on the challenging ISPRS dataset [1] and compare to other state-of-the-art results. We also investigate the effect of stronger image feature extractor on the semantic segmentation results. To the best of our knowledge, our work is the first applying NASNet [9] to semantic segmentation task.

Section 2 will describe the research using CNN in object recognition and semantic segmentation of aerial image. In the following, Sect. 3 we will explain our model in detail. The experiment results on the dataset of ISPRS challenge are demonstrated in Sect. 4. Our paper ends with conclusion in Sect. 5.

2   Related Work

In this section, we will briefly review some works using CNNs for object recognition and semantic segmentation task.

Currently, deep convolution neural network has dominated the ImageNet Large Scale Visual Recognition Competition (ILSVRC) since 2012, when the eight-layer CNN named AlexNet [10] was proposed. In ILSVRC 2014 competition, the VGGNets [11] consists of 19-layers or 16-layers, having smaller filter size than the filter size of AlexNet [10] but still get the same effective receptive field as large kernel size in AlexNet. GoogleLeNet [12] has more layer than the two previous, but using less parameters than AlexNet [10] 12 times. The idea of adding more layers for increasing accuracy became a revolution when ResNet [13] - a 152-layer network with top 5-error better than human performance was introduced. ResNet [13] used residual connection to ease the training of the networks. Inspired by residual connection in ResNet [13], DenseNet [14] established connection with other layer in each dense block to take advantage of feature reuse and reduce vanishing gradient problem. Usually, each novel architecture as in [10,12–14] requires a great amount of time to design architecture and do experiments. To ease the process of finding new neural network architecture, AutoML [15] has been developed and used by Google Brain to find the new CNN models achieving the highest accuracy in object recognition task.

Semantic segmentation task usually uses the object recognition network as feature extractor part before learning the prediction map for each pixel in different ways. In [8], FCN proposed by Long used the feature map from final and intermediate layers to learn the upsample feature map. Meanwhile, [16,17] created a symmetric encoder-decoder architecture and residual connection is added from feature extractor part to enhance detail features. Instead of upsampling small feature map to get the original size, [18–21] use dilated convolution [22] to keep the size of feature map unchanged and reduce the impact of field-of-view problem in normal convolution kernel. Other works [23] use prediction map at multiple scale to learn the model parameters.

In the past, neural network applied to aerial image segmentation by using patch-based approach. Neural network is considered as a classification for pixel in the center of a fixed-size window of pixels extracted from original high resolution images. Recent works based on the method that has gained successful results in semantic segmentation. [24] modified the FCN architecture by using no downsampling layer and increasing the kernel and padding size of pooling layer in the VGG network to reduce the computational cost but still achieved the same accuracy compare to FCNs. Ensemble prediction is also employed as in [25,26]. In [26], an ensemble of SegNet model is constructed by using multi - kernel convolution size at the last decoder layer to combine predictions at various scale, resulted in smoothing predictions. Additional channels such as Digital Surface Model (DSM), Normalized Difference Vegetation Index (NDVI), Normalize DSM (nDSM) are employed to the model to boost the accuracy. In [27], author proposed a method to increase the boundary-detection accuracy by using additional edge information extracted from boundary-detector network HED [28] to create edge-channel for image, achieving state-of-the-art results on ISPRS dataset.

3   Method

3.1   Neural Architecture Search Network (NASNet)

Finding a neural network architecture achieving the state-of-the-art results requires a great effort of designing and training from researchers. Different with other previous architectures, NASNet architecture is found automatically by AutoML system [15]. The main components of NASNet are two types of cell: Normal Cell and Reduction Cell. Reduction Cell will reduce the width and height of feature map by a half after forwarding the input feature map through. In contrast, Normal Cell will keep these two dimension the same as the input feature map. The general structure of NASNet is built by stacking N Normal Cell between Reduction Cell as in Fig. 1. There are two types of NASNet model, NASNet-large with N equal to 6 aims to get maximum possible accuracy and NASNet-mobile with N equal to 4 focus on running on limited resources devices.

Each cell in Normal Cell or Reduction Cell is composed of a number of blocks. Each block is built from the set of popular operations in CNN models with various kernel size e.g.: convolutions, max pooling, average pooling, dilated convolution, depth-wise separable convolutions. Finding best architecture for Normal Cell and Reduction Cell with 5 blocks is described details in [9]. The best structure of Normal Cell and Reduction Cell is described in Fig. 2.

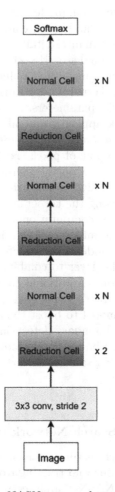

Fig. 1. NASNet general structure.

3.2 Fully Convolution Network (FCN)

FCN [8] is the pioneering work in applying CNN to semantic segmentation by taking advantage of succeed object recognition model. To satisfy the pixel-dense

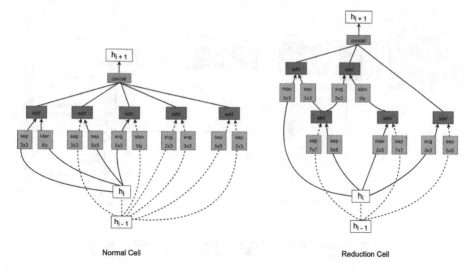

Fig. 2. Normal Cell and Reduction Cell architecture.

prediction requirement of semantic segmentation, FCN replace the last fully-connected layer in the object recognition network by convolution layer. By using convolution layer with kernel size 1 by 1, it can squash the number of channels in the last convolution layer to the number of classes. The feature map then is up-sampled by using deconvolution layer or bilinear upsampling operation. We can get the desired dense-pixel feature map from the previous predicted map, but the predicted label are too coarse. In order to overcome these issue, the authors combine the output prediction map with lower layers by summing feature maps of the same size, thus allow models make the local prediction that respect global structure. Also, it requires smaller stride step during deconvolution process, thus improves the details and accuracy of dense prediction.

3.3   Our Proposed Model

The idea of FCN [8] can be applied to other CNN for object recognition to solve pixel-dense classification task. As in [8], authors experiment with three different architectures: AlexNet [10], GoogleLeNet [12] and VGG [11]. The VGG [11] model illustrated in Fig. 3 achieved the best performance over these three models. For the aerial image segmentation, there are some works using FCN framework and ResNet [13], VGG [11] as the feature extractor and achieved competitive results. But none of the works apply NASNet [9] model as feature extractor part and compare results with other methods using FCN idea. Also as stated in [9], the accuracy of Faster-RCNN [29] model for object detection and localization task is boosted when plugin NASNet model to the Faster-RCNN. With all of that reasons, we want to investigate the effect when using NASNet model for aerial image segmentation task.

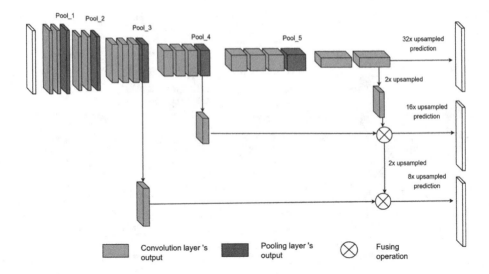

Fig. 3. Original FCN model based on VGG.

Our model follows the same design of FCN-8s as in [8]. The model architecture is shown in Fig. 4. By excluding the fully connected layer from the network and add the deconvolution layer with kernel size and stride equal to 4 and 2 respectively, we can double the feature map size. After that, we fuse the upsampled feature map with all of the output in Normal Cell of NASNet having the same size to encourage finer details in prediction map. The process of doubling feature map size and fusing them is continued in the same fashion as described before. For the last upsampling operation, we use the deconvolution layer with kernel size equal to 16 and stride equal to 8 to produce 8 times upsample feature map. Now the feature map has the same width and height as with the original input. The predicted feature map is then passed through a softmax function, resulting prediction probability vector for each pixels. The loss function is calculated by using average sum cross-entropy across dense-pixel of ground truth and the probability map. Back-propagation algorithm is employed for optimizing the loss function as usual. In this work, we use two verisons of NASNet: NASNet-large and NASNet-mobile to create semantic segmentation models called NASNet-large-FCN and NASNet-mobile-FCN respectively. The next section will describe experiments and results in details.

4   Experiment

4.1   Dataset

Our models are evaluated using ISPRS Vahingen 2D semantic segmentation dataset as in [1]. There are 33 patches, each of them contains very high resolution (more than 5 million pixels) true ortho photo (TOP) and Digital Surface

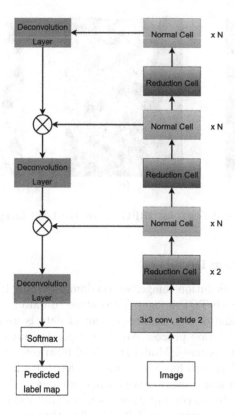

Fig. 4. NASNet-FCN architecture.

Model (DSM) data with 9-cm ground sampling distance. Each TOP image contain three information in three channels: infrared, red, green (IRRG). The goal of these challenges is to label each pixel of the image with one of six classes: building, low vegetation, tree, car, clutter and impervious surface. There are 16 images with groundtruth provided for training purpose out of all 33 patches. Illustration of data can be found in Fig. 5. This task is challenging because of complex appearance of objects e.g. buildings, streets, trees and cars in very high-resolution data.

4.2 Environment Setup

For training and prediction, we used a cluster with 2 x Intel(R) Xeon(R) CPU E5-2697 v4@ 2.30 GHz, 64 GB of RAM and Nvidia Tesla K40m GPU. The operating system is Cent-OS 7. For implementation, we use Python 2.7, Keras [30] framework with Tensorflow [31] backend.

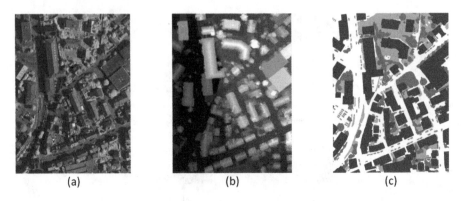

Fig. 5. Example of the dataset. (a) IRRG image, (b) DSM image, (c) Groundtruth image

4.3 Implementation Details

From the very high-resolution image, we randomly extract 1000 square regions of 224 by 224 from each TOP images. The extracted data is divided to two set: training set and validation set. Eighty-percent of data is used for training, the others is used for validation process. We do not employ any data augmentation technique for training process. Model is trained from scratch, using Adam [32] optimization algorithm with fixed learning of 0.0001, batch size of 10, and stop learning when model starts overfit. We do not put much effort to find the best hyper-parameter set due to computation resources limitation. For the prediction phase, we slide a square window of 224 by 224 through the test image and generate prediction map for each window image. We used overlap prediction to smooth the prediction map at boundary of extracted windows. The python code for model and training proces is publised at https://github.com/sugoi-ai/NASNet-FCN.

4.4 Results

The pixel-dense prediction maps are judged by the benchmark organizers. The competition website public the results and methods each team used in their submissions. For evaluation, each image the confusion matrix, precision, recall and F1 score for all six class is derived by comparing the ground truth with prediction results. After that, these results are accumulated to create the overall F1 score for each class and overall accuracy for test set as reported in Table 1.

Table 1 shows our prediction results over ISPRS Vaihingen dataset and some selected results from challenge website. We have three models named VNU1, VNU2, and VNU4 which used the original FCN-8s model [8], NASNet-mobile-FCN and NASNet-large-FCN respectively. As we can see, with deeper layers for learning image features, NASNet-large-FCN achieved higher accuracy than the two others. Meanwhile, the NASNet-mobile-FCN achieved the same accuracy with original FCN-8s model, but using fewer parameters (5 millions vs 134 millions). The NASNet-mobile-FCN model also surpass the performance of RIT_L8,

Table 1. Results on ISPRS Vaihingen dataset.

Submission	Imp suf	Building	Low veg	Tree	Car	Overall Acc
RIT_L8	89.6%	92.2%	81.6%	88.6%	76.0%	87.8%
ADL_3	89.5%	93.2%	82.3%	88.2%	63.3%	88.0%
BKHN_9	90.7%	94.4%	81.8%	88.3%	80.9%	88.8%
DLR_9	92.4%	95.2%	83.9%	89.9%	81.2%	90.3%
BKHN_4	92.7%	95.1%	84.7%	89.8%	86.6%	90.7%
VNU1	**89.2%**	**92.6%**	**80.1%**	**88.0%**	**74.6%**	**87.5%**
VNU2	**89.8%**	**92.0%**	**81.3%**	**88.2%**	**67.7%**	**87.8%**
VNU4	**91.2%**	**93.6%**	**81.5%**	**88.5%**	**77.7%**	**89.0%**

Fig. 6. Some prediction results from test set. Left: IRRG image, Middle: Our NASNet-large-FCN prediction, Right: BKHN_4 predictions.

which used an ensemble of FCN and random forest with the hand-designed feature. The NASNet-large-FCN model achieved slightly higher accuracy than the BKHN_9 and ADL_3 results, which used Fully Convolutional DenseNet [33] and patch-based prediction [34].

Compare with other methods achieved state-of-the-art results, our methods do not outperform the top accuracy e.g. DLR_9 and BKHN_4. Both of these methods used the additional data channel and ensemble learning, achieved greater than 1% compare with our current best overall accuracy prediction. While DLR_9 uses edge information extracted from original image as additional input channel for learning and prediction, BKHN_4 's method uses height information from nDSM and DSM data for learning ensemble of the FCN models. Our models do not use the height data, it leads to some mis-classified region where buildings are covered by shadow and is classified as clutter class. Examples of our prediction and other team prediction can be found in Fig. 6.

5   Conclusions

In this work, we employed the state-of-the-art object recognition model NASNet and FCN framework to tackle the aerial image segmentation problem. Experiment results show that the NASNet model boost the accuracy of original FCN-8s models and achieved state-of-the-art results with potential improvements. In the future, we will apply NASNet to other semantic segmentation framework and use post-processing technique e.g. Conditional Random Field to boost the performance of our models.

References

1. Cramer, M.: The DGPF-test on digital airborne camera evaluation-overview and test design. Photogrammetrie-Fernerkundung-Geoinformation **2010**(2), 73–82 (2010)
2. Porway, J., Wang, Q., Zhu, S.C.: A hierarchical and contextual model for aerial image parsing. Int. J. Comput. Vis. **88**(2), 254–283 (2010)
3. Dollar, P., Tu, Z., Belongie, S.: Supervised learning of edges and object boundaries. In: 2006 IEEE Computer Society Conference on Computer Vision and Pattern Recognition, vol. 2, pp. 1964–1971. IEEE (2006)
4. Nguyen, T.T., Grabner, H., Bischof, H., Gruber, B.: On-line boosting for car detection from aerial images. In: 2007 IEEE International Conference on Research, Innovation and Vision for the Future, pp. 87–95. IEEE (2007)
5. Kluckner, S., Bischof, H.: Semantic classification by covariance descriptors within a randomized forest. In: 2009 IEEE 12th International Conference on Computer Vision Workshops (ICCV Workshops), pp. 665–672. IEEE (2009)
6. Mnih, V., Hinton, G.E.: Learning to detect roads in high-resolution aerial images. In: Daniilidis, K., Maragos, P., Paragios, N. (eds.) ECCV 2010. LNCS, vol. 6316, pp. 210–223. Springer, Heidelberg (2010). https://doi.org/10.1007/978-3-642-15567-3_16
7. Rigamonti, R., Türetken, E., González Serrano, G., Fua, P., Lepetit, V.: Filter learning for linear structure segmentation. Technical report (2011)
8. Long, J., Shelhamer, E., Darrell, T.: Fully convolutional networks for semantic segmentation. In: Proceedings of the IEEE Conference on Computer Vision and Pattern Recognition, pp. 3431–3440 (2015)

9. Zoph, B., Vasudevan, V., Shlens, J., Le, Q.V.: Learning transferable architectures for scalable image recognition. arXiv preprint arXiv:1707.07012 (2017)
10. Krizhevsky, A., Sutskever, I., Hinton, G.E.: ImageNet classification with deep convolutional neural networks. In: Advances in Neural Information Processing Systems, pp. 1097–1105 (2012)
11. Simonyan, K., Zisserman, A.: Very deep convolutional networks for large-scale image recognition. arXiv preprint arXiv:1409.1556 (2014)
12. Szegedy, C., et al.: Going deeper with convolutions. In: CVPR (2015)
13. He, K., Zhang, X., Ren, S., Sun, J.: Deep residual learning for image recognition. In: Proceedings of the IEEE Conference on Computer Vision and Pattern Recognition, pp. 770–778 (2016)
14. Huang, G., Liu, Z., Weinberger, K.Q., van der Maaten, L.: Densely connected convolutional networks. In: Proceedings of the IEEE Conference on Computer Vision and Pattern Recognition, vol. 1, p. 3 (2017)
15. Zoph, B., Le, Q.V.: Neural architecture search with reinforcement learning. arXiv preprint arXiv:1611.01578 (2016)
16. Badrinarayanan, V., Kendall, A., Cipolla, R.: SegNet: a deep convolutional encoder-decoder architecture for image segmentation. IEEE Trans. Pattern Anal. Mach. Intell. **39**(12), 2481–2495 (2017)
17. Noh, H., Hong, S., Han, B.: Learning deconvolution network for semantic segmentation. In: Proceedings of the IEEE International Conference on Computer Vision, pp. 1520–1528 (2015)
18. Chen, L., Zhu, Y., Papandreou, G., Schroff, F., Adam, H.: Encoder-decoder with atrous separable convolution for semantic image segmentation. CoRR, vol. abs/1802.02611 (2018)
19. Chen, L., Papandreou, G., Schroff, F., Adam, H.: Rethinking atrous convolution for semantic image segmentation. CoRR, vol. abs/1706.05587 (2017)
20. Chen, L., Papandreou, G., Kokkinos, I., Murphy, K., Yuille, A.L.: Semantic image segmentation with deep convolutional nets and fully connected CRFs. CoRR, vol. abs/1412.7062 (2014)
21. Chen, L.-C., Papandreou, G., Kokkinos, I., Murphy, K., Yuille, A.L.: DeepLab: semantic image segmentation with deep convolutional nets, atrous convolution, and fully connected CRFs. IEEE Trans. Pattern Anal. Mach. Intell. **40**(4), 834–848 (2018)
22. Yu, F., Koltun, V.: Multi-scale context aggregation by dilated convolutions. arXiv preprint arXiv:1511.07122 (2015)
23. Zhao, H., Shi, J., Qi, X., Wang, X., Jia, J.: Pyramid scene parsing network. In: IEEE Conference on Computer Vision and Pattern Recognition (CVPR), pp. 2881–2890 (2017)
24. Sherrah, J.: Fully convolutional networks for dense semantic labelling of high-resolution aerial imagery. arXiv preprint arXiv:1606.02585 (2016)
25. Audebert, N., Le Saux, B., Lefèvre, S.: Beyond RGB: very high resolution urban remote sensing with multimodal deep networks. ISPRS J. Photogramm. Remote. Sens. **140**, 20–32 (2017)
26. Audebert, N., Le Saux, B., Lefèvre, S.: Semantic segmentation of earth observation data using multimodal and multi-scale deep networks. In: Lai, S.-H., Lepetit, V., Nishino, K., Sato, Y. (eds.) ACCV 2016. LNCS, vol. 10111, pp. 180–196. Springer, Cham (2017). https://doi.org/10.1007/978-3-319-54181-5_12
27. Marmanis, D., Schindler, K., Wegner, J.D., Galliani, S., Datcu, M., Stilla, U.: Classification with an edge: improving semantic image segmentation with boundary detection. ISPRS J. Photogramm. Remote. Sens. **135**, 158–172 (2018)

28. Xie, S., Tu, Z.: Holistically-nested edge detection. In: Proceedings of the IEEE international Conference on Computer Vision, pp. 1395–1403 (2015)
29. Ren, S., He, K., Girshick, R., Sun, J.: Faster R-CNN: towards real-time object detection with region proposal networks. In: Advances in Neural Information Processing Systems, pp. 91–99 (2015)
30. Chollet, F., et al.: Keras (2015)
31. Abadi, M., et al.: TensorFlow: a system for large-scale machine learning. OSDI **16**, 265–283 (2016)
32. Kingma, D.P., Ba, J.: Adam: a method for stochastic optimization. arXiv preprint arXiv:1412.6980 (2014)
33. Jégou, S., Drozdzal, M., Vazquez, D., Romero, A., Bengio, Y.: The one hundred layers Tiramisu: fully convolutional DenseNets for semantic segmentation. In: 2017 IEEE Conference on Computer Vision and Pattern Recognition Workshops (CVPRW), pp. 1175–1183. IEEE (2017)
34. Paisitkriangkrai, S., Sherrah, J., Janney, P., Van-Den Hengel, A.: Effective semantic pixel labelling with convolutional networks and conditional random fields. In: 2015 IEEE Conference on Computer Vision and Pattern Recognition Workshops (CVPRW), pp. 36–43. IEEE (2015)

Identifying Goals of Agents by Learning from Observations

Guillaume Lorthioir[2,3]([⊠]), Gauvain Bourgne[1], and Katsumi Inoue[2,3]

[1] Sorbonne Université, UPMC CNRS, UMR 7606, LIP6, 75005 Paris, France
[2] National Institute of Informatics, Tokyo, Japan
lorthioir@nii.ac.jp
[3] Department of Informatics, SOKENDAI (The Graduate University for Advanced Studies), Tokyo, Japan

Abstract. The intention recognition problem is a difficult problem which consists in determining the intentions and the goals of an agent. Solving this problem is useful when they are several agents which are interacting with each other and when they do not know each other. The effectiveness of an agents' work could be improved in this case. We present a method to infer the possible goals of an agent by observing him in a series of successful attempts to reach them. We model this problem as a case of concept learning and propose an algorithm to produce concise hypotheses. However, this first proposal does not take into account the sequential nature of our observations and we discuss how we can infer better hypotheses when we can make some assumption about the behavior of the agents and use background knowledge on the dynamics of the environment. We then provide a simple way to enrich our data by assuming the agent can compute the effects of his actions in the next step and study the properties of our proposal in two different settings. We show that our algorithm will always provide a possible goal if such a goal exists (meaning that there is indeed some set of states in which the agent always succeeds and stops in our observations).

Keywords: Intention recognition · Plan recognition
Goal recognition · Concept learning

1 Introduction

With the aging of the world population, the field of assistance to the elderly will evolve drastically. For this application, robotics will be useful, but to help a person, a robot must recognize the person's intentions, which is not trivial. There are many cases where the knowledge of an agent's intentions is useful, for cooperation or competition in a multi-agent system or even for a smartphone application which tries to help the user to do something. The ISS-CAD

This work was supported by JSPS KAKENHI Grant Number JP17H00763.

M. Kaenampornpan et al. (Eds.): MIWAI 2018, LNAI 11248, pp. 125–138, 2018.
https://doi.org/10.1007/978-3-030-03014-8_11

problem [11] is a good illustration of this problem, where a free-flying robot is observing an astronaut performing a task in the International Space Station (ISS) and he has to help him.

This problem is called "Plan recognition" or"Intentions recognition" and has been investigated in AI research and has many applications. Schmidt *et al.* [6] were the first ones to introduce the problem and treat it from a psychological point of view. Charniak and Goldman [7] use Bayesian models and Geib and Goldman [8] use also a probabilistic algorithm for the plan recognition. Carberry [9] describes the plan recognition problem and made a state of the art on the current ways to tackle this problem. Several other related recent works [1–5] show that goal recognition becomes more and more important.

However, although there are some works about inverse reinforcement learning used for related learning problems, there are only few works about learning techniques in plan recognition. So we have focused our work on this aspect of the plan recognition problem. We try to guess the goal of the agent, the state of things that the agent is trying to achieve. Indeed, many previous works try to solve the plan recognition problem by using a set of possible goals for the agent and try to guess which one is more likely, as it is the case for example in the work of Lang [10]. But often they assume that this set of possible goals is given, which is not really the case in reality.

In this paper a method is proposed to infer the possible goals of an agent by using concept learning. First Sect. 2 will explain how to formalize the problem of inferring goals from the observation of successful scenarios as a concept learning instance, then we will show and explain our algorithm in Sect. 3 and discuss, in Sect. 4, ways to take into account more data and improve the results by making some assumptions on the agent decision process and the environment. Section 5 then presents an experimental study of the proposed algorithm before concluding and discussing future works in Sect. 6.

2   Problem Formalisation

What is our problem exactly? Our objective is to infer the possible goals of an agent by observing him in a series of successful attempts to reach them. We thus assume some training process in which we observe the agent in a series of scenarios in which he performs actions in some environment until he satisfies one of the goals we are trying to guess. These observed scenarios will be modeled as a set of observed traces describing the successive states of the environment and actions of the agent. We consider environments with discrete time and no exogenous events: each action performed by the agent thus corresponds to a change of state. Here we model the state of the environment as a series of discrete-valued attributes: N variables var_i with $i \in \{1, \ldots, N\}$ taking their values in variable domains $D_j = \{val_1^i, \ldots, val_{N_i}^i\}$. We build an atomic representation by converting all the couples $var_i = val_j^i$ into atoms $var_i^{val_j^i}$, denoting by $\mathcal{L}$ the set of all these atoms. A *state* S is then defined as a set of atoms $var_i^{val_j^i}$

from $\mathcal{L}$ where each var_i appears once and a *trace* is defined as a sequence of couples (S_i, a_i) where $S_i \subset \mathcal{L}$ is a state and a_i an action (taken from a finite set of actions $\mathcal{A}$). We do not go into the detail of the environment's dynamics, but they can be abstracted away by some function $next$ from $2^{\mathcal{L}} \times \mathcal{A}$ to $2^{2^{\mathcal{L}}}$ which, given a state S and an action a gives the set of possible states that can be reached from S by performing a. When the environment is deterministic, $next(S, a)$ corresponds to a single state. Since they come from observations, traces are assumed to respect this dynamic, meaning that if i is not the last index of the trace, $S_{i+1} \in next(S_i, a_i)$.

To define successful traces we consider a special action $\mathsf{success}$ without effects $(\forall S, next(S, \mathsf{success}) = \{S\})$, which the agent performs whenever he reaches his goal. A successful trace is thus a trace $T = (S_0, a_0), \ldots, (S_K, a_K)$ where $a_K = \mathsf{success}$ and for $i < K$, $a_i \neq \mathsf{success}$. This means that a successful trace is a trace which ends in the first state where the goal of the agent is satisfied. Given a trace $T = (S_0, a_0), \ldots, (S_K, a_K)$, we denote by $endS(T)$ the last state S_K of a trace and by $intS(T)$ the set of intermediate states $\{S_0, \ldots, S_{K-1}\}$. The input of our problem is a set of successful traces $\Sigma = \{T_0, \ldots, T_L\}$ and our objective is to infer from that some hypothesis about the agent's goal, which will be expressed as a propositional formula over $\mathcal{L}$ which should be satisfied by some state (by interpreting states as the conjunction of their atoms) if and only if the goal is reached. We assume here that the goal depends only on the state and not on the way to reach it. The agent just needs to reach a state where the atoms composing the state satisfy his goal, no matter how he reaches it. However, the goal can be disjunctive, effectively we can have different sets of atoms to satisfy this one. We want the hypothesis written in the disjunctive normal form, more precisely we want hypotheses of the form $H = C_0 \vee C_1 \vee \ldots \vee C_m$ where each $C_i = a_0 \wedge \ldots \wedge a_n$ is a conjunction of atoms of $\mathcal{L}$. Then, given $H = C_0 \vee C_1 \vee \ldots \vee C_m$, a state $S = \{b_0, \ldots, b_n\}$ satisfies H if and only if $\bigwedge_{b_i \in S} b_i \models H$, that is, if and only if there exists $i \in \{0, \ldots, m\}$ such $C_i \subseteq S$.

Even without knowing anything about the behavior of the agents or the dynamics of the system, these observations give a series of states in which we know whether the goal is reached or not. Namely, we can build the set $S_{positive}$ of successful states by including in it all end-states of successful traces from Σ, that is, $S_{positive} = \{endS(T) | T \in \Sigma\}$. Likewise, we can build the set $S_{negative}$ of unsuccessful states by taking the union of all intermediate states, that is, $S_{negative} = \bigcup_{T \in \Sigma} intS(T)$. Given the definition of a successful trace, it means that the agent's goal is satisfied only by the elements of $S_{positive}$ and under no circumstances by an element of $S_{negative}$. The problem of inferring the goals of the agent is then equivalent to a concept learning problem where the states that we put in the set $S_{positive}$ are the positive examples and the states that we put in $S_{negative}$ are the negative ones. A hypothesis H will be said to be consistent with our data if it satisfied by all the elements of $S_{positive}$ and by none of the elements of $S_{negative}$. We want to obtain such a hypothesis as an output of our problem. We made an algorithm to treat this problem and produce such a hypothesis.

3   Concept Learning Algorithm

As we saw in the previous section, the problem of inferring the goal of an agent from observing a set of successful scenarios can be modeled as a concept learning problem, transforming the observed set of successful traces Σ into two sets of states $S_{positive}$ and $S_{negative}$. The objective is then to produce some hypothesis H expressed as a disjunction of conjunctive statements (sets of atoms) such that H is consistent with the data (ie satisfied by every states in $S_{positive}$ and not satisfied by any states in $S_{negative}$).

Given this, it would be possible to use existing symbolic concept learning algorithm such as Id3, Ripper or MGI [12–14]. As its output is very close to the form we want to produce, MGI could be a good candidate. However, this is a bottom-up algorithm where each conjunctive statement of the disjunctive hypothesis is obtained by the least-general generalization of some positive examples. Since in our specific case, we are likely to have much more negative examples than positive ones, we chose to adapt this algorithm by using different biases, favoring the generation of general terms. This concept learning process is described in Algorithm 1.

---

input : $S_{negative}$, $S_{positive}$
output: hypothesis

1 listOfPotentialGoals = list();
2 hypothesis = list();
3 i = 0;
4 **for** *state in $S_{positive}$* **do**
5   **if** *(an element of the list hypothesis is include in state)* **then**
6 | skip to next state;
7   **end**
8   **else**
9   i++;
10   listOfPotentialGoals.append(generation of all the subsets of atoms from state);
11   hypothesis.append(the subset of listOfPotentialGoals[i] with the minimum of cardinality and which is included in the most examples of $S_{positive}$);
12   **while** *hypothesis[i] is include in at least one element of $S_{negative}$* **do**
13   listOfPotentialGoals[i].remove(hypothesis[i]);
14   hypothesis[i] = the subset of listOfPotentialGoals[i] with the minimum of cardinality and which is included in the most examples of $S_{positive}$;
15   **end**
16   **end**
17 **end**

Algorithm 1. Goals deduction algorithm

This algorithm takes as input a set of positive examples $S_{positive}$ and a set of negative examples $S_{negative}$ that we will use for concept learning. First, we will use a positive example to create a possible goal, this possible goal will correspond to a set of atoms included in the positive example. We start from the smallest sets of atoms, selecting those which are included in as many positive examples as possible. Then we use the set of negative examples to see if the possible goal that we just extracted is valid or not by testing if this set of atoms is included in one of the negative examples. We repeat this process until all the positive examples are covered by at least one possible goal determined previously. In the end, the algorithm will return a hypothesis written in the disjunctive normal form that we described earlier.

This algorithm will always finish because in the worst case he will create a new possible goal for each positive example and for each of these goals it will go through all the negative examples. The complexity of our algorithm in term of time is therefore $|S_{positive}| * |S_{negative}|$ according to the number of examples and 2^n according to the number of atoms in $\mathcal{L}$, because of the possible goals generation phase.

4   Using Background Knowledge

In previous sections, our input Σ, a set of successful traces, is reduced to two sets of states $S_{positive}$ and $S_{negative}$. By doing so, we do not use the information contained in Σ about the order of the explored states and the actions performed by the agents at each step. The advantage of ignoring these aspects is that we can infer possible goals without assuming more about the agent than what is induced by the definition of successful traces, that is, the agent stops (with a **success** action) as soon as his goal is reached and this goal is dependent only on the current state. However, if we know the dynamics of the environment, it seems sensible to derive some information based on what the agent chose to do given what it could have done. This is only possible if we have at least some insight into the way the agent choose his actions. Generally, we can represent such insight by a function *estimDec*, which, given a current state S and some goal G, return a set of actions $estimDec(S, G)$ that we know the agent will consider in this context. Depending on our knowledge about the agent internal decision process, the smaller the cardinal of $estimEc(S, G)$ will be, a singleton answer meaning that we know exactly which action the agent would choose to do in the given context.

In such a general case, knowing some decision estimation function *estimDec*, we can impose an additional constraint on the formation of goal hypothesis. Indeed, the target goal G should be consistent with the decisions of the agent in each traces, meaning that for any $T \in \Sigma$ and any (S_i, a_i) in $intS(T)$ we should have $A_i \in estimDec(S_i, G)$. Therefore we can add this condition as an additional constraint for a candidate hypothesis to be consistent. We would then need a corresponding process in the learning algorithm checking, for each possible generated goal G_i, if it is consistent with the behavior that was actually observed in the trace. Using the function $estimDec(E_i, G_i)$ as an oracle, this can be done by checking for each (S_i, a_i) in the traces whether $estimDec(S_i, G_i)$ does contain the action a_i performed by the agent at step i.

But some specific deterministic cases can be pre-processed directly without the need to use such additional consistency checking process in the algorithm. For instance, we can consider the case of rational omniscient agents, in which we know that the agent we observe has a complete knowledge of his environment and its rules as well as a planner to find shortest plans to reach his goal. In such a case, if we know the environment dynamics, we can for each successful trace $T \in \Sigma$ of size K generate all the negative examples reachable from the state i in $K - i$ steps and add them to the set $S_{negative}$. This can be computed by using K_i times function $next$ with all possible actions to get all these reachable states.

Using the same principle with weaker assumptions, we consider here a case of a deterministic environment in which we assume that the agent is smart enough to reach his goal with only one move whenever this one is reachable with one move (with certainty since the environment is deterministic). This amounts to considering that the agent is at least able to plan one-step ahead, ie, to know the direct consequences of his actions and choose his actions accordingly. In this case, if we also know the environment and its dynamic, we can generate a lot of negative examples. Indeed, if we know the action model governing the effects of the agent's actions we can deduce from a state of the world the other states that the agent can reach at the next time step. Then, if we know that the agent did not reach his goal at the time step t that means that all the states that the agent could reach at the time step $t - 1$ are not final. And all these non-final states can thus be considered as negative examples and will allow us to refine the results of our algorithm. In such a case, we modify our algorithm by this pre-processing applied to each $T \in \Sigma$ to compute additional negatives examples (see Algorithm 2). Such a process improve learning by expanding initial input, allowing us to learn precise goals from fewer examples.

---

input : Set of successful traces Σ, function $next$, set of actions $\mathcal{A}$
output: $S_{newNegative}$

1 $S_{newNegative} = \text{list}()$;
2 **for** $T = (S_0, a_0), \ldots, (S_K, a_K)$ in Σ **do**
3   i=0 **for** $i < K - 1$ **do**
4        $S_{newNegative} = S_{newNegative} \cup \bigcup_{a \in \mathcal{A}} next(S_i, a)$
5   **end**
6 **end**

Algorithm 2. Pre-processing algorithm

Note that if we end up with $S_{positive} \cap S_{newNegative} \neq \emptyset$, we would have a contradiction (and no consistent hypothesis could be found). Such cases would mean that some assumptions are not met. In this case, it could mean that the agent is not in fact even planning one-step ahead, that his goal depends on more than the current states or that our observations are incomplete or wrong. If we have enough traces to learn precise goals without any assumptions on the agent's behavior, different assumptions could then be tested with the inferred goal to check which are compatible with the observed behavior, giving us some insight on the agent decision process.

5   Experiments

We made experiments with one agent in two different environments, a deterministic and a non-deterministic one. In each environment the goals of the agent and his decision model are different. The first environment is a grid of size $4 * 4$ and the second environment is a precision game represented by targets aligned on a line.

The first environment is, therefore, a grid of size $4 * 4$ where some walls are placed randomly between the cells of the grid. In this environment, the goal of the observed agent is to reach a dead-end, which means a cell of the grid surrounded by exactly three walls. For this, we assume that in each grid that we create that there is at least one dead-end and that there is a way for the agent to reach it from each starting position in the grid. The actions available for the agent in this environment are to move one cell to the left, to the right, to the top, to the bottom or stay at his current position. Obviously, the agent cannot move from a cell to another if there is a wall between this two cells, he is also not able to move outside from the grid even if there are not always some walls on the outlines of the grid. This environment is deterministic as the agent cannot fail his action, which means that if he tries to do a move which is not forbidden in his actual position, he will necessarily get to the corresponding position. To generate the observation trace, we implemented the agent as follows. First, the agent computes his path to reach a dead-end from his starting position by using the A^* algorithm and after he starts his journey, each state and action being recorded in the trace. The agent can only execute one action at each time step. To collect the trace of the journey of the agent we use the atomic formalization set out previously with the following variables. We use a variable *pos* which is related to the position of the agent in the environment and a set of variables *leftW*, *upW*, *rightW* and *downW* related to the presence or not of walls around the agent, each variable corresponding to a specific direction. For the experiments on this kind of environment we generated twelve different grids and we assume that the grids cover all the kinds of the possible dead-end (see for instance Fig. 1). Effectively there are four kinds of dead-end, depending on the direction of the exit. For each instance of a grid, we generated multiple traces depending on the agent starting position.

The second environment is a game where you have a line of ten cells and each cell has a color which is either black or white knowing that the colors of the cell's neighbors are different from her own color. We also have some jars which are placed randomly on some cells. A cell can only contain one jar. In this environment, the goal of the agent is to throw a ball into a jar which is

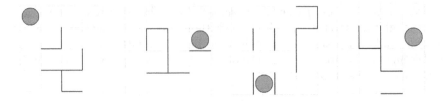

Fig. 1. Grids for the first experimentation (Color figure online)

above a white cell. For this, we assume that there is always at least a white cell with a jar on this one. This environment is quite different from the previous one because here the agent does not aim very well so at each try of the agent the ball has a possibility to reach each of the cells from the game. We also assume that after ten tries if the agent still not reach his goal he becomes more accurate and eventually reaches it. Figure 2 is an illustration of the environment, you can see in blue the jars and the cells in white or black. To collect the trace of this game we use a set of variable to describe the result of each ball thrown by the agent. The variable *pos* indicates which cell the ball arrived in, the variable *cellColor* corresponds to the color of the cell on which the ball has arrived, the variable *pot* indicates whether there is a jar on the cell that the ball hit and the variable *potOnLeft, potOnRight* indicate respectively whether there is a jar on the left or on the right of this one.

Fig. 2. An example of the second experimentation's environment (Color figure online)

Experimental Protocol: For all of our experiments, we have a set of negative and positive examples of data collected from the generated traces that we use as input for our algorithm. We start by using hundred percent of this data and we decrease the percentage of used data by two percent at each simulation (percentage of missing data range from 0% to 98%)). For each different percentage of used data, we run two hundred times our algorithm by taking randomly this percentage of data in our set of data and we make an average of the results for each percentage of data used. However, we use the same percentage of data for positive examples than for negative ones, for example, if we have to take randomly eighty percent of data we will take randomly eighty percent of the positive examples and eighty percent of the negative ones. For the experiments in the first environment, we use a set of 776 negative examples and a set of 192 positive ones, which correspond to a set of 192 successful traces. For the experiments in the second environment, we use a set of 452 negative examples and a set of 100 positive ones, which correspond to a set of 100 successful traces.

Measures: For our experiments, we used different types of measures. The first one is a *syntactic distance* between the hypothesis returned by our algorithm and the actual set of goals of the agent. It reflects the similarity between our hypothesis and the target goal. We defined this distance as such: for each goal in our hypothesis, we compute the symmetrical distance to each of the real goals of the agent. We then take for each of the goals of our hypothesis the minimum of this symmetrical distance, it defines the distance from a goal to the agent's goal set. Afterward, we compute the distance between the hypothesis and the agent's set of goals by summing the distance of each goal of the hypothesis to the agent's goal set that we computed previously. For example if our hypothesis is $H = (a \wedge b \wedge c) \vee (b \wedge d)$ and the real set of goals is $G = (a \wedge c) \vee (b \wedge c \wedge d)$, we have:

$$d(H, G) = d((a \wedge b \wedge c), G) + d((b \wedge d), G)$$
$$d(H, G) = min(Card(\{b\}), Card(\{a, d\})) + min(Card(\{a, b, c, d\}), Card(\{c\})) = min(1, 2) + min(4, 1) = 1 + 1 = 2$$

Since this measure makes no difference between cases in which the hypothesis is too specific and those where it is too general, we also made some size comparisons between the hypothesis and the target goal to refine our analysis. We thus also measure the difference of size between the goals which are included in our hypothesis and the real goals in the set of goals of the agent, allowing us to know if we produced some too small or too big goals in term of the number of atoms. A similar comparison is made on the size of the goals set themselves (number of conjunctive statements) in order to evaluate whether we generated too many or too few sub-goals. The last measure is a measure of the accuracy of our algorithm, it is calculated as follows:
(True Positives + True Negatives)/(total number of examples).

Results: Figure 3 is a graph of the evolution of the average syntactic distance introduced previously, between the results provided by our algorithm and the true goals of the agent that we observe. In this case for each hypothesis generated by our algorithm, we compute the syntactic distance to the set of goals of the agent. Then for each percentage of data used change, we make an average of this distance on the two hundred hypotheses generated by our algorithm.

We can see on Fig. 3 that as expected the performance of our algorithm decreases as the amount of data used for learning decreases. We can see that the average syntactic distance between the results provide by our algorithm and the real goals of the agent is pretty good because in the worse case this

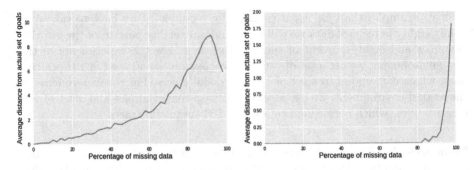

Fig. 3. Average syntactic distance from the true goals in function of the percentage of missing data, for the first environment.

Fig. 4. Average syntactic distance from the true goals in function of the percentage of missing data, second environment.

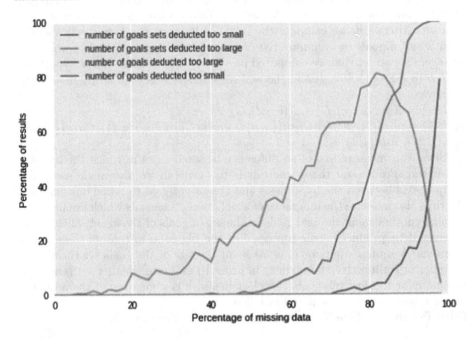

Fig. 5. Percentage of goals, sets of goals found by the algorithm, too small or too large compared to the true one in function of the percentage of missing data, for the first environment

average is little less than 9. Knowing that in this case, the agent has four goals of three atoms it means that in the worst case in average our algorithm finds almost one-third of the atoms of each real goals. Furthermore even with few data, twenty percent of the initial set of data, we still have effective results. Indeed the average syntactic distance is around 5. So even in this case we still deduct

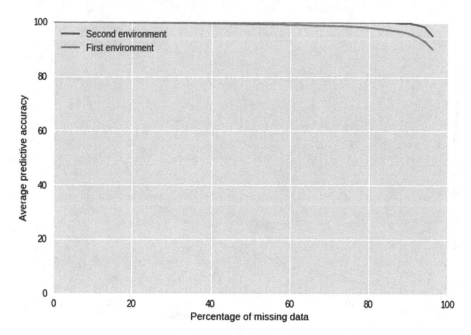

Fig. 6. Average predictive accuracy in function of the percentage of missing data

in almost two of the three atoms of each real goals of the agent. The accuracy decrease can be explained by the fact that with fewer negative examples, our algorithm might generate some possible goals from the positive examples which are not true and will not be removed of the final result. This is due to the lack of negative examples to invalid those wrong goals.

But our experiment with the second measure, Fig. 5 show us that the decrease in the amount of data used increases the number of goals too small in the hypothesis generated by our algorithm. This is also due to the fact that with less negative examples some goals too small could not be invalidated. However, given the results of Fig. 3, this suggests that the goals in our hypothesis are only a little bit smaller than the real ones. An interesting point is that we never obtain a goal with a higher number of variables than an actual one. This is due to the fact that our algorithm searches primarily for small cardinal goals and will gradually increment the size of these goals until it has found a valid goal. So by definition, our algorithm cannot find a greater goal than the real one. Otherwise, it would mean that this real goal is included in a negative example, which is impossible in our setting where the agent stops when he reaches his goal. We observe the same effect for the size of the generated hypotheses. More exactly after ten percent of missing data the percentage of hypotheses too big increases until we reach eighty percent of missing data, after which the number of generated hypotheses too big decreases to the benefit of the number of hypotheses too small. We can explain this by the fact that in a first time with the increase of the percentage

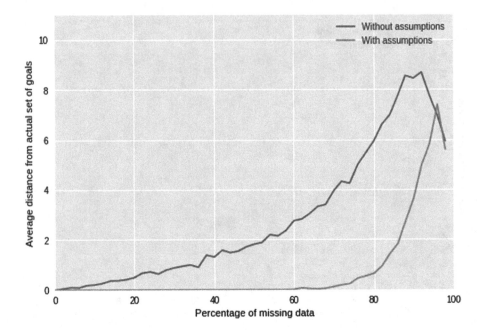

Fig. 7. Comparison of the average syntactic distance from the true goals in function of the percentage of missing data, for the first environment, with and without assumptions on the agent.

of missing data, the lack of negative examples could permit to generate goals of smaller size which will not be invalidated with the available negative examples. The problem is that these goals are too small to cover many positive examples so our algorithm will generate more goals and this is why we have some sets of goals too large in the end. But when we start to have really few data, some actual goals are no more covered by the positive examples, because of the lack of this last ones. Our algorithm will then generate fewer goals and we will obtain some too small goal sets.

The results that we can observe in Fig. 4 obtained with the second environment are quite similar to the ones that we got in the first environment. But here, since this goal is easier we obtain better results than for the previous environment. Even with few data, the precision of our algorithm is still good to deduce a goal like this. The only bad result obtained is when we use only two percent of the initial data, which is normal because it corresponds to only two games played by the agent. Figure 6 is a comparison of the average predictive accuracy for the two environments. As we explained before we can observe on this graph that our algorithm is far more accurate in the second environment than in the first one. Even with only fifteen percent of the initial data we still have around 96% of accuracy while it starts to decrease far more for the first environment. But even if we do not deduce exactly the actual goal, as we saw in our previous figure we are not far from this one if we have enough data. The accuracy of our algorithm is really important because we have far more negative examples than positive ones and our algorithm will never find a False Negative example, Which skews the accuracy a bit.

Figure 7 allows us to see the point to have some assumptions about the agent. Effectively for this case, we use the same experimental protocol than for Fig. 3, so we have 776 negative examples and 192 positive ones to give to our algorithm when we don't make assumptions about the agent. When we make two assumptions on the agent which are that we know the action model of the agent and that we know that if he can reach his goal with one move at the step $t - 1$ then at the step t he will reach it. These are not very strong assumptions. These assumptions allow us to generate more negative examples from the 192 itineraries followed by the agent during the simulation. In total, we obtain 2074 negative examples which is almost three times more than we have without the assumptions about the agent. As we can see in Fig. 7 it allows us to be closer to the actual goals than when we use no assumptions. In this case, the assumptions made on the agent are the last ones that we describe in the part 4 of our paper, so we use the algorithm 2 for pre-processing the data.

6   Future Works and Conclusion

We saw that the contribution of plan inference to the intelligent performance by computers could be useful in a wide variety of applications. Unfortunately, several serious problems still slow down the use of plan recognition in large-scale real-world situations. Carberry [9] describes these problems at the end of her paper. But we can also add another problem more related to our work, which is that in reality we do not really know when an agent reaches his goal, but we will come back on this problem later. We introduced our method and showed that it is quite different than the previous works on plan or goal recognition. Because few works are focused on learning in plan recognition and our formalisation of the problem allows us to use concept learning. This is very useful because the concept learning is well known and pretty easy to use, several algorithms already exist to treat concept learning. However, we made our own algorithm to control some generalization bias and explained his complexity which can be exponential in term of the number of variables describing the environment. But, since we first generate the smallest possible goals, we try to avoid a combinatory explosion. We saw that with our problem formalisation combined to our algorithm we can deduce the exact set of goals of an agent with enough traces of his behavior. In particular, if this set is composed of goals which are described by a few atoms, like in the second environment of our experiments, we need really few traces from the agent to infer his goals. Even when we do not deduce exactly the agent's goal set we can still deduce an approximate set of goals which is not so far from the actual one. We also showed that making some assumptions about the agent and his environment can drastically improve the goals deduction.

One of our future works is in fact to develop the decision function mentioned in Sect. 4. We were talking about the fact that in reality, we could not know when an agent reaches his goal. For this, a dynamic learning throughout the agent's actions might be efficient and more realistic. It could also be effective in a case where the agent changes goal along the way or in a case where the agent repeats the same cycle of actions, cases that we still can not solve with our method. So we will look into it later. We also plan to study about goals preference, effectively, the agent can have several goals and perhaps when he can reach two goals he will prefer one to the other. We must therefore, take this into account.

References

1. Vered, M., Pereira, R.F., Magnaguagno, M.C., Meneguzzi, F., Kaminka, G.A.: Online goal recognition as reasoning over landmarks. In: The AAAI 2018 Workshop on Plan, Activity, and Intent Recognition, New Orleans, Louisiana, USA (2018)
2. Goldman, R.P., Friedman, S.E., Rye, J.M.: Plan recognition for network analysis: preliminary report. In: The AAAI 2018 Workshop on Plan, Activity, and Intent Recognition, New Orleans, Louisiana, USA (2018)
3. E-Martin, Y., Smith, D.E.: Goal recognition with noisy observations. In: AAAI Workshop 2017, Palo Alto, California, USA (2017)
4. Mirsky, R., Stern, R., Gal, Y., Kalech, M.: Plan recognition design. In: AAAI Workshop 2017, Palo Alto, California, USA (2017)
5. Cardona-Rivera, R.E., Michael Young, R.: Toward combining domain theory and recipes in plan recognition. In: AAAI Workshop 2017, Palo Alto, California, USA (2017)
6. Schmidt, C.F., Sridharan, N.S., Goodson, J.L.: The plan recognition problem: an intersection of psychology and artificial intelligence. Artif. Intell. **11**(5), 45–83 (1978)
7. Charniak, E., Goldman, R.P.: A Bayesian model of plan recognition. Artif. Intell. **64**(5), 53–79 (1993)
8. Geib, C.W., Goldman, R.P.: A probabilistic plan recognition algorithm based on plan tree grammars. Artif. Intell. **173**, 1101–1132 (2009)
9. Carberry, S.: Techniques for plan recognition. User Model. User-Adap. Inter. **11**(5), 31–48 (2001)
10. Lang, J.: A preference-based interpretation of other agents' actions. In: International Conference on Automated Planning and Scheduling Conference 2004, vol. 04, pp. 33–42. AAAI, Whistler (2004)
11. E-Martin, Y., R-Moreno, M.D., Smith, D.E.: Practical goal recognition for ISS crew activities. In: International Workshop on Planning and Scheduling for Space 2015, Buenos Aires, Argentina (2015)
12. Henniche, M.: MGI: an incremental bottom-up algorithm. In: Australian New Zealand Intelligent Information Systems Conference 1994, pp. 347–351. IEEE, Brisbane (1994)
13. Quinlan, J.R.: Induction of decision trees. Mach. Learn. **1**(1), 81–106 (1986)
14. Cohen, W.W.: Trees and rules with set-valued features. In: AAAI Proceedings of the Thirteenth National Conference on Artificial intelligence 1996, Portland, Oregon, vol. 1, pp. 709–716 (1996)

Selection of Suitable PageRank Calculation for Analysis of Differences Between Expected and Observed Probability of Accesses to Web Pages

Jozef Kapusta[ID], Michal Munk[ID], and Peter Svec[(⊠)][ID]

Constantine the Philosopher University in Nitra, Nitra, Slovakia
{jkapusta,mmunk,psvec}@ukf.sk

Abstract. We describe various approaches how to calculate the value of PageRank in this paper. There are few methods how to calculate the PageRank, from the basic historical one to more enhanced versions. Most of them are using the original value of the damping factor. We describe the experiment we realised using our method for analysing differences between expected and observed probability of accesses to web pages of the selected portal. We used five slightly different methods for PageRank estimation using both the original value of damping factor and the value calculated from data in the web server log file. We assumed and confirmed that the estimation/calculation of the damping factor would have a significant impact on the estimation of the PageRank. We also wrongly assumed that the estimation/calculation of the damping factor would have a significant impact on the number of suspicious pages. We also compared the computational complexity of used PageRank methods, and the most effective method seems to be a method with the estimated value of the damping factor.

Keywords: Web usage mining · Web structure mining · PageRank
Damping factor · Support · Observed visit rate · Expected visit rate

1 Introduction

We can find many web mining methods that try to solve different issues of websites, like employing some personalisation, improve the structure of the website or reorganise web pages itself. Only a few of these methods try to combine the web structure and the web usage mining methods to achieve this aim. We developed method described in [1, 2] to analyse the differences between expected and observed probability of accesses to web pages of the selected portal. The expected rate of access to the web page was estimated using the PageRank (PR); the real visits were gotten from the web server log file. After the data pre-processing and user session identification [3], we calculated the value of support, which represent the real visits to the website. The method of calculating the PR is essential for our experiment. There are many different methods for calculating the PR [4–7], and we try to find the ideal one for our method of finding differences between expected and observed probability of accesses to web pages. We are also looking for the ideal value of the damping factor, which will be discussed later.

© Springer Nature Switzerland AG 2018
M. Kaenampornpan et al. (Eds.): MIWAI 2018, LNAI 11248, pp. 139–150, 2018.
https://doi.org/10.1007/978-3-030-03014-8_12

We combine various methods of PR calculation with different methods of setting the damping factor value – d in this paper.

2   Related Work

PR was developed at Stanford University by Larry Page and Sergey Brin [8, 9]. PR is a simple, robust and reliable way to measure the importance of web pages which can be computed offline using just the structure of web pages (sitemap) and the hyperlinks between pages. The PR form a probability distribution over web pages, so the sum of all web pages' PR will be one. PR can be thought of as a model of user behaviour. The original PR assume that there is a "random surfer" who is given a web page at random and keeps clicking on links, never hitting "back" but eventually gets bored and starts on another random page. The probability that the random surfer visits a page is its PR. Moreover, the damping factor is the probability at each page the "random surfer" will get bored and request another random page. The usual value of the damping factor is 0.85.

The literature does not offer the best value of the damping factor. When damping factor gets close to 1, the Markov process is closer to the "ideal" one, which would somehow suggest that damping factor should be chosen as close to 1 as possible. Boldi, Santini and Vigna [10] give several proofs of what happened when we choose the wrong value of the damping factor. When the value of d is close to 1, many important web pages will have rank 0 in the limit. Choosing d too close to 1 does not provide any good PR. Rather, PR becomes "sensible" somewhere in between 0 and 1.

The simplest and most basic algorithm that computes PR is an application of the Power Method. The PR algorithm including the crawler is in detail described in [11].

Some researchers try to use another approaches or enhancements to the PR. Deore and Paikrao [12] describe the UsersRank algorithm. While browsing the web, a user can save the link as a personal bookmark or as a social one. The social bookmark is shared among multiple users. UsersRank algorithm makes use of these bookmarks and produces valuable information for search engines. It believes in the logic that if the user is having some links as bookmarked, then those links are used by someone hence really valuable and gives useful results for web searches. Every bookmarked entry is considered as a vote given by the user to that page. UsersRank is achieved by summing up a total number of votes given by the users to that page.

Wang and Tao [13] create Personalised PR and combine the Monte-Carlo approach and group target nodes with similar PR together. They introduce a new notion called "PageRank heavy hitter" to quantify the importance of the second direction, and thereby, gives a convenient way to harness this direction for the recommendation. Personalised PR have been widely applied in social networking services to make friend recommendations; this is usually done by leveraging only the first "direction of importance".

The PR can be manipulated by the community of webmasters. They can create good links between pages and raise the rank. Yang, King and Lyu [14] tried to handle the manipulation problem, and they offer a DiffusionRank algorithm. This rank is motivated by the heat diffusion phenomena, which can be connected to web ranking because the activities flow on the web can be imagined as heat flow. They propose that link from a page to another can be treated as the pipe of an air-conditioner, and heat flow can embody the structure of the underlying web graph. Even in this idea, the authors used the value of 0.85 for the damping factor.

Yoseff and Mashiach [15] use Reverse PR based on the reverse graph (obtained by reversing the directions of all links) which is more suitable for local PR approximation and admits fast PR convergence.

Eiron, McCurley and Tomlin [16] propose some innovations (HostRank and Dir-Rank), to detect also pages that cannot be reached by crawlers. They call those pages as frontiers, and the consider them as significant – original PR algorithm deletes dangling pages. Their experiment was done on major newspapers in the U.S., and again they used the value of 0.85.

In our previous experiments [1, 2], we proved that there is a higher dependence of PR on the value of *support* in the visit rate of the examined web pages when the log file with identified user sessions is well-prepared. We also proved that the expected visit-rate of the individual web page (variable *PR*) correlated with the real visit-rate (*support*) obtained from the web server log file using the web usage mining method. We also proved that the dependence of PR on variable *support* would be higher when we pre-process the log file using user session identification methods. We utilized the potential advantages of joining web structure and the web usage mining methods in the residual analysis.

3   Materials and Methods

We developed a basic crawler, which went through and analysed web pages. The crawler created a sitemap which we have utilized later in the PR calculation of individual pages. The crawler was simple because it scanned only the hyperlinks between web pages. We consider this as the main limitation of the proposed method because the crawler did not regard the actual position of the hyperlinks within the web page layout, which has a strong influence on the probability of being accessed by a website visitor.

Consequently, we calculated PR for different web pages, based on several version of PR. We consider PR as a static evaluation of web pages, i.e. PR is calculated for each web page off-line, independently of search queries.

We divide the web page hyperlinks into two categories:

In-links – all hyperlinks that refer to the web page i from other web pages.
Out-links – all hyperlinks that refer to other web pages from the web page i.

The recursive hyperlinks are not considered. At the same time, we assume, the hyperlink from the web page, which referred to other web pages, transferred its importance to the target web pages implicitly. It means the web page is more relevant if other important web pages refer to it. We consider the web as an oriented graph G

$$G = (V, E), \tag{1}$$

where V is a set of nodes, i.e. a set of all web pages and E is a set of oriented edges, i.e. hyperlinks among web pages.

Let n ($n = |V|$) be the total count of web pages of the website. Then the PR of the web page i (p_i) is defined as

$$p_i(0) = \frac{1}{n},$$ (2)

$$p_i(t+1) = \sum_{(j,i) \in E} \frac{p_j(t)}{o_j}, j \in V,$$ (3)

where o_j is the count of hyperlinks referred (Out-links) to the other web pages from the web page j. This is the first, most simple version of the PR algorithm. We also used improved versions, employing the Random Surfer Model using the damping factor d using both available versions of calculating the PR. The first improved version is as follows

$$p_i(t+1) = 1 - d + d \sum_{(j,i) \in E} \frac{p_j(t)}{o_j}, j \in V,$$ (4)

where the value of d fits the interval $\langle 0, 1 \rangle$. The most common value of d is 0.85.

The second improved version of PR is the damping factor subtracted from 1 is divided by the number of pages, so the sum of PRs is equal to 1

$$p_i(t+1) = \frac{1-d}{n} + d \sum_{(j,i) \in E} \frac{p_j(t)}{o_j}, j \in V.$$ (5)

We can iterate this calculation until the difference between the two following values of $Pr(i)$ will be less than the desired accuracy ε.

We are calculating the internal PR, which is bounded by the domain of the website. We are interested only in links of the same portal. We are comparing different methods of calculating PR, including different values of damping factor in our methods of the analysis of differences between expected and observed probability of accesses to web pages.

3.1   Analysis of Differences Between Expected and Observed Probability of Accesses to Web Pages

We assume that the website is an oriented graph as stated in (1). We can identify suspicious pages using the following sequence:

1. **calculating the observed probability (s)** of accesses to web pages $i \in V$

$$s_i = \frac{number\ of\ identified\ sequences\ with\ i}{total\ number\ of\ identified\ sequences},$$ (6)

2. **estimation of expected probability** of access to web pages $i \in V$ with each method for calculating the PR as stated in (3), (4), (5).
3. **visualization of difference between the expected** *(p)* **and observed** *(s)* **probability**

$$r_i = s_i - p_i, \tag{7}$$

4. **identification of suspicious pages**

$$\bar{r} \pm 2s. \tag{8}$$

The analysis of the expected visit and observed visit combine data sources for web usage analysis and web structure analysis. Evaluating the structure of the web means to identify suspicious sites. Suspicious pages are pages where expected visit do not match to the observed one. We use the visualization of differences in observed and expected access probabilities (7) and the identification of extreme differences (8) for the evaluation. Observed page access probabilities are represented by the level of *support* for the frequent one-element item sets (6) and the expected access probabilities are represented by the PR (3), (4), (5). The PR for a particular page reflects the likelihood a random visitor will get to this page. While the observed access probability - *support* is calculated from the pre-processed portal web server log file, the PR for the examined web portal is calculated from the sitemap.

The PR method is based on the principle - the better the page is, the more links point to it. The PR value of page i depends on the extent to which is the recommender is important (pj) and how much recommendation it gives (oj). In other words, the PR value of one page depends on the PR of the referral page and the number of links it refers to (2). The value of t is the iteration number, given that PR is counted recursively. In the iteration process, all pages start with the same PR (2). If the page does not contain a link, e.g. document or image, then we assume that the user will go to any page, i.e. as if it contained n links (to all the pages of the examined portal).

4 Research Methodology

The value of damping factor d is significant in our experiment when using calculations (4) and (5). It indicates the probability that a random visitor comes to a page directly (not from a link). We have records from the web server log file in our experiment. The log file contains referrer information for each access, so we know where the visitor came from. We can estimate the value of the damping factor $\hat{d}$ as the proportion of pages with a referrer within the examined portal P.

$$\hat{d} = \frac{the\ number\ of\ accesses\ with\ referer\ i}{total\ number\ of\ access\ to\ the\ portal\ P}, i \in P. \tag{9}$$

Our aim is to compare different approaches to estimate the value of PR for the analysis of differences between expected and observed probability of accesses to web pages and to verify that the estimation of the damping factor has a significant effect on the reliability/accuracy of the expected page access. Using the experiment, we want to verify the following assumptions:

(1) *We assume that the estimate/calculation of parameter d will have a significant effect on PageRank estimation.*
(2) *We assume that the estimate/calculation of parameter d will have a significant impact on the number of identified suspicious pages.*

The experiment then consists of the following steps:

1. Determine the observed probability of access to web pages represented by the value of *support*;
2. Estimate of expected probability of access to web pages represented by the estimated value of PageRank:
   a. *PR A* - estimate the value of PR based on (3),
   b. *PR B* - estimate the value of PR based on (4) for $d = 0.85$,
   c. *PR C* - estimate the value of PR based on (4) with an estimated value of $\hat{d}$,
   d. *PR D* - estimate the value of PR based on (5) for $d = 0.85$,
   e. *PR E* - estimate the value of PR based on (5) with an estimated value of $\hat{d}$;
3. Make a linear transformation of results;
4. Identify dependence among examined variables;
5. Compare different value PR with considering the value of *support*.
6. Visualize the differences of observed and expected probabilities represented by different methods for estimation of PR;
7. Identify suspicious pages;
8. Qualitative evaluate identified suspicious sites using various PR methods.

5   Results

The sitemap of examined portal consists of 3996 pages. The damping factor calculated according to (9) is $\hat{d} = 0.35$. Kendall's coefficient of concordance represents the degree of concordance in values of the residuals using different PR estimations. The value of the coefficient (Table 1) is approximately 0.01 while 1 means a perfect concordance and 0 represents a discordance. Low values of the coefficient confirm statistically significant differences.

Based on multiple comparisons (LSD test) two homogenous groups (Table 1) were identified regarding the average residual for different PR estimations. Statistically significant differences were proved at the 5% significance level in the average residual between a basic estimation of *PR A* and estimations *PR C* and *PR E*, which were estimated based on calculated parameter $\hat{d}$.

Table 1. Homogeneous groups for residuals

residual	Mean	1	2
residual PR E	−0.1567	****	
residual PR C	−0.1567	****	
residual PR B	−0.1531	****	****
residual PR D	−0.1531	****	****
residual PR A	−0.1521		****
Kendall coefficient of concordance	0.00989		

Table 2. Homogeneous groups for residuals considering page level

Level	residual	Mean	1	2	3
Higher	residual PR E	−0.1922		****	
Higher	residual PR C	−0.1922		****	
Higher	residual PR B	−0.1880		****	****
Higher	residual PR D	−0.1879		****	****
Higher	residual PR A	−0.1868			****
Lower	residual PR C	0.0006	****		
Lower	residual PR E	0.0006	****		
Lower	residual PR B	0.0016	****		
Lower	residual PR D	0.0016	****		
Lower	residual PR A	0.0019	****		
Higher level: Kendall coefficient of concordance	0.01515				
Lower level: Kendall coefficient of concordance	0.76562				

A closer look at the results (Table 2) shows that

- A high concordance in residual values, when using different PR estimations is in the case of a lower page level (>2). The value of the coefficient of concordance (Table 2) is approximately 0.77, i.e. a high concordance. In the case of pages at the lower page level, statistically significant differences were not identified.
- On the contrary, statistically significant differences were identified in the case of pages with a high page level (<3). The value of the coefficient of concordance (Table 2) is approximately 0.02, i.e. discordance. Statistically significant differences were proved at the 5% significance level in the average residual between a basic estimation of *PR A* and estimations *PR C* and *PR E*.

Between the *support* measure and *PR* estimations (Table 3) was identified a moderate measure of direct proportional of dependency. The correlation coefficients for all PR estimations (Table 3) are statistically significant, with a slightly higher dependency between *support* and PR estimations *PR C* and *PR E*. In all cases, *PR* values (expected visit rate) and *support* values (observed visit rate) are changed together in the

Table 3. Correlations: support & PageRank

	Valid N	r	t	p-value
support & PR A	174	0.3196	4.4242	0.000017
support & PR B	174	0.3170	4.3837	0.000020
support & PR C	174	0.3204	4.4356	0.000016
support & PR D	174	0.3170	4.3829	0.000020
support & PR E	174	0.3205	4.4371	0.000016

Table 4. Kendall tau correlations for PageRank estimations at a high page level

Level = higher	PR A	PR B	PR C	PR D	PR E
PR A	1.0000	0.8851	0.7672	0.8853	0.7680
PR B	0.8851	1.0000	0.8820	0.9998	0.8829
PR C	0.7672	0.8820	1.0000	0.8818	0.9992
PR D	0.8853	0.9998	0.8818	1.0000	0.8827
PR E	0.7680	0.8829	0.9992	0.8827	1.0000

Table 5. Kendall tau correlations for PageRank estimations at a lower page level

Level = lower	PR A	PR B	PR C	PR D	PR E
PR A	1.0000	0.7686	0.5764	0.7686	0.5764
PR B	0.7686	1.0000	0.8079	1.0000	0.8079
PR C	0.5764	0.8079	1.0000	0.8079	1.0000
PR D	0.7686	1.0000	0.8079	1.0000	0.8079
PR E	0.5764	0.8079	1.0000	0.8079	1.0000

same direction, where the highest positive correlations were reached for *PR* estimates with the suggested *damping factor* estimate (Table 3).

The lowest measure of concordance was identified between a basic PR estimation *PR A* and estimations *PR C* and *PR E* for a high page level (<0.77) (Table 4) as well as for a lower page level (<0.58) (Table 5).

The first assumption was confirmed, the estimate/calculation of parameter *d* has a significant effect on PR estimation. PR estimations *PR C* and *PR E* provided the most accurate results - the highest degree of concordance was achieved with the variable *support*. Moreover, statistically significant differences in the values of residual were proved between a basic PR estimation *PR A* and estimations *PR C* and *PR E*, the highest differences being shown for a higher page level (<3). Similarly, the lowest measure of concordance was identified in values of PR between a basic PR estimation A and estimations *PR C* and *PR E*, which were estimated based on the calculated parameter *d*.

Figure 1 visualizes the differences between observed and expected probabilities of accesses of the web users, represented by the measure *support* and PR estimations *PR A* and *PR C*. Larger differences occurred in pages with a higher PR. After applying the "2

* standard deviation" rule, we identified 17 extreme cases- suspicious pages. In all cases, the expectations of the page creators were overestimated in terms of visit rate. Specifically, there are pages of level 1, which were characterized by a high PR (based on all examined PR estimations *PR A* - *PR E*) and the low observed visit rate (*support* < 2.2%).

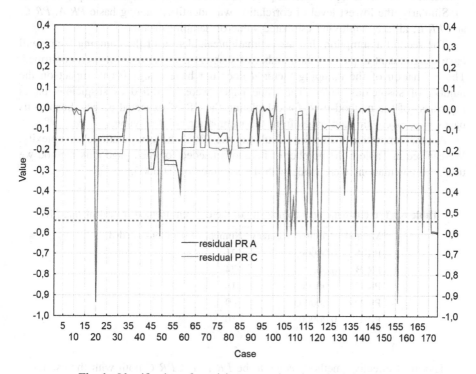

Fig. 1. Identification of suspicious pages based on the 2sigma rule

The second assumption was not confirmed, estimation of parameter d does not have a significant impact on the number of identified suspicious pages. Regardless of the used PR estimation, for the representation of the expected visit rate, the same suspicious pages were identified, i.e. the pages where the expectations of the web creators about the visit rate were overestimated.

6 Discussion

We realized experiment to verify the appropriateness of different methods for calculating the PR in the method of the analysis of differences between expected and observed probability of accesses to web pages. Before realizing the experiment, we defined two research assumptions. We assumed that the estimation/calculation of damping factor *d* would have a significant impact on the estimation of the PR. This assumption has been confirmed, the estimation/calculation of parameter d has a significant effect on PR estimation. Estimation of *PR C* and *PR E* have produced the most accurate results – we achieved the highest degree of correlation with the variable *support*. There were statistically significant differences in the residual value among the estimation of *PR A*, estimation of *PR C*, and estimation of *PR E* estimates. The largest differences were for a higher level of pages (a level lower than 3, the main page is level 0). Similarly, the lowest level of correlation was identified among basic *PR A*, *PR C*, and *PR E*; all are employing estimated value of damping factor.

The second assumption that the estimation/calculation of the damping factor will have a significant impact on the number of suspicious pages has not been confirmed. The estimation of the damping factor d does not have a significant impact on the number of suspicious pages. The same pages were identified as suspicious pages regardless of the method used for calculating the PR of expected access. Suspicious pages were overestimated pages from the webmaster point of view.

Another important factor for calculating the PR is the computational complexity. We can see in Table 6 the number of iterations needed for each page rank method we used. All calculations were made with the accuracy of 0.00005.

Table 6. The computational complexity of the different methods of calculating PR

Method	Required accuracy	Number of iterations needed
PR A	0.000005	121
PR B	0.000005	74
PR C	0.000005	18
PR D	0.000005	39
PR E	0.000005	10

The most effective method seems to be *PR E* and *PR C* both with the estimated value of the damping factor.

7   Conclusion

The different web mining methods and techniques can help to solve some typical issues of the contemporary websites, contribute to more effective personalization, improve a website structure and reorganize its web pages. The analysis of differences between expected and observed probability of accesses to web pages can give a hint if and how the combination of web structure mining method and web usage mining methods can identify misplaced pages and how they can contribute to the improvement of the website structure. The method analyses the relationship between the estimated importance of the web page from the webmaster point of view using the web structure mining method based on PR and visitors' real perception of the importance of that individual web page. The method compares the real access from the web server log file the estimated accesses using the PR algorithm. There are several options for calculation of PR. We compared these methods and proposed own modification of the PR algorithm. We employed the estimation of the damping factor and using the experiment we verified that this modification is most appropriate. Our calculated value of damping factor was 0.35 while to most commonly used value is 0.85. We compared the impact of the value of damping factor to PR estimations and methods with calculated damping factor provide the most accurate results with fewer iterations. The problem of the method may be the dynamics of the pages created. In most portals, new sites are growing every day. The PR calculation itself always works with the actual number of pages, i.e. new pages will automatically include in its calculation. However, it takes some time for the new pages of the portal to be visited and accesses will be part of the log file. This may slightly distort the estimate of the dumping factor needed for the calculation.

Acknowledgements. This work was supported by the Slovak Research and Development Agency under the contract No. APVV-14-0336, and Scientific Grant Agency of the Ministry of Education of the Slovak Republic and of Slovak Academy of Sciences under the contracts No. VEGA-1/0776/18, and by the scientific research project of the Czech Sciences Foundation Grant No. GA16-19590S.

References

1. Kapusta, J., Munk, M., Drlík, M.: Analysis of differences between expected and observed probability of accesses to web pages. In: Hwang, D., Jung, J.J., Nguyen, N.-T. (eds.) ICCCI 2014. LNCS (LNAI), vol. 8733, pp. 673–683. Springer, Cham (2014). https://doi.org/10.1007/978-3-319-11289-3_68
2. Kapusta, J., Munk, M., Drlík, M.: Identification of underestimated and overestimated web pages using PageRank and Web Usage Mining Methods. In: Nguyen, N.T. (ed.) Transactions on Computational Collective Intelligence XVIII. LNCS, vol. 9240, pp. 127–146. Springer, Heidelberg (2015). https://doi.org/10.1007/978-3-662-48145-5_7
3. Srivastava, M., Garg, R., Mishra, P.K.: Analysis of data extraction and data cleaning in web usage mining. In: Proc. 2015 Proceedings of the 2015 International Conference on Advanced Research in Computer Science Engineering & Technology (ICARCSET 2015), pp. 13:1–13:6. ACM, New York (2015). https://doi.org/10.1145/2743065.2743078
4. Migallón, H., Migallón, V., Palomino, J.A., Penadés, J.: A heuristic relaxed extrapolated algorithm for accelerating PageRank. Adv. Eng. Softw. **120**, 88–95 (2018). https://doi.org/10.1016/j.advengsoft.2016.01.024
5. Shen, Z.-L., Huang, T.-Z., Carpentieri, B., et al.: An efficient elimination strategy for solving PageRank problems. Appl. Math. Comput. **298**, 111–122 (2017). https://doi.org/10.1016/j.amc.2016.10.031
6. Csáji, B.C., Jungers, R.M., Blondel, V.D.: PageRank optimization by edge selection. Discret Appl Math **169**, 73–87 (2014). https://doi.org/10.1016/j.dam.2014.01.007
7. Buzzanca, M., Carchiolo, V., Longheu, A., et al.: Black hole metric: overcoming the pagerank normalization problem. Inf Sci (Ny) **438**, 58–72 (2018). https://doi.org/10.1016/j.ins.2018.01.033
8. Page, L., Brin, S., Motwani, R., Winograd, T.: The PageRank Citation Ranking: Bringing Order to the Web. Stanford InfoLab (1999)

9. Brin, S., Page, L.: The anatomy of a large-scale hypertextual Web search engine. Comput. Netw. ISDN Syst. **30**, 107–117 (1998). https://doi.org/10.1016/S0169-7552(98)00110-X
10. Boldi, P., Santini, M., Vigna, S.: PageRank as a function of the damping factor. In: Proceedings of the 14th International Conference World Wide Web, pp 557–566. ACM, New York (2005). https://doi.org/10.1145/1060745.1060827
11. Benincasa, C., et al.: Page Rank Algorithm. Department of Mathematics and Statics, University of Massachusetts, Amherst, Research (2006)
12. Deore, A.D., Paikrao, R.L.: Ranking Based Web Search Algorithms. Int. J. Sci. Res. Publ. **2** (10) (2012)
13. Wang, S., Tao, Y.: Efficient algorithms for finding approximate heavy hitters in personalized PageRanks. In: Proceedings of the 2018 International Conference on Management of Data - SIGMOD 2018, pp. 1113–1127. ACM Press, New York (2018). https://doi.org/10.1145/3183713.3196919
14. Yang, H., King, I., Lyu, M.R.: DiffusionRank: a possible penicillin for web spamming. In: Proceedings of the 30th Annual International ACM SIGIR Conference on Research and Development in Information Retrieval - SIGIR 2007, p. 431. ACM Press, New York (2007). https://doi.org/10.1145/1277741.1277815
15. Bar-Yossef, Z., Mashiach, L.-T.: Local approximation of Pagerank and Reverse Pagerank. In: Proceedings of the 17th ACM Conference on Information and Knowledge Management, pp. 279–288. ACM, New York (2008). https://doi.org/10.1145/1458082.1458122
16. Eiron, N., McCurley, K.S., Tomlin, J.A.: Ranking the web frontier. In: Proceedings of the 13th international conference on World Wide Web, pp. 309–318. ACM, New York (2004). https://doi.org/10.1145/988672.988714

Aggregating Crowd Opinions Using Shapley Value Regression

Yuko Sakurai[1(✉)], Jun Kawahara[2], and Satoshi Oyama[3,4]

[1] National Institute of Advanced Industrial Science and Technology,
Tokyo 135-0064, Japan
yuko.sakurai@aist.go.jp
[2] Nara Institute of Science and Technology, Nara 630-0192, Japan
jkawahara@is.naist.jp
[3] Hokkaido University, Hokkaido 060-0814, Japan
oyama@ist.hokudai.ac.jp
[4] Riken AIP, Tokyo 103-0027, Japan

Abstract. Crowdsourcing is becoming increasingly popular in various tasks. Aggregating answers from workers in crowsouring has been a widely used technique for providing many applications and services. To aggregate these answers, fair evaluation of workers is important to motivate them to give high quality answers. However, it is difficult to fairly evaluate workers if their answers show a high degree of correlation. In this paper, we propose to use the Shapley value regression as a means to address this problem. The regression technique is based on ideas developed from cooperative game theory to evaluate the relative importance of explanatory variables in reducing the error. We also exploit sparseness of worker collaboration graph to effectively calculate the Shapley value, since it requires an exponential computation time to calculate the Shapley value.

Keywords: Human computation · Crowdsourcing
Cooperative games · Shapley value regression

1 Introduction

Crowdsourcing is becoming increasingly popular in various tasks, such as classifying data, gathering opinions, and reviewing products. A requester can ask many workers around the world to do his/her tasks at relatively low cost by using crowdsourcing services, such as Amazon Mechanical Turk (AMT). Crowdsourcing has also been attracting attention from artificial intelligence (AI) and multi-agent systems (MAS) researchers as a platform for *human computation*, which tackles problems that can only be solved by computers. Human computation is based on the idea of the wisdom of crowds and solves problems by combining the forces of many people. It utilizes human intelligence as functions in computer programs [6,12,14]. Although an advantage of crowdsourcing is that

© Springer Nature Switzerland AG 2018
M. Kaenampornpan et al. (Eds.): MIWAI 2018, LNAI 11248, pp. 151–160, 2018.
https://doi.org/10.1007/978-3-030-03014-8_13

a large workforce is available at low cost, the quality of the results is occasionally problematic. For example, workers in image classification label sample images that are used as training data in machine learning. Although the cost of the labels incurred by workers in crowdsourcing is lower than that by experts, the possibility of errors in the former generally exceeds that of the latter. Thus, one of the most important and attractive research topics for crowdsourcing that has been studied is how to control the quality of the obtained results [3,4,9,10,13].

In this paper, we consider a way of controlling the quality of micro tasks in which task results are determined by aggregating multiple workers' opinions, such as the way they rate items. When they rate items workers often give the same scores to several items in accordance with their subjective evaluations. One straightforward way to accurately determine ratings obtained through crowd-sourcing is to ask multiple workers to rate items and use the majority of the scores they provided. This corresponds to treating the quality of the results given by different workers equally and simply considering the score that receives the largest number of votes as the true one. In crowdsourcing, however, since workers' abilities are not even, treating all ratings given by different workers equally is not always a good way to infer the true ratings.

For example, let us consider an online product review. Some online product review sites provide scores by professional reviewers as well as amateurs (community) reviewers. Professional reviews are reliable and consistent, but expensive and limited coverage. On the other hand, amateur reviews are sometimes unreliable and inconsistent but free and high coverage. Thus, we want to predict the professional scores for items for which only amateur scores are available. We will make a regression model to predict the professional score from amateur scores.

Recently, studies on false-name manipulations/sibyl attacks have been conducted by AI researchers, especially, with regard to multi-agent systems [15]. False-name manipulation means that a single worker inputs the identical answer multiple times by using multiple fictitious names, e.g., multiple e-mail addresses. Such a dishonest action is very difficult to detect, since identifying each worker on the Internet is virtually impossible. The workers can use multiple identities to write the same answer many times to influence the aggregated answer or to easily obtain more money. Even if the accuracy is relatively high in such cases, a requester needs to recognize that their contributions to obtain the correct answer are weak. Thus, in this research, we utilize the Shapley value which is the most popular solution concept in cooperative games to measure the contribution made by each worker.

The Shapley value indicates how to share the obtained profit among members in a coalition [11]. The Shapley value is the average marginal contribution of each agent, averaging over all possible order according to which the grand coalition built up from the empty coalition. The Shapley value is known as the unique solution concept that satisfies all desirable properties regarding fairness: efficiency, symmetry, null-player, and additivity.

In a supervised prediction model, it predict professional scores from amateur scores in the example of online review we explained above. Training data consists of items with both professional and amateur scores and test data consists of items with only amateur scores. Here, multicolinearity often occurs, i.e., there exist duplicated or highly correlated workers. For example, two different workers always give the same score. The weights in the regression model do not reflect contributions of workers: some workers can have too much influence. We determines weights for variables in a regression model with multicolinearity, since the weight reflects actual contribution of the variable in reducing the error. In this paper, we apply the Shapley value regression [7], which is based on the idea of the Shapley value.

Although the Shapley value has good properties, we must execute regression analysis for all possible subset for workers, that is, 2^n subsets when the number of workers is n. Thus, the Shapley value regression has been applied to small problems with less than 10 players in existing works. We have to develop the techniques to effectively calculate Shapley value regression for a crowdsourcing including a huge number of tasks and workers. In this paper, we utilize the frontier-based search developed in [5]. The frontier-based search constructs a zero-suppressed binary decision diagram (ZDD) [8] that concisely represents all the subgraphs of a given graph satisfying specified conditions. We use the frontier-based search to enumerate all connected components in a worker collaboration graph. We show that our approach can find all connected components efficiently.

The paper is organized as follows. We introduce the Shapley value in Sect. 2. and then we describe the Shapley value regression in Sect. 3. In Sect. 4, we propose the efficient computational method for the Shapley value by using worker collaboration graph. In Sect. 5, we introduce the frontier-based method to efficiently enumerate all connected components in a given graph. Finally, we show the experimental results by using the real-world crowdsourcing data.

2   The Shapley Value

Let $N = \{1, 2, \ldots, n\}$ be the set of agents. We assume a characteristic function game in this paper. The value of coalition S is given by characteristic function v, which assigns a value to each set of workers (coalition) $S \subseteq N$. The formal definition is as follows.

Definition 1 (Characteristic function). *A characteristic function assigns a real-value to each non-empty subset of agents:* $v\colon 2^N \to \mathbb{R}_+ \equiv \{x \in \mathbb{R} \mid x \geq 0\}$ *with* $v(\emptyset) = 0$.

In this paper, we assume that a characteristic function is non-negative. We also assume that a characteristic function is *super-additive*, i.e.,

$$\forall S, \forall S' \text{ s.t. } S \cap S' = \emptyset, \ v(S) + v(S') \leq v(S \cup S'). \tag{1}$$

Thus, grand coalition has the highest value among all coalitions.

Cooperative game theory provides a number of solution concepts that represent the way of assigning the obtained profit to the participants, such as the

Shapley value, the core and the nucleolus. These solution concepts have already been adopted in the computer science literature. In particular, the Shapley value has attracted the most attention. It is the unique solution concept that satisfies the axioms of Pareto efficiency, the null property, symmetry, and additivity.

Here, we will introduce the Shapley value [11]. Let $\gamma_i(v)$ be a distributed payoff of agent i for a given characteristic function v. The Shapley value is well-known as a unique division scheme in cooperative games with characteristic functions that satisfy the following four axioms:

Efficiency. The entire available payoff is distributed among players:

$$\sum_{i \in N} \gamma_i(v) = v(N).$$

Symmetry. Distributed payoffs do not depend on the agents' identities. The agents who have the contribution obtain the same payment.

Null player. Agents that contribute nothing to the value of any coalition get nothing.

Additivity. The sum of payoffs in two different games is equal to the payoff in the combined game:

Definition 2 (The Shapley Value). *Let s be the number of agents in subset $S \subseteq N$. The Shapley value for agenti is defined as follows:*

$$\gamma_i(v) = \sum_{S \subseteq N \setminus \{i\}} \frac{|S|!(|N| - |S| - 1)!}{|N|!} [v(S \cup \{i\}) - v(S)]. \tag{2}$$

Intuitively, the Shapley value the average marginal contribution of each agent over all possible orders in which the agents may join the coalition.

Example 1. We consider that a characteristic function game is for two agents, 1 and 2. The characteristic functions are $v(\{1\}) = 8$, $v(\{2\}) = 8$, $v(\{1,2\}) = 20$. The Shapley value for agent 1 is calculated as follow: Her marginal contribution is $8 - 0 = 8$ when agent 1 makes a coalition from an empty coalition, and her marginal contribution is $20 - 8 = 12$ when she joins a coalition after agent 2. The probability that each case happens is $1/2$. As a result, the Shapley value of agent 1 is $4 + 6 = 10$. As a similar manner, the Shapley value of agent 2 is 10. The Shapley value of each agent is identical since these agents are symmetry. Furthermore, the sum of the Shapley value for both agents is 20, which is equal to the value of grand coalition.

3   The Shapley Value Regression

In this section, we will introduce the Shapley value regression to estimate the contributions made by each worker. This regression was proposed in Lipovetsky and Conklin [7] and has been widely applied to the analysis of real-world data sets. The *Features Games* proposed by Azari Soufiani *et al.* [2] share a similar problem setting with the Shapley value regression.

Assume we have I items and J workers. Worker j give a numeric score x_{ij} for item i. Let t_i be the true score for item i given by a specialist. Our objective is to aggregate workers' scores to approximate the true scores. To aggregate workers' scores, we adopt a linear model

$$y_i = \sum_j w_j x_{ij}. \tag{3}$$

The weight w_j for worker j can be determined by minimizing the error function

$$E^2 = \sum_i (t_i - y_i)^2 = \sum_i (t_i - \sum_j w_j x_{ij})^2. \tag{4}$$

However, the weights determined by this approach do not reflect the true importance of workers if there are two or more workers who gave the similar scores for the items. Let vectors $\boldsymbol{x}_j$ and $\boldsymbol{x}_k$ denote sets of scores given by worker j and k respectively. This assume that $\boldsymbol{x}_j = \boldsymbol{x}_k$, $w_j \boldsymbol{x}_j + w_k \boldsymbol{x}_k$ take the same value for any values w_j and w_k that satisfy $w_j + w_k = constant$. For example $w_j \boldsymbol{x}_j + w_k \boldsymbol{x}_k$ takes the same value both for $w_j = 0, w_k = 1$ and $w_j = 1, w_k = 0$ and so is the loss function. Therefore, if we use conventional regression, weight w_j does not always reflect the importance of the worker.

The Shapley value regression determines the weight for workers based on their Shapley values. In this case, the characteristic function for a coalition (set of workers) is $1 - E_S^2$, where E_S^2 is the error of regression using the set of workers S. (We assume scores are centered and normalized so that E_S^2 takes a value in $[0, 1]$). Then the weight for worker j is determined by

$$w_j = \frac{SV_j}{r_j} \tag{5}$$

where SV_j is the Shapley value for worker j and r_j is the correlation between the scores of worker j and the true scores.

Example 2. Let's consider a task of quality scores for wines. The score for each wine is assigned from 1 to 10 as shown in Table 1. We want to predict scores of the professional taster by aggregating scores of amateur tasters. In this example, scores by amateur taster 3 and amateur taster 4 are examples of multicollinearity. By applying the Shapley value regression, we give the identical weight to both amateur tasters 3 and 4.

Table 2 shows the values of the characteristic function obtained from regressions using subsets of workers. We can see that even if worker 4 joins the coalition including worker 3, the value of the characteristic function does not change. For example, the values of the characteristic function for $\{2, 3\}$ and $\{2, 3, 4\}$ are the same.

Table 3 shows the Shapley values of workers computed from the values of the characteristic functions in Table 2. We can see that workers 3 and 4 have the same Shapley value. The Shapley values of all workers sum up to one.

Table 1. Score of each wine

	Pro	Amateur			
		1	2	3	4
Wine A	8	10	9	7	7
Wine B	9	9	6	10	10
Wine C	7	8	5	6	6
Wine D	10	6	5	8	8

Table 2. Values of the characteristics function for the example

Set of workers S	Characteristic function $v(S)$
$\{1\}$	0.2800
$\{2\}$	0.0419
$\{3\}$	0.4629
$\{4\}$	0.4629
$\{1,2\}$	0.4118
$\{1,3\}$	0.7641
$\{1,4\}$	0.7641
$\{2,3\}$	0.4861
$\{2,4\}$	0.4861
$\{3,4\}$	0.4629
$\{1,2,3\}$	1.0000
$\{1,2,4\}$	1.0000
$\{1,3,4\}$	0.7641
$\{2,3,4\}$	0.4861
$\{1,2,3,4\}$	1.0000

4   Efficient Computation of the Shapley Values Using the Worker Collaboration Graph

In computing the Shapley value, we have to perform a regression analysis for every subset of workers. Therefore, if the number of workers is large, computing the Shapley value becomes intractable. For this reason, the Shapley value regression has been applied only to problems with a small number of explanatory variables. To apply the Shapley value regression to integrate opinions of many crowd workers, it is necessary to reduce the cost of computing the Shapley value. One of the traditional approach is approximating the Shapley value by sampling coalitions. Recently, Azari Soufiani it et al. [2] proposed a way to compute approximate the Shapley value by clustering workers on the basis of their similarity.

Table 3. Shapley values of workers

Worker i	Shapley value $\gamma_i(v)$
1	0.3903
2	0.1255
3	0.2421
4	0.2421

In crowdsourcing, however, the numbers of workers assigned to a task is usually limited even if the total number of workers is very large. For example, we usually ask five workers at most to answer the same question because of the monetary cost. In general, crowdsourced data have the following characteristics.

- A worker does not necessarily perform all the tasks.
- A task is not necessarily done by all the workers.

The number of workers who worked on the same task is much smaller than the total number of workers. Therefore, the set of all workers can be divided into disjoint sets of workers who have worked together. Preceding studies on the Shapley value regression did not consider such situations. We can exploit this *sparseness* of relations among workers to efficiently compute exact Shapley value.

If no one in a worker set S has never worked on the same task with anyone in another worker set S', the value of the characteristic function of the union of the two sets can be computed by the sum of the values of functions of each set:

$$v(S \cup S') = v(S) + v(S'). \qquad (6)$$

Thus, we do not have to perform computationally expensive regression analysis for $v(S \cup S')$ if we have already performed regression for S and S'.

We represent relationships between workers in a worker collaboration graph, where a node represents a worker and a link between two nodes represents that the two workers have worked on the same task. Since the value of the characteristic function of a set of workers is calculated as the sum of the values of the function of its connected components, we have to perform regression analysis only for the connected components.

5   The Frontier-Based Search

Recently an efficient method called the frontier-based search has been proposed for enumerating all the subgraphs of a graph satisfying given conditions [5]. We utilize the frontier-based search to find sets of workers for which we have to actually perform regression analysis. This can largely reduce the time to compute the Shapley value since regression analysis accounts for a large part of computation in evaluating the characteristic function.

Table 4. Number of connected components

Num. of workers	Num. of connected components	Max. Num. of coalitions	Reduction rates
10	86.6	1013	8.5%
15	3072.6	32752	9.3%
20	96585.8	1048555	9.2%

The frontier-based search constructs a zero-suppressed binary decision diagram (ZDD) [8] that concisely represents all the subgraphs of a given graph satisfying specified conditions. A ZDD is a variation of the binary decision diagram (BDD) which is a graph structure that represents a logic function [1]. A ZDD can efficiently represent a set of combinations by applying the following two reduction rules: (1) delete all nodes whose high-edge directly points to the 0-terminal node and (2) share all equivalent nodes. A high-/low-edge means the presence/absence of an element in a combination. While a path from the root node to the 1-terminal node in a ZDD represents that a combination with corresponding elements exists in a set of combinations, a path from the root node to the 0-terminal node represents that such a combination does not exist in a set of combinations.

Given a graph, we can regard a subgraph of the graph as a set of edges, and a set of subgraphs as a set of (edge) combinations, which can be represented as a ZDD. The frontier-based search directly constructs such a ZDD in a breadth-first manner. By storing some information into nodes of a ZDD in the process of the construction, the frontier-based search can impose various conditions on subgraphs such as the number of edges, the number of connected components, the connectivity of specified vertices, and so on. Utilizing this property, Kawahara *et al.* [5] proposed an algorithm based on the frontier-based search for enumerating all connected components. We apply this algorithm to enumerate all connected components, i.e., sets of workers who have done the same tasks.

6   Analysis of Real Crowdsourcing Data

To confirm how much computation is reduced by only considering connected components, we conducted experiments using real crowdsourcing data. *Web Search Relevance Judging Dataset* [16] consists of 2,665 query-URL pairs with five-grade relevance judgments by workers. The total number of workers is 177 and each query-URL pair receives six judgments on average. In addition, the ground truth by the agreement of nine experts is provided.

We randomly selected 10, 15 and 20 workers and made adjacency matrices that represent whether two workers have ever labeled the same data. The Frontier Method was used to enumerate all connected components of the graph. Table 4 shows the average of the numbers of components found in five trials and the

number of possible coalitions. We can see that the number of coalitions we have
to consider in calculating the Shapley value was largely reduced to less than 10%
in all cases.

7 Conclusion

Aggregating answers from workers in crowdsouring has been a widely used technique for providing many applications and services. We proposed to use the
Shapley value regression as a means to address the issue of fair evaluation for
crowd workers. The regression technique is based on ideas developed from cooperative game theory to evaluate the relative importance of explanatory variables
in reducing the error. We exploited the sparseness of worker collaboration graph
to effectively calculate the Shapley value. In experimental evaluations, by applying the frontier-based search, we showed that the computational cost is reduced
by only considering connected components.

While the computational cost of the Shapley value regression can be largely
reduced by performing regression analysis only for connected components in a
worker collaboration graph, further improvement in computational efficiency is
needed to apply it for aggregating the opinions of workers in large crowd. One
possible approach is restricting regression analysis only for k-connected components in a worker collaboration graph. Another research direction is extending
our approach to classification problems.

Acknowledgement. This work was partially supported by JSPS KAKENHI Grant
Numbers JP18H03 299, JP18K04610, JP15H02782, Kayamori Foundation of Informa-
tional Science Advancement, and the Telecommunications Advancement Foundation.

References

1. Akers, S.B.: Binary decision diagrams. IEEE Trans. Comput. **C-27**(6), 509–516
   (1978)
2. Azari Soufiani, H., Chickering, D.M., Charles, D.X., Parkes, D.C.: Approximating
   the shapley value via multi-issue decompositions. In: Proceedings of the 2014 International Conference on Autonomous Agents and Multi-agent Systems (AAMAS
   2014), pp. 1209–1216 (2014)
3. Baba, Y., Kashima, H.: Statistical quality estimation for general crowdsourcing
   tasks. In: Proceedings of the 19th ACM SIGKDD International Conference on
   Knowledge Discovery and Data Mining (KDD 2013), pp. 554–562 (2013)
4. Duan, L., Oyama, S., Sato, H., Kurihara, M.: Separate or joint? Estimation of
   multiple labels from crowdsourced annotations. Expert Syst. Appl. **41**(13), 5723–
   5732 (2014)
5. Kawahara, J., Inoue, T., Iwashita, H., Minato, S.: Frontier-based search for enumerating all constrained subgraphs with compressed representation. IEICE Trans.
   Fundam. Electron. Commun. Comput. Sci. E **100.A**(9), 1773–1784 (2017)
6. Law, E., Ahn, L.V.: Human Computation. Morgan & Claypool Publishers (2011)
7. Lipovetsky, S., Conklin, M.: Analysis of regression in game theory approach. Appl.
   Stoch. Model. Bus. Ind. **17**(4), 319–330 (2001)

8. Minato, S.: Zero-suppressed BDDs for set manipulation in combinatorial problems. In: The 30th Design Automation Conference (DAC 1993), pp. 272–277 (1993)

9. Oyama, S., Baba, Y., Sakurai, Y., Kashima, H.: Accurate integration of crowd-sourced labels using workers' self-reported confidence scores. In: Proceedings of the 23rd International Joint Conference on Artificial Intelligence (IJCAI 2013), pp. 2554–2560 (2013)

10. Sakurai, Y., Okimoto, T., Oka, M., Shinoda, M., Yokoo, M.: Ability grouping of crowd workers via reward discrimination. In: Proceedings of the First AAAI Conference on Human Computation and Crowdsourcing (HCOMP 2013) (2013)

11. Shapley, L.S.: A value for n-person games. In: Kuhn, H., Tucker, A. (eds.) In Contributions to the Theory of Games, vol. II, pp. 307–317. Princeton University Press (1953)

12. Shaw, A.D., Horton, J.J., Chen, D.L.: Designing incentives for inexpert human raters. In: Proceedings of the ACM 2011 Conference on Computer Supported Cooperative Work (CSCW 2011), pp. 275–284 (2011)

13. Sheng, V., Provost, F., Ipeirotis, P.: Get another label? Improving data quality and data mining using multiple, noisy labelers. In: Proceeding of the 14th ACM SIGKDD International Conference on Knowledge Discovery and Data Mining (KDD 2008), pp. 614–622 (2008)

14. Snow, R., O'Connor, B., Jurafsky, D., Ng, A.Y.: Cheap and fast - but is it good? Evaluating non-expert annotations for natural language tasks. In: Proceedings of the Conference on Empirical Methods in Natural Language Processing (EMNLP 2008), pp. 254–263 (2008)

15. Yokoo, M., Sakurai, Y., Matsubara, S.: Robust combinatorial auction protocol against false-name bids. Artif. Intell. **130**(2), 167–181 (2001)

16. Zhou, D., Basu, S., Mao, Y., Platt, J.C.: Learning from the wisdom of crowds by minimax entropy. In: Advances in Neural Information Processing Systems 25 (NIPS 2012) (2012)

A Hierarchical Conditional Attention-Based Neural Networks for Paraphrase Generation

Khuong Nguyen-Ngoc[1], Anh-Cuong Le[2(✉)], and Viet-Ha Nguyen[1]

[1] VNU University of Engineering and Technology, Ha Noi City, Vietnam
khuongnn@dhhp.edu.vn, hanv@vnu.edu.vn
[2] NLP-KD Lab, Faculty of Information and Technology, Ton Duc Thang University,
Ho Chi Minh City, Vietnam
leanhcuong@tdtu.edu.vn

Abstract. Sequence-to-Sequence (Seq2Seq) learning has immense interest in recent years. The prosperous approach of end-to-end training fashion using encoder-decoder neural networks like machine translation has sprouted active research in transduction tasks such as abstractive summarization or especially Paraphrase Generation (PG). Dealing with paraphrase generation problem, one of the most intrinsic obstruction of existing solutions do not pay enough attention to the fact that words and sentences in particular context own differential importance. Consequently, the loss of crucial information probably occurs and irrelevant paraphrasing components are generated. To overcome these barriers, an emerging Hierarchical Conditional Attention-based Neural Networks (HCANN) architecture to construct end-to-end text generation framework is proposed. More specifically, included method in that represents hierarchy of document along with conditional decoder for paraphrase generation processes. Quantitative evaluation of the method on several benchmark paraphrase datasets demonstrates its efficiency and performance capability by a significant margin.

Keywords: Sequence-to-sequence learning
Hierarchical Conditional Attention-based Neural Networks
Paraphrase generation

1 Introduction

Paraphrase generation concerns the Natural Language Processing (NLP) task of detecting and generating paraphrases. Concretely, re-statements of a text or passage are obtained, however it must convey the same meaning and its component parts consist different words from the source. It recently extends to plenty tasks as answering question, summarizing and reasoning in natural language [19]. There are several traditional methods for paraphrase generation such as automatically learned complex paraphrase patterns [39], hand-crafted

© Springer Nature Switzerland AG 2018
M. Kaenampornpan et al. (Eds.): MIWAI 2018, LNAI 11248, pp. 161–174, 2018.
https://doi.org/10.1007/978-3-030-03014-8_14

rules and thesaurus-based [20], semantic-driven natural language generation [13] or a leverage Statistical Machine Learning (SML) method [37].

More recently, a popular approach to Seq2Seq learning [33] have been effectively used to solve various tasks in NLP as below: language modeling [34], machine translation [4], speech recognition [15], and dialogue systems [30]. The essence of PG can be formulated machine translation task that is performed within a single language and totally can be considered as a Seq2Seq learning task. However, not much work has been done in this area with regard to cutting edge deep neural networks like Neural Machine Translation (NMT) [21]. In sequel, Neural Attention Mechanism (NAM) has been used for textual entailment generation [12] which has brought impressive results. In fact, PG is also a type of bi-directional semantic relation between text fragments and thus the methods of using NAM in Neural Paraphrase Generation (NPG) [26],[9] have significantly outperformed over previous works. Notably, Bahdanau et al. [1] proposed a prevailing attention mechanism that achieved in NMT.

Moreover, Prakash et al. [26] has proposed using the prevailing attention mechanism in stacked residual Long-Short-Term-Memory (LSTM) networks architecture for paraphrase generation. It outperformed state-of-the-art models for Seq2Seq learning problem but the authors also stated that the attention-based neural network for machine translation is not suitable for paraphrase generation because not all words in the source sequence should be substituted for paraphrasing.

Based on the latest achievements of both the generator by adopting the attentive Seq2Seq architecture with copy mechanism [1,28] and the evaluator by adopting the deep matching model based on the decomposable attention model [8,24], Zichao Li et al. [16] are improved significantly its performance over previous works. However, the understanding and paraphrasing of long documents is still far from satisfactory wish [38]. So far, almost no research has investigated the effectiveness of the representation of long document and the role of each part of paraphrasing sequences on the performance of paraphrase generation.

A novel neural network architecture being able to yield paraphrasing sequence through a fully paraphrase generation is proposed in this article. More specifically, a encoder-decoder model is built by adopting hierarchical Long-Short-Term-Memory mentioned in [18] for paraphrase generation. In that, uni-directional LSTMs is substituted by bidirectional GRUs (Bi-GRUs), in which the representations of sentences are learned by a Bi-GRUs model whose inputs are words and the representation of the document is learned by another Bi-GRUs model whose inputs are sentences. A conditional attention decoder [29] is accepted within paraphrases sequence at two-level attention of word and sentence respectively.

Consequently, the following contributions to paraphrase generation are achieved:

- firstly, presenting a novel approach by casting the role of hierarchical representation of documents in the encoder-decoder framework

- secondly, proposing an new end-to-end conditional attention-based neural networks architecture
- finally, exploring potentialities of HCANN with word-level and sentence-level modeling. Overall, the performance of suggested model is rather competitive with the existing cutting edge attention-based neural paraphrase generation solutions.

2 Related Work

There are several different approaches to address the paraphrase generation as below: knowledge-driven approaches [19], hand-crafted rules [20], automatically learned complex paraphrase patterns [39], thesaurus-based, semantic analysis-driven [13]. In another case, Wubben et al. [37] have crawl news headlines from Google News to build a large aligned monolingual corpus that were used in a phrase-based machine translation framework for sentential paraphrase generation. Subsequently, Zhao et al. [40] proposes learning phrase-based paraphrase tables and devising a log-linear SMT model based on combining multiple resources and feature functions. In term of a specific application [39], bilingual parallel corpora [2], determining candidate paraphrases by applying a multi-pivot approach [41] are considered.

So far, investigating impact and effectiveness of dataset size to paraphrase generation problem has failed or not mentioned in prior works except for this article. Recently, in Weiting [35], PPDB 2.0 so-called Annotated-PPDB developing from PPDB 1.0's paraphrasability is revealed. It has 6 common sizes respectively (S, M, L, XL, XXL, XXXL). Besides, the author also publishes another paraphrase dataset namely ML-Paraphrase for the purpose of evaluating performance of bigram paraphrase generation task. The research points out that the smaller dataset contains only better-scoring, high-precision paraphrases, while the larger ones aim at high coverage. In comparison with baseline methods, admittedly, numerous experiments with merely L-sized dataset from PPDB 2.0 for training and testing are utilized and carried out in the proposed model.

Further more, there are several works based on usage of residual connections combined with LSTM neural networks. DenseNet et al. [10] utilized dense connections over every layer in image recognition. By contrast, Wu et al. [36] proposed deep residual LSTM with attention mechanism for machine translation. Last but not least, Prakash et al. [26] have used residual connections with stack LSTMs for paraphrase generation tasks which achieved perspective results in PPDB, WikiAnswer and MSCOCO datasets. It is worth noting that it is the first and foremost work that exploiting the role of the attention mechanism in paraphrase generation issue.

3 Model Description

3.1 Problem Formalization

Let D denote a paragraph or a document, which is comprised of N_D sentences, $D = s_1, s_2, ..., s_{N_D}, < eod >$. An additional "$< eod >$" token is appended to each document. Each sentence s is comprised of a sequence of tokens $s_i = w_{i,1}, w_{i,2}, ..., w_{i,N_{i,s}}$ where $N_{i,s}$ denotes the length of the sentence i, each sentence ending with an "$< oes >$" token. The word w is associated with a K-dimensional embedding $x_w, x_w = x_w^1, x_w^2, ..., x_w^K$. Let V denote vocabulary size. Each sentence s is associated with a K dimensional representation e_s.

An encoder is a neural model where output units are directly connected with or identical to input units. Typically, inputs are compressed into a representation using neural models (encoding), which is then used to reconstruct it back (decoding). The encoder first compresses document D into a vector representation e_D and then reconstructs D based on e_D.

For clarification, the following notations are used in encoder and decoder at first:

- $h_{i,j}^w$ and $h_{k,m}^s$ denote hidden vectors from LSTM models in encoder component; h_t^{dw} denotes hidden vectors from LSTM models in decoder component, the subscripts of which indicate time-step t, the second character of superscripts of which indicate operations at word level (w) or sequence level (s).
- x_t^w denote word-level embedding for word at position t in terms of its residing sentence or document at encoding stage.
- y_t^w denotes word-level embedding for word at position t decoding stage.

Aiming to estimate a generation probability $p(y_1, ..., y_T | D)$ of a given document D, a paraphrases sequence $Y = \{y_1, ..., y_T\}$ is generated in accordance to $p(y_1, ..., y_T | D)$. In the following section, how to construct $p(y_1, ..., y_T | D)$ and how to learn will be elaborated.

3.2   Conditional Attention-Based Encoder-Decoder Model

An overview of the proposed model is presented in the Fig. 1. It takes D as input and consists of 2 main components: encoders for D using word and sentence embedding and the conditional dual-attention decoder that takes the learned annotations of the input sequences and its previous hidden state to estimate the conditional probability $p(y_t | D, Y_{t-1})$ where $Y_{t-1} = (y_1, y_2, ..., y_{t-1})$

The Encoder and Word Attention. The new model as illustrated in the Fig. 1, contains two related encoders. The first encoder's task is to transform the input sequence words ($w_{i,1}, ..., w_{i,N_{i,s}}$) into a sequence of annotations ($h_{i,1}^w, ..., h_{i,N_{i,s}}^w$). The second encoder's task is to transform the input sequence sentences ($c_{1,t}', ..., c_{N_D,t}'$) into a sequence of annotations ($h_{1,t}^s, ..., h_{N_D,t}^s$) that are fed later to the attention mechanism in the decoder. These encoders have the same architecture presented in Fig. 3 with one difference. The only difference is in the encoder responsible for learning annotations for the sentence vectors sequence X, where the embedding layer is removed because the model is directly fed with embedding vectors is given by

$$h_{i,k}^w = concat(\overrightarrow{h_{i,k}^w}, \overleftarrow{h_{i,k}^w}) \tag{1}$$

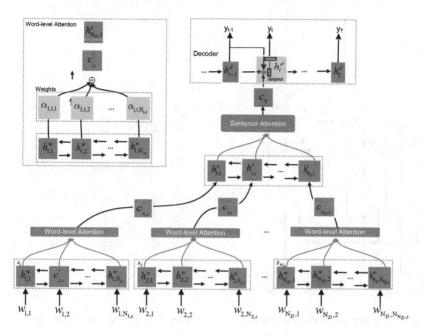

Fig. 1. Hierarchical Conditional Attention-based Neural Networks

Let consider $c'_{i,t}$ as a sentence represent vector. $\forall i \in \{1, ..., N_D\}, c'_{i,t}$ is designed by

$$c'_{i,t} = \sum_{j=1}^{N_{i,s}} \alpha_{i,t,j} h_{i,j} \tag{2}$$

$\{c'_{i,t}\}_{i=1}^{N_D}$ are then utilized as input of an sentence level encoder and transformed to $h_{1,t}^s, ..., h_{N_D,t}^s$ as hidden vectors of the context.

Different from the classic attention mechanism, conditional word level attention in HCANN depends on both the hidden states of the decoder and the hidden states of the sentence level encoder. It works in a reverse order by first weighting $\{h_{N_D,j}^w\}_{j=1}^{N_D,s}$ and then moving towards $\{h_{1,j}^w\}_{j=1}^{N_{1,s}}$ along the sentence sequence. $\forall i \in N_D, ..., 1, i \in \{1, ..., N_{i,s}\}$, weight $\alpha_{i,t,j}$ is calculated as

$$e_{i,t,j} = \eta(h_{t-1}^d, h_{i+1,t}^s, h_{i,t}^s, h_{i-1,t}^s, h_{i,j}^w)$$
$$\alpha_{i,t,j} = \frac{exp(e_{i,t,j})}{\sum_{k=1}^{N_{i,s}} exp(e_{i,t,k})} \tag{3}$$

where $h_{N_D+1,t}^s$ and $h_{0,t}^s$ is initialized with a isotropic Gaussian distribution, h_{t-1}^d is the $(t-1)$-th hidden state of the decoder, and $\eta()$ is a Multi-Layer Perceptron (MLP) with tanh as an activation function.

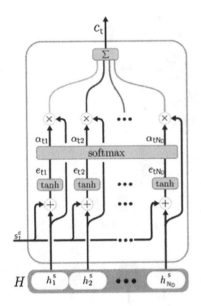

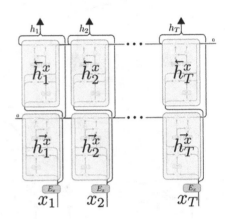

Fig. 2. The attention decoder model   **Fig. 3.** Bidirectional RNN encoder

The Decoder. The decoder is in charge of estimating the conditional probability $p(y_t|D, Y_{t-1})$ at each time step t. It is also a RNN, but with many small components with an architecture partially similar to the architecture proposed by Sennrich et al. [29] and Khuong et al. [22]. Herein, the main differences between the existing architectures are presented. It takes as input the annotations $H^w = (h^w_{i,1}, ..., h^w_{i,N_{i,s}})$ and $H^s = (h^s_{1,t}, ..., h^s_{N_D,t})$ of respectively the sequence word W and sequence sentence S. The sentence annotation are the output of the previously presented encoders, its own previous hidden state h^d_{t-1} and the previous predicted target word y_{t-1}. Different from previous work of Khuong et al. [22], replacing the standard RNN decoder and sentence attention mechanism with a new conditional Gated Recurrent Unit (GRU) with attention is carried out in the proposed model. As a result, the new architecture has 3 components and takes as input its previous state h^d_{t-1}, the previous predicted word y_{i-1} and the annotations $H^s = (h^s_{1,t}, ..., h^s_{N_D,t})$ to compute its new hidden state s_i that is later used to predict y_t:

$$h^d_t = cGRU_{att}(h^d_{t-1}, y_{t-1}, H^s) \qquad (4)$$

The first component is a classic GRU architecture Cho et al. [3] that computes an intermediate hidden state s^d_t using the following equations:

$$s^d_t = GRU_1(y_{t-1}, h^d_{t-1}) = (1 - z'_t) \odot \tilde{s}^d_t + z'_t \odot h^d_{t-1} \qquad (5)$$

where

$$\tilde{s}_t^d = tanh(W'E_{y_{t-1}} + r_t' \odot U'h_{t-1}^d)$$
$$r_t' = \sigma(W_r'E_{y_{t-1}} + U_r'h_{t-1}^d) \tag{6}$$
$$z_t' = \sigma(W_z'E_{y_{t-1}} + U_z'h_{t-1}^d)$$

E is the target words embedding matrix, $W', U', W_r', U_r', W_r', U_r'$ are weights and σ is the sigmoid activation function.

The second component is almost the same attention mechanism as Bahdanau et al. [1]. It takes $H^s = (h_{1,t}^s, ..., h_{N_D,t}^s)$ and s_t^d and computes the new context vector c_t. The goal of the attention mechanism is to generate a context vector c_t conveying information from a given annotations sequence $H^s = (h_{1,t}^s, ..., h_{N_D,t}^s)$. It takes also the intermediate hidden state s_t^d as input. The Fig. 2 provides an illustration of the model. The first step is to compute the energies e_{tj} from each annotation $h_{t,j}^s$ using the alignment model:

$$e_{tj} = v_a^{N_D} tanh(U_a s_t^d + W_a h_{j,t}^s) \tag{7}$$

where v_a, U_a, W_a are learned weights. Then, the energies are used to compute the probabilities $\beta_{t,j}$ defined by:

$$\beta t, j = \frac{exp(e_{t,j})}{\sum_{k=1}^{N_D} exp(e_{t,k})} \tag{8}$$

These probabilities determine the importance of the influence that each element from the input has on the context c_t computed through this weighted sum:

$$c_t = \sum_{i=1}^{N_D} \beta_{i,t} h_{i,t}^s \tag{9}$$

The third and last component of the conditional GRU with attention, is a second classic GRU that takes s_t^d and the context vector c_t to finally produce the new hidden state h_t^d

$$h_t^d = GRU_2(s_t^d, c_t) = (1 - z_t) \odot \tilde{h}_t^d + z_t \odot s_t^d \tag{10}$$

where

$$\tilde{h}_t^d = tanh(Wc_t + r_t \odot Us_t^d)$$
$$r^t = \sigma(W_r c_t + U_r s_t^d) \tag{11}$$
$$z_t = \sigma(W_z c_t + Uz s_t^d)$$

in which W, U, W_r, U_r, W_z, U_z are weights and σ is the sigmoid activation function. Notably, the recurrence in this architecture is not produced at the level of each GRU but is assured for the whole cGRUatt thanks to the intermediate hidden state s_t^d that assures the link between the 3 different components.

Where a maxout layer Goodfellow et al. [6] is used by Bahdanau et al. [1] to compute the conditional probability $p(y_t | h_{t-1}^d, c_t)$ before applying a softmax layer. Sennrich et al. [29] uses a feedforward hidden layer. Once the new hidden state h_t^d and the context vector c_t are computed, they are fed to the deep out layer in addition to a vector representing the previously generated word y_{t-1}.

$$p(y_t|h_{t-1}^d, c_t) = softmax(d_t W_o) \qquad (12)$$

where

$$d_t = tanh(h_t^d W_{d1} + E_{y_{t-1}} W_{d2} + c_t W_{d3}) \qquad (13)$$

where $W_{d1}, W_{d2}, W_{d3}, W_o$ are weights.

4   Experimental Settings

4.1   Dataset

Experiments are conducted on two different well-known paraphase datasets PPDB 2.0 [25] and WikiAnswers.

PPDB 2.0 has pre-packaged in 6 sizes: S to XXXL. Although, for the purpose of conducting experiments to compare with the existing works, only the paraphrase dataset PPDB 2.0 with size L [25] is utilized. It contains about 18 million paraphrases. According to that, 5.3 million paraphrases (mainly short phrases) are selected that makes it appropriate for paraphrase generation following statement in [19].

The paraphrases in WikiAnswers[5] have existed as different questions which were tagged by the users as similar questions. Although, WikiAnswers consists of more than 29 million instances, random choice of 5.3 million paraphrases (mainly long phrases) are carried out for both training and testing of the model.

In these datasets, K-Fold Cross-Validation method has been used to evaluate effectiveness of the proposed model. Regarding K-fold cross-validation, the original corpus is randomly partitioned into K sections. Among the K sections, a single section is retained as the validation data for testing the model, and the remaining $K - 1$ sections are utilized as training data. The cross-validation process is then repeated K times (the folds), each of the K sections uses exactly once as the validation data. The K results from the folds are averaged (or otherwise combined) to final results. In these experiments, constant $K = 10$ is preferred to choose [11].

4.2   Models

Table 1 describes six different models which are used for the purpose of benchmark. For each model, both the encoder and decoder were used two and four LSTM layers. At first, model 1 is a sequence to sequence model from Sutskeveret et al. [33]. Subsequently, model 2 from Bahdanau et al. [1] is the model of sequence-to-sequence with attention mechanisms for bilingual machine translation which was used for generating paraphrase and achieved the state-of-the-art results in this problem. While, model 3 from Graves et al. [7] uses stacked LSTMs.

Table 1. List of existing models.

#	Models	Reference
1	Sequence to Sequence	(Sutskeveret et al. 2014)
2	Seq2Seq with Attention	(Bahdanau et al. 2015)
3	Bi-directional LSTM	(Graves et al. 2013)
4	Residual LSTM	(Praksh et al. 2016)
5	PCA-RLSTM	(Khuong et al. 2018)
6	HCANN	(The proposed model)

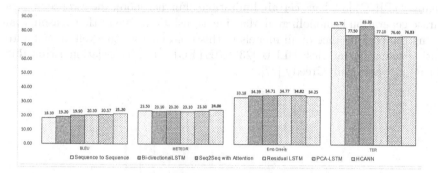

Fig. 4. Evaluation results on PPDB with beam size of 5 (best results in **bold**).

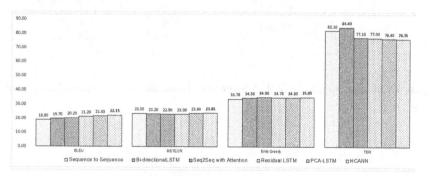

Fig. 5. Evaluation results on PPDB with beam size of 10 (best results in **bold**).

On the contrary, model 4 from Prakash et al. [26] chooses residual connections between LSTM layers. Recent work of Khuong et al. [22] constructs a Penalty Coefficient Attention-based Residual Long-Short-Term-Memory (PCA-RLSTM) neural network in model 5. Last but not least, proposal model of HCANN is emerged as major contribution of this article.

In encoder-decoder models, the computational complexity is inversely proportional to the size of the beam search algorithm. Herein, the most common beam size (5 and 10) has been used as mentioned in the literature [33]. Training all models uses the implementation of the Stochastic Gradient Descent (SGD) algorithm with the one-hot vector of words as input. In addition, the learning rate in the interest of 1.0 is chosen.

5   Evaluation

5.1   Metrics

Prakash et al. [26] shows that some paraphrase generation evaluation metrics, such as Paraphrase Evaluation Metric (PEM) [17] and Paraphrase In Ngram Changes (PINC) [32] have certain limitations. Further more, the essence of paraphrase generation is monolingual Machine Translation. Due to that reason, evaluating the performance of all models in this work chooses the well-known automatic evaluation metrics: BLEU [23], METEOR [14], Translation Error Rate (TER) [31] and Emb Greedy [27].

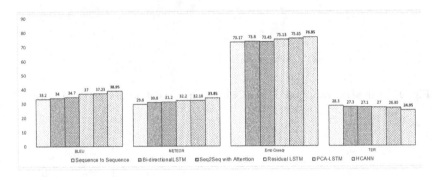

Fig. 6. Evaluation results on WikiAnswer with beam size of 5 (best results in **bold**).

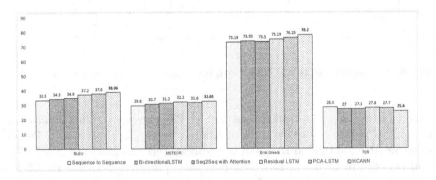

Fig. 7. Evaluation results on WikiAnswer with beam size of 10 (best results in **bold**).

5.2   Results

Using the above explained setting, experiments of six models using PPDB 2.0 and WikiAnswer paraphrase datasets were conducted and delivered result in Figs. 4, 5, 6 and 7 as described and discussed in the following section. The performance of HCANN model is better than other models on measurement of three metrics (BLEU, TER and METEOR). Especially, as to Emb Greedy metric, the proposed model outperforms almost other models with the exception of PCA-LSTM when beam size of 5 is considered. Obtained results could be explained by observing the PPDB 2.0 dataset which contains mostly short phrases. What is more, the Emb Greedy metric is generally appropriate with long phrases on WikiAnswer dataset in comparison with parallel corpora. By virtue of majority of long phrases in WikiAnswer dataset, model of 6 outperforms all other models. As a consequence, it obviously proves that HCANN model fits with long document. Above all, these experimental results also transparently reveal that the performance of conditional attention-based model architectures have been enhanced by juxtaposing to traditional attention counterparts.

6   Conclusion and Future Work

A contribution to paraphrase generation issue in natural language processing aspect has been made. A proposal of contemporary model, namely HCANN based on conditional attention-augmenting hierarchical neural network is presented. Ultimately, to demonstrate the practicability and performance of the model, an application was introduced via empiric experimental analysis by a set of simulations in term of BLUE, TER, METEOR and Emb Greedy evaluation metrics. In most cases, better results have been obtained and pointed out from two selected dataset sources PPDB2 2.0 and WikiAnswers in comparison with prior methods. Given the discussed results, there still a lot of improvements and future work that could be a continuity of this work. Here we used only one algorithm of sentence vector representation which is based on the word vector. We think that it would be interesting to test the same architectures with other existing sentence representation approaches. We believe that better results are achievable if we find a way to improve the quality of the used sentences representations. Finally, we think that our model is useful for other NLP tasks, especially for the sequence to sequence learning problems.

Acknowledgment. This paper is supported by The Vietnam National University, Hanoi (VNU), under Project No. QG.17.69 and The Vietnam National Foundation for Science and Technology Development (NAFOSTED) under grant number 102.01-2014.22.

References

1. Bahdanau, D., Cho, K., Bengio, Y.: Neural machine translation by jointly learning to align and translate. arXiv preprint arXiv:1409.0473 (2014)
2. Bannard, C., Callison-Burch, C.: Paraphrasing with bilingual parallel corpora. In: Proceedings of the 43rd Annual Meeting on Association for Computational Linguistics, pp. 597–604. Association for Computational Linguistics (2005)
3. Cho, K., Van Merriënboer, B., Bahdanau, D., Bengio, Y.: On the properties of neural machine translation: Encoder-decoder approaches. arXiv preprint arXiv:1409.1259 (2014)
4. Chorowski, J.K., Bahdanau, D., Serdyuk, D., Cho, K., Bengio, Y.: Attention-based models for speech recognition. In: Advances in Neural Information Processing Systems, pp. 577–585 (2015)
5. Fader, A., Zettlemoyer, L., Etzioni, O.: Paraphrase-driven learning for open question answering. In: Proceedings of the 51st Annual Meeting of the Association for Computational Linguistics (Volume 1: Long Papers), vol. 1, pp. 1608–1618 (2013)
6. Goodfellow, I.J., Warde-Farley, D., Mirza, M., Courville, A., Bengio, Y.: Maxout networks. arXiv preprint arXiv:1302.4389 (2013)
7. Graves, A., Wayne, G., Danihelka, I.: Neural turing machines. arXiv preprint arXiv:1410.5401 (2014)
8. Gupta, A., Agarwal, A., Singh, P., Rai, P.: A deep generative framework for paraphrase generation. arXiv preprint arXiv:1709.05074 (2017)
9. Hasan, S.A., et al.: Neural clinical paraphrase generation with attention. In: ClinicalNLP 2016, p. 42 (2016)
10. Huang, G., Liu, Z., Weinberger, K.Q., van der Maaten, L.: Densely connected convolutional networks. arXiv preprint arXiv:1608.06993 (2016)
11. Kohavi, R.: A Study of Cross-validation and Bootstrap for Accuracy Estimation and Model Selection, pp. 1137–1143. Morgan Kaufmann (1995)
12. Kolesnyk, V., Rocktäschel, T., Riedel, S.: Generating natural language inference chains. arXiv preprint arXiv:1606.01404 (2016)
13. Kozlowski, R., McCoy, K.F., Vijay-Shanker, K.: Generation of single-sentence paraphrases from predicate/argument structure using lexico-grammatical resources. In: Proceedings of the Second International Workshop on Paraphrasing, vol. 16, pp. 1–8. Association for Computational Linguistics (2003)
14. Lavie, A., Agarwal, A.: Meteor: An automatic metric for MT evaluation with high levels of correlation with human judgments. In: Proceedings of the Second Workshop on Statistical Machine Translation, pp. 228–231. Association for Computational Linguistics (2007)
15. Li, X., Wu, X.: Constructing long short-term memory based deep recurrent neural networks for large vocabulary speech recognition. In: IEEE International Conference on Acoustics, Speech and Signal Processing (ICASSP) 2015, pp. 4520–4524. IEEE (2015)
16. Li, Z., Jiang, X., Shang, L., Li, H.: Paraphrase generation with deep reinforcement learning. arXiv preprint arXiv:1711.00279 (2017)
17. Liu, C., Dahlmeier, D., Ng, H.T.: PEM: a paraphrase evaluation metric exploiting parallel texts. In: Proceedings of the 2010 Conference on Empirical Methods in Natural Language Processing, pp. 923–932. Association for Computational Linguistics (2010)
18. Liu, P., Qiu, X., Chen, X., Wu, S., Huang, X.: Multi-timescale long short-term memory neural network for modelling sentences and documents. In: EMNLP, pp. 2326–2335 (2015)

19. Madnani, N., Dorr, B.J.: Generating phrasal and sentential paraphrases: a survey of data-driven methods. Comput. Linguist. **36**(3), 341–387 (2010)
20. McKeown, K.R.: Paraphrasing questions using given and new information. Comput. Linguist. **9**(1), 1–10 (1983)
21. Manning, C.D., Luong, M.-T., Pham, H.: Effective approaches to attention-based neural machine translation. CoRR abs/1508.0402 (2017)
22. Nguyen-Ngoc, K., Le, A.-C., Nguyen, V.-H.: An attention-based long-short-term-memory model for paraphrase generation. In: Huynh, V.-N., Inuiguchi, M., Tran, D.H., Denoeux, T. (eds.) IUKM 2018. LNCS (LNAI), vol. 10758, pp. 166–178. Springer, Cham (2018). https://doi.org/10.1007/978-3-319-75429-1_14
23. Papineni, K., Roukos, S., Ward, T., Zhu, W.-J.: BLEU: a method for automatic evaluation of machine translation. In: Proceedings of the 40th Annual Meeting on Association for Computational Linguistics, pp. 311–318. Association for Computational Linguistics (2002)
24. Parikh, D.M.: Handbook of Pharmaceutical Granulation Technology. CRC Press, Boca Raton (2016)
25. Pavlick, E., Rastogi, P., Ganitkevitch, J., Van Durme, B., Callison-Burch, C.: PPDB 2.0: Better paraphrase ranking, fine-grained entailment relations, word embeddings, and style classification (2015)
26. Prakash, A., et al.: Neural paraphrase generation with stacked residual LSTM networks. arXiv preprint arXiv:1610.03098 (2016)
27. Rus, V., Lintean, M.: A comparison of greedy and optimal assessment of natural language student input using word-to-word similarity metrics. In: Proceedings of the Seventh Workshop on Building Educational Applications Using NLP, pp. 157–162. Association for Computational Linguistics (2012)
28. See, A., Liu, P.J., Manning, C.D.: Get to the point: Summarization with pointer-generator networks. arXiv preprint arXiv:1704.04368 (2017)
29. Sennrich, R., et al.: Nematus: a toolkit for neural machine translation. arXiv preprint arXiv:1703.04357 (2017)
30. Serban, I.V., et al.: Multiresolution recurrent neural networks: An application to dialogue response generation. arXiv preprint arXiv:1606.00776 (2016)
31. Snover, M., Dorr, B., Schwartz, R., Micciulla, L., Makhoul, J.: A study of translation edit rate with targeted human annotation. In: Proceedings of Association for Machine Translation in the Americas, vol. 200 (2006)
32. Socher, R., Huang, E.H., Pennington, J., Ng, A.Y., Manning, C.D.: Dynamic pooling and unfolding recursive autoencoders for paraphrase detection. In: NIPS, vol. 24, pp. 801–809 (2011)
33. Sutskever, I., Vinyals, O., Le, Q.V.: Sequence to sequence learning with neural networks. In: Advances in Neural Information Processing Systems, pp. 3104–3112 (2014)
34. Vinyals, O., Kaiser, Ł., Koo, T., Petrov, S., Sutskever, I., Hinton, G.: Grammar as a foreign language. In: Advances in Neural Information Processing Systems, pp. 2773–2781 (2015)
35. Wieting, J., Bansal, M., Gimpel, K., Livescu, K., Roth, D.: From paraphrase database to compositional paraphrase model and back. arXiv preprint arXiv:1506.03487 (2015)
36. Wu, Y., et al.: Google's neural machine translation system: Bridging the gap between human and machine translation. arXiv preprint arXiv:1609.08144 (2016)

37. Wubben, S., Van Den Bosch, A., Krahmer, E.: Paraphrase generation as monolingual translation: data and evaluation. In: Proceedings of the 6th International Natural Language Generation Conference, pp. 203–207. Association for Computational Linguistics (2010)
38. Xu, K., et al.: Show, attend and tell: neural image caption generation with visual attention. In: International Conference on Machine Learning, pp. 2048–2057 (2015)
39. Zhao, S., Lan, X., Liu, T., Li, S.: Application-driven statistical paraphrase generation. In: Proceedings of the Joint Conference of the 47th Annual Meeting of the ACL and the 4th International Joint Conference on Natural Language Processing of the AFNLP: Volume 2-Volume 2, pp. 834–842. Association for Computational Linguistics (2009)
40. Zhao, S., Niu, C., Zhou, M., Liu, T., Li, S.: Combining multiple resources to improve SMT-based paraphrasing model. In: ACL, pp. 1021–1029 (2008)
41. Zhao, S., Wang, H., Lan, X., Liu, T.: Leveraging multiple MT engines for paraphrase generation. In: Proceedings of the 23rd International Conference on Computational Linguistics, pp. 1326–1334. Association for Computational Linguistics (2010)

Ontology Based Approach for Precision Agriculture

Quoc Hung Ngo[✉], Nhien-An Le-Khac, and Tahar Kechadi

School of Computer Science, College of Science, University College Dublin,
Belfield, Dublin 4, Ireland
hung.ngo@ucdconnect.ie, {an.lekhac,tahar.kechadi}@ucd.ie

Abstract. In this paper, we propose a framework of knowledge for an agriculture ontology which can be used for the purpose of smart agriculture systems. This ontology not only includes basic concepts in the agricultural domain but also contains geographical, IoT, business subdomains, and other knowledge extracted from various datasets. With this ontology, any users can easily understand agricultural data links between them collected from many different data resources. In our experiment, we also import country, sub-country and disease entities into this ontology as basic entities for building agricultural linked datasets later.

Keywords: Agriculture ontology · Knowledge base
Precision agriculture

1 Introduction

The Internet of Things (IoT) is growing quickly in developing the smart grids, such as home, health care, transportation, and environment systems as well as smart cities. According to a new forecasts update of International Data Corporation (IDC) [4], worldwide spending on IoT reaches $772 Billion in 2018; an increase of 11.5% over the $674 billions that were spent in 2017, and this number is predicted to be over $1 trillion by 2020. Moreover, 60% of global manufacturers will use data analytics from connected devices to analyze processes and identify optimization possibilities.

Similarly, IoT in agriculture also grows quickly to improve farm productivity and increase farm profitability. IoT applications in agriculture include vehicle tracking, farm and livestock monitoring, storage monitoring, and much more in producing food products [5]. Considering the future vision of the food lifecycles are well recorded from seeds, cultivation, products, transportation, food processing, sales in supermarket, it is exciting to have public confidence on food security and high added value to the agriculture and food suppliers.

IoT systems are playing an increasingly important role in smart farms, allowing different organizations and information technology facilities create different datasets. These different datasets create enormous challenges to integrate them into a workable system so that the midstream firms and the end consumers can

© Springer Nature Switzerland AG 2018
M. Kaenampornpan et al. (Eds.): MIWAI 2018, LNAI 11248, pp. 175–186, 2018.
https://doi.org/10.1007/978-3-030-03014-8_15

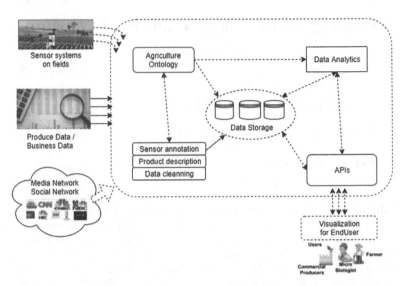

Fig. 1. Architecture of agriculture system

query the history of the agricultural products unhindered by the bounds of the previous vendors. One of the most important requirements of such integration is that the data semantics are not consistent among different phases of products. As shown in Fig. 1, to achieve such target, an unified ontology of agriculture should be utilized by all the information systems of the different phases. Ontology is a concept that is emerging from the various Semantic Web initiatives, which can be defined as a semantic system that contains terms, the definitions of those terms, and the specification of relationships among those terms.

In this research, we propose an agriculture ontology for the purpose of smart agriculture systems, namely AgriOnt. This ontology will describe basic concepts in the agricultural domain and related thematic subdomains. To keep the ontology light-weight, we ignore the complexity of the specific agriculture activities or food processing. Only the environments of the agriculture products are considered so that all the history can be queried quickly and easily.

The next section gives an overview of an open access linked data, AGROVOC, and its related knowledge base in the agriculture domain. Section 3 describes in details our AgriOnt, Agricultural Ontology. Then, Sect. 4 discusses the results of several experiments on AgriOnt. Finally, we conclude the paper and give some future work in Sect. 5.

2   AGROVOC and Related Knowledge Base

There are several ontologies in precision agriculture. The most popular ontology is AGROVOC. AGROVOC[1] is a well-known vocabulary system that has

---

[1] http://aims.fao.org/standards/agrovoc/linked-data.

international interoperability and it consists of over 32,000 concepts available in over 20 languages [1]. The AGROVOC is aligned from 16 vocabularies related to agriculture and is published and managed by the Food and Agriculture Organization of the United Nations (FAO). Detailed information about AGROVOC thesaurus is available from the FAO website, while the RDF version of AGROVOC can be downloaded at: http://aims.fao.org/aos/agrovoc/ or https://datahub.io/dataset/agrovoc-skos.

However, AGROVOC is only a good vocabulary system to start building an agricultural ontology rather than being used as an ontology for agriculture because some of its relations are inconsistently assigned and others are too broadly defined. For example, there are some insufficient features that can be used as core vocabulary. First of all, the relationship between concepts is not clear or well defined. Most of narrower and broader relationship is attached only by considering the pair-wise relationship. Thus hierarchy by these relationships are not so consistent [6]. This vague relationship between concepts can lead to the difficulty when adding new terms. In addition, it is difficult to define relations for concepts in AGROVOC, i.e., to find the best position for new terms. Secondly, the number of activity names about rice farming are insufficient. These disadvantages come from the combination of all vocabularies into one vocabulary like AGROVOC.

Adding to AGROVOC, there are several smaller ontologies for agricultural studies. For example, Plant Ontology of Cooper, et al. [10], Animal Ontology, and Animal Disease Ontology of Fauré, et al. [3] are built for living entities in agriculture. They are very useful database resources for all plant and animal scientists. According to [10], the Plant Ontology consists of over 1,300 rigorously-defined ontology terms and their relations that describe plant anatomy, morphology and developmental stages. Its relations include *partOf* and *hasPart* pair, *precedes* and *precededBy* pair, participates and *hasParticipant* pair, in which *dry_seed_stage* concept is *precededBy* some seed maturation stages. Moreover, more specific ontologies like Crop Ontology [11] or knowledge models of AgroPedia[2] [12] (supported and certified by the Indian Council of Agricultural Research) defined very specific concepts and relations (as a screen shot shown in Fig. 2 for knowledge model of wheat).

For environmental monitoring, IoT architectures use a collection of numerous active physical things, sensors, actuators, cloud services, and communication layers. These architectures base on SSN ontology to describe sensors and their measurement processes, observations [2]. When applying IoT architectures into agriculture, IoT applications still need a general ontology in the agriculture domain. This ontology can link entities in agriculture (such as animals, plants, fertilizer, diseases), producing aspects (such as weather or soil conditions), and their observations. In fact, HuSiquan, et al. [9], or Roussey Catherine, et al. [20] also introduced ontologies for agriculture domain. However, these ontologies only contain basic concepts in agriculture, such as *Farm, Product, Crop*, or

---

[2] http://agropedia.iitk.ac.in.

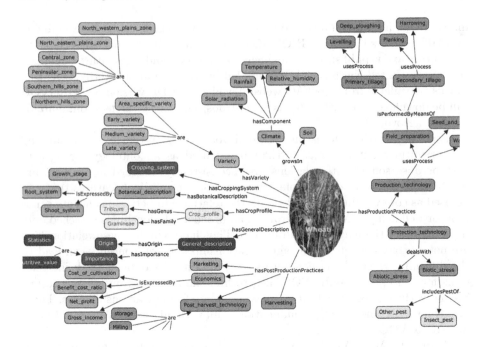

Fig. 2. A screenshot of knowledge model for wheat

Condition. Therefore, these studies will be a brief ontology to build a bigger ontology containing all aspects of the agriculture domain.

To summarise, there are several available resources as knowledge-bases in specific topics of the agriculture domain, however, building an agricultural ontology is necessary for applying data science into agricultural management and improving crop yields. Firstly, for example, this knowledge-base can be used to build a data schema for a data warehouse [22]. Secondly, it can link available resources based on its hierarchy and semantic relations.

3   AgriOnt: Agricultural Ontology

Based on needs of a knowledge-base for precise agricultural applications, an agricultural ontology has an important role in developing its applications. According to Nengfu Xie [16], an intelligent agricultural knowledge-based service system has an agriculture-specific ontology and a method for agricultural knowledge acquisition and representation. Xie and coauthors [16] also describe ontology developing progress which includes three steps:

(1) Building a domain-specific knowledge hierarchy;
(2) Defining slots of the categories and representing axioms;
(3) Knowledge acquisition filling in the value for slots of instances.

In general, our new agricultural ontology includes four thematic subdomains: agriculture part, geographical ontology, IoT subdomain, and business subdomain (as shown in Fig. 3). Concepts or classes in each subdomains are inherited from a general class, *Entity*, and two its sub-classes (*VirtualEntity* and *PhysicalEntity*).

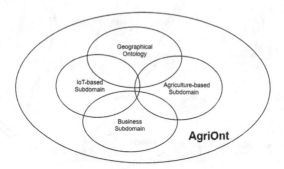

Fig. 3. Components of agricultural ontology

Entity: In several ontologies, *Entity* is also called *Thing* and it includes two sub-classes, *VirtualEntity* and *PhysicalEntity* (as shown in Fig. 4).

3.1   Agricultural Subdomain

Agricultural subdomain includes basic classes in agriculture domain, such as *Farm, Crop, Product, Fertilizer,* or *Condition*. Figure 4 shows an overview of agricultural ontology with its main concepts and relationships.

Farm (also called *Field*) mentions a place for planting crops or feeding animals.

Product and its sub-classes are used to describe agricultural products. Main sub-classes of *Product* are *Food* (*DairyFood* and *ProcessedFood*), *Oil* (*AnimalOil* and *PlantOil*), and *Nutrient*.

Crop, Livestock and their sub-classes are agricultural classes and entities which make products, such as *Cereal, Flower, Fruit, Vegetable* (Crop), *Poultry, Cattle* (Livestock), *Fishery*. These concepts can be built based on Plant Ontology[3], Animal Ontology[4].

Process or **Phase** class is used to capture positions in the lifecycle of agricultural products. This class has sub-classes, such as *SoilProcess, Plainting, Spraying, Fertilizering, Harvesting, Marketing,* and *Transportation*.

Condition includes everything related to agricultural conditions for producing, such as weather, soil, water, or physiographic features (as shown in

---

[3] http://www.plantontology.org.

[4] http://www.cs.man.ac.uk/~rector/tutorials/Biomedical-Tutorial/Tutorial-Ontologies/Animals/Animals-tutorial-complete.owl.

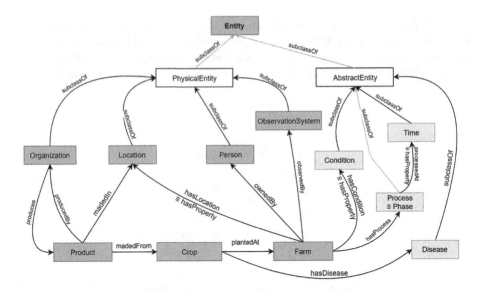

Fig. 4. An overview of agricultural ontology architecture

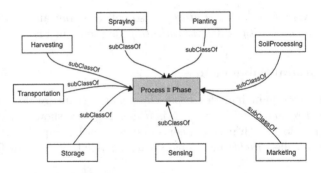

Fig. 5. Process and its sub-classes

Fig. 6). These conditions are implemented into *WeatherCondition*, *SoilCondition*, *WaterCondition* classes and their features, such as wind speed, temperature, humidity value, chemical properties, and physical properties of soil.

3.2 IoT Subdomain

The role of IoT subdomain is connecting sensor systems and linking to observed objects. For this purpose, the Semantic Sensor Network[5] (SSN) ontology is a suitable choice to extend and integrate into an agriculture ontology. SSN ontology was developed by W3C Semantic Sensor Networks Incubator Group [2], and provides a schema that describes sensors, observation, data attributes, and other

---

[5] https://www.w3.org/2005/Incubator/ssn/ssnx/ssn.

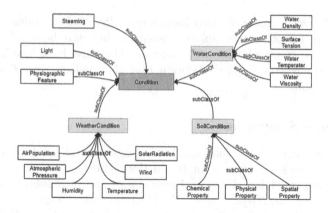

Fig. 6. Condition and its sub-classes

related concepts at https://www.w3.org/2005/Incubator/ssn/ssnx/ssn. By using the SSN ontology as a framework to implement IoT aspects into an agricultural system, main classes for this subdomain are:

ObserveSystem or **System:** A *System* is a unit of IoT infrastructure, it includes a set of sensors or sub-systems. It observes *FeatureOfInterests*, generates observation values for monitoring *Conditions* (such as weather, water, soil) during processing.

Sensor: A sensor is any entity that can follow a sensing method and thus observe several properties of a *FeatureOfInterest*. Sensors may be physical devices, computational methods, a laboratory setup with a person following a method, or any other thing that can follow a Sensing Method to observe a *Property*.

FeatureOfInterest: A *FeatureOfInterest* is a set of *Properties* and it is considered as a *Condition* object in the agricultural part.

ObservationValue: The value of the result of an *Observation*. An *Observation* has a result which is the output of some sensors, the result is an information object that encodes some values for a *FeatureOfInterest*.

3.3 Geographical Subdomain

In this ontology, geographical classes includes two main administrative levels (**Country** and **Subcountry** classes) and free control locations (**geo:SpatialThing** and **geo:Point**). Relationships are longitude/latitude, population, area properties, part-whole relationships among geographical instances, and *hasLocation, isLocationOf,* and *isProducedAt* relationships between geographical instances and other instances (plants, animals, products, etc). In fact, a **Country** is a political division that is identified as a national entity. It also has an unique ISO 3166-1 code in the ISO 3166 standard published by the International Organization for Standardization (ISO). A **Subcountry** is a subdivision (e.g., province, city or state) of all countries coded in ISO 3166-1, and most of *Subcountry* instances also have unique ISO 3166-2 codes in the ISO 3166 standard. For other geographical instances, they have basic relations, such as longitude, latitude, address, and postcode. They also have *hasCountry* and *hasSubCountry* relationships to mention that they belong with *Country* and *Subcountry* instances.

3.4 Business Subdomain

When building agriculture ontology, linking agricultural subdomain and IoT subdomain is necessary to monitor production. This connection can be implemented by **Organization, Person, Farm** classes and their sub-classes, such as *Company, GovernmentOrganization, NonGovernmentOrganization* (sub-class of *Organization*), *Farmer, LandOwner* (sub-class of *Person*) classes. Relationships between these classes and *Product* class include *hasProduct, produces, isProducedBy, isProducedAt* relations. With these classes and relationships, the ontology can describe factors contributed to produce agricultural products.

4 Experiments

With three main steps in building a core ontology (as mentioned in Sect. 3), we have built an agriculture ontology with 447 classes and over 700 axioms related to agriculture (as shown in Table 1). It not only provides an overview of the agriculture domain but also describes agricultural concepts, and lifecycles between seeds, plants, harvesting, transportation, and consumption. It also gives relationships between agricultural concepts and related concepts, such as weather, soil conditions, fertilizers, farm descriptions.

Table 1. Ontology metrics

Figure	Core	with Geo-data	with Diseases
Axiom	1843	64,805	108,062
Logical axiom count	749	50,876	75,316
Declaration axioms	728	9,240	15,951
Class count	447	447	447
Object property count	69	69	69
Data property count	27	27	27
Individual count	101	8,615	15,392

To provide basic geo-location data in this ontology, we extract countries and sub-countries, and then import them into our AgriOnt ontology based on studies of Quoc Hung, et al. [17–19,21]. Most of them contain ISO 3166-1 codes for country level instances and ISO 3166-2 codes for sub-country level instances.

Table 2. Detail of geographial part

Entry	Detail	Count
Country	With ISO 3166-1 code	243
Sub-country	With ISO 3166-2 code	4,085
	Without ISO 3166-2 code	142
Relations	Longitude, Latitude, ISO code, Wikipedia, population, area, climate	23,991

Geographical data (as shown in Table 2) also contains longitude, latitude, population, area, agricultural land area, climate condition information, and Wikipedia links.

For smart agriculture systems, chemical and biological control of plant and animal diseases is remarkably high. Therefore, agricultural ontologies contain knowledge-bases about diseases and related sectors is necessary. In this ontology, animal disease instances are imported from Animal Disease Ontology[6] of Fauré Marie-Colette and Aubin Sophie [3] while plant disease instances are extracted from Plant Disease pages of APS Journals[7].

With existing resources, we have built an agricultural ontology with geographical instances (countries and sub-countries), diseases, micro-organisms. Moreover, we also manually collect and create main instances in the agricultural domain, such as crops, animals, and related typical products.

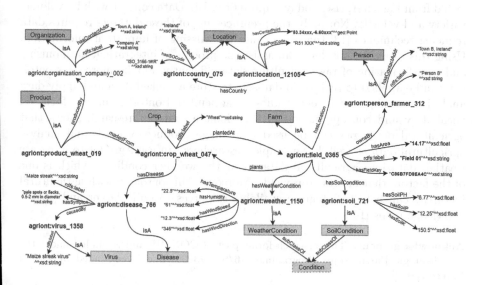

Fig. 7. Example of linked data based on AgriOnt.

---

[6] http://lovinra.inra.fr/2015/09/28/maladies-animales/.
[7] https://apsjournals.apsnet.org.

In our scenario, this ontology will be a semantic framework to build a linked data for agriculture applications and analytics. As shown in Fig. 7, the process relates to products, crops, farms, farmers, diseases, affected aspects and producing conditions. In fact, this linked data example shows features of field *"Field 01"* (has URI *agriont:field_0365*), such as its basic characteristics, location, weather condition (*agriont:weather_1150*), and soil condition (*agriont:soil_721*).

Moreover, ontologies can be used to build data warehouse schema. According to Thenmozhi [22], database tables can be inherited ontology classes while attributes of tables are mapped to properties of the equivalent classes or relationships between classes. In our scenario, *Product, Crop, Farm* or *Field, Farmer, SoilCondition,* and *Weather* are considered to be database tables in the data warehouse schema and their descriptions and relations will help to define features of database tables [23]. Similarly, relationships between concept classes are presented as relations between database tables in whole schema of the data warehouse.

5   Conclusion and Future Work

We presented an ontology architecture for agriculture domain. We describe four main thematic subdomains of an agricultural ontology and give descriptions of typical concepts of each subdomain. The architecture of our proposed ontology with these four sub-domains aims to tackle the challenges in pre-processing and analysing real-world agriculture datasets. In addition, raw argriculture data collected from big enterprises today is quite fit in Big Data context with its volume, variety and velocity. Normally, the preprocessing of these datasets requires data reducing techniques [13] that may cause the missing of important information. Using this proposed ontology can assist the process of integrating, harmonising and transformation of raw agriculture data efficiently. Furthermore, this ontology can be applied to real-world datasets to store as linked data and apply data analytics techniques. Current studies on agricultural ontology mostly focus on vocabulary and concept models of this domain, but our research shows that agricultural ontologies can be used to manage produce progress and analyse agricultural data as well. For example, researchers can use AgriOnt to integrate weather data into agricultural datasets as the weather condition which is one of the factors that affects crop yields. Moreover, this ontology with agricultural hierarchy can help to integrate available resources to build larger and precise knowledge maps [14].

Acknowledgement. This research forms part of CONSUS and is funded under the SFI Strategic Partnerships Programme (16/SPP/3296) and is co-funded by Origin Enterprises Plc.

References

1. Caracciolo, C., et al.: The AGROVOC linked dataset. Semant. Web **4**(3), 341–348 (2013)
2. Michael, C., et al.: The SSN ontology of the W3C semantic sensor network incubator group. Web Semant. Sci. Serv. Agents World Wide Web **17**, 25–32 (2012)
3. Faure, M.C., Zundel, E., Aubin, S., Millox, M.: The animal diseases reference system: from CERISA to Linked Data. In: Animal Health: News and Quality, p. 97 (2011). Presented at Scientific Animation Days of the Department of Animal Health, Fréjus, France, 22–25 May 2011 (in French)
4. International Data Corporation (IDC) Ltd. Forecasts Worldwide Spending on the Internet of Things 07 December 2017. https://www.idc.com/getdoc.jsp?containerId=prUS43295217. Accessed 30 April 2018
5. Jayaraman, P.P., Yavari, A., Georgakopoulos, D., Morshed, A., Zaslavsky, A.: Internet of things platform for smart farming: experiences and lessons learnt. Sensors **16**(11), 1884 (2016)
6. Joo, S., Koide, S., Takeda, H., Horyu, D., Takezaki, A., Yoshida, T.: Agriculture activity ontology: an ontology for core vocabulary of agriculture activity. In: International Semantic Web Conference (Posters & Demos) (2016)
7. Kawtrakul, A.: Ontology engineering and knowledge services for agriculture domain. J. Integr. Agric. **11**(5), 741–751 (2012)
8. Du, H., et al.: An ontology of soil properties and processes. In: Groth, P., et al. (eds.) ISWC 2016. LNCS, vol. 9982, pp. 30–37. Springer, Cham (2016). https://doi.org/10.1007/978-3-319-46547-0_4
9. Hu, S., Wang, H., She, C., Wang, J.: AgOnt: ontology for agriculture internet of things. In: Li, D., Liu, Y., Chen, Y. (eds.) CCTA 2010. IAICT, vol. 344, pp. 131–137. Springer, Heidelberg (2011). https://doi.org/10.1007/978-3-642-18333-1_18
10. Cooper, L., et al.: The plant ontology as a tool for comparative plant anatomy and genomic analyses. Plant Cell Physiol. 54(2), e1, 1–23 (2012). https://doi.org/10.1093/pcp/pcs163
11. Matteis, L., et al.: Crop ontology: vocabulary for crop-related concepts. In: The First International Workshop on Semantics for Biodiversity (S4BioDiv) (2013)
12. Sini, M., Yadav, V., Singh, J., TV, P., Awasthi, V.: Knowledge Models in Agropedia Indica. FAO (2009)
13. Le-Khac, N.-A., Bue, M., Whelan, M., Kechadi, M.-T.: A clustering-based data reduction for very large spatio-temporal datasets. In: Cao, L., Zhong, J., Feng, Y. (eds.) ADMA 2010. LNCS (LNAI), vol. 6441, pp. 43–54. Springer, Heidelberg (2010). https://doi.org/10.1007/978-3-642-17313-4_5
14. Le-Khac, N.-A., Aouad, L., Kechadi, M.-T.: Distributed knowledge map for mining data on grid platforms. Int. J. Comput. Sci. Netw. Secur. **7**(10), 98–107 (2007)
15. Xie, N., Wang, W., Ma, B., Zhang, X., Sun, W., Guo, F.: Research on an agricultural knowledge fusion method for big data. Data Sci. J. **14**, 2–9 (2015)
16. Xie, N., Wang, W., Yang, Y.: Ontology-based agricultural knowledge acquisition and application. In: Li, D. (ed.) CCTA 2007. TIFIP, vol. 258, pp. 349–357. Springer, Boston, MA (2008). https://doi.org/10.1007/978-0-387-77251-6_38
17. Collier, N.: Detecting web rumours with a multilingual ontology-supported text classification system. J. Adv. Dis. Surveill. **4**, 242 (2007)
18. Hung Ngo, Q., Doan, S., Winiwarter, W.: Building a geographical ontology by using Wikipedia. In: Proceedings of the 13th International Conference on Information Integration and Web-based Applications & Services, pp. 345–348. ACM (2011)

19. Ngo, Q.-H., Doan, S., Winiwarter, W.: Using Wikipedia for extracting hierarchy and building geo-ontology. Int. J. Web Inf. Syst. **8**(4), 401–412 (2012)
20. Roussey, C., Soulignac, V., Champomier, J.-C., Abt, V., Chanet, J.-P.: Ontologies in agriculture. In: AgEng 2010, International Conference on Agricultural Engineering. Cemagref, pp. 1–10 (2010)
21. Doan, S., Ngo, Q.H., Collier, N.: Building and using geospatial ontology in the BioCaster surveillance system. In: Workshop on Bio-Ontologies 2008: Knowledge in Biology, July 2008
22. Thenmozhi, M., Vivekanandan, K.: An ontological approach to handle multidimensional schema evolution for data warehouse. Int. J. Database Manag. Syst. **6**(3), 33 (2014)
23. Ngo, V.M., Le-Khac, N.-A., Kechadi, T.M.: An efficient data warehouse for crop yield prediction. In: 14th International Conference on Precision Agriculture, International Society of Precision Agriculture (2018)
24. Zheng, Y.: Construction of the ontology-based agricultural knowledge management system. J. Integr. Agric. **11**(5), 700–709 (2012)

Learning Generalized Video Memory
for Automatic Video Captioning

Poo-Hee Chang$^{(\boxtimes)}$ and Ah-Hwee Tan$^{(\boxtimes)}$

School of Computer Science and Engineering, Nanyang Technological University,
Singapore 639798, Singapore
{phchang,asahtan}@ntu.edu.sg

Abstract. Recent video captioning methods have made great progress
by deep learning approaches with convolutional neural networks (CNN)
and recurrent neural networks (RNN). While there are techniques that
use memory networks for sentence decoding, few work has leveraged on
the memory component to learn and generalize the temporal structure
in video. In this paper, we propose a new method, namely Generalized Video Memory (GVM), utilizing a memory model for enhancing
video description generation. Based on a class of self-organizing neural
networks, GVM's model is able to learn new video features incrementally. The learned generalized memory is further exploited to decode
the associated sentences using RNN. We evaluate our method on the
YouTube2Text data set using BLEU and METEOR scores as a standard benchmark. Our results are shown to be competitive against other
state-of-the-art methods.

Keywords: Memory model · Video captioning · Deep learning
Adaptive Resonance Theory · LSTM · CNN

1 Introduction

Automatic video captioning has a wide array of applications, such as artificial consciousness, videos categorization and aids for the visually impaired.
It involves the understanding and translation of temporal visual features into
words. While video captioning is a challenging task for both computer vision
and language, recent progress with deep neural networks have led to many possibilities in regards to automatic video captioning.

Current deep learning approach to the video captioning task typically
involves a deep visual encoder using convolutional neural networks (CNN)
such as AlexNet [17] and a sentence decoder using Long-Short Term Memory (LSTM) [14], a variant of recurrent neural network (RNN). For example,
the mean pool approach [34] which takes the average of the AlexNet features
across the video frames. The mean pooled vector trains the LSTM network and
decodes a sequence of words. The mean pooling approach serves as a baseline
to many of the recent state-of-the-art algorithms. Further research has explored

© Springer Nature Switzerland AG 2018
M. Kaenampornpan et al. (Eds.): MIWAI 2018, LNAI 11248, pp. 187–201, 2018.
https://doi.org/10.1007/978-3-030-03014-8_16

the temporal representation of the videos [33], the temporal representation of the sentence decoder [41] and the visual attention mechanism [18] for improving the quality of video captions.

Another area of research involves the introduction of memory into deep neural models. Weston et al. introduced the Memory Networks [40] which enabled RNNs to memorize long sequences. The general model of the memory network is to generalize inputs, to retrieve memories, and to interpret the stored memories. Memory networks have shown to be able to tackle textual and visual question and answering tasks [39]. While there are some video captioning work involving the memory component, such as Iterative Attention/Memory [9] which is a memory model based attention mechanism, there is a lack of a memory model that focused on generalizing and storing the temporal structure of the video. Previous memory model for video captioning have a fixed pre-defined number of memory slots which may limit the number of useful memories stored.

To address the issue, we adapt from an earlier work, the Adaptive Resonance Theory (ART) [2] which is a class of self-organizing neural network. The ART model is able to stores input patterns in a content addressable way with unlimited categories or memory slots. To our best knowledge, the use of ART neural network as the external memory module for general deep learning tasks are not explored. One possible reason may be the difficulty of integrating the ART network with deep learning methods as the ART model does not learn by back-propagation.

In this paper, we present the video captioning architecture, with a memory model named the Generalized Video Memory (GVM) that is able to generalize and store the temporal video features using the ART framework. GVM is able to store memory incrementally, in which are retrieved for improving caption decoding. Our main contribution of this paper is to show that how a memory model based on the ART is integrated with the deep learning approach. The GVM is able to generalize and retrieve the temporal structure of the video to improve the quality of the video description base on a deep learning framework. We construct our framework that is based on the mean pool approach [34], with the integration of the GVM model. The mean pooled features are the representation of the visual features within a video. Our method explores on the representation and storage of similar video features into memories. The idea is analogous to a human drawing past experiences and knowledge to conduct an informed judgement based on a limited sensory information. By recalling memory of similar videos, the LSTM caption decoder is able to utilize the additional information and generate better quality sentence. Using the publicly available YouTube2Text data set [5], we show that by combining GVM with the basic mean pool approach, we can obtain competitive results as compared to the current state-of-the-art methods.

The organization of this paper is as follows. We report the related work for video captioning in Sect. 2. In Sect. 3, we introduce our GVM network and the video captioning framework. In Sect. 4, we discuss the details of the experiment set up. We then illustrate the performance of GVM by comparing other state-of-the-art methods in Sect. 5. We then finalize our paper with concluding remarks in Sect. 6.

2   Related Work

Early research on video captioning has focused on using various image processing techniques to extract the best subject, verb and object tuples from the video. Together with rule based, statistical modeling and sentence templates [12,16], they are able to produce grammatically correct sentences. However, these methods has focused on a narrow domain with limited vocabularies describing the objects and its the activities.

Recent success with large-scale image recognition using convolutional neural networks (CNN) [17,22,27] and language modeling and translation using variants of the RNN [10,25,26] have inspired researchers to combine both deep learning domains for work regarding image captioning [15,35].

The natural progression of image captioning using deep learning approach is to extend to the video domain. Venugopalan et al. [34] used the AlexNet to extracts frame by frame features. Mean pooling or averaging is applied to the frame features. The mean pooled vector is presented as input to a two-layer LSTM network for generating descriptions. While this method of averaging frame features loses the representation in the temporal aspects, it has provided a good baseline result for other video captioning work.

To address the temporal representations of video for generating description, a sequence to sequence LSTM framework is proposed for temporal modeling of videos and language [33]. Recent work include the attention mechanism [18,41] which are able to selectively focus on the given input video features. However, these models do not attend to other videos which have similar visual features.

There is a trend in deep learning to integrate the use of memory into neural network models. Weston et al. introduced the Memory Networks [40] which can help RNNs to memorize long sequences. This memory model is known to be difficult to train by backpropagation. Sukhbaatar et al. [24] proposed an end-to-end memory network that requires less supervision in training. Memory networks have been shown to be able to do textual and visual question and answering tasks [39]. However, these memory models do have limited slots to store memories.

The ART network [2] was proposed to learn memory or cognitive nodes by encoding input patterns and to support the recognition and recall of the stored patterns. A vigilance parameter is used to control the level of generalization on the stored patterns. Tan et al. proposed the fusion ART [30], which is an ART variant with multi input fields. The fusion ART model has been applied to the modeling of episodic memory [4,23,37,38] as well as to the reinforcement learning [28,29,31,36] domain. Given that the ART network does not learn by backpropagation, it may present a challenge to integrate the ART model into an end-to-end neural network. Our work focuses on how the ART-based memory module is able to integrate into a deep learning approach to the video captioning domain.

3 Video Captioning Using Generalized Video Memory

The video captioning task encodes visual features from an image sequences $(v_1, v_2, ..., v_n)$ and decodes a sequence of words $(y_1, y_2, ...y_m)$. The length of both input and output sequences are variable. In this paper, we propose a memory model named Generalized Video Memory (GVM) network for storing and recalling of the generalized video features. Our automatic video captioning framework is based on Venugopalan et al. [34] mean pooling approach. Firstly, a CNN based image encoder is used for extracting frame features. The extracted frames features are averaged (mean pooled). The mean pooled vector representing the video are presented to the GVM for memory generalization storage. The mean pool vector and the generalized video memory features are provided as the inputs to a two-layer LSTM caption decoder. By using additional information from the memory, the caption decoder is able to generate better captions. Figure 1 shows our video captioning framework integrating with the GVM network. In the following sections, we describe our video captioning framework with the GVM network.

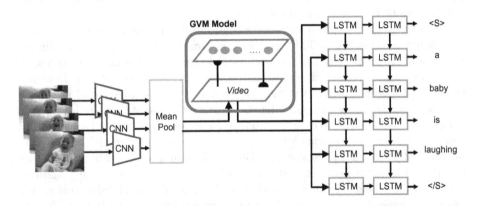

Fig. 1. Video captioning framework with Generalized Video Memory (GVM) model. The token <S> represents the start-of-sentence and the token </S> represents the end-of-sentence.

3.1 The CNN Video Encoder

The 16-layer CNN based image encoder, VGG16 [22], is used for encoding the image features from the video clip. The VGG16 network is loaded with pretrained parameters trained with the 1.2M subset images from the ImageNet data set [21]. We use the publicly available VGG16 implementation from Caffe [8] and converted the implementation to tensorflow. Image features (4096 dimensional vector) are extracted from the fully connected layer (fc2) after ReLU activation. To encode the entire video, image features extracted are averaged (mean pooled) across the video frames to form a mean pooled vector fc_{mean}.

3.2 The Generalized Video Memory Network

The GVM network proposed in this paper is based on Adaptive Resonance Theory (ART) neural network [2] and fusion ART [30]. Figure 2 shows architecture of the GVM network. The GVM network consists of a input field, namely the *video* field, and a category field. The network is designed to learn cognitive nodes at the category layer (F_2), while encoding the input patterns at the input field layer (F_1). During learning, the input vector presented to the input field is matched against the cognitive nodes at the F_2 layer. The matching criteria is controlled by the vigilance parameter. When a match is found, the matched cognitive node adapts its weights to the new input vector. If no match is found, a new cognitive node is recruited which learns the newly presented input vector. Thus, the GVM performs fast and stable learning in response to a continual stream of input patterns, and learns new patterns incrementally. It supports the recognition and recall of the stored patterns based on similarity of the search cue. For completeness, the network dynamics are described below.

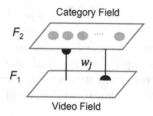

Fig. 2. The Generalized Video Memory (GVM) network.

Input vectors: Let $\mathbf{I} = (I_1, I_2, \ldots, I_n)$ denote an input vector, where $I_i \in [0, 1]$ indicates the ith input element. Let the complement coded vector be $\bar{\mathbf{I}}$, such that $\bar{I}_i = 1 - I_i$.

Input fields: Let F_1 denote an input field that holds the input pattern for the video features. Let $\mathbf{x} = (x_1, x_2, \ldots, x_{2n})$ be the activity vector of F_1 receiving the input vector $\mathbf{I}$ (including the complement) such that $\mathbf{x} \leftarrow (I_1, I_2, \ldots, I_n, \bar{I}_1, \bar{I}_2, \ldots, \bar{I}_n)$.

Category field: Let F_2 denote the category field. Let $\mathbf{y} = (y_1, y_2, \ldots, y_m)$ be the activity vector of F_2.

Weight vectors: Let $\mathbf{w}_j$ denote the weight vector associated with the jth node in F_2 for learning the input pattern in F_1.

Parameters: Each field's dynamics is determined by choice parameters $\alpha \geq 0$, learning rate parameters $\beta \in [0, 1]$, contribution parameters $\gamma \in [0, 1]$ and vigilance parameters $\rho \in [0, 1]$.

The dynamics of the GVM network can be considered as a system of continuous resonance search processes comprising the basic operations as follows.

Code activation: A node j in F_2 is activated by the choice function

$$T_j = \gamma \frac{|\mathbf{x} \wedge \mathbf{w}_j|}{\alpha + |\mathbf{w}_j|}, \tag{1}$$

where the fuzzy AND operation $\wedge$ is defined by $(\mathbf{p} \wedge \mathbf{q})_i \equiv min(p_i, q_i)$, and the norm $|.|$ is defined by $|\mathbf{p}| \equiv \sum_i p_i$ for vectors $\mathbf{p}$ and $\mathbf{q}$.

Code competition: A code competition process follows to select a F_2 node with the highest choice function value. The winner is indexed at J where

$$T_J = \max\{T_j : \text{for all } F_2 \text{ node } j\}. \tag{2}$$

When a category choice is made at node J, $y_J = 1$; and $y_j = 0$ for all $j \neq J$ indicating a *winner-take-all* strategy.

Template matching: A template matching process checks if resonance occurs. It checks if the *match function* m_J of the chosen node J meets its vigilance criterion such that

$$m_J = \frac{|\mathbf{x} \wedge \mathbf{w}_J|}{|\mathbf{x}|} \geq \rho. \tag{3}$$

If the vigilance constraint is violated, a mismatch reset occurs and T_J is set to 0 for the duration of the input presentation. Another F_2 node J is selected using choice function and code competition until a resonance is achieved. If no selected node in F_2 meets the vigilance, an uncommitted node is recruited in F_2 as a new category node.

Template learning: Once a resonance occurs, the weight vector $\mathbf{w}_J$ is modified by the following learning rule:

$$\mathbf{w}_J^{(new)} = (1 - \beta)\mathbf{w}_J^{(old)} + \beta(\mathbf{x} \wedge \mathbf{w}_J^{(old)}). \tag{4}$$

Activity readout: The chosen F_2 node J may perform a readout of its weight vectors to an input field F_1 such that $\mathbf{x}^* = \mathbf{w}_J$.

Using the described network dynamics, our memory model is able to generalize video representations and store memories incrementally at the category field F_2. For our framework, we use the mean pooled vector, fc_{mean} as inputs to the GVM model. The mean pool vector, fc_{mean} is normalized by dividing the vector by a scaling factor of M, subjected to a ceiling of one. The normalized mean pool vector $\mathbf{I}_{norm}$, is complement coded such that the input vector $\mathbf{x}$ is $[\mathbf{I}_{norm}, \overline{\mathbf{I}_{norm}}]$ (8192 dimensional vector). The overall learning process is summarized in Algorithm 1. Each created category node weight vector $\mathbf{w_j}$ represents a new memory of a class video features. During learning, the closeness of which the category nodes are categorized are determined by the vigilance parameter ρ. The higher the vigilance parameter, the more specific the category nodes are learned.

Algorithm 1. Encoding of the Generalized Video Memory

1: Input: The normalized mean pooled vector
2: Present the normalized mean pooled vector to the *video* field at F_1
3: Perform code activation in the category field F_2 ▷ see (1)
4: **repeat**
5:     Perform code competition and template matching ▷ see (2 & 3)
6: **until** resonance occurs ▷ see (3)
7: Perform template learning ▷ see (4)

To recall the generalized video memory, the vigilance parameter, ρ is set to zero. The recalling process is described in Algorithm 2 for retrieving the matching memory $\mathbf{x}^*$ from the input $\mathbf{x}$. The retrieved memory represents a generalized feature most similar to the input. With the use of complement coding and fuzzy AND operations, the memory node is able to represent the range values of the stored category [3]. The generalized memory is complement coded, such that $\mathbf{x}^* = [w^*, \overline{w_c^*}]$, where w^* is the lower bound of the memory vector, and $1 - \overline{w_c^*}$ is upper bound of memory vector. We averaged both the upper and lower bound memory vector and rescaled the vector back by M to form the *generalized memory vector*, $\mathbf{m}^*$. In this case, $\mathbf{m}^*$ has a dimension of 4096. The vector $\mathbf{m}^*$ is used as part of the input to the caption decoder as described in later sections.

Algorithm 2. Retrieval of the Generalized Video Memory

1: Input: The mean pooled vector to the *video* field
2: Perform code activation in the category field ▷ see (1)
3: Select the winner code with highest choice value ▷ see (2)
4: **return** The readout of the winner's memory $\mathbf{x}^*$

3.3   Caption Decoder

A standard RNN in principle is able to map a sequence of inputs to a sequence of outputs. For our work, a RNN is useful in mapping out a sequence of words to form the video description. Practically however, training a standard RNN with long-term dependency is difficult as it suffers from vanishing gradient problem [1]. The Long Short-Term Memory (LSTM) [14], a variant of RNN addresses the vanishing gradient problem with nonlinear gating units and memory cell c_t to maintain its state over time. As there are many variants of LSTM [11], to avoid confusion, we denote the exact LSTM equations used in our work. The LSTM unit used are described by Graves et al. [10]. The vector formulas for the LSTM unit are written as:

$$
\begin{aligned}
i_t &= \sigma(W_{ix}x_t + W_{ih}h_{t-1} + b_i) \\
f_t &= \sigma(W_{fx}x_t + W_{fh}h_{t-1} + b_f) \\
o_t &= \sigma(W_{ox}x_t + W_{oh}h_{t-1} + b_o) \\
c_t &= f_t \odot c_{t-1} + i_t \odot \phi(W_{cx}x_t + W_{ch}h_{t-1} + b_c) \\
h_t &= o_t \odot \phi(c_t)
\end{aligned}
\tag{5}
$$

where σ is the sigmoid function, ϕ is the hyperbolic tangent function and $\odot$ denotes pointwise multiplication of two vectors. The LSTM weight matrices are denoted by W_{ij}, and its biases bj. Each LSTM unit has three gates to compute the hidden state h_t. For an input of x_t at time step t, the input gate i_t controls how much of the input x_t is to be considered. The forget gate f_t controls how much to forget on the previous memory state c_{t-1}. The output gate o_t controls how much information in the memory state c_t is to be transferred to the hidden state h_t.

To have a direct comparison with the original mean-pool technique, we use the same two-layer LSTM designs as described in the mean pool approach [34]. A two-layer LSTM captures the structure of time series more naturally than a single-layer LSTM [13]. From the mean pool method, the mean pooled vector fc_{mean} is repeatedly presented as inputs to the LSTM caption decoder. In our work, during training, we present the *generalized memory vector*, $\mathbf{m}^*$ as the first input of the sequence, followed by the fc_{mean} vector repeatedly. This allows to prime the LSTM model to learn similar experiences from the generalized video memory vector, while learning the exact representation from the mean pooled vector. The LSTM model outputs the hidden state per time step. To predict a word from the hidden states, a word embedding is trained. The word embedding formula is represented as:

$$z_t = \phi(Wh_t + b) \tag{6}$$

where z_t is the predicted word output vector, W is the word embedding vector, b is the bias for the embedding vector, and h_t is the hidden states from the second LSTM layer. The words are represented as one-hot vectors y_t with a vector length D, where D is the size of the vocabulary. The sentence is prepended with a start-of-sentence (<S>) token, and appended with a end-of-sentence </S>) token. We use the softmax function to compute the probability distribution of the words w:

$$p(w|h_t) = \frac{\exp(W_w h_t + b)}{\sum_{w' \in D} \exp(W_{w'} h_t + b)} \tag{7}$$

During training, the LSTM model maximizes the log-likelihood objective function which is formulated as,

$$\max_{\theta} \sum_{t=1}^{T} \log\ p(y_t|z_t, y_{t-1}; \theta) \tag{8}$$

where θ denotes the model parameter which is to be optimized over the entire training data set.

During testing, the first input of the sequence to the LSTM model is the *generalized memory vector* $\mathbf{m}^*$, followed by the fc_{mean} vector repeatedly until the (</S>) token is emitted.

4 Experiment

4.1 Data Set

The YouTube2Text data set [5] contains 1,970 YouTube video clips annotated with multiple language descriptions. The descriptions are created by crowd sourcing using the Amazon's Mechanical Turk. We use only the English descriptions from the data set, which is about 80,000 video-sentence pairs. Each clip is usually less than 10 seconds long which depicts a main activity, accompanied with about 40 sentences. Following mean pool approach [34], we split the data set by randomly picking a training set of 1,200 videos, a testing set of 670 videos and a validation set of 100 videos.

4.2 Preprocessing

Video Preprocessing: We conducted frame sampling for one in every ten frames. We resized the sampled frames to 224×224 pixels, which is the input size for the VGG16 network. The video clips are zero padded to maintain the original aspect ratio.

Text Preprocessing: We tokenized the sentences, removed punctuations and converted the words to lower case. The vocabulary size is about 5,000 after removal of rare words that appeared less than four times. Due to batch training, sentences are padded with </S>) tokens to align with the longest length of the word sequence of each batch.

4.3 Training Details

For the visual encoder, we fix the weights of the VGG16 network to reduce computation work load. For each video, the outputs vectors of the VGG16 fc2 layer are mean pooled to form the mean pooled vector.

To learn the generalized video memory vector, the mean pooled vectors are used for memory encoding. The scaling factor M for normalization is set to 64.0. One shot learning is enabled by setting the GVM's learning rate β to 1.0. The choice parameter, α is set to 0.001. With the vigilance parameter ρ set at 0.99, GVM learns a total of 576 categories after learning training set.

The training of the caption decoder proceeds after learning the GVM's memories. The two-layer LSTM caption decoder has 1,000 hidden units for each layer. To avoid over-fitting, a dropout of 0.5 is used on both the inputs and the outputs of both LSTM layers. Training of the caption decoder with GVM model is described in Sect. 3.3. We stopped training the LSTM caption decoder when the validation loss does not improve. For our baseline comparison, we have also replicated the results using the mean pool method with VGG16 video encoder with our data set splits.

4.4   Evaluation Metrics

We use two model-free evaluation metrics, BLEU [20] and METEOR [7] to evaluate the results against the ground truth sentences. The two metrics are chosen as most prior work with YouTube2Text data set report their results with BLEU and METEOR scores, therefore a direct comparison can be done. Both BLEU and METEOR are typically used for evaluating machine translation and image captioning tasks. Generally, the higher the scores, the better the correlation of the predicted descriptions are against human judgement. We employed the codes from the Microsoft COCO Caption Evaluation Server [6] to obtain both BLEU and METEOR scores.

5   Experimental Results

The evaluation metric scores are shown in Table 1. While other methods may have trained with more image/video captioning data set, we only compare the evaluation results that are trained purely on the YouTube2Text data set, with the use of pre-trained visual encoder. We report the scores of the compared algorithms along with the type of visual encoder as the evaluation scores can differ by employing a different visual encoder. The BLEU scores for both the mean pool (VGGNet) and the S2VT methods are omitted as they are not reported in the original work. The results are shown in Table 1.

5.1   Compared Algorithms

The following describes briefly on the compared algorithms:

- **Factor Graph Model (FGM)** [32]. FGM first employs vision recognizers to obtain the subject, object, activity and place (SOVP) elements. The Factor

Table 1. Evaluation results based on the YouTube2Text data set, with compared methods with its visual encoder. (*) represents our replicated results.

Model	BLEU@4	METEOR
FGM	13.68	23.9
Mean pool (AlexNet)	31.2	26.9
Mean pool (VGGNet)	-	27.7
Our Experiments		
Mean pool (VGGNet) *	42.5	27.6
GVM (VGGNet)	**42.5**	**28.1**
Recent Methods		
S2VT (VGGNet) (AlexNet)	-	29.8
LSTM-E (VGGNet) (C3D)	45.3	31.0
HRNE-Attention (GoogLeNet) (C3D)	46.7	33.9

Graph Model further refines the co-occurring SOVP elements by maximum a posteriori (MAP) estimation. A template is used for sentence generation based on the refined SOVP elements.

- **Mean Pool (AlexNet)** [34]. The visual features are extracted using AlexNet. The features are averaged (mean pooled) across the frames of the entire video. The mean pooled feature is used as the input to the LSTM caption decoder continuously until a end-of-sentence token is omitted.
- **Mean Pool (VGG)** [33]. Similar to the above, with the exception of utilising the VGGNet visual encoder.
- **S2VT (VGG & AlexNet)** [33]. The VGGNet is used to extract RGB features, and the AlexNet for to extract optical flow features. Both RGB and flow features are presented as the input to an encoder-decoder model of LSTM. The first encoding phase processes the sequences of the visual features. The second decoding phase generates the captions until a end-of-sentence token is omitted.
- **LSTM-E (VGG & C3D)** [19]. Visual-semantic embeddings using LSTM are used to maximize the probability of next word given the previous word and visual content. A joint learning of relevance and coherence objective functions are utilized to minimize losses between the visual and textual content.
- **HRNE-Attention (GoogLeNet & C3D)** [18]. The Hierarchical Recurrent Neural Encoder (HRNE) exploits the temporal structure of the video. The 2-layer hierarchical LSTM structure is analogical to a convolutional network. Information flows to the next layer by a fixed time step. Along with attention mechanism, HRNE decodes the captions from the video feature sequences.

As the data set split of the training, testing and validation set is randomly picked, it may affect the metric scores when compared to other work due to the data set differences. For a fair comparison, we also replicated the result of the mean pool (VGG16) approach using our data set splits.

5.2 Analysis

With training done on the YouTube2Text data set alone, our framework with GVM model is able to achieve a METEOR score of 28.1. This is better than the reported baseline method Mean pool (VGG) at 27.7 and our replicated result at 27.6. It should be noted that these results are trained only with the YouTube2Text data set. The result shows that the GVM model is able to enhance the video captioning quality. While the magnitude of the evaluation scores may not be intuitive to interpret, by comparing with the latest algorithms that combines multiple visual features, we can gauge that minor differences in score do make significant contribution to the quality of captions.

When inspecting the test output, there are a number of sentences that do not contain the verbs of the activities. We attribute this issue to the mean pooling method as it does not fully capture the order of visual events which is important for activity recognition.

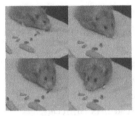

Test Example (1)
GVM: a hamster is eating a seeds
BL: a hamster is cutting seeds
GT: A hamster is eating sunflower seeds

Test Example (2)
GVM: a band is playing on stage
BL: man is playing
GT: A man is dancing on a stage

Test Example (3)
GVM: a man is shooting a gun
BL: a man is shooting a
GT: Someone is shooting a gun

Test Example (4)
GVM: a cat is meowing
BL: a cat is licking
GT: A cat is licking its lips

Test Example (5)
GVM: a man is cutting a pineapple
BL: a man is a a
GT: A man is seasoning a chicken

Test Example (6)
GVM: a woman is dancing
BL: a woman is eating
GT: A man is serving some food

Fig. 3. Example 1 to 3 (top left to right) and Example 4 to 6 (bottom left to right) with screenshots of the video against text generated by the Generalized Video Memory Network (GVM); the replicated mean pool baseline (BL); and the ground truth (GT).

The one drawback of the ART based network is that the category nodes learned are dependent on the order of which the inputs are presented. This issue is mitigated by shuffling the order of the training data during the encoding stage of the GVM network.

5.3   Test Examples

Figure 3 shows some examples of the generated captions with our framework using GVM, the replicated mean pool method and the ground truth. Interestingly for test example 2, while the focus is on the dancing man, GVM is able to pick up the background activities depicting a group of musicians performing on the stage. Our current framework do not have the attention mechanism which may improve the focus of the subjects in the video clips. For the test example 4 and 5, while our GVM model captions are invalid, it generates related captions that are similar to the video scene. The invalid output suggests a down side of over-generalization of the video memory.

6   Conclusion

We have proposed a memory framework GVM for video captioning. Our experiments have shown that GVM is able to enhance on the BLEU and METEOR scores using a similar baseline design based on mean pooling. We have demonstrated the potential of enhancing the accuracies of a deep learning model using memory modules based on ART. We believe by integrating the concepts investigated in this paper to the latest state-of-the-art video captioning architecture, we can further enhance the scores as well. In future work, we will like to introduce GVM into the latest state-of-the-art methods and expand the use of multi-channel input fields to represent multi-modal memories.

Acknowledgments. This research is supported in part by a research grant (DSOCL16006) from DSO National Laboratories, Singapore and a joint project funded by ICT Virtual Organization of ASEAN Institutes and NICT (ASEAN IVO).

References

1. Bengio, Y., Simard, P., Frasconi, P.: Learning long-term dependencies with gradient descent is difficult. IEEE Trans. Neural Netw. **5**(2), 157–166 (1994)
2. Carpenter, G.A., Grossberg, S.: Adaptive Resonance Theory. In: Arbib, M.A. (ed.) The Handbook of Brain Theory and Neural Networks, pp. 87–90. MIT Press, Cambridge (2003)
3. Carpenter, G.A., Grossberg, S., Rosen, D.B.: Fuzzy ART: fast stable learning and categorization of analog patterns by an adaptive resonance system. Neural Netw. **4**(6), 759–771 (1991)
4. Chang, P.-H., Tan, A.-H.: Encoding and recall of spatio-temporal episodic memory in real time. In: Proceedings of the International Joint Conference on Artificial Intelligence, pp. 1490–1496 (2017)
5. Chen, D.L., Dolan, W.B.: Collecting highly parallel data for paraphrase evaluation. In: Proceedings of the 49th Annual Meeting of the Association for Computational Linguistics: Human Language Technologies, vol. 1, pp. 190–200 (2011)
6. Chen, X., et al.: Microsoft COCO captions: Data collection and evaluation server. arXiv preprint arXiv:1504.00325 (2015)
7. Denkowski, M., Lavie, A.: Meteor universal: language specific translation evaluation for any target language. In: Proceedings of the ninth workshop on Statistical Machine Translation, pp. 376–380 (2014)
8. Donahue, J., et al.: DeCAF: a deep convolutional activation feature for generic visual recognition. In: International Conference on Machine Learning, pp. 647–655 (2014)
9. Fakoor, R., Mohamed, A., Mitchell, M., Kang, S.B., Kohli, P.: Memory-augmented attention modelling for videos. arXiv preprint arXiv:1611.02261 (2016)
10. Graves, A., Mohamed, A., Hinton, G.: Speech recognition with deep recurrent neural networks. In: Proceedings of the IEEE international conference on Acoustics, Speech and Signal Processing, pp. 6645–6649 (2013)
11. Greff, K., Srivastava, R.K., Koutník, J., Steunebrink, B.R., Schmidhuber, J.: LSTM: a search space odyssey. IEEE Trans. Neural Netw. Learn. Syst. **28**(10), 2222–2232 (2017)
12. Guadarrama, S., et al.: YouTube2Text: recognizing and describing arbitrary activities using semantic hierarchies and zero-shot recognition. In: Proceedings of the IEEE International Conference on Computer Vision, pp. 2712–2719 (2013)
13. Hermans, M., Schrauwen, B.: Training and analysing deep recurrent neural networks. In: Advances in Neural Information Processing Systems, pp. 190–198 (2013)

14. Hochreiter, S., Schmidhuber, J.: Long short-term memory. Neural Comput. **9**(8), 1735–1780 (1997)
15. Karpathy, A., Fei-Fei, L.: Deep visual-semantic alignments for generating image descriptions. In: Proceedings of the IEEE Conference on Computer Vision and Pattern Recognition, pp. 3128–3137 (2015)
16. Krishnamoorthy, N., Malkarnenkar, G., Mooney, R.J., Saenko, K., Guadarrama, S.: Generating natural-language video descriptions using text-mined knowledge. In: Association for the Advancement of Artificial Intelligence, vol. 1, p. 2 (2013)
17. Krizhevsky, A., Sutskever, I., Hinton, G.E.: ImageNet classification with deep convolutional neural networks. In: Advances in Neural Information Processing Systems, pp. 1097–1105 (2012)
18. Pan, P., Xu, Z., Yang, Y., Wu, F., Zhuang, Y.: Hierarchical recurrent neural encoder for video representation with application to captioning. In: Proceedings of the IEEE Conference on Computer Vision and Pattern Recognition, pp. 1029–1038 (2016)
19. Pan, Y., Mei, T., Yao, T., Li, H., Rui, Y.: Jointly modeling embedding and translation to bridge video and language. In: Proceedings of the IEEE Conference on Computer Vision and Pattern Recognition, pp. 4594–4602 (2016)
20. Papineni, K., Roukos, S., Ward, T., Zhu, W.J.: BLEU: a method for automatic evaluation of machine translation. In: Proceedings of the 40th Annual Meeting on Association for Computational Linguistics, pp. 311–318 (2002)
21. Russakovsky, O., et al.: ImageNet large scale visual recognition challenge. Int. J. Comput. Vis. **115**(3), 211–252 (2015)
22. Simonyan, K., Zisserman, A.: Very deep convolutional networks for large-scale image recognition. In: Proceedings of the International Conference on Learning Representations (2015)
23. Subagdja, B., Tan, A.-H.: Neural modeling of sequential inferences and learning over episodic memory. Neurocomputing **161**, 229–242 (2015)
24. Sukhbaatar, S., Weston, J., Fergus, R., et al.: End-to-end memory networks. In: Advances in Neural Information Processing Systems, pp. 2440–2448 (2015)
25. Sundermeyer, M., Schlüter, R., Ney, H.: LSTM neural networks for language modeling. In: Conference of the International Speech Communication Association (2012)
26. Sutskever, I., Vinyals, O., Le, Q.V.: Sequence to sequence learning with neural networks. In: Advances in Neural Information Processing Systems, pp. 3104–3112 (2014)
27. Szegedy, C., et al.: Going deeper with convolutions. In: Proceedings of the IEEE Conference on Computer Vision and Pattern Recognition, pp. 1–9 (2015)
28. Tan, A.-H.: Falcon: a fusion architecture for learning, cognition, and navigation. In: Proceedings of the IEEE International Joint Conference on Neural Network, vol. 4, pp. 3297–3302. IEEE (2004)
29. Tan, A.-H.: Direct code access in self-organizing neural networks for reinforcement learning. In: Proceedings of the International Joint Conference on Artificial Intelligence, pp. 1071–1076 (2007)
30. Tan, A.-H., Carpenter, G.A., Grossberg, S.: Intelligence through interaction: towards a unified theory for learning. In: Liu, D., Fei, S., Hou, Z.-G., Zhang, H., Sun, C. (eds.) ISNN 2007. LNCS, vol. 4491, pp. 1094–1103. Springer, Heidelberg (2007). https://doi.org/10.1007/978-3-540-72383-7_128
31. Teng, T.H., Tan, A.-H., Zurada, J.M.: Self-organizing neural networks integrating domain knowledge and reinforcement learning. IEEE Trans. Neural Netw. Learn. Syst. **26**(5), 889–902 (2015)

32. Thomason, J., Venugopalan, S., Guadarrama, S., Saenko, K., Mooney, R.: Integrating language and vision to generate natural language descriptions of videos in the wild. In: Proceedings of the International Conference on Computational Linguistics, pp. 1218–1227 (2014)
33. Venugopalan, S., Rohrbach, M., Donahue, J., Mooney, R., Darrell, T., Saenko, K.: Sequence to sequence-video to text. In: Proceedings of the IEEE International Conference on Computer Vision, pp. 4534–4542 (2015)
34. Venugopalan, S., Xu, H., Donahue, J., Rohrbach, M., Mooney, R., Saenko, K.: Translating videos to natural language using deep recurrent neural networks. In: Proceedings of the Conference of the North American Chapter of the Association for Computational Linguistics: Human Language Technologies, pp. 1494–1504 (2015)
35. Vinyals, O., Toshev, A., Bengio, S., Erhan, D.: Show and tell: a neural image caption generator. In: Proceedings of the IEEE International Conference on Computer Vision, pp. 3156–3164 (2015)
36. Wang, P., Zhou, W.J., Wang, D., Tan, A.-H.: Probabilistic guided exploration for reinforcement learning in self-organizing neural networks. In: Proceedings of International Conference on Agents, pp. 109–112 (2018)
37. Wang, W., Subagdja, B., Tan, A.-H., Starzyk, J.A.: A self-organizing approach to episodic memory modeling. In: Proceedings of the IEEE International Joint Conference on Neural Networks, pp. 1–8. IEEE (2010)
38. Wang, W., Subagdja, B., Tan, A.-H., Starzyk, J.A.: Neural modeling of episodic memory: encoding, retrieval, and forgetting. IEEE Trans. Neural Netw. Learn. Syst. **23**(10), 1574–1586 (2012)
39. Weston, J., et al.: Towards ai-complete question answering: a set of prerequisite toy tasks. arXiv preprint arXiv:1502.05698 (2015)
40. Weston, J., Chopra, S., Bordes, A.: Memory networks. In: Proceedings of the International Conference on Learning Representations (2015)
41. Yu, H., Wang, J., Huang, Z., Yang, Y., Xu, W.: Video paragraph captioning using hierarchical recurrent neural networks. In: Proceedings of the IEEE Conference on Computer Vision and Pattern Recognition, pp. 4584–4593 (2016)

Short Papers

An Efficient Hash-Based Method for Time Series Motif Discovery

Pham Thanh Xuan and Duong Tuan Anh[(✉)]

Faculty of Computer Science and Engineering,
Ho Chi Minh City University of Technology, Ho Chi Minh City, Vietnam
xuan_pham_thanh@yahoo.com, dtanh@cse.hcmut.edu.vn

Abstract. In this paper, we propose a new efficient method for discovering 1-motifs in large time series data that can perform faster than Random Projection algorithm. The proposed method is based on hashing with three improvement techniques. Experimental results on several benchmark datasets show that our proposed method can discover precise motifs with high accuracy and time efficiency on large time series data.

Keywords: Time series · Motif discovery · Feature extraction
Hashing-based

1 Introduction

Time series motifs are frequently occurring but previously unknown subsequences of a longer time series. Motif discovery is one of the most important data mining tasks in time series data. Some well-known algorithms for motif discovery are Random Projection by Chiu et al. [2]; EMD by Tanaka et al. [8] which applies Minimum Description Length principle; MK by Mueen et al. [7] which is an exact motif discovery algorithm; and an algorithm by Gruber et al. (2006) which is based on time series segmentation and clustering [3]. Among these above-mentioned algorithms for motif discovery, Random Projection has been considered as the most popular algorithm and is the basis of many other approaches that deal with this problem. However, Random Projection still suffers from high computational cost and cannot satisfy the requirement of real applications with large time series datasets.

   In this paper, we propose a new efficient hash-based method for discovering motif in large time series data. The method first reduces the dimensionality using Piecewise Aggregate Approximation (PAA) ([6]) and discretizes the time series using Symbolic Aggregate Approximation (SAX) ([6]) and extracts features from the discretized time series through a sliding window and then hashes the features into a hash table. The matching features are placed into the same bucket. After hashing, the features which are stored in the bucket with the largest number of matching features are instances of the 1-motif. Our motif discovery method, called Feature Matching Grouping (FMG), has three important features: (i) FMG uses less data structures than Random Projection, (ii) FMG applies a new way of shifting the sliding window, and (iii) FMG aims to find the motifs with good shape. Experimental results on several benchmark datasets show

© Springer Nature Switzerland AG 2018
M. Kaenampornpan et al. (Eds.): MIWAI 2018, LNAI 11248, pp. 205–211, 2018.
https://doi.org/10.1007/978-3-030-03014-8_17

that our proposed method can discover precise motifs with high accuracy and time efficiency on large time series data.

2 Background

2.1 Some Definitions

A time series $T = t_1, t_2, \ldots, t_n$ is an ordered set of n real values measured at equal intervals. Given a time series T of length n, a subsequence C is a subsection of length $m < n$ of contiguous positions from T, i.e., $C = t_p, t_{p+1}, \ldots, t_{p+m-1}$, for $1 \leq p \leq n - m + 1$.

Definition 1. *Sliding Window*: Given a time series T of length n, and a user-defined subsequence length w, a list S of all possible subsequences can be built by sliding a window of size w ($w \ll n$) across T. The size of list S is $n-w + 1$.

Definition 2. *Match*: Given a positive real number R (called *range*, supplied by user) and a time series T containing a subsequence C beginning at p and a subsequence M at q, if the distance from C to M, $D(C, M) \leq R$, then M is called a matching subsequence of C. (In this work, we use Euclidean distance).

Definition 3. *Trivial match*: Given a time series T containing a subsequence C beginning at position p and a matching subsequence M beginning at q, we say that M is a trivial match to C if $p = q$ or there does not exist a subsequence M' beginning at q' such that $D(C, M') > R$ and $q < q' < p$ or $p < q' < q$.

Definition 4. *1-Motifs*: Given a time series T of length n, and a range R, the most significant *motif* in T (called the *1-Motif*) is a subsequence C_1 that has highest count of non-trivial matches. All the subsequences that are similar to the 1-motif are called *instances* of the 1-motif.

The above definitions are from Lin et al. [5].

2.2 PAA and SAX

A time series $C = (c_1, \ldots, c_n)$ of length n can be represented in a reduced w-dimensional space as another time series $C' = (\mu_1, \ldots, \mu_w)$ by segmenting C into w equally-sized segments and replacing each segment by its mean value μ_i. This dimensionality reduction technique is called Piecewise Aggregate Approximation (PAA) [6]. After this step, the time series C is transformed by SAX ([6]) into a symbolic sequence $A = a_1 \ldots a_w$ in which each real value μ_i is mapped to a symbol a_i from an alphabet of size a.

Given two SAX representations of the same length, to check if they match with each other, we need to compute the difference between them. This difference needs the *dist*() function for each pair of symbols. The *dist*() function for a pair of symbols can be implemented using a table lookup as shown in [6].

2.3 The Random Projection Algorithm for Time Series Motif Discovery

Random Projection, developed by Chiu et al. [2], is the first algorithm that can find motifs in linear time. This algorithm is an iterative approach and uses as base structure a *collision matrix* whose rows and columns are the SAX representation of each time series subsequence. The subsequences are obtained using a sliding window approach. At each iteration, it selects certain positions of each word as the *mask* and traverses the word list. For each match, the collision matrix entry is incremented. In the end, the largest entries in the collision matrix are selected as motif candidates.

3 The Proposed Method

Our proposed method, called Feature Matching Grouping (FMG), for time series motif discovery is based on hashing technique. Our FMG method is somewhat similar in spirit to Random Projection (RP) algorithm. However, there are some major differences between our proposed method and RP. First, our FMG uses less data structures than RP: while RP uses a hash table and a collision matrix, our FMG uses only a hash table. Second, FMG aims to find motifs with good shape. Finally, FMG speeds up the motif discovery process by a new way of shifting the sliding window.

We need some more definitions before explaining the algorithm.

Definition 5. *Feature Match*: Two features match with each other if they do not overlap and for each corresponding symbol pair, their difference is not greater than 1.

Example: Given a discretized time series T = '*aacbaccacbc*', and the sliding window of length 3 (w = 3). If we have two features f_1 = '*aac*', f_4 = '*bac*' then their difference $|f_{1i} - f_{4i}| = 100$. Notice that this difference can be computed based on *dist* function (see Sect. 2.2). The two features f_1 and f_4 match with each other, they are put in the same bucket as illustrated in Fig. 1. If we have two features f_1= '*aac*', f_5 = '*acc*' then their difference $|f_{1i} - f_{5i}| = 020$, then the two features f_1 and f_5 do not match with each other, and they are put in two different buckets as shown in Fig. 1.

Definition 6. *Trivial Feature Match*: One feature is a trivial match of another feature if the two features *overlap* and match with each other.

Notice that subsequences whose shapes are almost close to straight lines should not be selected as motif candidates. Therefore, we need a definition of a good motif candidate as follows.

Definition 7. *Good motif candidate*: A feature is a good motif candidate if the difference between the maximal symbol and the minimal symbol in the feature is greater than s, a *good motif score* supplied by user.

In practice, we set a default value for good motif score s by the formula: $s = a/2$ where a is the size of the alphabet in SAX. The constraint in Definition 7 helps user determine a reasonable shape for the motif candidates.

The outline of the FMG algorithm is given as follows.

Step 1. Normalizing the input time series.

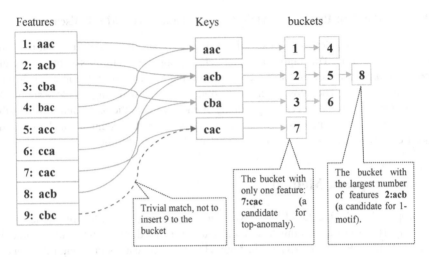

Fig. 1. The process of extracting features, putting them in the hash table, and finding motif candidate from the discretized time series $T = aacbaccacbc$, with window size $w = 3$.

Step 2. By sliding a window of size w across the time series, extracting subsequences, converting the subsequences to PAA representation and converting them to SAX words.

Step 3. Building the hash table with the features extracted from the time series.

Step 4. Identifying the motif candidate based on the hash table and discovering 1-motif of the time series from the motif candidates.

Figure 1 illustrates the process of extracting features from the time series, and putting them into the hash table. Given the discretized time series $T = $ 'aacbaccacbc' and with the window size $w = 3$, the FMG can extracted nine SAX words when sliding the window across the time series: 'aac', 'acb', 'cba', 'bac', 'acc', 'cca', 'cac', 'acb', 'cbc'. After hashing, these features are put in the hash table at 4 locations and the buckets associated with these locations are shown as in Fig. 1. From the hash table, FMG can identify the candidate for 1-motif.

3.1 Building the Hash Table

FMG begins by creating a SAX representation of the entire time series, by sliding a window of length w across the time series one PAA segment at a time, extracting subsequences, converting them to SAX words (also called *features*). For each feature, FMG also keeps its position in the original time series as its *index*. During hashing, the *key* of each feature is the feature itself. In hashing, if there exist some other features that are non-trivial match with this feature and these features have been already stored in some bucket, then the feature is also hashed to that bucket. Otherwise, there exists no other feature matching with the feature in question, this feature will be hashed to a new bucket. The key of the bucket with the largest number of features is selected as the motif candidate.

In FMG, we apply a new way to shift the sliding window. Random Projection creates a SAX representation of the entire time series by sliding a window of length w across the time series T one data point at a time. But FMG shifts the sliding window across the time series one PAA segment at a time in order to speed up the motif discovery process. This new way to shift the sliding window is the same as in EMD algorithm by Tanaka et al. [8] and Improved-RP algorithm by Binh and Anh [1].

3.2   Identifying the Motif Candidate and Finding the 1-Motif

Finding the motif candidate from the hash table needs at most two scans of the hash table. In the first scan, we aim to find the *good motif candidate* by using the parameter s (*good motif score*) to ensure the motif candidates have a good shape. At the end of this scan, if we can find the bucket with enough features (greater than 2), we finish the procedure with the motif candidate corresponding to that bucket. Otherwise, we start the second scan of the hash table without applying the criterion of good motif candidate in this scan. Notice that applying the criterion of good motif candidate is just optional. At last, the key of the bucket with the largest number of features is selected as a motif candidate.

After obtaining the motif candidate, FMG builds *the set of motif instances* from the key of the bucket with the largest number of features. It scans through all the features in the discretized time series to check if there exist some more features that are non-trivial matches with all the features in the set of motif instances. If there is any such feature, it is inserted to the set of motif instances. From the set of motif instances, FMG can determine the 1-motif of the time series by selecting the first instance in the set (i.e. the key of the bucket with the largest number of features).

4   Experimental Evaluation

In this experiment we compare FMG to RP algorithm in motif discovery. The RP is selected as a baseline for comparison in motif discovery due to its popularity.

4.1   Datasets and Parameter Setting

We tested the algorithms on seven publicly available datasets: ECG (100,000 data points), ECG (300,000 data points), ERP (198,400 data points), EEG (10,750 data points), MEMORY (6,875 data points), POWER (35,040 data points), STOCK (12,640 data points). All these seven datasets are obtained from the two time series data mining archives: the UCR Time Series Clustering/Classification Home page [4], and Web page for Analysis of Financial Time Series (http://faculty.chicago.booth.edu/ruey.tsay/teaching/fts). The datasets are from different areas such as medicine, industry and finance.

The FMG algorithm requires the following parameters: the length of each PAA segment (*paa_ratio*), the alphabet size (a), the SAX word length (w), the MINDIST distance threshold (R_{max}), the good motif score for the motif candidate (s), the number of iterations in RP algorithm (i). These parameters depend on the dataset, for example,

$w = 25$ for ECG dataset and $w = 20$ for MEMORY dataset. The parameter settings for all seven dataset are given in Table 1. The default value for the number of iterations i is $w/5$.

Table 1. The parameter settings for all seven datasets

Parameter	ECG	EEG	ERP	MEMORY	POWER	STOCK
paa_ratio	16	10	16	16	15	20
a	6	6	6	6	6	8
w	25	25	20	20	45	20
R_{max}	1.0	3.0	1.0	3.0	0.0	0.0
s	4	default	4	4	4	2
i	default	default	default	default	default	default

4.2   Experimental Results

We check the accuracy of motif discovery algorithms by using human inspection. On the seven tested datasets, the 1-motifs discovered by FMG have exactly the same shapes as those discovered by RP.

The experimental results of comparing FMG to the RP algorithm in motif discovery over the seven datasets are shown in Table 2. The fourth column reports the number of motif instances discovered by the two methods.

Table 2. Experimental results in comparing FMG, RFMG to RP over the seven datasets.

Dataset	Length	Method	Number of Motif instances	Runtime (ms)
ECG	100000	RP	23	1295
		FMG	37	200
	300000	RP	N/A	N/A
		FMG	200	787
EEG	10750	RP	4	63
		FMG	5	67
ERP	198400	RP	12	5807
		FMG	37	1682
MEMORY	6875	RP	4	16
		FMG	4	7
POWER	35040	RP	51	342
		FMG	51	159
STOCK	12640	RP	13	24
		FMG	10	15

From these experimental results we can see that:

- FMG is more effective than RP in terms of accuracy. In most of the datasets, the number of motif instances for the 1-motif found by FMG is more than that of RP. The reason of this fact is that in the last step, FMG performs a thorough scan in all discretized subsequences to find the instances for the 1-motif.
- FMG is more time efficient than RP. For example, with large datasets such as ECG (300,000 data points), RP cannot work since it fails to tackle this large dataset while FMG can find the 1-motif in a very short time (0.787 s). In average on six datasets, FMG runs about 2.816 times faster than RP.

5 Conclusions

In this paper, we proposed an efficient algorithm FMG that can discover time series motifs much faster than Random Projection algorithm. The proposed algorithm is based on hashing with three improvement techniques. The experimental results on the several benchmark datasets demonstrate that our proposed method can discover precise 1-motif in high time efficiency on large time series data.

In the future we intend to extend our algorithm in order that it can discover 1-motif and 1-discord at the same time with the strategy that discord detection is a by-product of motif discovery process.

References

1. Binh, D.X., Anh, D.T.: A suite of techniques to improve Random Projection in time series motif discovery. In: Proceedings of 2016 IEEE RIVF International Conference on Computing and Communication Technologies, Research, Innovation and Vision for Future, 7–9 November, Hanoi, Vietnam, pp. 13–16 (2016)
2. Chiu, B., Keogh, E., Lonardi, S.: Probabilistic discover of time series motifs. In: Proceedings of 9th International Conference on Knowledge Discovery and Data Mining (KDD 2003), pp. 493–498 (2003)
3. Gruber, C., Coduro, M., Sick, B.: Signature verification with dynamic RBF network and time series motifs. In: Proceedings of 10th International Workshop on Frontiers in Hand Writing Recognition (2006)
4. Keogh, E., et al.: The UCR Time Series Classification/Clustering. http://www.cs.ucr.edu/~eamonn/time_series_data/. Accessed 2017
5. Lin, J., Keogh, E., Patel, P., Lonardi, S.: Finding motifs in time series. In: Proceedings of 2nd Workshop on Temporal Data Mining, at the 8th ACM SIGKDD International Conference on Knowledge Discovery and Data Mining (2002)
6. Lin, J., Keogh, E., Lonardi, S., Chiu, B.: Symbolic representation of time series, with implications for streaming algorithms. In: Proceedings of 8th ACM SIGMOD Workshop on Research Issues in Data Mining and Knowledge Discovery, San Diego, CA, 13 June (2003)
7. Mueen, A., Keogh, E., Zhu, Q., Cash, S., Westover, B.: Exact discovery of time series motif. In: Proceedings of SIAM International Conference on Data Mining, pp. 1–12 (2009)
8. Tanaka, Y., Iwamoto, K., Uehara, K.: Discovery of time series motif from multi-dimensional data based on MDL principle. Mach. Learn. 58(2–3), 269–300 (2005)

One-Dimensional Camera Calibration Based on PSO Algorithm

Yuhuang Zhang, Lijun Wu[✉], Zhicong Chen, Shuying Cheng, and Peijie Lin

College of Physics and Information Engineering, Fuzhou University, Fuzhou, China
lijun.wu@fzu.edu.cn

Abstract. Camera calibration is an essential process in visual measurement. 1D target based camera calibration can great facilitate the operating procedure especially when multiple vision sensors should be calibrated. However, the current one-dimensional calibration algorithm is still imprecision in practice. In this work, the PSO algorithm is employed to improve the precision of one-dimensional camera calibration. Since the swarm intelligence algorithm is initial value sensitive, in this work, a data cluster algorithm is proposed to get a better initial value. To overcome the over optimizing problem accounted in swarm intelligence algorithm, prior knowledge, such as the picture's size, is employed to make sure the parameters will converge toward the true values.

Keywords: One-dimensional calibration · Cluster · PSO

1 Introduction

Camera calibration makes it possible to obtain 3D information from 2D images. Generally, those camera calibration algorithms are divided into three-dimensional calibration [1], two-dimensional calibration [2,3], one-dimensional [4,5] and self-calibration [6] in terms of the different dimensions of the calibration target. Compare with other algorithms, calibration based on one-dimensional target can provide much better precision than self-calibration and more flexibility than two dimensional or three-dimensional calibration, which has attracted widely attention since its first proposed by Zhang [5].

Since the image is inevitably corrupted by noise during the acquisition procedure, camera parameters obtained by the linear calibration algorithm often have severe errors. In order to solve this problem, nonlinear optimization, such as LM optimization [7], are applied to improve the calibration precision via reducing the back-projection errors. However, nonlinear optimization algorithm is still sensitive to initialization and easy to fall into local minimum. Meanwhile, mathematical optimality sometimes makes the optimized parameters lose their physic meaning, which has been over optimized.

In recent years, researchers have proposed camera parameters optimization algorithms based on heuristic algorithms [8–11]. For example, Deng et al. put

© Springer Nature Switzerland AG 2018
M. Kaenampornpan et al. (Eds.): MIWAI 2018, LNAI 11248, pp. 212–218, 2018.
https://doi.org/10.1007/978-3-030-03014-8_18

forward a PSO (Particle Swarm Optimization) optimization algorithm based on differential heredity [8]. Li et al. combine the variation characteristic of genetic algorithm with PSO algorithm, and propose the GA-PSO algorithm [9]. Based on back propagation (BP) and automatically weight optimization via gradient descent, Jiang et al. take calibration process as a black box towards minimizing the back-projection errors [11]. Although those works have increased the precision of calibration to some extern, it is still not good enough for one dimensional camera calibration since heuristic algorithms are sensitive to initialization and over optimization happens occasionally.

2 The Principle of One-Dimension Calibration

Providing a point's coordinate M in real world is $[X, Y, Z]^T$, and then its homogeneous coordinates is $\widetilde{M} = [X, Y, Z, 1]^T$; the corresponding imaging point is $m = [u, v]^T$ while its homogeneous coordinates is $\widetilde{m} = [u, v, 1]^T$. According to the pinhole imaging model, point $\widetilde{M}$ and point $\widetilde{m}$ satisfy (1),

$$\alpha \widetilde{m} = K\left[R, t\right], \quad K = \begin{bmatrix} f_x & s & u_0 \\ 0 & f_y & v_0 \\ 0 & 0 & 1 \end{bmatrix}. \tag{1}$$

where α is an arbitrary scale factor, (R, t) is the extrinsic parameters, and K called the camera intrinsic matrix, with (u_0, v_0) the coordinates of the principal point, f_x and f_y the scale factors in image u and v axes, and s the parameter describing the vertical relationship of the two image axes. Generally, it is assumed that the camera coordinate system coincides with the world coordinate system, that is $R = \mathbf{I}_3(\mathbf{I}$ is unit matrix), $t = \mathbf{0}_{3 \times 1}$, then we have

$$\alpha \widetilde{m} = KM. \tag{2}$$

Suppose that there is a fine stick with three marked points A, B and C, and its length is L, that is

$$\|B - A\| = L, \tag{3}$$

$$C = (1 - \lambda)A + \lambda B. \tag{4}$$

Assuming the projected points of A, B and C is a, b, and c respectively, and their Z coordinate values is z_A, z_B and z_C, from (1), one has

$$A = z_A K^{-1}\widetilde{a}, \quad B = z_B K^{-1}\widetilde{b}, \quad C = z_C K^{-1}\widetilde{c}. \tag{5}$$

Substituting (5) into (4), then one can obtain

$$z_B = -z_A \frac{(1 - \lambda)(\widetilde{a} \times \widetilde{c})(\widetilde{b} \times \widetilde{c})}{\lambda(\widetilde{b} \times \widetilde{c}) \cdot (\widetilde{b} \times \widetilde{c})}. \tag{6}$$

From (3), (5) and (6), one has

$$z_A \| K^{-1} (\tilde{a} + \frac{(1-\lambda)(\tilde{a} \times \tilde{c})(\tilde{b} \times \tilde{c})}{\lambda(\tilde{b} \times \tilde{c}) \cdot (\tilde{b} \times \tilde{c})} \tilde{b}) \| = L \tag{7}$$

$$z_A^2 h^T K^{-T} K^{-1} h = L^2, \quad h = \tilde{a} + \frac{(1-\lambda)(\tilde{a} \times \tilde{c})(\tilde{b} \times \tilde{c})}{\lambda(\tilde{b} \times \tilde{c}) \cdot (\tilde{b} \times \tilde{c})} \tilde{b}. \tag{8}$$

Let $B = A^{-T} A^{-1}$. Since the matrix product B is a symmetric matrix, B can be defined as 6-dimension vector $b = \begin{bmatrix} B_{11}, B_{12}, B_{22}, B_{13}, B_{23}, B_{33} \end{bmatrix}^T$. Where B_{ij} represents the i-th row, j-th column elements of matrix B. If one denotes x by $z_A^2 b$, then (8) becomes

$$V^T x = L^2 \tag{9}$$

with $V = \begin{bmatrix} h_1^2, 2h_1 h_2, h_2^2, 2h_1 h_3, 2h_2 h_3, h_3^2 \end{bmatrix}^T$, $h = \begin{bmatrix} h_1, h_2, h_3 \end{bmatrix}^T$. Supposed the stick rotates N times around a fixed-point A, then one has $2N + 8$ unknown parameters and can get $2 + 3N$ equations. If N is no less than 5, the correlation parameters of one-dimensional calibration are solved.

3   Our Work

3.1   Brief Introduction of PSO Algorithm

The particle swarm optimization algorithm originated from the information sharing in bird foraging and the real-time changing information of position. First, the large number individual's uniform distribution allows the population to step in each interval. Second, information sharing makes the population not satisfied with the temporary optimal value. Finally, the real-time updating of the position is advantageous to the population moving towards the global best. The way that the real-time position updating is shown in (10).

$$x_{id}^{n+1} = x_{id}^n + v_{id}^{n+1}, \quad v_{id}^{n+1} = w v_{id}^n + c_1 r_1^n (p_{id}^n - x_{id}^n) + c_2 r_2^n (p_{gd}^n - x_{id}^n) \tag{10}$$

where w, c_1, c_2 are constants, represent inertial weight and acceleration constant respectively, and v is for velocity, r is usually a random number that satisfies the uniform distribution of $U(0,1)$, x is the position of the particle, p_{id}^n is the best fitness for the particle at the time of n, and p_{gd}^n is the best fitness for the population at n time.

3.2   Data Preprocessing

Due to noise corrupted, one dimensional camera calibration results are normally not good enough in precision, sometimes even have singularities. Multiple experiments are necessary for the purpose of obtaining a better solution. To get good initial value, calculating the average of multiple calibration results could be a straight-forward approach. However, this approach works only when the results are basically correct or else the average could be biased by the singularities. Therefore, a self-cluster algorithm based on Euclidean distance is proposed to find out the 'good enough' camera calibration results which is averaged to provide a better initialization for PSO. In here, we assume that 'good enough' calibration results should gather around the ground truth while the others should be far away from the ground truth in contrast, which is reasonable in practice. Therefore, the key point is how to draw the line between the 'good enough' results and others. In this work, the different calibration results are regarded as the points distributed in a high dimensional sphere, and the desired 'line' is obtained via looking for the appropriate radius and the center of the sphere. The proposed self-cluster algorithm is listed as follows.

(1) Sort the matrix of multiple calibration results by the first column, named P, and find out its maximum, named P_{MAX}, and minimum element, named P_{MIN}. Let the Euclidean distance between P_{MAX} and P_{MIN} is d.

(2) Take different calibration results as different points distributed in a high dimensional sphere, determine the ratio of points that is treated as 'good enough' points. One calculates the ratio N based on the d according to (11),

$$N = \frac{e^{-d}}{(1 + e^{-d})}. \tag{11}$$

(3) Determine the 'good enough' sphere: Set iteration $i = 0$, the radius is $d/10$, and the step size as $d/100$.

(4) Set the start center point for C_{ij}, as the first camera calibration result($j = 1$). Filter out the 'good enough' points: Determine if the point is within the 'good enough' sphere one by one, according to its Euclidean distance to C_{ij}.

(5) Calculate the number N_{ij} of 'good enough' points of C_{ij}.

(6) Repeat step (4) and (5) for setting all camera calibration results as the center points one by one, and make N_{imax} equal to max of N_{ij}.

(7) If N_{imax} equal to N, then the center point is the corresponding center point while the radius is the radius for i−th iteration. And then exit the loop. If N_{imax} is larger than N, then decrease the radius by one step. If N_i is smaller then N, then increase the radius. And make $i = i + 1$, repeat step (4)–(7).

(8) Takes the average of the filtered out 'good enough' sphere as the initialization for PSO.

3.3   Optimization of Calibration Parameters Using PSO Algorithm

The camera parameters P are solved via (9), and repeated experiments were done to obtain the camera parameter matrix. Since the camera parameters are obtained via solving equations, the results may deviate from the real value. Even though a better initial value has been acquired by applying the algorithm proposed in Sect. 3.2. However, the better initial value still cannot guarantee the optimized result after employed PSO will converge to the real value.

In reality, there is some prior knowledge of some parameters in camera calibrated, which can be used to help the optimization converge toward the true value. For example, with the progress of science and technology, the skewness factor s, which stand for the ability of camera representation the vertical relationship of reality, should approach to zero. This can be used as a start value to make sure the PSO optimization converge to a result with physical meaning. Therefore, the prior knowledge should be fully mined as a qualification in PSO optimization. The optimization process in this work is presented as follows.

(1) Obtain the better initial value through the proposed self-clustering algorithm.
(2) Using the prior knowledge to limit the value of the relevant parameters. For example, let the u_0, v_0 equal to half of picture size and the start value of skew factor to be zero.
(3) PSO initialization. Initialize a population with 8 particles, for example, i−th particle has a random location x_i in specified space and random velocity v_i.
(4) Evaluation. For each particle, evaluate the fitness according to (12).

$$fitness = |\sum_{i=1}^{N}[(x_{pi} - x_i) + (y_{pi} - y_i)]| \tag{12}$$

(5) Compare the evaluated fitness value of each particle with its p_{id}^n. If current value is better than p_{id}^n, then replace current location using the p_{id}^n location. Furthermore, if current value is better than p_{gd}^n, then reset p_{gd}^n to the current index in particle array.
(6) According to the (10), change the particle's location and velocity.
(7) $iters = iters + 1$, loop to step (4) until a stop criterion is met, usually a sufficiently good fitness value or iterates achieved a predefined maximum generation max iterations.
(8) Return the camera parameters.

4   Experiment Results

In this work, we verify the feasibility of the proposed algorithm via a simulated camera whose parameters are set as below: $f_x = f_y = 1000$, $s = 0$, $u_0 = 320$, $v_0 = 240$, and the fixed rotation point A's coordinates is $[0, 45, 150]$.

First, we test the performance of proposed self-cluster algorithm. 20 random orientations of the stick, whose azimuthal angle θ and polar angle ϕ vary in the range $[0, \pi]$ according to uniform distribution, are sampled for each camera calibration. To simulate the practice image collection condition, gaussian noise with 0 mean and "standard deviation is added to the projected image points. 100 calibrations are repeated to obtain a parameter matrix which provide redundancy for the proposed self-cluster algorithm.

The noise level is varied from 0.1 pixel to 0.5 pixel. For each noise level, 100 independent trials are performed and parts of camera calibration results shown in Table 1 are average. From Table 1, one can see error increase almost linearly as the noise level increases both in take-the-mean and self-cluster method. But it is also clear that results obtained by the proposed self-cluster algorithm is also closer to the actual value even in severely corrupted condition.

Table 1. The partial results of different methods in different standard deviation.

σ	Method	1000	1000	0	320	240
0.1	Mean	986.89	998.17	-2.80	304.79	275.68
	Cluster	**998.10**	**1001.34**	**2.50**	**321.33**	**245.20**
0.3	Mean	928.75	945.87	33.85	373.05	235.13
	Cluster	**993.04**	**983.10**	**-0.84**	**313.48**	**259.34**
0.5	Mean	856.43	854.55	21.65	398.11	365.64
	Cluster	**963.79**	**1002.72**	**23.13**	**319.06**	**290.67**

Then both the take-the-mean results and the self-cluster results are used as the PSO input parameters, and let the u_0, v_0 equal to half of picture size and the start value of skew factor to be zero. In PSO optimization, we set $N = 30$, $G = 500$, $w = 0.8$, $c_1 = 2.8$, $c_2 = 1.3$. The experiment results are shown in Fig. 1. According to reference [12], the relative errors in (u_0, v_0) is with respect to f_x. From Fig. 1, one can find that both solution's relative errors increase almost linearly with the noise level. However, compare with the mean solution, the algorithm proposed in this paper refine the cluster results and has significantly higher precision (with about 500% less errors). From the Fig. 1b, one can find that that the errors of camera parameters are about 3.5% in 0.5 pixels noise while the value in Fig. 1a is about 15%.

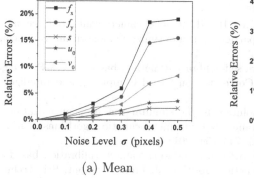

(a) Mean

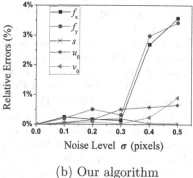

(b) Our algorithm

Fig. 1. Calibration errors with respect to the noise level of the image points.

5   Conclusions

In this paper, we propose a self-cluster algorithm which can find a better initialize value for the PSO algorithm, and prior knowledge about the center point and skewness factor is also employed to make sure the optimization result converge to the real values. Compared with traditional methods, the results show that the algorithm proposed in this paper is feasible, accurate and practical.

Acknowledgements. The authors would like to acknowledge the supports by the National Natural Science Foundation of China (Grant No. 61601127, 51508105, and 61574038), the Fujian Provincial Department of Science and Technology of China (Grant No. 2016H6012, and 2018J0106), the Fujian Provincial Economic and Information Technology Commission of China (Grant No. 830020, 83016006), and the Science Foundation of Fujian Education Department of China (Grant No. JAT160073).

References

1. Tsai, R.Y.: An efficient and accurate camera calibration technique for 3D machine vision. In: Proceedings of IEEE Conference on Computer Vision & Pattern Recognition, pp. 364–374 (1986)
2. Zhang, Z.: A Flexible New Technique for Camera Calibration. IEEE Computer Society (2000)
3. Duan, F., Fuchao, W., Zhanyi, H.: Pose determination and plane measurement using a trapezium. Pattern Recognit. Lett. **29**(3), 223–231 (2008)
4. Fuchao, W., Zhanyi, H., Zhu, H.: Camera calibration with moving one-dimensional objects. Pattern Recognit. **38**(5), 755–765 (2005)
5. Zhang, Z.: Camera calibration with one-dimensional objects. IEEE Trans. Pattern Anal. Mach. Intell. **26**(7), 892–899 (2004)
6. Pollefeys, M., Van Gool, L., Oosterlinck, A.: The modulus constraint: a new constraint for self-calibration. In: International Conference on Pattern Recognition, vol. 1, pp. 349–353 (1996)
7. Moré, J.J.: The levenberg-marquardt algorithm: implementation and theory. Lect. Notes Math. **630**, 105–116 (1977)
8. Deng, L., Lu, G., Shao, Y., Fei, M., Hu, H.: A novel camera calibration technique based on differential evolution particle swarm optimization algorithm. Neurocomputing **174**(PA), 456–465 (2016)
9. Li, J., Yang, Y., Fu, G.: Camera self-calibration method based on GA-PSO algorithm. In: IEEE International Conference on Cloud Computing and Intelligence Systems, pp. 149–152 (2011)
10. Safaei, A., Fazli, S.: A novel solution in the simultaneous deep optimization of RGB-D camera calibration parameters using metaheuristic algorithms. Turk. J. Electr. Eng. Comput. Sci. **26**(2), 743–754 (2018)
11. Jiang, X., Fan, Y., Wang, W.: BP neural network camera calibration based on particle swarm optimization genetic algorithm. J. Front. Comput. Sci. Technol. **8**(10), 1254–1262 (2014)
12. Triggs, B.: Autocalibration from planar scenes. In: European Conference on Computer Vision, pp. 89–105 (1998)

Evaluating Named-Entity Recognition Approaches in Plant Molecular Biology

Huy Do[1], Khoat Than[3], and Pierre Larmande[1,2(✉)]

[1] University of Science and Technology of Hanoi (USTH), ICT Lab, Hanoi, Vietnam
[2] Institute of Research for Development (IRD), LMI RICE, DIADE,
Montpellier, France
pierre.larmande@ird.fr
[3] Hanoi University of Science and Technology (HUST), Hanoi, Vietnam
khoattq@soict.hust.edu.vn

Abstract. Text mining research is becoming an important topic in biology with the aim to extract biological entities from scientific papers in order to extend the biological knowledge. However, few thorough studies are developed for plant molecular biology data, especially rice, thus resulting a lack of datasets available to exploit advanced machine learning methods able to detect entities such as genes and proteins. In this article, we first developed a dataset from the Ozyzabase - a database of rice gene, and used it as the benchmark. Then, we evaluated the performance of two Name Entities Recognition (NER) methods for sequence tagging: a Long Short Term Memory (LSTM) model, combined with Conditional Random Fields (CRFs), and a hybrid method based on the dictionary lookup combining with some machine learning systems to improve result. We analyzed the performance of these methods when apply to the Oryzabase dataset and improved the results. On average, the result from LSTM-CRF reaching 86% in F_1 is more exploitable.

Keywords: Text mining · LSTM-CRF · NER · Bioinformatics
Plant genomics

1 Introduction

1.1 Problem Statement

The last few decades have witnessed the massive explosion of information in life science. However, an important proportion of information relevant to this field is not available from databases but is instead present in unstructured scientific documents, such as journal articles and reports. Agronomy is an overarching field, that comprises of diverse domains such as genetics, plant molecular biology, ecology and soil science. Despite the advancement in information technologies, scientific communication in agronomy is still largely based on text because it is the common way to report scientific advancements. To effectively develop applications to improve crop production through sustainable methods, it is important

© Springer Nature Switzerland AG 2018
M. Kaenampornpan et al. (Eds.): MIWAI 2018, LNAI 11248, pp. 219–225, 2018.
https://doi.org/10.1007/978-3-030-03014-8_19

to overlay research findings from these fields as they are highly inter-connected. However, the collection of content is growing continuously and the information are currently available as unstructured text. Several text mining methods and tools have been developed to solve the problem of named entity recognition by using different approaches [11] such as rule-based, dictionary lookup or hybrid methods. Identifying biological entities is not trivial. Despite the fact that there exists many available approaches to handle this problem in general and in the Biomedical domain, few thorough studies have been implemented for plants, especially rice. Moreover, we found rare benchmarks available for plant species and none for rice. Thus, we faced several difficulties exploiting advanced machine learning methods for accurate analysis of rice scientific papers.

1.2   Objective

In the large scale, we are currently building an RDF knowledge base, Agronomic Linked Data (AgroLD - www.agrold.org) [12]. The knowledge base is designed to integrate data from various publicly plant centric databases such as Oryzabase [13] to name a few. The aim of AgroLD project is to provide an integrated portal for domain experts to exploit the homogenized data model towards filling the knowledge gaps. In this landscape, we aim to extract relevant information from the scientific literature in order to enrich the content of integrated datasets.

In this article, we identified two relevant approaches: LSTM-CRF and the hybrid method based on dictionary lookup associated with machine learning, has been chosen for further analysis due to their relevance and efficiency compared to others.

2   Material and Method

In this section, we describe the architecture of the LSTM-CRF and the hybrid method for sequence tagging. The input going through model is sentences; each word is considered as a token, given in the following lines including three tabs: word, the part-of-speech (POS) tag and the entity type in IOB format. For LSTM-CRF, model map each word into a vector using pre-trained model, and concatenate it with vector of char embedding. The output is feature vectors.

2.1   LSTM-CRF

LSTM. When Recurrent Neural Network (RNN) are applied in practice for sequence prediction, they tend to fail to predict input that are depended on long previous sequences. This problem is called "The long-term dependencies" has been explored by Hochreiter [6] and Bengio *et al.* [2] Long Short Term Memory, a special kind of RNN, was introduced to avoid the long-term dependency problem of RNN by Hochreiter & Schmidhuber (1997) [7]. With the addition of more sigmoid layers, it becomes more complex than a traditional RNN but it proves that it works effectively to solve the problems of long-term dependencies. The sigmoid layers with output between $[0, 1]$ decide which information will be forgotten while the tanh layer use that output to create a vector of candidates during the training process [7].

CRF. Conditional random fields, introduced by Lafferty *et al.* [8], is a statistic modeling method for labeling and segmenting structured data, such as sequences, trees and lattices. The general idea of this model [10] is to make independent tagging decisions for each output y_t using the features h_t. However, for NER tagger, using traditional CRFs with independent classification decisions is insufficient and impossible with numerous constraint because of the strong dependencies cross the output labels.

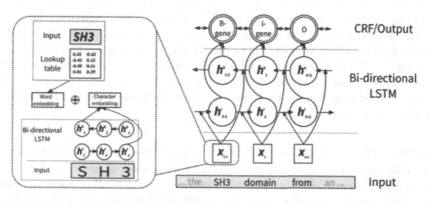

Fig. 1. bi-LSTM-CRF model from Habibi *et al.* [5]

bi-LSTM-CRF. The workflow follows a bidirectional LSTM (bi-LSTM) [4] which is a pair of forward and backward LSTM. With the input as a set of d-dimensional vector, the forward LSTM layer computes the representation $\overrightarrow{h}_t$ of the left context of the sentence at every word while the backward LSTM reads the same input sequence in reverse to obtain the representation $\overleftarrow{h}_t$ of the right context. Next step, the model concatenates its left and right context representations, $h_t = [\overrightarrow{h}_t \overleftarrow{h}_t]$ to achieve the vector of a word. The architecture of bi-LSTM-CRF is illustrated in Fig. 1 [5]. Every embedding vector regarding distinct word is a concatenation of two components: word- and a character-level embedding. We retrieved the word-level embedding using a Google's Word2vec pre-trained model meanwhile, we applied a same bi-LSTM for characters in word to achieve the character-level embedding. The final output from this layer is obtained by applying the classical Viterbi algorithm [3].

2.2 NER-hybrid Approach

This approach is based on a dictionary lookup entity recognizer combined with machine learning classifiers. The OGER entity recognizer is used to annotate the objects in some selected domain ontologies. Next, the Distiller framework is applied to extract this information as a feature for a machine learning algorithm to select relevant entities. For this step, we implemented two different machine learning algorithms: CRFs and Neural network (NNs).

OGER. The Onto Gene group has developed an approach for biomedical entity recognition based on dictionary lookup and flexible matching [1]. OGER performs a flexible interface for dictionary based annotation. For the given input, we implemented OGER as a web service. OGER architecture is configured to have a strategy towards to a greater false positive (FP) which leads to a lower precision value, but less false negative (FN) which can get an high recall.

The aim of the project focus on the information of plant genes and proteins and their relationship, we used the Gene Ontology Consortium[1] and the Protein Ontology[2] as the lookup table. In OGER, the entities of the term dictionary were preprocessed in the same way as the documents with respect to tokenization, stemming, and case sensitivity. Next, the input documents will be compared to the dictionary with an exact-match strategy.

Distiller. The Distiller framework is an open-source project developed to build a flexible, extensible system for natural language processing fields [1]. The main process of Distiller is based on the performance of Automatic Key-phrase Extraction (AKE) to extract information from text. AKE seems to be different from NER, as while the former is focus on finding the small set of the most relevant information in a document, and then find all the information of selected types. Besides, AKE can be performed both as unsupervised and supervised algorithms. Actually, the Distiller derives from an unsupervised approach.

Models and Features. In our project, we proposed two machine learning algorithms: NN and CRF which are considered to perform the exploitable results [1]. The workflow for the hybrid approach will be implement as follow: Based on traditional dictionary lookup, annotate object from text data using OGER for a given input. Integrate output from OGER with Distiller framework to assign new features, prepare them to be processed by a machine learning system. Apply machine learning system including a Neural network and a CRF, select the relevant entities in the document using the information generated in the previous steps. The list of features from each system is shown in the Table 1.

---

[1] http://geneontology.org/.

[2] https://pir.georgetown.edu/pro/.

Table 1. The details of features

	CRF	Neural network
Input	Single tokens	n-grams from OGER
Features		
Candidate POS-tagger	Yes	
Candidate tag (IOB format)	Yes	Yes
Candidate contains numbers	Label yes/no	Count
Candidate ends with numbers	Label yes/no	Label yes/no
Candidate selected by OGER	Label yes/no	
Neighbor tokens	Yes	
Neighbor token POS-taggers	Yes	
Distiller features		Yes
Total features for each tokens	23	13

2.3 Dataset

In this project, we built and implemented methods on dataset collected from Oryzabase[3], an integrated scientific database for Oryza sativa species (or rice) published online since 2000 [13]. The lasted version of Oryzabase contains 21, 739 of rice genes, collected from 44, 837 distinct scientific articles. The PubMed database is used as resource to collect the raw text which is pre-processed later to form the input data. After filtering, over 10, 000 articles were processed. Next, concentrating on the entities of rice genomes, we took the Oryzabase gene list as the ground truth to built our dataset by keyword matching term respectively.

3 Implementation

Text Pre-processing. To tokenize data, raw text is splited into sentences, and from sentences into words. Each word is considered as a token, given in the following lines; one token per line, and included 3 tabs: the first one being the word itself, the POS tag and the last one being the entity type. Each token is on a separated line, ends with dots and has an empty line after each sentence. To avoid errors, data is converted into lower case; and "non-alphabet" characters are ignored. Then, we matched words of the Oryzabase list gene by keys and applied the IOB format to determine the token be entity or not.

NER-tagger. The bi-LSTM (with CRF) work at word level which include an entity tag to determine itself and the input data going through model is embedding sequences. The bi-LSTM (with CRF) used for NER built based on the model of Lample *et al.* [9]. To start the training process, we have done several

---
[3] https://shigen.nig.ac.jp/rice/oryzabase/.

experiments to find the best parameters for this model. Some results were very exploitable at a specific value of learning rate and dropout.

Hybrid Methods. For the hybrid method, OGER, a dictionary tool supported by Gene Ontology Consortium and Protein Ontology dictionary, used to annotate all objects in the dataset. The output was formatted into tables which contains full information of genes. Next, evaluation was applied to evaluate the performance of OGER on the whole dataset to see how OGER effectively work on this dataset and based on that to improve the results. For CRF and NN, we also started with POS-tag and candidate tag prepared in the pre-processing part and combined with features that are generated and listed above.

Evaluation Parameters. Dataset was separated it into 3 subsets with different ratio: 75% for training set, 15% for testing set, and the last 10% of dataset for validation set. To evaluate a deep learning model, as usual, we also used the precision, recall and $F_1 - score$ on the test set. By evaluating the set of true positive, false positive and false negative, we computed the value of $F_1 - score$.

4   Results

We assessed the performance of NER tagger methods by evaluating the LSTM-CRF and hybrid methods on the Oryzabase dataset covering different types of rice genomes. LSTM-CRF used low-dimension vector, created by mixing word-level embeddings with character-level embeddings. Results were compared between a original LSTM model; LSTM with CRF which have the same function to recognize entity in the text using tag information; OGER with CRF and NN. The performance of all methods was evaluated on Oryzabase dataset. Results in terms of precision, recall, $F_1 - score$ for each model are shown in Table 2. LSTM-CRF achieved the best performance on average when its F_1-score is 86.72% for the LSTM-CRF method, while 80.44% for the LSTM method. Result of hybrid method is very exploitable. The performance of OGER with CRF got the best result on testing set among 3 approaches which is 85.08% on average. The second rank is OGER combining with Neural Network, which has reached 67% accuracy on average. Although the improvements are not high as we expected but it still has some improvement rather than the only OGER which is around 58.5%.

Table 2. Result of performance of both method in terms of precision, recall and $F_1 - score$

	Precision(%)	Recall(%)	$F_1 - score(\%)$
LSTM	78.06	82.97	80.44
LSTM-CRF	87.32	**86.13**	**86.72**
OGER	53.03	65.23	58.50
OG+NN	63.93	71.10	67.32
OG+CRF	**88.39**	82.24	85.08

5   Related Work

For the first method, our work is close to the work of Habibi *et al.* [5] when we built a deep neural network to extract information of gene, proteins of plant from scientific article instead of human genes which are researched by many scientists. Similar to the model of Lample *et al.* [9], our model work for sequence tagging. For the second method, following Basaldella *et al.* article, we also applied the hybrid method on a dataset of rice genomes to see how efficiency it work.

In recent years, pattern- and dictionary-based methods have been replaced by new approaches based on machine learning. Methods relying the combination of deep neural network with other techniques are used to develop applications which are able to detect entities automatically rather than manually as the traditional ways. It makes a lot of benefits for the research works as well as for human life. For instances, it can help people to extend the databases which can be used for several purposes of human, or can help scientists finds some new entities. However, scientists normally focus more on the biomedical or somethings that related to human genes. The research in Agronomy now is very popular and plays an important role for human nutrition.

References

1. Basaldella, M., Furrer, L., Tasso, C., Rinaldi, F.: Entity recognition in the biomedical domain using a hybrid approach. J. Biomed. Semant. **8**, 51 (2017)
2. Bengio, Y., Simard, P., Frasconi, P.: Learning long-term dependencies with gradient descent is difficult. IEEE Trans. Neural Netw. **5**(2), 157–166 (1994)
3. Forney, G.D.: The viterbi algorithm. In: Proceedings of the IEEE, pp. 268–278 (1973)
4. Graves, A., Schmidhuber, J.: Framewise phoneme classification with bidirectional LSTM networks. In: 2005 IEEE International Joint Conference on Neural Networks, 2005. IJCNN 2005. Proceedings, vol. 4, pp. 2047–2052. IEEE (2005)
5. Habibi, M., Weber, L., Neves, M., Wiegandt, D.L., Leser, U.: Deep learning with word embeddings improves biomedical named entity recognition. Bioinformatics **33**(14), i37–i48 (2017)
6. Hochreiter, S.: Untersuchungen zu dynamischen neuronalen netzen. Diploma, Technische Universität München **91**, 1 (1991)
7. Hochreiter, S., Schmidhuber, J.: Long short-term memory. Neural Comput. **9**(8), 1735–1780 (1997)
8. Lafferty, J., McCallum, A., Pereira, F.C.: Conditional Random Fields: Probabilistic Models for Segmenting and Labeling Sequence Data (2001)
9. Lample, G., Ballesteros, M., Subramanian, S., Kawakami, K., Dyer, C.: Neural architectures for named entity recognition. arXiv preprint arXiv:1603.01360 (2016)
10. Ling, W., et al.: Finding function in form: Compositional character models for open vocabulary word representation. arXiv preprint arXiv:1508.02096 (2015)
11. Nadeau, D., Sekine, S.: A survey of named entity recognition and classification. Lingvisticae Investigationes **30**(1), 3–26 (2007)
12. Venkatesan, A., Ngompe, G.T., Hassouni, N.E.l., Chentli, I., Guignon, V., Jonquet, C., et al.: Agronomic Linked Data (AgroLD): a Knowledge-based System to Enable Integrative Biology in Agronomy. BioRxiv. (2018). https://doi.org/10.1101/325423
13. Yamazaki, Y., Sakaniwa, S., Tsuchiya, R., Nonomura, K.I., Kurata, N.: Oryzabase: an integrated information resource for rice science. Breeding Science (2010)

Reconstruction of a 3D Model from Single 2D Image by GAN

Lei Si[(⊠)] and Yoshiaki Yasumura[(⊠)]

Electrical and Electronic Information Department,
Shibaura Institute of Technology, Tokyo, Japan
sileiisi@yahoo.co.jp, yasumura@shibaura-it.ac.jp

Abstract. In this paper, we propose a method for reconstructing the 3D model from a single 2D image. The current cutting-edge methods for 3D reconstruction use the GAN (Generative Adversarial Network) to generate the model. However, the methods require multiple 2D images to reconstruct the 3D model, because all the information of a real object cannot be obtained from only one side, especially the back of the object is invisible. Since rebuilding a 3D model from a single view is an important issue in practical applications, the system requires the ability to obtain information about the surrounding environment of the object more quickly without the need for the object to move around.

Therefore, we propose a method for reconstructing 3D models from an image by learning the relationship between 3D model and 2D image. Mainly this method consists of three parts. The first part is the view layer, observing real-world objects and capturing 2D images. The layer searches the related 2D image of the 3D model that exists in the 3D model library. The second part is the corresponding layer. The 2D image corresponding to the 3D model is taken out, and contrast with real-world 2D images of objects. The 2D cross-section of the 3D model is found as the most similar one to the 2D image of the real-world object. The third part is generative layer that based on the model library to find the corresponding 3D model, reconstructing a 3D model that corresponds to the real object by using the GAN.

Keywords: 3D reconstruction · GAN · View layer · Corresponding layer
Generative layer

1 Introduction

In recent years, the research goal of computer vision is creating computer that has the ability of sensing, abstracting and judging the space objects in the world so as to achieve the purpose of recognition and comprehension. 3D model reconstruction is of great significance to computer vision. There are already many related papers for reconstructing 3D models. Some researchers reconstruct point cloud images. For example, Haoqiang Fan [4] achieved 3D point cloud model reconstruction based on 2D images. That is generated by a point cloud. However, the generated model itself has a large deviation. At present, the traditional method is better to use multiple images. The traditional methods of generating 3D models like papers [5, 6, 9–12] provide the ability to reconstruct 3D models from a single 2D image or multiple 2D views. However, most

© Springer Nature Switzerland AG 2018
M. Kaenampornpan et al. (Eds.): MIWAI 2018, LNAI 11248, pp. 226–232, 2018.
https://doi.org/10.1007/978-3-030-03014-8_20

of these methods only reconstruct the 3D model and do not acquire objects from the real world and reconstruct 3D models from a single image. Some methods are collecting multiple images to generate different faces of the 3D model from the front, side, and top view. Then the system combines them to get a complete 3D model. The disadvantage of the method is that the generated model is not well reconstructed. Bo Yang [1] realizes the reconstruction of three-dimensional data based on the existing data using the method similar to DCGAN. Although using GAN is popular method to reconstruct 3D models, it also cannot reconstruct the object's invisible information. The problem of information loss is caused by a single view in 2D images. For example, we cannot see from a single view that a cube has a prominent triangular back, or a back having a line of text information. When the 3D model is reconstructed, the fluctuating part is more difficult to reconstruct only according to the training set. At present, the method of restoring the 3D model from a single image is still less, and the actual effect remains to be improved. The back part of the reconstructed models is randomly reconstructed punctate shapes, and the surface is not a smooth plane.

In this paper, we propose a method for reconstructing 3D model from an image by learning the relationship between 3D model and 2D image. This method finds a similar 3D model from dataset by a single 2D image and uses this model to reconstruct the back-part and object's invisible information of the target object by GAN. This method simulates the human brain's ability to perceive the 3D model, and to solve the problem that if the object is confirmed from the real world.

2 3D Reconstruction Method

This section describes a method for reconstructing 3D model from a single image by GAN. Figure 1 shows an overview of the proposed method. The first part is the view layer. The function is equivalent to the retina of the human eye that is used for capturing the images. The second part is the corresponding layer, which is equivalent to searching the corresponding object images in the human brain. In other words, it is based on the corresponding cross section of 3D objects, and then finds a parallel 3D model. For example, we can obtain the images from the real-world information by eyes. From Fig. 1 After we saw the chair, we searched the corresponding images in the brain such as the bench in the park or the office chair in the room. Then we are according to the information seen in the past, image the look of the 3D model of the

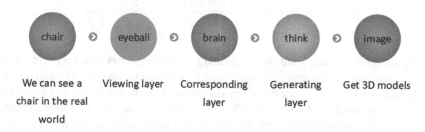

Fig. 1. Overview of the proposed method.

brain. This is the third part of the generative layer with 3D model reconstruction function. In other words, in the first part, we get the object's 2D images in the real world. Comparing with the 2D cross section of the model in the 3D database, the system finds similar objects according to the similarity of the images.

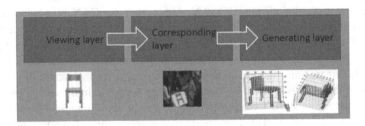

Fig. 2. Overview of the three layers.

2.1   View Layer

From Fig. 2, the main function of the view layer is to determine the object that we reconstruct from the 2D image of the real-world perspective. From its 2D cross-section, this part is mainly used OpenCV Cascades to achieve. Here we get the real-world chair's motif, which we will reconstruct it to 3D model for later. This section describes the same function of our real eyeball, observing the surroundings and identifying the objects to be captured. The main function of this section is responsible for identifying and extracting the real world 2D images of the chair. Cascades algorithm is an effective object detection method by using haar feature classifier based on the machine learning algorithm. The view layer of this method uses Cascades to create an algorithm to detect the chair.

2.2   Corresponding Layer

The main function of the corresponding layer is based on the 2D image of the object found in the view layer. Searching images in the 3D model database, the system gets 2D images of the 3D model. The system can find similar graphs based on 2D images. The highest value in the matrix is the image area with the highest matching degree.

$$R(x,y) = \frac{\sum_{x',y'}(T'(x',y') * I'(x+x',y+y'))}{\sqrt{\sum_{x',y'} T'(x',y')^2 * \sum_{x',y'} I'(x+x',y+y')^2}} \tag{1}$$

Equation (1) is x and y are the x-axis and y-axis coordinates of pixel points on the image respectively. We brought two image's information into Eq. (1) and get the similarity of two images. After the 3D model obtained by the corresponding layer. This part is mainly based on the corresponding 3D model extracted by the GAN algorithm for 3D model reconstruction. Then the system selects one of the reconstructed models that has the highest similarity to the real world as the best effect reconstruction model.

2.3   Generating Layer

Generative adversarial nets (GANs) is an unsupervised machine learning algorithm. The advantage of using the GAN network to build a 3D reconstruction model is that the system does not need hidden information. Reconstructing confrontation network includes a generator and a discriminator. The generator reconstructs the data from the noise-added raw data. The resulting data are then compared to the original data. If the discriminator does not recognize whether it is original data or generated data, the generated result is valid.

$$\min_G \max_D V(D, G) = E_{x-p_{data}(x)}[\log D(x)] + E_{z \sim p_z(z)}[\log(1 - D(G(Z)))] \quad (2)$$

In Eq. (2), P is the target data, Z is a normal distribution vector, and X is a sample.

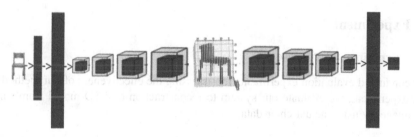

Fig. 3. This is the reconstructing 3D models of architecture by GAN.

Figure 3 shows the GAN algorithm, the left side is the data of the original 3D models, and then the pooling processes the information. Multiple encodings generate the final 3D model. Then, it is decoded into information multiple times to the GAN to discriminate the effect of the reconstructing 3D model.

$$Y = \int (I)\left(I, Y \in Z_2^{30^3}, \text{ where } Z_2 = \{0, 1\}\right) \quad (3)$$

Equation (3) indicates the amount of data in a 30 * 30 * 30 coordinate system.

$$L_{ae} = -xy\log(y') - (1 - x)(1 - y)\log(1 - y') \quad (4)$$

Equation (4) shows the relationship between positive and negative cases in the loss function. The correct result is multiplied by a positive probability. The wrong result is multiplied by the negative probability.

2.4 Metrics

$$\text{IoU} = \frac{\sum_{ijk}[I(y'_{ijk} > p) * I(y_{ijk})]}{\sum_{ijk}[I(I(y'_{ijk} > p) * I(y_{ijk})]}$$

$$\text{CE} = \frac{1}{ijk} \sum_{ijk} \left[y_{ijk}\log\left(y'_{ijk}\right) + \left(1 - y'_{ijk}\right)\log\left(1 - y'_{ijk}\right) \right] \tag{5}$$

Equation (7) is Intersection-over-Union (IoU) and cross-entropy loss (CE) is the metrics. Ijk are the output 3D models in the voxel dimension sizes. The lower CE value is the best 3D reconstruction model. But the highest IoU value is the best 3D reconstruction model.

3 Experiment

3.1 Experimental Purpose

We conducted evaluation experiments for assessing the effectiveness of our method. In this experiment, we evaluate our system to reconstruction of a 3D model from single 2D image by using actual chair data.

3.2 Experimental Setting

Now we use the data sets based on ShapeNet and ModelNet data sets. Although the amount of data is huge, the data type of the data set is not conducive to experimentation. In the view layer, we first need to identify the image of the chair in the image and cut it off. Because the focus of this paper is not to improve the accuracy of recognizing chairs. We use OpenCV Cascade algorithm to recognize chair. The experimental results successfully identified the image of the chair in the image and cut it out, leaving it to the next layer of contrast for processing. In the corresponding layer, we use the captured chair image by the view layer. We use Template Matching algorithm to compare with the template that existing in the 2D image data. Find the highest similarity image, then output the image's 3D model data to the reconstruction layer for reconstructing. In the generating layer, using the previously processed ModelNet 3D model as a data set, the GAN algorithm was used to reconstruct the 3D model.

3.3 Experimental Results

Figure 5 Shows the experimental results of this method. Figure 4 shows the accuracy of the experimental results. There were 150 epochs in the experiment and each epoch was updated 40 times. The appendix shows the resulting 3D model for every 100 appochs.

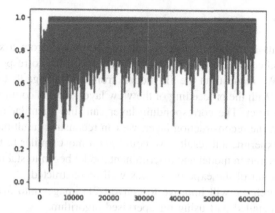

Fig. 4. The accuracy of the experimental results during training.

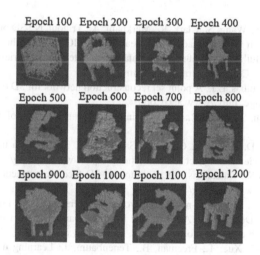

Fig. 5. The result pictures of the reconstructed model by MeshLab during training.

3.4 Experimental Consideration

We can see that as the epoch progresses, the loss of the generation and the loss of the discriminant continue to decrease in the overall trend. Because there is no point generated at the 0 epoch, so the error is at the beginning of full value, then due to excessive generation point, the point is also coincident with the increase, the error will be small at about short epoch 100. However, as the experiment progresses, the points generated by the GAN gradually have the appearance of a chair, and the overall trend of errors gradually decreases. The accuracy of the final experimental results was between 70 and 80%.

4   Conclusion

This paper presents a method for reconstructing 3D model from a single image by GAN. This method consists of three parts, the view layer, the corresponding layer, the generative layer. We reconstruct the 3D models from a 2D image that is different with other researchers. With the proceeding of the view layer, we can confirm the object that we need to reconstruct. The corresponding layer can find a similar model in the 3D model database. In the reconstruction layer, we can reconstruct multiple 3D models by GAN. From the experimental results, we could get a most similar to the target object model. GAN's generation model and discriminant model began to stabilize after 40,000 times. The final result of the experiment was well reconstructed.

In future research we will improve to convert 2D images into 3D models and to reconstruct more detailed part using unsupervised algorithm.

References

1. Yang, B., Wen, H., Wang, S., Clark, R., Markham, A., Trigoni, N.: 3D object reconstruction from a single depth view with adversarial learning. In: ICCV Workshops (2017)
2. Li, Y., Dai, A., Guibas, L., Nießner, M.: Database-assisted object retrieval for real time 3D reconstruction. In: Computer Graphics Forum (2015)
3. Fan, H., Su, H., Guibas, L.J.: A point set reconstruction network for 3D object reconstruction from a single image. http://www.arxiv.org/
4. Gadelha, M., Maji, S., Wang, R.: 3D shape induction from 2D views of multiple objects. In: CVPR (2017)
5. Choy, C.B., Xu, D., Gwak, J., Chen, K., Savarese, S., 3D-R2N2: a unified approach for single and multi-view 3D object reconstruction. http://www.arxiv.org/
6. Dou, P., Shah, S.K., Kakadiaris, I.A.: End-to-end 3D face reconstruction with deep neural networks. http://www.arxiv.org/
7. Chen, Z., Tong, Y.: Face super-resolution through Wasserstein GANs. http://www.arxiv.org/
8. Tatarchenko, M., Dosovitskiy, A., Brox, T.: Machine learning multi-view 3D models from single images with a convolutional network. http://www.arxiv.org/
9. Wu, J., Zhang, C., Xue, T., Freeman, B., Tenenbaum, J.: Learning a probabilistic latent space of object shapes via 3D generative-adversarial modeling. In: NIPS (2016)
10. Smith, E., Meger, D.: Improved adversarial systems for 3D object reconstruction and reconstruction. In: CORL (2017)
11. Wu, J., Wang, Y., Xue, T., Sun, X., Freeman, B., Tenenbaum, J.: MarrNet: 3D shape reconstruction via 2.5D sketches. In: NIPS (2017)
12. Qi, C. R., Su, H., Nießner, M., Dai, A., Yan, M., Guibas, L.J.: Volumetric and multi-view CNNs for object classification on 3D data. http://www.arxiv.org/

Inverse Ant Algorithm

Jaymer M. Jayoma[✉][iD], Bobby D. Gerardo, and Ruji M. Medina[✉]

Graduate Programs, Technological Institute of the Philippines, Quezon City,
Philippines
jmjayoma@carsu.edu.ph, bgerardo@wvsu.edu.ph,
ruji.medina@tip.edu.ph

Abstract. This paper presents a swarm optimization algorithm (SOA) which is specifically an enhanced version of the ant algorithm that solves shortest path problem. Ant Algorithm finds the shortest path through its pheromone deposits. However, its solutions are less effective if implemented in actual scenario like road traffic management and others because it stagnates when using large data. Variants of the ant algorithm where being developed to address the stagnation issue like Ant Colonization Optimization, Rank Based Ant Algorithm, Max-Min Ant Algorithm, Inverted Ant Colonization Algorithm and etc. However, each development failed to integrate real-world scenarios that can contribute to stagnation when applied to traffic management. Thus, the proposed algorithm addresses the stagnation issue when applied to traffic management and can adapt and be used in an actual event that requires shortest path solution by incorporating rules and constraints and other scenarios that may contribute to the delays.

Keywords: Inverse ant algorithm · Rules · Constraints

1 Introduction

Shortest path problem, which finds the path with the least cost distance from the source to destination, is one fundamental problem in graph theory. It arises from various practical problems from network optimization [1] and etc. Several algorithms are Kruskal Algorithm and etc. yet they are not efficient when handling in large data and real-time environment [2] which why Ant Colony Algorithm was first introduced by E. Bonabeau, M. Dorigo, V. Mahiezzo and A. Colorni in 1991 [4] the algorithm is a simulation based evolution process of the real ant colonies seeking food. They can communicate information about the paths they found to food sources by marking these paths with pheromone [6].The algorithm has been widely used in Job-shop scheduling problem [2], in telecommunications [7] such as routing and load balancing. However, because the ant algorithm may stagnate when ants are concentrated on local optimum path so modifications were made to solve the problem like ACO, MaxMin, Rank Bases and Inverted ACO(IACO) [9]. Section 2 discusses the differences between ant algorithm variance. Section 3 discusses the inverse ant algorithm our solution. Section 4 discusses the comparison of the three ant algorithms variants lastly Sect. 5 discusses the conclusion and future research.

© Springer Nature Switzerland AG 2018
M. Kaenampornpan et al. (Eds.): MIWAI 2018, LNAI 11248, pp. 233–239, 2018.
https://doi.org/10.1007/978-3-030-03014-8_21

2 Shortest Path Problem

2.1 Ant Colony Algorithm

Ant Colony Algorithm, designed Marco Dorigo in his PHD thesis in 1992, was inspired by the behavior of real ants seeking food [3, 5] which use their sense of smell to follow on a trail and focus on the immediate vicinity and their ability to deposit pheromone along the trail.

$$a_{ij} = \tau_{ij}^{\alpha} \eta_{ij}^{\beta} \tag{1}$$

Where a_{ij} measures the attractiveness of the route from node i to j, τ_{ij} is the pheromone concentration in edge ij [2]. The higher pheromone concentration that path becomes attractive where it is weighted by the power term α and η_{ij} is the heuristic information of the path such that $\eta_{ij} = 1/d_{ij}$ where d_{ij} is the Euclidean distance [8]. The longer the path the less it is attractive which is weighted by the power term β. The probability of the next move in shown in Eq. 2.

$$P_{ij}^{k} = \begin{cases} \dfrac{a_{ij}}{\sum_{s \in w_k} a_{is}} & j \in w_k \\ 0 & otherwise \end{cases} \tag{2}$$

Where a_{ij} is the pheromone concentration from node i to j and $\sum_{s \in w_k} a_{is}$ is the sum of all possible routes from node i to s and P_{ij}^{k} is the next move probability. The attractiveness that approaches zero will likely be infrequently visited. However, some ants may follow an alternative long route that will make pheromone deposits evaporate (3) overtime if path are not trodden which may lead to similar result and will be updated if it is trodden.

$$\tau_{ij}(t+1) = (1-\rho)\tau_{ij}(t) + \Delta\tau_{ij}, \text{ where } \Delta\tau_{ij} = \begin{cases} \dfrac{1}{L_k}, & \text{if ant k passed ij} \\ 0, & \text{otherwise} \end{cases} \tag{3}$$

2.2 Stagnation Problem

The basic ant algorithm solution is easy to fall into its optimum with the initial value of each path is set to 0. Some path will accumulate more pheromones compared to other paths that becomes more attractive hence movement of the ants always towards where the most pheromone concentration that causes the algorithm to stagnate [9, 12]. One of the solutions for the stagnation is the Ant Colony Algorithm that was introduced by Dorigo and Gambardella in 1997. The major difference is the release of pheromone during each round and during the end of the round which is according to the global optimum solution which is a local pheromone update rule and more realistic compared the basic ant system. Second solution is the Rank Based Ant Algorithm. It was introduced by Bullnheimer, Hartl, & Strauss in 1999. It has combined the rule gene algorithm and rank order into the Ant Algorithm in which the solution derived from N ants will be given automatic sequence according to the length of their respected tour and the pheromone release rule is according to the rank of ordered solutions. Third solution for stagnation problem is the Max Min Ant Algorithm that was introduced by Stuetzle and Hoos in 2000. The mechanism is to set the interval $[\tau_{min}, \tau_{max}]$ the upper bound and lower bound pheromone update where τ_{max} is set as the initial trail update. Fourth solution, for stagnation was IACO [11] where ants get repelled when too much pheromone is detected in the edge.

3   Proposed Method

Ants seeking food follows a trail of pheromone deposits left behind by its companions in the path [3]. The more pheromone the more likely the path will be selected by the ants. However, though the path is identified, it is not necessarily the best path at all times. If we apply the concept to a road traffic it will stagnate [9]. Road conditions at a specific instance differs from time to time like speed, visibility, passability and etc. that will become a constraint along the road. Traffic rules among others will be an input as well that will guide proper traffic management that will cause delays and congestion as time goes by. To adapt to the actual needs in the streets the rules and constraints (as discussed Sects. 3.1 and 3.2) are integrated in the inverse ant algorithm which will help it decide the best available path in which the ant should tread upon.

3.1   Inverse Ant Algorithm Rules

Rules identification is an essential part that governs movements of ants. Rules like ant velocity, ways (1-way/2way) traffic, pheromone volume an ant should deposit, path restriction and etc. Velocity rule will define how much time an ant will spend in the current path from node i to j. In consequence, it will also define how much time a pheromone stays in the path ij. Depending on the ant's velocity, the path may accumulate more pheromone as time progress. If the velocity is slow, it will accumulate more pheromone at shortest possible time that will reach to the maximum allowable concentration in the path. Way rule will define whether or not an ant can pass through and/or can go back in the path ij. It is defined in a directed graph $G(V,E) = \{(v_1,v_2),$ $(v_2,v_3), (v_3,v_4),\dots (v_{n-1},v_n)\}$ [4, 10]. Way rule will shorten the ant's selection process of best path because automatically eliminates unpassable path. Pheromone rule will define how much an ant can deposit in the path it is currently treading. The pheromone capacity of an ant will help identify which path it can accommodate at any given time. Thus, providing it foreknowledge what path it should undertake whether or not it will violate the path constraints. A pheromone rule is an attribute added to an agent in the inverse ant algorithm which will be one of the factors in determining the best path to take. Path restriction rule can be determined in the way rule. If there is no vertex between the nodes indicates that the path is not passable because of in-time conditions that may activate restrictions on the path. This rule can be implemented my deleting the node between ij by substituting the current value of a_{ij} to zero.

3.2   Inverse Ant Algorithm Constraints

Constraints are present conditions in which also affect ant's movements like path capacity, path closures at any given time, sudden change of routes and among others.

Path capacity constraints is defined under the limits a path can accept deposited pheromones. Though in theory, a path cannot be overwhelmed with pheromones but in practice it gets overwhelmed that will cause a stagnation [9]. Thus, a capacity will limit ants in the path. It is represented in a constraints matrix C where element c_{ij} contains the maximum pheromone concentration the path ij can contain. It is compared against the weighted matrix W element w_{ij} such that if w_{ij} is less than c_{ij} means that the path ij is still passable at that instant. Path closures and sudden changes of routes will be defined when a path capacity is reached thus restricting the ants from treading in the path thus the inverse ant will find an alternative path.

3.3   Inverse Ant Algorithm Input and Graph Representations

The input derived by computing the Euclidean distance [10]. That is represented by distance matrix A where elements a_{ij} contains the distance between $edge_{ij}$. Then the weight Matrix B is initialized that contains the pheromone concentration of each node ij. Its initial value could be defined between 0 and 1 and can increase as time progress as where pheromones are added when ants tread in b_{ij} and pheromones are subtracted from b_{jk} as it leaves b_{jk}. The weight matrix is always compared to the constraints matrix when ant choose the next node to tread. Constraints matrix C is initialized base on the rules definition like path capacity, number of lanes, speed limit and distance. The more it is subjected to these rules; constraints value gets smaller. However, the lesser the value of element c_{ij} the lesser the path ij can accommodate pheromone deposits in the weight matrix W element w_{ij}.

3.4   Inverse Ant Algorithm Updating Policy

Ant algorithm provides updating of pheromone in the nodes during an ant visit where the level of concentration will attract more ants to take that path. While nodes that are not frequently visited also requires updating which pheromone decays overtime [3]. However, in reality pheromone deposits and its decay can be dictated by the presence of the ant in the path. Thus, in the inverse ant algorithm, upon the entrance of the ant in the node it deposits its pheromone and upon its exit the pheromone is subtracted also. So, the updating Eq. 3 can be simplified and rewritten as:

$$\tau_{ij}, \tau_{jk} = \begin{cases} \tau_{ij} - ant.pher, & \tau_{jk} + ant.pher \\ 0, & otherwise \end{cases} \qquad (4)$$

Equation 4 reflects that as the ant moves from node ij to node jk it subtracts its pheromone from node ij and add it to node jk.

3.5   Inverse Ant Algorithm Path Selection

Ant algorithm selects an appropriate next node base on the Eq. 2. However, when rules and constraints are integrated it will not serve its purpose. Thus, in inverse ant algorithm the Eq. 2 we can be rewrite as

$$
P_{ij}^k = \begin{cases} \frac{a_{ij}\rho}{\sum_{s\epsilon w_k} a_{is}} j\epsilon w_k, & \text{if } a_{ij} < c_{ij} \text{ Then } \rho = 1 \text{ else } (0 < \rho < 1) \\ 0 & \text{otherwise} \end{cases}
\tag{5}
$$

Where c_{ij} is the value for the set of rules and constraints and ρ is the inverse rate factor for choosing the lesser pheromone concentration. The inverse rate factor ρ value will identify which nodes are to be eliminated from the next node selections of the probable next move.

4   Experimental Results and Discussion

The proposed algorithm was developed using java. Its ancestor was derived from the work of Thomas Jungblut. Windows 7 Professional OS is used with Interl iCore 7 CPU M 640@ 2.8 GHz and 8 GB RAM. For demonstration purposes, the research uses the Berlin52 Traveling Sales Person (TSP) data. Three applications where compared namely; Ant Algorithm as A1, Modified Ant Algorithm as A2, and Inverse Ant Algorithm as A3. The algorithms were inputted with ants at 5 increments per processing to get their response time and best distance discovered from their point of origin. Parameters were set for Alpha = 0, Beta = 9, Q = 0.0001 and Inverse Num = 1×10^{-31}. The test is done to showcase until what number of ants each algorithm can accommodate without any problem with stagnation and the result shows. The three data were tested using Wilcoxson signed-rank Test and the result shows that their no significant difference between the running of A1, A2 and A3 respectively. In addition, the test shows the distance derived from each algorithm has no significant difference between A1, A2 and A3 respectively.

4.1   Running Time Comparison

Ants algorithm and Inverse Algorithm shows good results as the ants are increased.

Initially, the classic ant algorithm performs better when ants are less 40 compared to the other experiments. However, when the number of ants reached within 90 ants, it stagnates as shown in Fig. 1. While the Inverse ant cruise beyond 100 ants and even performs better compared the ant algorithm that is not subjected to constraints.

4.2   Distance Comparison

Distance is a factor when choosing a path. The shorter the path the better. The three experiments showed a downward pattern of path distance as the number of ants traversing the map increases. This indicates that the more ants are deployed the more chances it would yelled a shorter distance. However, in the case of the ant algorithm

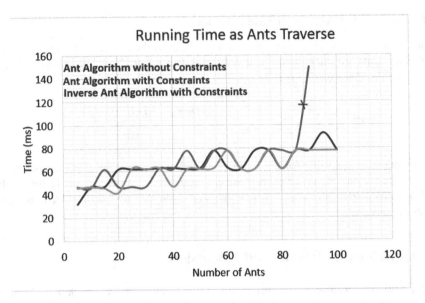

Fig. 1. Running time comparison

that is employed with constraints, it is not reliable when introduced with 90 or more ants because it stagnates (Fig. 2).

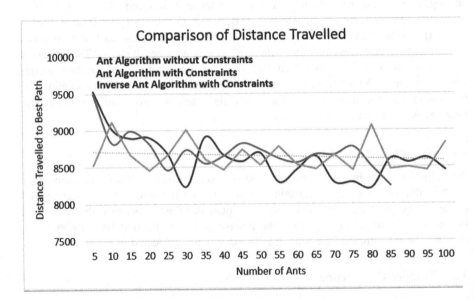

Fig. 2. Shortest distance found by ants.

5   Conclusion and Future Work

The study presented in this paper implements an enhanced ant algorithm which is the inverse ant algorithm. At a given time, instead of looking for the most frequently used path it will provide a path that is less trodden to avoid stagnation which is reliable when applied to traffic management. In addition, when travelling time is essential. So, regardless of distance, time is vital when deciding which path you should take. The test showed that the performance of inverse ant algorithm is comparable to the previous implementations. Future research directions include testing the algorithm to a specific city traffic condition. Moreover, this algorithm will be tested in data communications network, traffic management and others. Enhancement of the inverse ant algorithm is also intended for time and memory complexity issues.

References

1. Adubi, S.A., Sanjay, M.: A comparative study on the Ant Colony Optimization Algorithms. In: 2014 11th International Conference on Electronics, Computer and Computation (ICECCO), 29 September–1 October 2014 (2014). 978-1-4799-4106-3/14/$31.00 © 2014 IEEE
2. Collin, A.: Ant Colony Algorithms: solving optimization problems. Dr. Dobb's J. **31**(9) 46–51 (2006)
3. Dias, J.C., Machado, P., Silva, D.C., Abreu, P.H.: An Inverted Ant Colony Optimization approach to traffic. Eng. Appl. Artif. Intell. **36**, 122–133 (2014)
4. Gu, S., Zhang, X.: An Improved Ant Colony Algorithm with Soldier Ant. In: 11th International Conference on Natural Computation (ICNC), Hubei, China, pp. 206–209 (2015)
5. Huang, M., Ding, P.: An Improved Ant Colony Algorithm and its application in vehicle routing problem. In: Mathematical Problems in Engineering, pp. 1–9 (2013)
6. Min, H., Dazhi, P., Song, Y.: An improved hybrid ant colony algorithm and its application in solving TSP*, pp. 423–427. IEEE (2014)
7. Ping, G., Chunbo, X., Yi, C., Jing, L., Yanqing, L.: Adaptive Ant Colony Optimization Algorithm. International Conference on Mechatronics and Control (ICMC), pp. 95–98. IEEE, Jinzhou (2014)
8. Su Hlaing, Z.C., Khine, M.A.: An Ant Colony Optimization Algorithm for Solving Traveling Salesman Problem. In: 2011 International Conference on Information Communication and Management, pp. 54–59 (2011)
9. Yong, L., Guangzhou, Z., Fanjun, S.: Adaptive Ant-based dynamic routing algorithm. In: 5th World Congress on Intelligent Control, pp. 2694–2697. IEEE, Hangzhou (2004)
10. Yonghua, Z., Jin, X., Wentong, Y., Yong, C.: The Advanced Ant Colony Algorithm and Its Application. 2011 Third International Conference on Measuring Technology and Mechatronics Automation, pp. 664–667 (2001)
11. Yuan, Y., Liu, Y., Wu, B.: A modified Ant Colony algorithm to solve the shortest path problem. In: International Conference on Cloud Computing and Internet of Things (CCIOT 2014), pp. 148–151. IEEE,Changchun (2014)
12. Zhaoa, D., Luob, L., Zhanga, K.: An improved ant colony optimization for the communication network routing problem. Math. Comput. Model. **52** (2010)

Enhanced Texture Representation for Moving Targets Classification Using Co-occurrence

Chit Kyin Htoo$^{(\boxtimes)}$ and Myint Myint Sein

University of Computer Studies, Yangon, Myanmar
chitucsy@gmail.com, myintucsy@gmail.com

Abstract. This paper presents a moving targets identification system in more effective computational cost by using Gray Level Co-occurrence Matrix (GLCM) instead of using the other texture descriptors: the conventional LBP histograms and LBPs with co-occurrence matrix. The aim of this work is to develop an enhanced texture analysis based method for the detection and classification of the moving targets in real environment. Firstly, the system distinguished the moving regions from the background regions by using an Adaptive Gaussian Mixture Model (GMM). The gray level (grayscale intensity or Tone) texture features on a co-occurrence matrix will be extracted from each segmented moving block by the four texture features, energy, homogeneity, correlation and contrast in four directions ($0°$, $45°$, $90°$, and $135°$) and quantized into a feature vector. These exploited texture features will be used to classify the moving objects using the Support Vector Machine (SVM) classification learner. The walking-dog-14-0-3 test sequence from UCF11 dataset is used in experimentation to show the effectiveness of the proposed feature method.

Keywords: Image texture feature representation
Gray level Co-occurrence matrix · Moving targets classification

1 Introduction

Texture can be defined as the visual information concerning to the variation such as shapes, illumination, shadows, absorption and reflectance of an image's surface. The texture information for a digital image or the selected region of an image is the information about the repetitive patterns of the structurally arranged surface of an image in spatial domain. These texture features are also analyzed to be more effective image classification, recognition and retrieval. Among many texture feature extraction techniques, the LBP histogram is one of the robust texture descriptions against uniform changes in illumination. T. Ojala, M. Pietikäinen, and D. Harwood firstly describe LBP in 1994 and worked the comparative study on LBP for image texture classification in [1, 2] and LBP has been proposed in many researches [3, 4]. However, there is no consideration for spatial relation of adjacent LBPs. Therefore, the co-occurrence among adjacent LBPs was proposed in [5, 6]. A co-occurrence matrix or co-occurrence distribution is noticed as the distribution of co-occurring values for a specified offset in an image. Co-occurrence matrix is often used to extract image's textual information via the various local regions in [7, 8].

M. Kaenampornpan et al. (Eds.): MIWAI 2018, LNAI 11248, pp. 240–246, 2018.
https://doi.org/10.1007/978-3-030-03014-8_22

The Gray Level Co-occurrence Matrix (GLCM) operator has been recently interested in many image textural feature extraction for many visual applications such as image retrieval, identification, classification, and cars or pedestrians detection in traffic monitoring and automotive safe applications. The GLCM is the spatial texture information extracted from each local region in the entire image. It is a calculating method how often a pixel with gray-level value i occurs to its neighboring pixels with the value j either in horizontally, vertically or diagonally. Ramamurthy [9] and Bino Sebastian, et al. [10] proposed texture based image retrieval using GLCM in global analysis. Metty Mustikasari [11] also locally analyzed texture feature using GLCM over four image sub-blocks. This paper will show that the proposed gray level co-occurrence matrix method has significantly cost-effective in computation time over the original LBP and LBP along with co-occurrence.

2 Proposed System Architecture and Methodologies

The proposed system architecture is shown in Fig. 1 and its processing flows and methodologies are detail discussed in next sessions.

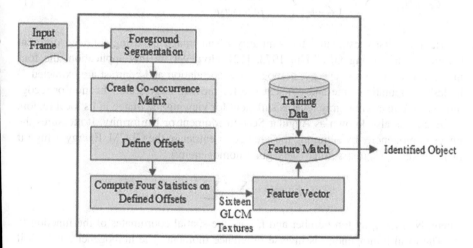

Fig. 1. The proposed system architecture for moving targets identification.

The foreground segmentation is the first pre-processing step of the image recognition system. Morphological operations are useful mathematical tools for removing the noise and filling the gaps in the detected objects as the foreground extraction and detection process often generates undesirable noise and may objects split as multiple objects. After applying these some fuzzy based morphological filtering operations, segmentation result has achieved more effective in this work. The left unwanted blocks are removed by thresholding their area from Mathlab's regionprops function. Next, the only moving targets in an image can be detected and tracked with the help of blob-analysis. Then, the system extracted the gray level texture features in each local region from the segmented moving objects. Next, we template SVM model with Gaussian kernel based on the binary class model (Human or Dog) over the extracted texture features and the ten-fold cross validation is used to avoid the data bias. Next, the test images are predicted with the trained SVM files of each feature method as a moving target labeling.

3   The Proposed Gray Level Co-occurrence Matrix

Gray Level Co-occurrence Matrix (GLCM) is a useful second order feature extraction method in the low level features analysis of the image processing. GLCM shows the distance and angular spatial information of a specified local region in an image. It is mentioned by measuring the spatial relationship between the reference pixel with intensity value j and the neighbor pixel with the value i. It measures the changes of the relative spatial positions, p and q of the neighboring pixels for a given local region in an image at direction θ and interval distance d to create a co-occurrence matrix as follows:

$$C_{\delta x, \delta y}(i,j) = \sum_{p=1}^{n} \sum_{q=1}^{m} \begin{cases} 1, & \text{if } I(p,q) = i \text{ and } I(p+\delta x, q+\delta y) = j \\ 0, & \text{otherwise} \end{cases}, \quad (1)$$

Haralick firstly estimated the similarity of an image by using fourteen different texture features using GLCM in 1973, [12]. However, in this application, the four major statistic features: energy, homogeneity, correlation and contrast are extracted to be less computation time and efficient use for moving targets classification or recognition as the using few gray level is sufficient for viewing the image in its local region.

Energy is also known as Angular Second Moment or Uniformity. It measures the image homogeneity by summing the squared of entries in the GLCM. Energy is high if image pixels are quite similar (very good homogeneity).

$$Energy = \sum_{i}^{N} \sum_{j}^{N} P_{ij}^2, \quad (2)$$

where, N is the gray ton number and i, j are the spatial coordinates of the function P.

The local homogeneity is inverse difference moment. The homogeneity is high if local gray level become into uniform and inverse gray level matrix is high.

$$Homogenity = \sum_{i} \sum_{j} \frac{1}{1 + (i-j)^2} g_{ij} \quad (3)$$

Correlation is one of the statistic features that measure the linear dependency of grey levels of neighboring pixels. It is also an optical method which employs image registration and tracking techniques for many image processing applications.

$$Correlation = \frac{\sum_i \sum_j (ij)g_{ij} - \mu_x \mu_y}{\sigma_x \sigma_y}, \tag{4}$$

Contrast a measure the intensity variation between a pixel and its neighboring pixel in the entire image. It returns a magnitude local intensity contrast in the GLCM.

$$Contract = \sum_i \sum_j (i - j)^{2g_{ij}}, \tag{5}$$

These four features are measured in a different co-occurrence matrix for the same (rotated) image by four directions (see Fig. 2): horizontal $(0°)$, vertical $(90°)$, diagonal (bottom left to top right, $45°$ and top left to bottom right, $135°$) for each local region of the segmented target and all GLCM histograms are stored into a vector. Doing extract, GLCM feature method has achieved more computation time over the other features, LBP and co-occurrence of adjacent LBPs (CoALBP). The processing flow of GLCM texture feature extraction over each segmented target of original input image can be seen in Fig. 3.

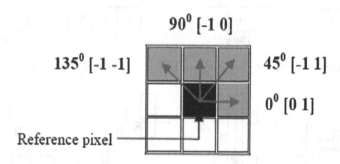

Fig. 2. The four rotated directions for co-occurrence matrix.

In order to compare GLCM with LBP along with co-occurrence, we use Nosaka's co-occurrence concept for adjacent LBPs in [5]. The co-occurrence of adjacent LBPs means that how often they combine each other in the entire image. Instead of considering the eight neighboring pixels of a given center pixel in the original LBP, the method uses the two sparse LBP configurations: LBP (+) and LBP (x) to extract LBP with co-occurrence by making the threshold the image's local region based on a set of two horizontally pixels and two vertically pixels and a set of four diagonally pixels respectively (see Fig. 4).

Next, all the considered LBPs are quantized into a feature vector for all possible number of LBPs (N_p) and we create the $N_p \times N_p$ auto-correlation matrix to calculate the LBP with co-occurrence by calculating the combination of adjacent LBP_i and LBP_j via the displacement vector (a) which is a set of all the configuration patterns: $\{(\Delta r, 0)^T, (\Delta r, \Delta r)^T, (0, \Delta r)^T, (-\Delta r, \Delta r)^T\}$ (see Fig. 5).

Next, we also sum up all the column vector of the auto-correlation matrix to obtain the original LBP histogram combining with co-occurrence spatial information. These

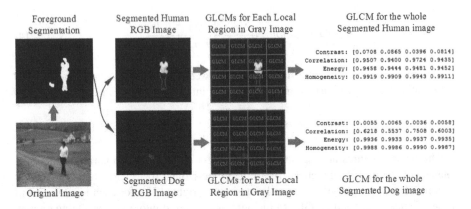

Fig. 3. Processed flow for GLCM texture feature extraction.

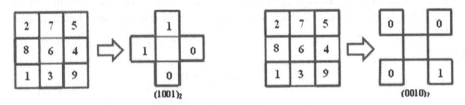

Fig. 4. Two sparse configurations: LBP (+) in Left and LBP(x) in Right.

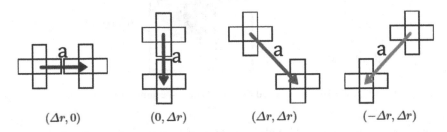

Fig. 5. CoALBP's configured patterns.

auto-correlation matrices are converted to vector form and quantized into a feature vector with high dimensionality in $4N_p^2$ due to the use of the sparse LBPs. The extraction process flow of co-occurrence among LBPs is shown in Fig. 6.

4   Evaluation Results

Some testing resulted images in this experimenting are described with their annotations and moving targets tracking results for some original images (see Fig. 7). The system extracted the texture features for GLCM, LBP and CoALBP from the segmented moving objects over the walking-dog-14-0-3 test sequence from UCF11 dataset as shown in Figs. 3 and 6. The feature length of the proposed GLCM texture

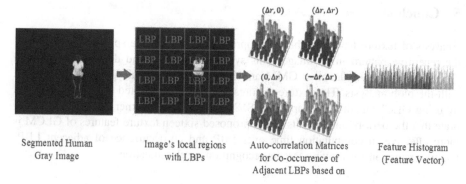

Fig. 6. Processed flow for co-occurrence matrix among adjacent LBPs.

representation has moderated than LBP and CoALBP and so, the computation time over GLCM is desirably achieved over them in this moving targets classification. The results of their classification performance via SVM model are reported (see Table 1).

Fig. 7. The moving targets detection and tracking results: original images in left, moving region detection in middle, and moving region tracking.

Table 1. Classification results of the proposed GLCM feature.

Dataset	v_walk_dog_14_03			
Feature method	**Propoed GLCM**	LBP	CoALBP (+)	CoALBP (x)
Feature extraction time	**3.107023 s**	3.900115 s	2.038923 s	1.938923 s
Feature length	**16**	884	1024	1024
Training time	**0.6706 s**	2.5039 s	3.2487 s	3.0583 s
Classification accuracy	**98%**	98%	98%	98%
Classification speed (obs/sec)	**2200**	180	150	150

5   Conclusion

Analysis of texture feature is the best approach to measure the spatial information of the repetitive pattern in an image. This system segmented and detected the moving objects based on the adaptive GMM and fuzzy morphological operators are tracked with the blob analysis. The texture features from each segmented object are extracted by using GLCM method. By applying SVM classification learner, the system collaborate that the performance results of the proposed sixteen texture features of GLCM is more effective in computation time over LBP and co-occurrence of adjacent LBPs feature extraction for moving targets recognition or classification.

References

1. Ojala, T., Pietikäinen, M., Harwood, D.: A comparative study of texture measures with classification based on feature distributions. Pattern Recogn. **29**, 51–59 (1996)
2. Ojala, T., Pietikainen, M., Maenpaa, T.: Multiresolution gray-scale and rotation invariant texture classification with local binary patterns. IEEE Trans. Pattern Anal. Mach. Intell. **24** (7), 971–987 (2002)
3. Maenpaa, T.: The local binary pattern approach to texture analysis-extensions and applications, Oulu University, Finland (2003). ISBN 951-42-7075-4, ISSN 0355-3213
4. Satpathy, A., Jiang, X., Eng, H.L.: LBP-based edge-texture features for object recognition. IEEE Trans. Image Process. **23**(5), 1953–1964 (2014)
5. Nosaka, R., Ohkawa, Y., Fukui, K.: Feature Extraction Based on Co-occurrence of Adjacent Local Binary Patterns. In: Ho, Y.-S. (ed.) PSIVT 2011. LNCS, vol. 7088, pp. 82–91. Springer, Heidelberg (2011). https://doi.org/10.1007/978-3-642-25346-1_8
6. Xie, Z.: Infrared Face Recognition based on LBP Co-occurrence Matrix, Proceedings of the 33rd Chinese Control Conference (2014)
7. Kobayashi, T., Otsu, N.: Image feature extraction using gradient local auto-correlations. In: Forsyth, D., Torr, P., Zisserman, A. (eds.) ECCV 2008, Part I. LNCS, vol. 5302, pp. 346–358. Springer, Heidelberg (2008)
8. Watanabe, T., Ito, S., Yokoi, K.: Co-occurrence histograms of oriented gradients for pedestrian detection. In: Proceedings of the 3rd IEE Pacific-Rim Symposium on Image and Video Technology, pp. 38–47 (2009)
9. Ramamurthy, B., Chandran K.R.: Content based medical image retrieval with texture content using gray level co-occurrence matrix and k-means clustering algorithms. J. Comput. Sci. **8**(7), 1070–1076 (2012). ISSN 1549-3636
10. Sebastian, V.**B.**, Unnikrishnan, A., Balakrishnan, K., Grey level co-occurrence matrices: generalization and some new feature. Int. J. Comput. Sci. Eng. Inf. Technol. (IJCSEIT) **2**(2), (2012)
11. Mustikasari, M., Madenda, S.: Texture based image retrieval using GLCM and image sub-block. Int. J. Adv. Res. Comput. Sci. Softw. Eng. **5**(3) (2015). ISSN 2277 128X
12. Haralick, R.M., Shanmugan, K., Dinstein, I.: Texture features for image classification. IEEE Trans. Syst. Man Cybern. **SmC-3**(193) 610–621 (1973)

An Adequate Dietary Planning Model Using Particle Swarm Optimization

Edmarlyn Porras[1](✉), Arnel Fajardo[2](✉), and Ruji Medina[1](✉)

[1] Technological Institute of the Philippines, Manila, Philippines
edz17@yahoo.com, ruji.medina@tip.edu.ph
[2] School of Engineering and Information Technology, Manuel L. Quezon University, Manila, Philippines
acfajardo2011@gmail.com

Abstract. This study aims to develop a linear programming optimization model that will effectively assist dietitians in preparing a meal plan for adults with the variety of foods that include appropriate food group proportion and at the same time meets his/her total daily energy requirement, macronutrients and micronutrients needs. The objective function of the programming model is designed to minimize food cost. The model was solved by Particle Swarm Optimization written in Matlab. As a result, a low-cost meal for a day was selected.

Keywords: Optimization · Particle Swarm Optimization
Dietary planning

1 Introduction

Inadequate nutrition is described as "a scourge in our world" [1]. The record shows almost 1.9 billion individuals around the world who suffer from various kinds of nutritional deficiencies [2] and these are due to many causes like starvation, an insufficient amount of food and nutrients in the body and for not taking good care of one's health [3]. These are often related to overeating, a bad habit which may later lead to overweight and obesity. Hence, this condition is now considered as a public health problem for it leads the global burden of disease [4,5], since it causes shortness of breath, prevents blood circulation, weakens the muscle, increases the risk of infections, inhibits recovery, aggravates the improper functioning of various physiological processes, etc. [6,7].

In the Philippines, the common features of malnutrition are chronically poor diets, high intake of fats, oils, sugars and syrups, meats and processed meat products and other cereal products and low consumption of fruits and vegetables [8]. Further, this is due to a sedentary lifestyle, the convenience of fast food, and the planning and preparation of healthy and nutritious food are not of prime importance [9]. Consequently, it becomes an alarming issue for it increases one's

Supported by MIWAI 2018.

M. Kaenampornpan et al. (Eds.): MIWAI 2018, LNAI 11248, pp. 247–254, 2018.
https://doi.org/10.1007/978-3-030-03014-8_23

vulnerability to lifestyle diseases such as cardiovascular diseases, cancer, diabetes and chronic respiratory diseases [10]. Hence, awareness of proper nutrition through a healthy diet, balanced energy intake with the essential amount of vitamins and minerals coupled with appropriate food choices, gives an individual a protective result [11] since, it fosters good health, good quality of life and it keeps individuals away from diseases [6]. Moreover, a healthy diet at a reasonable price is an additional burden [12]; however, there are still some nutrient-rich foods that can be bought at a lower price and much more healthful such as fruits and vegetables which contain lower amount of calories and are packed with vitamins, minerals, dietary fiber and antioxidants [13].

In the previous years, there are several studies that were patterned from the classical diet problem where the nutritional needs of an individual or of an organization were satisfied while minimizing the cost such as; minimizing food cost while satisfying the nutritional constraints and maximizing the rating given by the users based on their daily meals [14]. An optimization model wherein nutrient needs of the referenced man and woman were met and it is subject to available household budget [15]. In another study, a recommended diet plan was created whereby necessary nutrients intake for the high school students were satisfied while minimizing government budget [16]. In separate work, nutritional requirements were satisfied by a model while minimizing the cost, cooking and preparation time [17]. Another model was created where the cost was lessened while meeting all nutritional requirements, maintaining nutrient contents and preserved eating practices [18]. In addition, the work of [19] stresses that a daily menu should be provided to the users to satisfy the required amount of nutrients, to reduce cost and to maximize rating. Indeed, expanding the current knowledge of diet planning, having a variety of foods through appropriate food group proportion in every meal, meeting the required total calories and satisfying the nutrients at least cost were the focused of the study.

In this research, the meal plan was determined based on the recursive dietary pattern of Filipino people where rice, fish, and vegetables constitute the usual diet. The 2012 Nutritional Guidelines for Filipinos emphasizes a need to consume a wide variety of foods every day purposely to get the nutrients that a body needs. Variety must come from each of the three basic food groups: Go Foods (Rice and Alternatives), Grow Foods, (Fish and alternatives) and Glow foods (Vegetables and Fruits). Therefore, eating a variety of foods in the right proportions can build a healthy plate at meal times [8, 20].

2   Materials and Methods

This healthy diet meal plan is for every active and healthy individual. The total energy requirement for a day was used based on the desired body weight of an individual.

2.1   Diet Planning Method

Particle Swarm Optimization (PSO) [22,23] was used as a searching algorithm to traverse search space created by the model to find the best combination of foods. PSO is a member of the Si-based algorithm family; it mimics the behavior of flock birds. The algorithm's main idea is that there are set of particles wherein every particle is defined with a position and a velocity and moves around the search space in the direction of the current best solution of an NP-hard problem. The positions of the particles are updated according to their optimal local position and the optimal global position visited. The mathematical formula for updating the position of a particle is defined as:

$$x_i^{t+1} = x_i^t + v_1^{t+1} \tag{1}$$

where $x_i{}^t$ is the current position of the particle, and $v_i{}^{t+1}$ is the new velocity of the particle. The formula for the velocity of a particle is defined as:

$$v_i^{t+1} = w * v_1^{t+1} + c1 * (x_t^p - x_1^t) + c2 * (x_j^g - x_i^t) \tag{2}$$

where *(i)* $v_i{}^{t+1}$ is the current velocity of the particle, $x_t{}^p$ is the best position encountered by the particle, $x_i{}^t$ is the current position of the particle, $x_j{}^g$ is the best position encountered by a particle at the swarm level and w, c1 and c2 are scalar constants that weight the importance of each component part of the velocity formula.

3   Model Formulation

Each food contains nutrients, thus nutrients are represented by $i = 1, \ldots, m$. Then, consider a non-negative matrix $A = A_{(ij)}$, meaning the quantity of nutrients i in one unit of food item j, for all $i = 1, \ldots, m$ and for all $j = 1, \ldots, n$. Total energy intake, macronutrients and micronutrients should be based on the recommended nutrient intakes.

Objective Function: A candidate solution is a least cost dietary plan, thus, the total cost F is minimize,

$$F = \sum_{i=1}^{n} Y_j * C_j \tag{3}$$

where Y_j, this value means the amount of food item j; while C_j is the cost of food item j. This objective function has several constraints. The quality of the solution is the basis of penalty constraints, as if it violates more constraints the penalty will also increase.

Constraints: There is a need to satisfy the person's level of energy intake; thus it must not exceed to the lower and upper limit of the total energy requirement, where A_{Ej} is the quantity of energy in every serving of the food item j, E denotes the total energy allowance for a day of an individual while n is the number of foods per meal.

$$c_1 = \sum_{j=1}^{n} A_{Ej} * Y_j \leq E, \qquad \sum_{j=1}^{n} A_{Ej} * Y_j \geq E \qquad (4)$$

For macronutrients, there are an adequate intake values based on the recommend-ed energy and nutrient intakes [24]. Thus, daily intakes of macronutrients should be within the range of intakes based on Acceptable Macronutrient Distribution Range (AMDR).

$$c_2 = \sum_{j=1}^{n} A_{Pj}4Y_j \leq 0.1E, \qquad \sum_{j=1}^{n} A_{Pj}4Y_j \geq 0.15E$$

$$c_3 = \sum_{j=1}^{n} A_{Pj}4Y_j \geq 0.15E, \qquad \sum_{j=1}^{n} A_{Pj}4Y_j \geq 0.15E \qquad (5)$$

$$c_4 = \sum_{j=1}^{n} A_{Cj}4Y_j \leq 0.55E, \qquad \sum_{j=1}^{n} A_{Cj}4Y_j \geq 0.75E$$

where A_{Pj}, A_{Fj}, A_{Cj} denote the quantity of proteins, fats and carbohydrates in every serving of food items j, and n is the number of courses in the meal. Since the quantities are expressed in grams, conversion factors are required to attain to calories (e.g. 4 for protein and carbohydrates and 9 for fats). While E is the recommended calorie requirement value for a day. On the other hand, the micronutrients should be according to the Recommended Nutrient Intake (RENI) per day which is considered adequate for the maintenance of health and well-being of a person. There are 8 nutrients that were considered based on Philippine Dietary Reference Intake (PDRI) such as, Calcium, Phosphorous, Iron, Vitamin A, Thiamin, Riboflavin, Niacin, and Vitamin C.

$$c_5 = \sum_{j=1}^{n} A_{ij}Y_j \leq RENI \qquad i = 1, 2...8 \qquad (6)$$

where a_{ij} means the quantity of nutrient i in one unit of the food item j , for all item $i = 1, \ldots m$, and for all $j = 1,..n$.

To ensure that an individual can consume variety of foods, food groups are well represented in every meal by a quantity that is equivalent to its portion size (e.g. 1/2 of the plate is for glow foods with 1/3 for fruits and 1/6 for vegetables, 1/3 for grow foods and 1/6 for go foods). Y_{Goj}, Y_{Grj}, Y_{Frj}, Y_{Vj} denote the amount of food item j that belongs in the food group Go, Glow, Fruits and Vegetables used in a meal and n is the number of foods in that group. While A_{Ewj} is the amount of energy in serving of food i that belong in group w, thus the need to satisfy the equalities as shown in Eq. 7.

$$c_6 = \sum_{j=1}^{n} Y_{Goj} A_{EGoj} = 0.33E, \qquad \sum_{j=1}^{n} A_{Grj} A_{EGRj} = 0.17E$$

$$c_7 = \sum_{j=1}^{n} Y_{Frj} A_{EFrj} = 0.17E, \qquad \sum_{j=1}^{n} A_{Vj} A_{EVj} = 0.33E \qquad (7)$$

The foods are categorized into 3: Go foods, Glow foods (fruits and vegetables) and Grow foods. However, there are foods that contain a combination of Grow foods (e.g. fish, meat, seafood) and vegetables. It is called a one-dish meal. This food can already represent both the Grow foods and vegetables; thus, if the food generated was a one-dish meal then its proportion in one meal will increase and it is expressed as:

$$c_8 = \sum_{j=1}^{n} Y_{Odj} A_{EOdj} = 0.50E \qquad (8)$$

And each food category will contribute one dish aside from Glow foods with two dishes on a per meal basis. Thus, there is a need to specify the food requirements, since 4 dishes are needed for every meal.

$$c_9 = \sum_{j=1}^{n} Types of Foods(Y_j) = n \qquad (9)$$

There are also other specific recommendations that must be maintained at a certain level such as dietary fiber, sodium and potassium:

The amount of sodium intake should be limited to only less than 2 g, where A_{Sj} is the amount of sodium S in every serving of food item j; thus, the Eq. 10 shows.

$$c_{10} = \sum_{j=1}^{n} A_{Sj} Y_j \leq 2 \qquad (10)$$

While the amount of potassium must be increased to 3,510 mg, where A_{Tj} is the amount of potassium T in every serving of food item j (Eq. 11).

$$c_{11} = \sum_{j=1}^{n} A_{Tj} Y_j \geq 3510 \qquad (11)$$

On the other hand, a daily intake of 25 g of dietary fiber is highly recommended for adults and this can be expressed as:

$$c_{12} = \sum_{j=1}^{n} A_{Bj} Y_j \geq 25 \qquad (12)$$

where A_{Bj} is the amount of fiber B in every serving of food item j.

4   Results and Discussion

Let's consider the data of a particular adult. A 30 years old woman who stands 154.94 cm, weighs 54 kgs and maintain a sedentary activity, and her total energy requirement for a day is 1500 calories a day.

The results of the experiment is illustrated in Table 1, It consists of 147 food items which come from the three food groups, PSO that was written in Matlab was used to solve the optimization model. It can be seen that PSO algorithm is able to plan and generate meals for adults successfully amounting to 19.33 with 12 food items; 3 food items in every food group to be consumed for a day that is good for breakfast, lunch and dinner and it has a total calories of 1499.9. However, repetitions of the same food is visible but it can be solved by means of extending the food databases. Thus, dietitian can used the model and eventually help them in preventing inaccuracies in creating an adequate dietary plan for adult that would help him/her in maintaining his/her overall health.

Table 1. List of food items to be consumed for a day.

Food group	Food item	Serving size
Go foods	Sinangag fried rice with egg	1 cup
	Brown rice	1/2 cup
	Brown rice	1/2 cup
Grow foods	Clam soup	1 cup
	Pork tocino	100 g
	Clam soup	1 cup
Vegetables	Utan	1 cup
	Veggie fritters	3 pieces
	Utan	1 cup
Fruits	Banana	1 piece
	Apple	1 piece medium
	Apple	1 piece medium
Food cost	19.33	

5   Conclusion

This research work provides a new method that will help dietitian improve the effectiveness of their work. Through this tool, dietitians can save time and effort in preparing a meal plan for their clients. For future work, PSO can still be improved through hybridization. It is done by combining fuzzy logic to allow better decision making capabilities and efficiency in selecting a global best solutions to the problem. The optimization model can also be extended to cater to children, adolescents, elderly and pregnant and lactating mothers.

References

1. DFID: Scaling Up Nutrition: The UK's position paper on undernutrition (2011)
2. World Health Organization: WHO—Obesity and overweight, WHO (2017). http://www.who.int/mediacentre/factsheets/fs311/en/
3. Fanzo, J.: Ethical issues for human nutrition in the context of global food security and sustainable development. Glob. Food Secur. **7**, 15–23 (2015)
4. Chan, R.S.M., Woo, J.: Prevention of overweight and obesity: how effective is the current public health approach. Int. J. Environ. Res. Public Health **7**(3), 765–783 (2010)
5. International Food Policy Research Institute (IFPRI): Global Nutrition Report 2016 From Promise to Impact Ending Malnutrition by 2030 Summary (2016)
6. Schaynová, L.: A nutrition adviser's menu planning for a client using a linear optimization model. Acta Polytech. Hung. **14**(5), 121–137 (2017)
7. Saghir Ahmad, K.Y.: Malnutrition: causes and strategies. J. Food Process. Technol. **6**(434), 2 (2015)
8. Food and Nutrition Research Institution-Department of Science and Technology: The Double Burden of Malnutrition in the Philippines (2016)
9. National Nutrition Council-NCR: 8th National Nutrition Survey reveals increasing number of overweights in Metro Manila (2016)
10. Dahly, D.L., Gordon-Larsen, P., Popkin, B.M., Kaufman, J.S., Adair, L.S.: Associations between multiple indicators of socioeconomic status and obesity in young adult Filipinos vary by gender, urbanicity, and indicator used. J. Nutr. **140**(2), 366–370 (2010)
11. Roberto, Z.-F., Alexis, P.-N.: Diet generator using genetic algorithms. Res. Comput. Sci. **75**, 71–77 (2014)
12. Ferrero, F., Hsieh, E., Wagner, A.: Diet Optimization Problem IEMS 310 Professor Armbruster Spring 2009 (2009)
13. Maillot, M., Darmon, N., Drewnowski, A.: Are the lowest-cost healthful food plans culturally and socially acceptable? Public Health Nutr. **13**(08), 1178–1185 (2010)
14. Kahraman, A., Seven, H.A.: Healthy daily meal planner. In: Proceedings of the 7th Annual Workshop on Genetic Evolutionary Computation, pp. 390–393 (2005)
15. Pasic, M., Catovic, A., Bijelonja, I., Bathanovic, A.: Goal programming nutrition optimization model. In: Katalinic, B. (ed.), vol. 23(1), pp. 243–246 (2012)
16. Ali, M., Sufahani, S., Ismail, Z.: A new diet scheduling model for Malaysian school children using zero-one optimization approach. Glob. J. Pure Appl. Math. **12**(1), 413–419 (2016)
17. Leung, P., Wanitprapha, K., Quinn, L.A.: A recipe-based, diet-planning modelling system. Br. J. Nutr. **74**(2), 151–62 (1995)
18. Sklan, D., Dariel, I.: Diet planning for humans using mixed-integer linear programming. Br. J. Nutr. **70**(01), 27–35 (1993)
19. Kaldirim, E.: Application of a multi-objective genetic algorithm to the modified diet problem. Comput. Eng. 10–13 (2006)
20. Levine, E., Abbatangelo-Gray, J., Mobley, A., McLaughlin, G., Herzog, J.: Evaluating MyPlate: an expanded framework using traditional and nontraditional metrics for assessing health communication campaigns. J. Nutr. Educ. Behav. **44**, S2–S12 (2012)
21. Bonito, S., Dones, L.B.: A training manual for health workers for the prevention and control of noncommunicable diseases (2009)

22. Pop, C.B., Chifu, V.R., Salomie, I., Cozac, A., Mesaros, I.: Particle swarm optimization-based method for generating healthy lifestyle recommendations. In: Proceedings - 2013 IEEE 9th International Conference on Intelligent Computer Communication and Processing, ICCP 2013, pp. 15–21 (2013)
23. Xu, X., Rong, H., Trovati, M., Liptrott, M., Bessis, N.: CS-PSO: chaotic particle swarm optimization algorithm for solving combinatorial optimization problems. Soft Comput. **3**, 1–13 (2016)
24. Food and Nutrition Research Institution-Department of Science and Technology: Recommended Energy Intakes per day Acceptable Macronutrient Distribution Ranges Recommended Nutrient Intakes per day (Macronutrients) (2015)

An Agent Cooperation Model and Dependency Measurement Based on Merge & Synthesis on Shared Timed Task Environments

Hürevren Kılıç[✉]

Computer Engineering Department, Engineering Faculty, Doğuş University,
Acıbadem, Kadıköy, 34722 İstanbul, Turkey
hkilic@dogus.edu.tr, hurevren@gmail.com

Abstract. In this paper, we analyze cooperation phenomena based on agent synthesis on merge of timed two-input discrete transition systems. The model allows handling of possible incomplete task environment descriptions and representation of nondeterministic directive effects and/or deviating (or blocking) disturbances defined over agent capabilities. Also, we propose an agent dependency measure that uses the result of additive Merge&Synthesis operation for quantification purpose.

Keywords: Timed task environments · Agent Merge & Synthesis
Two input transition systems · Agent dependency measurement

1 Introduction

The task of agent cooperation is known to be a difficult problem especially when the environment is dynamic, unpredictable, and complex. Goal-commonality and result sharing are common basis for establishment of cooperation in most multi-agent models [1, 2]. On the other hand, cooperation with partially matching goal(s) and task environment sharing are observable organizational behavior and requires further elaborations on model. Representation of agent capabilities (i.e. agent actions) and a common understanding of mutually agreed known agent decision points (i.e. states) are required to be specified together with task type (i.e. achievement or avoidance). Moreover, based on its (possibly incomplete) description, environment may generate some useful directive effects and/or deviating (or blocking) disturbances defined over agent capabilities that represents its nondeterministic nature. Still further, a model with time attribute provides a more realistic representation.

In this paper, we introduce a general purpose agent cooperation model based on agent merge and synthesis of possibly incomplete, shared and timed task environment descriptions. Basic motivation behind the study is to provide a new perspective on cooperation definition based on state level agreement of agents that refers and exploits information e.g. kept in a shared state/task ontology. Our perspective is; before any action there is a state. The existence of agents' common understanding and agreement points (i.e. states) forms a natural basis for mutual empathy that results in establishment of further possible cooperation and dependencies. To be able to understand the other's

M. Kaenampornpan et al. (Eds.): MIWAI 2018, LNAI 11248, pp. 255–262, 2018.
https://doi.org/10.1007/978-3-030-03014-8_24

situation/state supports both cooperation (if agents prefer). Also, figuring out mutual dependencies is useful for agents to build possible further cooperative task executions. For our purpose, we use two-input discrete transition system definition given in [3] and extend it by adding merge operator and time attribute. In literature, one-input transition system (i.e. without disturbance consideration) has been introduced as a process matchmaking model in unstructured, decentralized environments [4]. An approach to agent dependency definition based on social dependency theory is given in [5]. Bidirectional dependencies among agents due to task environment sharing imply a basis for cooperation. Also, we introduce an alternative agent dependency measurement based on the proposed agent cooperation model that uses the result of synthesis operation to quantify dependencies among the agents.

In Sect. 2, we give basic definitions for the agent cooperation model. Algorithms for cooperative agent synthesis are introduced in Sect. 3. Section 4 discusses different types of inter-agent dependencies and their proposed measurement. The last section is conclusion. Throughout the text, we used terms capability and action, interchangeably.

2   The Model

Definition 1: Let Z be a finite set of states. *Two-input transition system* $S = (X, U, V, \delta)$ is a quadruple where $X \subseteq Z$ is a finite set of environment states; U and V are finite sets that represents agent's controllable capabilities and uncontrolled disturbances generated by environment, respectively; $\delta : X \times U \times V \to X$ is the system's state transition function [3].

Definition 2: *Timed Task Environment* $T = (S, P, L)$ is a triple where S is a two-input transition system; $P \subseteq X$ is agent's goal/avoidance state set; $L = [i, f)$ is agent's execution interval starting at i, ending at f such that $i < f$ and $i, f \in N$.

Let us define two example timed task environments T_1 and T_2 as below:

$$X_{T_1} = \{x_1, x_3, x_4\}; \qquad U_{T_1} = \{u_{T_1}^1\}; \qquad V_{T_1} = \{v_{T_1}^1, v_{T_1}^2\};$$

$$\delta_{T_1} = \{\left((x_1, u_{T_1}^1, v_{T_1}^1)\right) \to x_4\right), \ \left((x_1, u_{T_1}^1, v_{T_1}^2) \to x_3\right), \ \left((x_3, u_{T_1}^1, v_{T_1}^1) \to x_3\right),$$
$$\left((x_3, u_{T_1}^1, v_{T_1}^2) \to x_1\right), \ \left((x_4, u_{T_1}^1, v_{T_1}^1) \to x_4\right), \ \left((x_4, u_{T_1}^1, v_{T_1}^2) \to x_1\right)\};$$

$$P_{T_1} = \{x_4\}; \qquad L_{T_1} = [2, 6);$$

$$X_{T_2} = \{x_1, x_2, x_3, x_5\}; \qquad U_{T_2} = \{u_{T_2}^1, u_{T_2}^2\}; \qquad V_{T_2} = \{v_{T_2}^1\};$$

$$\delta_{T_2} = \{\left((x_1, u_{T_2}^1, v_{T_2}^1) \to x_2\right), \ \left((x_2, u_{T_2}^1, v_{T_2}^1) \to x_3\right), \ \left((x_3, u_{T_2}^1, v_{T_2}^1) \to x_5\right),$$
$$\left((x_1, u_{T_2}^2, v_{T_2}^1) \to x_5\right)\}, \qquad P_{T_2} = \{x_5\}; \qquad L_{T_2} = [3, 8)$$

T_1 and T_2 are incompletely defined timed task environments since states x_2 and x_5 are missing in T_1 and state x_4 is missing in T_2. An example application of our proposed approach is cooperative transportation task environment in which spatial locations represented by states; capabilities of moving commodities to different locations refers controlled actions; possible inevitable commodity movements to alternative locations due to uncontrolled disturbances (e.g. company or government decision to close and/or direct traffic flow before or during transportation time). The target geographical locations for transport and those high risk locations due to for example security reasons represented by goal/avoidance states. Finally, the time interval that commodity transport should be done can be represented by agent's execution time interval component of the model. Notice that if the time interval for the execution of transportation task is too short transportation cannot be realized, cooperatively. A timed task can be taken as a two-person game played by agent and environment in a time interval. Agent cooperation occurs by the help of other agents situated in the environment and realized via capability sharing during common time interval. Goal of single agent is to decide on a task execution strategy such that whatever the uncontrolled environmental disturbances are, its induced behavior (possibly by the help of other agent(s)) satisfies avoidance-from or reaching-to some distinguished set of states. Single agent does not execute outside but only in its defined time interval.

Definition 3: Given timed task environments T_1 and T_2, operator $merge(T_1, T_2)$ returns timed task environment T_3 such that $X_{T_3} = X_{T_1} \cup X_{T_2}, U_{T_3} = U_{T_1} \cup U_{T_2}, V_{T_3} = V_{T_1} \cup V_{T_2}, \delta_{T_3} = \delta_{T_1} \cup \delta_{T_2}, P_{T_3} = P_{T_1} \cup P_{T_2}$ and $L_{T_3} = L_{T_1} \cap L_{T_2}$.

Note that $merge$ operation is idempotent i.e. $T_i = merge(T_i, T_i)$ and symmetric i.e. $merge(T_i, T_j) = merge(T_j, T_i)$. The result of operation $T_3 = merge(T_1, T_2)$ is given below:

$$X_{T_3} = \{x_1, x_2, x_3, x_4, x_5\}; \quad U_{T_3} = \left\{ u_{T_1}^1, u_{T_2}^1, u_{T_2}^2 \right\}; \quad V_{T_3} = \left\{ v_{T_1}^1, v_{T_1}^2, v_{T_2}^1 \right\};$$

$$\delta_{T_3} = \begin{cases} \left(\left(x_1, u_{T_1}^1, v_{T_1}^1 \right) \to x_4 \right), & \left(\left(x_1, u_{T_1}^1, v_{T_1}^2 \right) \to x_3 \right), & \left(\left(x_3, u_{T_1}^1, v_{T_1}^1 \right) \to x_3 \right), \\ \left(\left(x_3, u_{T_1}^1, v_{T_1}^2 \right) \to x_1 \right), & \left(\left(x_4, u_{T_1}^1, v_{T_1}^1 \right) \to x_4 \right), & \left(\left(x_4, u_{T_1}^1, v_{T_1}^2 \right) \to x_1 \right), \\ \left(\left(x_1, u_{T_2}^1, v_{T_2}^1 \right) \to x_2 \right), & \left(\left(x_2, u_{T_2}^1, v_{T_2}^1 \right) \to x_3 \right), & \left(\left(x_3, u_{T_2}^1, v_{T_2}^1 \right) \to x_5 \right), \\ \left(\left(x_1, u_{T_2}^2, v_{T_2}^1 \right) \to x_5 \right) \}; & P_{T_3} = \{x_4, x_5\}; & L_{T_3} = [3, 6) \end{cases}$$

In terms of cooperative transportation, merge operation produces a joint transportation task on which commodities are moved cooperatively while avoiding from defined locations.

3 Algorithms for Cooperative Agent Synthesis

It can be argued that there exists no such thing as state since it is nothing but a result of labeled sequence of actions. Also, one can assume that states are atoms of common understanding. In most of their interactions, human (or organizations) communicate over and care about publicly known contexts defined by states without knowing their originating action sequences. We also know that human can reach (at least temporarily) an agreement on states (or believe so) while their inaccessible action sequences alone may not be sufficient to define agreed states (i.e. incomplete task environment description) but by using the others', only. Inspired from human cooperation, our agents show cooperative behavior by state-level merge of task environments as the first step of agent cooperation before its synthesis.

Definition 4: A *strategy* c is a mapping from a state sequence set to capability set, $c : X^* \rightarrow U$. A strategy is called a *state strategy* if the state sequence set is restricted to only the current state (i.e. $c : X \rightarrow U$).

Agent using a state strategy is called *reflexive* (or *memoryless*) agent. Winning strategy is the one using which agent for example, can avoid from states in set P during its execution. Here, we assumed that agents are cooperative entities that share their task description with others; aim to be successful in a timed task environment. In order to simplify the cooperation model and especially its further dependency formulation, we consider state strategies, only. The approach can further be extended to identification of strategies with memory via necessary elaborations on the algorithms and measures. An algorithm for agent synthesis that returns maximum cardinality possible set of states while avoiding from sates of P during its execution is given in [3]. Controllable predecessors set $\pi(F)$ of a given set $F \subseteq X$ of a two-input transition system S is the set on which proper selection of action u can enforce the system into F. Before giving our proposed *Merge&Synthesis* algorithm, we give the following algorithm that returns controllable predecessors state set π and its selected *(state, action)* tuples set R [3].

Algorithm *Controllable_Predecessors* (F, S, π, R)
Inputs: Current set $F \subseteq X$ of two-input transition system $S = (X, U, V, \delta)$ to reduce
Outputs: Controllable predecessors state set π of F; Set R of *(state, action)* tuples
```
{     π = R = φ
      for each xᵢ ∈ F
          for each uⱼ ∈ S.U {
              take_x = true
              for each vₖ ∈ S.V
                  if δ(xᵢ, uⱼ, vₖ) ∉ F {
                      take_x = false
                      break }
              if take_x {
                  π = π ∪ {xᵢ}
                  R = R ∪ {(xᵢ, uⱼ)}}}
      return π, R
}
```

In terms of cooperative transportation, the induced state strategy defines a route and resource usage plan (which agent's what capability to use) during transportation plan execution. The following *Merge&Synthesis* algorithm returns all *(state, action)* tuples set M from which alternative winning strategies can be induced; maximal winning state set W (a.k.a. maximal control invariant set) on which winning strateg(y/ies) can be executed safely while avoiding from P and the time interval L_T that synthesized agent can execute. If there is no such synthesizable agent or no executable time interval exists, the algorithm returns null.

Algorithm *Merge&Synthesis* (T_1, T_2, W, M, L_T)
Inputs: Timed task environments T_1 and T_2 to be merged & synthesized for an agent
Outputs: Maximal winning state set W; Winning strategies set M of *(state, action)* tuples; Time interval L_T during which synthesized agent can execute.
{ /* Merge operation */
$\quad X_T = X_{T_1} \cup X_{T_2}$
$\quad U_T = U_{T_1} \cup U_{T_2}$
$\quad V_T = V_{T_1} \cup V_{T_2}$
$\quad \delta_T = \delta_{T_1} \cup \delta_{T_2}$
$\quad P_T = P_{T_1} \cup P_{T_2}$
$\quad L_T = L_{T_1} \cap L_{T_2}$
$\quad$ **if** $L_T \neq \phi$ {
/* Synthesis operation */
$\qquad F_0 = X_T - P_T$
$\qquad$ **repeat**
$\qquad\quad$ *Controllable_Predecessors* (F_k, S_T, π, R)
$\qquad\quad F_{k+1} = F_k \cap \pi$
$\qquad$ **until** $F_{k+1} = F_k$
$\qquad$ **if** $F_k \neq \phi$
$\qquad\quad W = F_k$
$\qquad\quad M = R$
$\qquad\quad$ **return** W, M, L_T
$\qquad$ **else return null** }
$\quad$ **else return null**
}

The results of operation *Merge&Synthesis* (T_1, T_2, W, M, L_T) for the example inputs T_1, T_2 are $W = \{x_1, x_2, x_3\}$; $M = \left\{ \left(x_1, u^1_{T_2}\right), \left(x_2, u^1_{T_2}\right), \left(x_3, u^1_{T_1}\right) \right\}$; $L_T = [3, 6)$. Notice that both *Merge&Synthesis* (T_1, T_1, W, M, L_T) and *Merge&Synthesis* (T_2, T_2, W, M, L_T) return null since there are no synthesizable agents that can avoid from the states in their avoidance sets. It is easy to define a synthesis algorithm *Synthesis(T, W, M)* for a single timed task environment to check problem solving capability of a single agent by itself.

4 Agent Dependency Measurement

Inter-agent dependency is closely related to the need for cooperation in problem solving. We can say that there exists dependence between two agents if at least one of them needs the other in order to be successful in its task. In multi-agent systems context, dependence networks and dependence graphs provide useful tools to visualize the dependency relationship between agents [6–8]. In [8], potential dependencies between agents *Agent$_i$* and *Agent$_j$* with their assigned task environments T_i and T_j are defined as: *No dependency:* No need for the other's action for its own task achievement/maintenance; *Unilateral dependence:* One agent needs cooperation of the other for its task achievement/maintenance but the other doesn't; *Mutual dependence:* Both agents depend on each other with respect to the same goal(s) to achieve/maintain their assigned task environments (i.e. need/avoidance equivalent task environments, $P_{T_i} = P_{T_j}$); *Reciprocal dependence:* Both agents depend on each other with respect to their goal(s) to achieve/maintain in their assigned task environments (i.e. need/avoidance disjoint task environments, $P_{T_i} \neq P_{T_j}$). In our context, dependency between two agents in their task execution can be related to the result of application of *merge* operation followed by *synthesis* operation defined in Sect. 3. Existence of synthesizable agent(s) in merged timed task environments implies possible existence of dependency among them. However, remember that agent cooperation; dependency and its measurement are valid and meaningful only for time-overlapping task environments assigned to the agents. Otherwise, we cannot talk about existence of an agent cooperation and dependence measurement as its consequence. In terms of our cooperative transportation example, dependence measurement gives a useful feedback for further cooperation and cost calculation for the shared commodity move capabilities.

Assume that we applied algorithms *Synthesis(T, W$_S$, M$_S$)* for both agents individually and *Merge&Synthesis $(T_i, T_j, W_{M\&S}, M_{M\&S}, L_T)$* for *Agent$_i$* and *Agent$_j$* together using their assigned time-overlapping timed task environments T_i and T_j. Merge&Synthesis operation provides only new alternative action options for agents to be used in their current states and neither replaces nor damages existing agent capabilities. Therefore, it is an additive operator in terms of agent synthesizability. As a consequence of this, if an agent is synthesizable in a given single timed task environment, it is not possible to obtain a null result by its Merge&Synthesis with another. So, $|W_S| \leq |W_{M\&S}|$ and $|M_S| \leq |M_{M\&S}|$ holds. Quantification of dependency among two agents in their task execution is important at least for further possible cooperative actions to be taken among them or in any multi-agent set up, in general. For our purpose, we give a measure that is useful to quantify the dependency description based on contribution of agents to their winning strategies set size via their capabilities. It is clear that dependency relation requires at least two agents. Their contribution to the joint additive problem solving performance provide a useful input for their dependency computation. A similar basis can be found in [9] where individual trade share of state (or country) i is defined by the ratio between dyadic trade between states i & j and total trade of i. We measure dependence of *Agent$_i$* to *Agent$_j$* based on winning strategies as below:

$$D_{ij} = 1 - \frac{|C_i|}{|M_{M\&S}|} \text{ where } C_i = \left\{ \left(x_l, u_{T_k}^m \right) \in M_{M\&S} | k = i, x_l \in X, m \in N^+ \right\}$$

Note that $D_{ij} + D_{ji} = 1$. In a special case, when $|M_{M\&S}| = 0$, we assume $D_{ij} = D_{ji} = 0$. However, $|C_i| = 0$ and $0 < |M_{M\&S}|$ together implies full dependency of *Agent$_i$* to *Agent$_j$*. For the example environments, we measure $D_{12} = 1 - \frac{|C_1|}{|M_{M\&S}|} = 1 - \frac{1}{3} = \frac{2}{3}$; similarly $D_{21} = 1 - \frac{|C_2|}{|M_{M\&S}|} = 1 - \frac{2}{3} = \frac{1}{3}$. As a consequence, in terms of sizes of the obtained winning strategies set size, there is a bilateral reciprocal dependency between two agents.

It is important to consider that to be able to understand the other's situation/state (i.e. empathy) and benevolence are distinguishing human capabilities that effects formation of short/long term human cooperation in different forms. Suppose that our example timed task environment definition T_2 modified as avoidance state set $P_{T_2} = \emptyset$. In this case, $Agent_2$ does not need $Agent_1$ in its task execution and may not prefer to cooperate. Alternatively, it may cooperate although it creates a dependency to $Agent_1$ due to its added capability $\left(x_3, u_{T_1}^1\right)$ owned by $Agent_1$. Such a deliberate human-like benevolent dependency preference on the other hand may lead to further possible agent cooperation even to formation of trust among them, especially when both agents are designed so. The rationale behind such benevolent human preference is faith and belief of not episodic but sequential nature of human life. Agents are for humans and should reflect their different preferences.

5   Conclusions

An agent cooperation model that extends two-input discrete transition system definition by merge operator and time attribute is developed. Handling of possible incomplete task environment descriptions and representation of its nondeterministic directive effects and/or deviating (or blocking) disturbances defined over agent capabilities are distinguishing characteristics of the model. Shared task environment descriptions of the proposed cooperation model enable us to develop an agent dependency measure that uses the result of additive Merge&Synthesis operation for quantification purpose. Figuring out dependencies in our setup can be useful for agents to build possible further cooperative task executions. The proposed primitive dependency measure description is based on contribution of agents to the induced winning strategy set size via by their capabilities. In future, one can develop alternative dependency measures based on cooperating agents' contributions to all possible (finite/infinite) length discrete solution strategies defining a (noisy/noiseless) language/channel. Still further, we are planning to define different characteristics of dependencies including interdependence, symmetry and asymmetry.

Acknowledgements. Author of the paper would like to thank the anonymous reviewers for their valuable comments and suggestions to improve the quality of the paper.

References

1. Andrejczuk, E., Rodriguez-Aguilar, J.A., Sierra, C.: A concise review on multiagent teams: contributions and research opportunities. In: Criado Pacheco, N., Carrascosa, C., Osman, N., Julián Inglada, V. (eds.) EUMAS/AT - 2016. LNCS (LNAI), vol. 10207, pp. 31–39. Springer, Cham (2017). https://doi.org/10.1007/978-3-319-59294-7_3
2. Golpayegani, F., Clarke, S.: Goal-based multi-agent collaboration community formation: a conceptual model. In: 4th Workshop on Goal Reasoning at IJCAI-2016, New York, USA (2016)

3. Maler, O.: Control from computer science. Ann. Rev. Control **26**, 175–187 (2002)
4. Cakir, B., Kilic, H.: An investigation about process matchmaking performances of unstructured and decentralized digital environments. In: 2007 Inaugural IEEE-IES Digital EcoSystems and Technologies Conference, pp. 81–87 (2007)
5. Sichman, S.J., Demazeau, Y.: On social reasoning in multi-agent systems. Rev. Ibero-Am. de Inteligencia Artif. **13**, 68–84 (2001)
6. Sichman, J.S., Conte, R.: Multi-agent dependence by dependence graphs. In: AAMAS, pp. 483–490 (2002)
7. Lau, B.P.L., Singh, A.K., Tan, T.P.L.: A review on dependence graph in social reasoning mechanism. Artif. Intell. Rev. **43**(2), 229–242 (2015)
8. Sichman, J.S.: Depint: dependence-based coalition formation in an open multi-agent scenario. J. Artif. Soc. Soc. Simul. **1**(2), 1–3 (1998)
9. Barbieri, K.: International trade and conflict: the debatable relationship. In: Paper presented at the 39th Annual Convention of the International Studies Association, Minneapolis, MN, 17–21 March 1998

Design and Development of Real-Time Video Transmission System Using Visual IoT Device

Ken T. Murata[1]($\boxtimes$), Takamichi Mizuhara[2], Praphan Pavarangkoon[1], Kazunori Yamamoto[1], Kazuya Muranaga[3], and Toshiki Aoki[2]

[1] National Institute of Information and Communications Technology, Tokyo, Japan
ken.murata@nict.go.jp
[2] CLEALINKTECHNOLOGY Co., Ltd., Kyoto, Japan
[3] Systems Engineering Consultants Co., Ltd., Tokyo, Japan

Abstract. Visual Internet of Things (IoT) is a class of IoT that collects rich visual data over the Internet. In general, the visual IoT device is equipped with video transmission equipment such as a mobile camera. Both advanced video transmission techniques and information extraction from images by image recognition techniques are key techniques for the visual IoT. However, since the video data size is larger than the sensor data size in general, one of the issues of visual IoT is high-performance video transmission in networks in which the bandwidths are limited. In this paper, we design a real-time video transmission system using visual IoT device. Our system is based on a novel protocol, named high-performance video transmission (HpVT), for field monitoring via 4G LTE mobile networks. Our implementation of the system is based on Raspberry Pi boards, which are single-board computers with ARM processor. We evaluate the performance of our system in real fields to conclude that we can achieve full high-definition (full HD) resolution video transmission with as high frame rate as 30 fps even from a vehicle moving on a highway.

Keywords: Internet of Things (IoT) · Raspberry Pi
Mobile virtual network operator (MVNO) · Video transmission
Mobile networks · HpVT

1 Introduction

With the rapid growth in information and communication technologies, a large amount of sensing information in real (physical) space is generated by a variety

This research and development work was supported by the MIC/SCOPE #165009001 and JSPS KAKENHI Grant Number JP17K00158. We also thank Inoue computer service, Japan to develop the system in this work and thank Economical Co., Ltd., Japan to provide us with a set of SIM modules. The 3D printer cases are designed by HalloweenJack, Co., Ltd., Japan.

M. Kaenampornpan et al. (Eds.): MIWAI 2018, LNAI 11248, pp. 263–269, 2018.
https://doi.org/10.1007/978-3-030-03014-8_25

of sensors, and is accumulated in cyberspace (e.g., cloud system). Nevertheless, the data size over network becomes bigger and bigger. Internet of Things (IoT) is an important concept that realizes the cyber-physical systems by connecting many objects (things) to the Internet. An IoT sensor oughts to be small and portable enough to be placed anywhere to collect a variety of information.

Visual IoT is a class of IoT, where the first-tier sensors are specified to image or video sensors rather than generalized sensors. According to [1], the visual IoT device is equipped with video transmission equipment such as a mobile camera, and is connected to the Internet. In the visual IoT, critical challenges must be addressed, such as the wide bandwidth needs of visual data and the tradeoff between computing and communication. The solutions are (1) advanced video transmission technology and (2) information extraction from images by image recognition techniques. In addition, they point out that (3) consideration for privacy issues are important. This paper mainly focuses on a video transmission technology.

In this paper, we design and develop a real-time video transmission system using visual IoT device. The concept of the proposed system is shown in Fig. 1. Our targets of real-time outdoor monitoring are such as power plants, transportations, airports, and rivers. To achieve real-time monitoring, we address six issues: (1) multi-directional monitoring via multi-camera network, (2) location-free data transfer via mobile networks, (3) adaptive data transfer control depending on objective, immediacy and network condition, (4) real-time image processing, information extraction and privacy protection via edge computing, (5) augmented reality (AR) display via extracted information overlaid on video and image and (6) integrated data service on cloud mixed with rich data set.

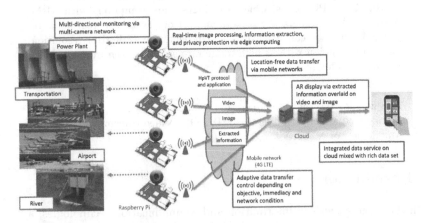

Fig. 1. Concept of visual IoT for real-time outdoor monitoring.

2   Proposed Real-Time Video Transmission System

We design and develop a real-time video transmission system using visual IoT device. The proposed system, which is based on high-performance video transmission (HpVT) protocol, consists of camera system and our original web application.

2.1   HpVT Protocol

We develop a new application, named HpVT protocol, specifically designed for Raspberry Pi (hereafter RPi) [2] on the mobile networks based on H.264 codec. The RPi is a cheap (about $10 to $50) and general-purpose microcomputer providing Raspbian (Linux) environment and high-performance H.264 encoder/decoder. The HpVT is a connection-oriented protocol based on user datagram protocol (UDP) via H.264. Using acknowledgment (ACK) packets to get feedback information of network conditions, the HpVT enables to control encoding parameters dynamically, such as frame ratio, resolution among full high-definition (full HD), HD, and standard-definition (SD), etc. Generally, Internet Protocol (IP) camera systems need to terminate video decoding once the encoding parameters are changed. The decoder is intelligent enough to catch up with the change of the transmitted frames. Even in case of dynamic parameter changes, the decoded image changes its quality depending on the parameter without any termination or blackout. Furthermore, in unstable wireless networks such as WiFi or mobile network (4G LTE), the HpVT enables smooth video streaming in quasi real time.

For user's development of applications or systems using the HpVT protocol, we develop an application to utilize the HpVT. Figure 2 shows an overview of the HpVT application. In the HpVT application, video input from MIPI/CSI-2, which is a standard camera signal format of the RPi, is transmitted remotely by the HpVT. Especially in wireless environments where the network bandwidth and delay amount are unstable and fluctuate greatly, the HpVT protocol guarantees high real-time performance and video transmission quality exceeding those on the ordinary surveillance camera system so far (e.g., full HD/high quality video transmission becomes possible at 30 fps). The HpVT application is designed so that a developed applicant based on the HpVT enables to transmit video mostly in real time.

2.2   Camera System

The camera system is originally developed using RPi in this study, named smart sight camera. A RPi specified lens (camera module) is on sale in low price, but is known that the quality is not enough for many practical uses. We have originally designed a lens mount module for the smart sight cameras. We select M12 mount lens for this study, since the size and cost of M12 lens are reasonable to be mounted and used for IoT type of smart sight camera deployments.

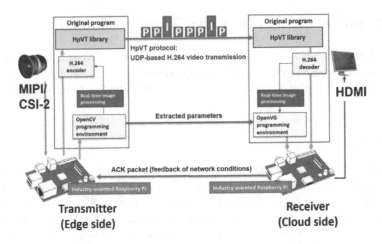

Fig. 2. Overview of HpVT application on RPi.

3   Outdoor Experiments

3.1   Objective

In order to examine the basic performance of the HpVT protocol and the smart sight camera systems, we study the video transmission via the HpVT application on outdoor experiments. The objective of the outdoor experiments is to examine the qualities and usabilities of video transmission from a transmitter to a receiver in Fig. 1. We use Rocket Mobile service, one of the mobile virtual network operators (MVNOs) in Japan, provided by Economical Co., Ltd. This service is interesting that there is no charge limitation to uplink data amount, which is a reasonable service for visual IoT devices.

3.2   Results

The advantages of our smart sight camera are its easy use and high performance on a mobile condition. We examine the performance by transmitting video via our smart sight camera system both at fixed locations with WiFi or wired network services and on a mobile condition using a mobile network service.

Fixed Camera Results #1. As a fixed location model, we set up a smart sight camera system in a garden of an individual (one of the authors) house. Figure 3 shows an outlook of the camera and a picture taken by the smart sight camera system. Herein we use a RPi zero based smart sight camera wrapped in a waterproof pouch, as shown in Fig. 3(a). The archived images are available on web application developed for the smart sight camera system, as shown in Fig. 3(b). One may choose a date and time to preview picture or movie on the web. Automatic time-lapse movies creation service is available as well.

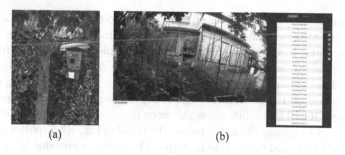

(a)   (b)

Fig. 3. Outlooks of (a) smart sight camera installed in a garden and (b) archived image preview web.

Fixed Camera Results #2. Figure 4(a) is another installation sample of the smart sight camera. Four cameras set in housing cases are mounted to a X-band weather radar system [3]. The cameras are connected to the Internet via wired network. The pictures and movies taken by them are transferred to a cloud server to show up on a web application immediately after imaging. Figure 4(b) is a captured image of the web top page. On the page, if there are more than two cameras connected, thumbnail images are listed. One may make a choice of one thumbnail to get detailed information and set up parameters to control the camera on the web as well. Time interval to transfer picture, Image resolutions, frame rates, bit rate for H.264 encoding, buffering sizes and other parameters are selectable.

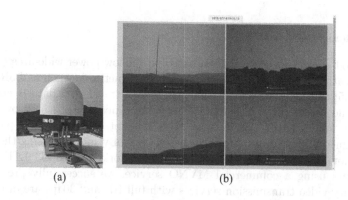

(a)   (b)

Fig. 4. Outlooks of (a) X-band weather radar site in Kochi, Japan with four smart sight cameras installed in housing cases and (b) top web application of smart sight camera system with four thumbnails.

Mobile Camera Results. For the mobile condition, we settle the camera on a vehicle to run a highway in Japan. Figures 5(a) and (b) show a route map of the trajectory on the highway and a time-dependent behaviors of the video transmission from the transmitter on the highway to the receiver at cloud. What should be noted is that this real-time image is obtained on the receiver side, not transmitter side. In these days, a variety of portable drive recorder movies on consumer vehicles become popular, which supply rather high-quality movies. However, these are recorded movies on the cameras without enabling our real-time monitoring on the cloud side. Figure 5(b) implies that the HpVT protocol is available on (4G LTE) mobile networks since no other way to transmit video in real time from a highway. As indicated on the panel of Fig. 5(b), spatial resolution is 1080p (full HD) and frame rate is 30 fps. The movie is encoded in H.264 with 6 Mbps. The given buffer size is as low as 300 ms suggesting that time delay in video transmission is less than few seconds.

(a)   (b)

Fig. 5. Video transmission experiment on highway in Japan: (a) trajectory and (b) transmitted video in real time.

3.3 Discussion

General IoT sensor devices are often based on the low-power wide-area (LPWA) communication technology on narrow-bandwidth networks such as LoRa [4] or Wi-SUN [5] since the amount or time interval of transferred data is not large, whereas the use of (4G LTE) mobile networks especially provided by MVNO is effective for visual IoT device with large amount of data. In this paper, we have designed a system to reproduce the concept of visual IoT using the HpVT protocol for video transmission over mobile network such as 4G LTE. In our experiments using a commercial MVNO service, we successfully proved that high-quality video transmission services with full HD and 30 fps are in real use. On the other hand, there are disadvantages in RPi systems based on the HpVT protocol. One of the most significant issues is its power consumption. Since the HpVT protocol works on Raspbian OS, a Linux distribution, on RPi, which is not a micro-computer but a normal single-board computer. The Linux-based OS is good for development of general applications using general program languages, such as C++ or Python[1]. The work in [6] presented an original low-power

---

[1] Python is an interpreted high-level programming language for general-purpose programming.

processing architecture to obtain several examples of large-, medium- and small-scale visual IoT. However, IoT module based on RPi eliminates the need of a microcontroller and wireless transceiver module in sensor node, thus it makes a node flexible for programming, cost effective and easy to use. Our future work is to develop a new RPi carrier board using compute module (Compute Module 3 [2]) that has functions to control external power supply and power consumption onboard.

4   Conclusion

So far many IoT studies have been reported to use RPi for monitoring air pollution, healthcare, fingerprint, home security, and so on. In most of the studies RPi has been used as a sensor device, not as a video transfer device. The CPU onboard RPi is ARM based and both H.264 hardware encoder and decoder are mounted, but not many studies have reported yet to use this property for visual IoT systems. The RPi camera system has high potential to play significant roles in many industrial uses such as transportation, disaster mitigation, education, welfare, tourism, and security.

In order to realize the concept of visual IoT, we developed a new H.264-based protocol, named HpVT protocol, which is specifically designed for RPi to achieve real-time video streaming. We then designed and implemented a camera system using the HpVT on RPi for field monitoring based on mobile networks via 4G LTE. We examined it to conclude that the camera system has a potential to transmit full HD video in 30 fps in many outdoor environments. A web application to preview images in real time and control camera system is available.

References

1. Iyer, R., Ozer, E.: Visual IoT: architectural challenges and opportunities; toward a self-learning and energy-neutral IoT. IEEE Micro **36**(6), 45–49 (2016)
2. Raspberrypi.org: Raspberry Pi - Teach, Learn, and Make with Raspberry Pi. https://www.raspberrypi.org/
3. Murata, K.T., et al.: Real-time 3D visualization of phased array weather radar data via concurrent processing in Science Cloud. In: 7th Annual Information Technology, Electronics and Mobile Communication Conference (IEMCON). IEEE (2016)
4. Sinha, R.S., Wei, Y., Hwang, S.-H.: A survey on LPWA technology: LoRa and NB-IoT. ICT Express **3**(1), 14–21 (2017)
5. Wi-sun.org: Wi-SUN Alliance. https://www.wi-sun.org/
6. Chua, V.S., Esquivel, J.Z., Paul, A.S.: Visual IoT: ultra-low-power processing architectures and implications. IEEE Micro **37**(6), 52–61 (2017)

Author Index

Printed in the United States
By Bookmasters